Handsome Heroes & Vile Villains

Handsome Heroes & Vile Villains

Men in Disney's Feature Animation

Amy M. Davis

British Library Cataloguing in Publication Data

Handsome Heroes & Vile Villains: Men in Disney's Feature Animation

A catalogue entry for this book is available from the British Library

ISBN: 978 0 86196 704 9 (Paperback)

Cover design: Jonny Wood.

Published by
John Libbey Publishing Ltd, 3 Leicester Road, New Barnet, Herts EN5 5EW,
United Kingdom   e-mail: john.libbey@orange.fr; web site: www.johnlibbey.com

Direct orders: **Marston Book Services Ltd:** direct.orders@marston.co.uk

Distributed in Asia and North America by **Indiana University Press**, Herman B Wells
Library—350, 1320 E. 10th St., Bloomington, IN 47405, USA. www.iupress.indiana.edu

Printed and bound in China by 1010 Printing International Ltd.

Contents

Acknowledgements

Though this book may have a single author, undoubtedly there has been a team of people who have been of help and support at various points during the book's creation. I cannot name individually everyone who has been there for me during this process, but if you played a part and you know it, I thank you from the bottom of my heart. Special mention must go to some who helped in enormous ways, often above and beyond the call of duty. They are my mother, Kathleen Davis, my grandmother, Betty Erwin, and my brother, Brian Davis, who bought me many of the dvds (and some of the books) that were to play a part of the research for this project, talked Disney with me, and kept me going; special thanks to my mother for reading drafts and giving detailed feedback, too! Likewise, I must thank colleagues (many of whom are also friends) past and present for their giving me space and encouragement, and for letting me bounce ideas off of them from time to time (not to mention letting me complain when I realised just how useless Prince Charming is!). Special mention must go to Máire Messenger-Davies, David Eldridge, and James Zborowski, who discussed ideas and themes at various stages of the process. I must also thank John Libbey, the publisher of this book, for his unending patience when teaching, administrative, and life commitments meant that the manuscript's submission "deadline" had to be changed again and again. I promise never to mention another new book to you before it is *at least* ninety percent completed (if not actually done)! Also, a very special thank you must go to my students, past and present, who studied on my American Animation History module and my Disney Studies module. On more than one occasion, our classroom discussions helped me to work through ideas, sometimes see things in a new light, or remind me of something I'd forgotten because I first thought about it or read about it quite some time ago, and it had since slipped away from my poor, tired brain. One of the greatest joys of teaching – apart from sharing with others a subject you love – is that, invariably, you learn from your students themselves, as well as from the process of explaining things to your students. For that, know that you have my sincere appreciation; I hope that you, too, have benefited from our time together. There are, of course, others (colleagues and/or friends) who deserve to be singled out for thanks for discussing (formally and informally) all sorts of things about the world of Disney (films, parks, and merchandise), gender roles, handsome princes, animation, bad guys, the process of academic writing, and the like. In no particular order, I would like to thank Rachael Kelly, Dorene Koehler, Iris Kleinecke-Bates, James Aston, Jemma Gilboy Alexander Ornella, Georgina Waterhouse, Charlotte Waterhouse, and Emma Waterhouse (and Cara & Rob, too!).

My most sincere thanks to each and every one of you whom I've mentioned here, whether or not I've listed you by name. Without you, as they say, it would not have been possible.

Introduction

"Story-wise, we sharpen the decisive triumph of good over evil with our valiant knights – the issues which represent our moral ideals. We do it in a romantic fashion, easily comprehended by children. In this respect, moving pictures are more potent than volumes of familiar words in books."
– Walt Disney.[1]

When many people think of the Disney studio's animated feature films, they think of princesses. And on the surface, it's no wonder. The films which were key financial, critical, and popular successes for Disney – *Snow White and the Seven Dwarfs* (1937), *Cinderella* (1950), *The Little Mermaid* (1989), *Beauty and the Beast* (1991), *Aladdin* (1992), *Tangled* (2010) – as well as turning points in the studio's history, all feature young women who are either born or become princesses. The young women around whom these stories centre are charismatic, beautiful, interesting, and beset with monumental problems, and so they have what it takes to capture much of our interest. The problems they face, by and large, in most of the examples cited above,[2] are caused by equally-compelling women: evil to the point of monstrous, their determination, jealousy, and dynamism nearly steal the show from the heroines who are the targets of their animosity.

But what about the men? The young boys who go on amazing adventures? The princes and heroes who win the hearts of the princesses and heroines and who, we just know by the ends of the films, will go on to live in love and romantic unity happily ever after? The friends and companions who assisted them along the way? Villains who bring danger – and in most cases excitement – to the story? Yes, they're remembered by the public, to a degree. Being able to name all seven of the dwarfs is something of a trivia game in some quarters (Doc, Happy, Bashful, Sleepy,

1   Jeff Kurtti, *The Art of Tangled* (San Francisco: Chronicle Books LLC, 2010), p. 104.

2   *Beauty and the Beast* and *Aladdin* are the exceptions, and in both of these cases, they are scene-stealing men, villains who have both great comic timing and genuine auras of menace and danger.

1

Sneezy, Grumpy, and Dopey, in case you can't *quite* remember). Characters such as Snow White's Prince, Cinderella's Prince Charming, and other royal suitors comes up (though many would have trouble naming character traits for any of them). Those who are that bit more "into" Disney will remember that the prince with whom Ariel falls in love has an actual name, Prince Eric, but he is not the most memorable character in the story, even though we would never have the story at all if he had not been there for Ariel to rescue and fall head-over-heels for (once she got her legs, anyway).

Certainly, the Disney Company has recognised this: their marketing strategies include the incredibly-successful "Princess Collection" which, in-and-of itself, has spawned numerous parodies and references (my personal favourite is the 2012 *Saturday Night Live* sketch featuring Lindsay Lohan, "The Real Housewives of Disney"[3]), and the memorable Disney Villains Collection, an idea which has become associated with Halloween in particular but, in some circles, is popular all year round. But there is no official Disney Princes Collection, or Disney Boys Collection. When heroes are merchandised and marketed, it is almost always as counter-parts to the heroines and not as a group worth celebrating.

But *why* have the "princesses"[4] come to dominate the public's imagination? It is not down to marketing as such: when Cinderella was reinvented as a Disney heroine in the 1950 film, she was perceived in the popular press – and presumably by many amongst the general public – as being a typical Disney princess, despite the fact that she is preceded by only one other Disney princess – Snow White. Indeed, the princesses were outnumbered by the commoners throughout the history of Disney feature animation, so much so that not even all of the characters who comprise the official "Disney Princess Collection" marketing are actually princesses. Mulan, for example, is from a high-status family, but they are by no means royalty. There have been a great many more princesses to join the Disney character family beginning with Ariel in 1989, but this seems to have become a trend in Disney animated feature films simply because the idea of the Disney princess had so captured the public imagination. Ariel, in fact, is the fifth princess,[5] but is followed (as of the time of writing this) by another seven: Belle, Jasmine, Pocahontas, Kida, Tiana, Rapunzel and Vanellope.

And princes? Where do they figure into all of this? What about male heroes generally? Looking at the list of the twenty-eight films analysed in this study,[6] nine are actually named after a male

[3] *Saturday Night Live*, Season 37, Episode 16, Original US Air Date 3 March 2012.

[4] Not all of the characters in the "Princess Collection" are princesses in their films. Mulan, for example, is not of royal birth, nor does she marry a prince. The young man who is likely to become her husband someday, Shang, is not a prince; so even upon marriage to him, Mulan would continue to be of the same social rank as that which she held at the start of the film. Likewise, some princesses – to include characters who are princesses in their own right – have been left out of the Princess Collection entirely, such as Princess Kida from *Atlantis* , 2001. By the end of *Atlantis*, Kida's father has died and she has inherited the throne of Atlantis in her own right, thereby becoming the only one of the Disney princesses to become a reigning queen before her film's end.

[5] The previous four are Snow White, Cinderella, Aurora (from *Sleeping Beauty*, 1959), and Eilonwy (from *The Black Cauldron*, 1985).

[6] See Appendix A.

character; only five are named for a single female character, three make reference to both the male and female leads in the title, and eleven are gender neutral. When you include all fifty-two films to date,[7] the number of male to female designated titles is in even sharper contrast: twenty-one films are named solely for their male leads, six for their female leads, five titles make explicit reference to having both a male and a female lead, and twenty titles are gender neutral. *All* of the films with a female character's name as the title are humans (if you count Ariel, the Little Mermaid, as human; for our purposes here, since she spends most of her film human and is human at the end of the story, I consider her human). Titles which name only the male lead, however, have a mix of species: humans, an elephant, a deer, several bears, a lion, a chicken, and a dog. As of the time of writing this book, titles which are either male or gender neutral are the overwhelming majority: forty-one. While this does not always reflect the importance of lead characters – for example, Wendy is as important as Peter in *Peter Pan* (1953), just as Jasmine is vital to *Aladdin* (1992) – on the surface, it appears that male characters are more important to titles than females, and possibly male or neutral names are safer for attracting audiences. The likelihood is that this trend against featuring a female character as the single-named character in a film looks likely to continue, too. In a *Los Angeles Times* article published on 9 March 2010, the article's authors make the argument – which they support by quotes from people like Ed Catmull (at that time president of the Pixar and Disney Animation Studios) and Roy Conli (the producer for the 2010 film *Tangled*) – that the reason that *Tangled* was chosen as a title instead of *Rapunzel* (the film's original title) was precisely because it was not a girl's name, and the perception was that boys would not want to see a film which featured a female name in its title. Even the article treats this revelation with a disdainful attitude of mock shock: "After the less-than-fairy tale results for its most recent animated release, *The Princess and the Frog*, executives at the Burbank studio believe they know why the acclaimed movie came up short at the box office. Brace yourself: Boys didn't want to see a movie with 'princess' in the title."[8] The article goes on to quote Catmull's claim that, "Based upon the response from fans and critics, we believe it [*The Princess and the Frog*] would have been higher [in its box office takings] if it wasn't prejudged by its title".[9] Mentioning that, at that time, the planned movie based on "The Snow Queen" had been shelved because the studio had concluded that "it had too many animated girl flicks in its lineup [*sic*]",[10] the article concludes with a rather interesting claim:

7 See Appendix B.

8 Chmielewski, Dawn C., and Claudia Eller, "Disney Restyles 'Rapunzel' to Appeal to Boys", from *The Los Angeles Times*, 9 March 2010; found at: http://articles.latimes.com/2010/mar/09/business/la-fi-ct-disney9-2010mar09

9 Chmielewski and Eller, "Disney Restyles 'Rapunzel' to Appeal to Boys", *LT* online.

10 In fact, the film – under the gender neutral title *Frozen* – is set to be released in November 2013.

> But princesses have played an integral role in Disney's animation division since the 1937 debut of *Snow White and the Seven Dwarfs* all the way to last year's *Princess and the Frog*. Princesses and other female protagonists helped lead the 1980s and '90s revival of the animation unit with *The Little Mermaid*, *Beauty and the Beast* and *Mulan*. The difference between those releases and *Princess and the Frog* is that those earlier films weren't marketed as princess movies.[11]

This is a particularly interesting claim in light of the analysis of Disney titles. When you look at who the lead characters are in the Disney animated films of the 1980s and 1990s – the period cited specifically by Dawn Chmielewski and Claudia Eller – what you find is that, far from it being the case that "female protagonists helped lead the 1980s and '90s revival", just the opposite is true. In the fourteen official animated feature films Disney released in this period, eight of them (*The Fox and the Hound*, 1981, *The Great Mouse Detective*, 1986, *Oliver and Company*, 1988, *The Rescuers Down Under*, 1990, *The Lion King*, 1994, *The Hunchback of Notre Dame*, 1996, *Hercules*, 1997, and *Tarzan*, 1999) focus primarily on a male lead, and three (*The Black Cauldron*, 1985, *Beauty and the Beast*, 1991, *Aladdin*, 1992, and *Pocahontas*, 1995) construct the narratives so that the male and female leads share the spotlight more or less equally. Yes, of those eight focusing on male leads, there *are* important female characters; however, each functions primarily in a supporting role, with the narrative focus featuring the male lead. Of the 1980s and 1990s, in fact – in contrast to the claim in Chmielewski and Eller's article – only two films, *The Little Mermaid* (1989) and *Mulan* (1998), allow narrative focus to centre primarily on a female lead. Some – perhaps a great many – may perceive Disney films as being primarily female-driven narratives. And of course women have *always* played important roles in these films; even when their names fail to show up in the titles, they are vital. But this idea that the titles of films might put off boys (and possibly men) is what I am addressing here, along with the idea that female characters dominate Disney animated feature films. Analysis shows that they are not the studio's primary set of characters.

Instead, where female characters lead in the world of Disney is in the merchandising of the films. In a line of products numbering more than 25,000 items, Disney Princess merchandising has been a marketer's dream and a mainstay of the Disney Company's merchandising division since its debut at the turn of the twenty-first century. According to Andy Mooney, who began the Disney Princess merchandise line, his inspiration came when he attended a "Disney on Ice" show in Phoenix. As he would later recall,

11 Chmielewski and Eller, "Disney Restyles 'Rapunzel' to Appeal to Boys", *LT* online.

4

Standing in line in the arena, I was surrounded by little girls dressed head to toe as princesses. They weren't even Disney products. They were generic princess products they'd appended to a Halloween costume. And the light bulb went off. Clearly there was latent demand here. So the next morning I said to my team, "O.K., let's establish standards and a color palette and talk to licensees and get as much product out there as we possibly can that allows these girls to do what they're doing anyway: projecting themselves into the characters from the classic movies".[12]

So little girls were wanting to play princess, and Disney was more than happy to help them. But what about the princes? Where do they figure into this? Interestingly, according to Peggy Orenstein in her article on Disney Princess merchandising, "It's true that, according to Mattel, one of the most popular games young girls play is 'bride', but Disney found that a groom or prince is incidental to that fantasy, a regrettable necessity at best. Although they keep him around for the climactic kiss, he is otherwise relegated to the bottom of the toy box, which is why you don't see him prominently displayed in stores."[13] Part of this trend may well be that girls are merchandised to more than boys, even when a filmic/televisual text is known to have cross-gender (and even cross-generational) appeal. In her article on the merchandising of *The Powerpuff Girls* (1998-2005), Joy Van Fuqua discusses this phenomenon at length, noting that, "Although the relationship of girl viewers to the main program text extends to consumption of *Powerpuff Girls* 'intertexts' (merchandise), the relationship of boy viewers with the program does not necessarily include consumption of accompanying commodities. In other words, boys may be encouraged to watch, but they are not encouraged to consume the commodity intertexts – all that shopping stuff is strictly for girls (or so the merchandise suggests)."[14] Van Fuqua goes on to say that such commodification is, in and of itself, "neither positive nor negative, neither progressive nor reactionary". Rather, she argues that such trends are a reflection of normal contemporary ideas about gender, and – particularly interesting in light of ideas about the function of fairy tales for child audiences and Disney's role therein – that such contradictions between target audience for the film/television show and the target audience for the attendant merchandise "may work to reframe primary cultural texts that appear to question the very definition of girlhood".[15]

So while it *might* be the case that the "Boys didn't want to see a movie with princess in the title",[16] the girls – apparently – were never terribly interested in the boys and the princes, either. And perhaps it wasn't just the girls who wanted to focus on princesses and forget about the prince. Orenstein quotes Miriam Forman-

12 Peggy Orenstein, "What's Wrong With Cinderella?" from *The New York Times* online, published 24 December 2006. http://popcultureand americanchildhood. com/wp-content/up loads/2012/04/ What%E2%80%99s-Wrong-With-Cinderella_-NY Times.pdf.

13 Orenstein, "What's Wrong With Cinderella?", *NY Times* online.

14 Van Fuqua, Joy. "'What Are Those Little Girls Made Of?': *The Powerpuff Girls* and Consumer Culture", in Carol A. Stabile and Mark Harrison (eds), *Prime Time Animation: Television Animation and American Culture* (London: Routledge, 2003), p. 207.

15 Van Fuqua, p. 207.

16 Chmielewski and Eller, "Disney Restyles 'Rapunzel' to Appeal to Boys", *LT* online.

Brunell, a historian at the University of Missouri, Kansas City, who has argued that western societies typically have turned to the archetype of the Princess during difficult times. "Francis Hodgson Burnett's original 'Little Princess' was published at a time of rapid urbanization, immigration and poverty; Shirley Temple's film version was a hit during the Great Depression. 'The original folk tales themselves,' Forman-Brunell says, 'spring from medieval and early modern European culture that faced all kinds of economic and demographic and social upheaval – famine, war, disease, terror of wolves. Girls play savior during times of economic crisis and instability."[17] For Cashdan, however, the reason may be even more fundamental – more part of our personal development than our society's development: "Fairy tales are essentially maternal dramas in which witches, godmothers, and other female figures function as the fantasy derivatives of early childhood splitting. By transforming splits in the self into an adventure that pits the forces of good against the forces of evil, not only do fairy tales help children deal with negative tendencies in the self, they pay homage to the pivotal role that mothers play in the genesis of the self."[18] So while men's names (or names which do not specify the characters' gender) may possibly bring in a wider audience (presumably the men and boys who would find it threatening to their sense of their own masculinity – they don't want anyone to think that they're "girlie" – to be seen going to see a film that might be about a woman, or even worse, a girl), the characters we seem collectively to focus on and remember are those very same women who are missing or invisible in the film's title. It is an interesting contrast, and full of contradictions. Why focus on the male characters in the titles, but leave the stories to the women? What are male characters in Disney films like, and how as a group have they evolved since The Prince came walking into Snow White's life back in 1937? In order to answer such questions, it is important to understand the Disney studio, its audiences, the industry in which it operated, and how the public's and the studio's perceptions of "Disney", fairy tales, and masculinity shaped the studio's films, characters, and marketing decisions.

Disney, Its Audiences, and the Hays Code

Marina Warner has noted that:

> Fairy tale's historical realism has been obscured. One of the reasons may be the change in audience that took place through the nineteenth century, from the mixed age group who attended the *veillée* or the nursery reading of the tales, as in seventeenth- and eighteenth- and early nineteenth-century evidence, towards an exclusively young audi-

17 Orenstein, "What's Wrong With Cinderella?", *NY Times* online.

18 Cashdan, p. 28.

ence who had great enterprises like marriage still ahead of them. Furthermore, certain tales which star children have gained world-wide popularity ('Cinderella' and 'Jack and the Beanstalk'), while the range of the familiar problems dramatized in the stories reflects the youth of the dominant target audience of the times. The increasing identification of fantasy with the child's mentality has also contributed to the youth of the protagonists.[19]

Though not all of the Disney films to be examined in this book are based on fairy tales (only nine are based on traditional fairy tales[20]), Disney films as a group seem to be perceived as being predominately fairy tale adaptations. This is something of a falsehood: of the fifty-two animated feature films realised by Disney from *Snow White and the Seven Dwarfs* (1937) to *Wreck-It Ralph* (2012), only nine are based on fairy tales. Even if one expands this idea to encompass traditional stories, legends, mythology, and folk-/tall tales, this includes only thirteen of the fifty-two films. The rest are either literary adaptations or original screenplays (or, in the cases of some of the package features, combinations of adaptations, folk-/tall tales, and screenplays).

And yet ... Disney animated films are perceived as being fairy tales, and one could certainly make the argument, should one so choose, that they *function* as fairy tales, relying as many of them do on archetypal characters, and telling stories which abound with themes of life, death, good versus evil, and the elevation of ideals such as devotion, loyalty, kindness, friendship, family, honesty, patience, tenacity, and the value of hard work. That these are classic aspects of most fairy tales is, by and large, accepted. That they are values which most people wish to convey to their children is equally accepted; certainly they are to be found in numerous examples of children's literature. But not all films strive to shoulder a didactic burden, nor (regardless of the morals they may or may not wish to convey) are all films suitable for a younger and/or family audience. For decades, Disney has been seen as family-friendly entertainment, a position which it has maintained very carefully. Just as the editors of successive printed versions of fairy tales have been willing to alter the actual selection of which stories are on offer, as well as aspects of the stories themselves, to remain in keeping with what was deemed acceptable to their target audiences, so too has the Disney studio, in translating those printed versions to the medium of cinema, continued that tradition of cultural and social adaptation and selection. In the story meeting for *Snow White and the Seven Dwarfs* held on 22 December 1936, Walt Disney commented that, "In our version of the story we follow the story very closely. We have put in certain twists to make it more logical, more convincing and easy to swallow."[21] In this quote, Walt does not mention certain

19 Marina Warner, *From the Beast to the Blonde: On Fairy Tales and Their Tellers* (London: Vintage, 1995), p. 237.

20 They are *Snow White and the Seven Dwarfs* (1937), *Cinderella* (1950), *Sleeping Beauty* (1959), *The Little Mermaid* (1989), *Beauty and the Beast* (1991), *Aladdin* (1992), *Mulan* (1998), *The Princess and the Frog* (2009), and *Tangled* (2010). Of the rest, four are based on Myths/Folk/Tall Tales, two are based on original screenplays, one is an original screenplay based on Plato's account of Atlantis (*Atlantis: The Lost Empire*, 2001), and twelve – nearly half – are adaptations of books.

21 Story-Conference Notes for *Snow White and the Seven Dwarfs*, Dated 26 July 1934 through 8 June 1937. Transcription from the Original Story-Meeting Notes held at the Disney Studio Archives in Burbank, California, copied by David R. Williams, August 1987, and held in the collection of the British Film Institute Library, 20 Stephen Street, London. Excerpt from p. 21, notes from meeting held on December 22, 1936.

alterations which were made when the Disney story team adapted it from the Grimm Brothers' version to their film. For instance, the death of the evil Queen occurs off-screen in the Disney version, rather than showing her being forced to dance herself to death in a pair of red-hot iron shoes at Snow White's wedding (in the Disney film, we know she is killed in a landslide when she falls from a cliff and is crushed by a boulder, but we only see the Queen and the rocks fall; we never actually see her crushed and killed, but her death is signified by the circling vultures who look ravenously down to where the Queen has fallen).[22] One can argue that the reasons many of these changes were made was so that they would comply with the Code, which could have banned the Grimms' version of the Queen's death as being excessively violent. The studio's first feature film, *Snow White and the Seven Dwarfs*, premiered only three and a half years after the implementation of the Hays Code, and naturally Disney sought to ensure that the studio's output was in line with the Code: without the Code seal of approval, a film was unlikely to be distributed in the 1930s and 1940s. Their adherence to the Code meant more, however, than a guarantee of their distribution and an audience. Increasingly, as other studios' films began to challenge the Code, and as the Hays office lost influence as the 1950s and 1960s progressed, Disney films – both live-action and animated – eventually evolved as a film "brand" who stood out as "safe" in a film market which, increasingly in the 1960s, in the years leading up to the adoption of a ratings system in November 1968, offered fewer and fewer films which the whole family would feel comfortable watching together. What kept Disney films "safe" as a brand was not just their initial adherence to the Hays Code back in the 1930s, but also because of the studio's recognition that, for most of the American film-going public, the basic principles underlying the Code were principles with which they agreed, and which they wished to stress to their children not *in spite of*, but rather *because of*, the many social, political, and cultural changes which characterised the United States in the 1960s and 1970s. The ideals of the Code may, on the surface, have appeared to be the ideals of an earlier generation, but that generation, still alive and well, had raised a subsequent generation to uphold those same ideals and beliefs. Our modern perception of these ideals as "old-fashioned" and "outmoded" would *not* be an accurate reflection of the attitudes of many Americans in the 1960s.

The first of the General Principles listed in the Motion Picture Production Code of 1930 (a.k.a. the Hays Code) states that: "No picture shall be produced that will lower the moral standards of those who see it. Hence the sympathy of the audience should

22 Iona and Peter Opie, *The Classic Fairy Tales* (New York: Oxford University Press, 1980), p. 228.

never be thrown to the side of crime, wrongdoing, evil or sin." That Walt Disney ensured that his studio adhered to this is, of course, unquestionable. As a producer of mainstream entertainment, not to mention as the head of an independent studio which depended on Walt's being able to make a distribution deal with one of the major studios so that Disney films would be exhibited in mainstream cinemas in the United States, to have rejected the Code would have been suicidal. Beyond that, however, I think it is important to remember that, in many ways, the idea of highlighting what might be considered to be "upstanding moral values" is *still* an approach that holds sway in mainstream American cinema; some of the things we consider to be moral or immoral may have changed since 1930, but the idea that we uphold our society's moral standards and reject those who oppose them is one which would make sense to most modern audiences, as well as to those who entertain them. Much of the modern western audience may no longer consider having sex (or even starting a family) outside of marriage as morally wrong, for example, but we do now treat racism as a moral failing for which characters must be punished in some way, if they cannot be reformed.

As Richard Maltby has noted, "The Production Code became the industry's guarantee that it manufactured 'pure' entertainment, amusement that was not harmful to its consumers, in much the same way as the purity of meat or patent medicines was guaranteed by the US Food and Drug Administration".[23] Something which scholars and critics sometimes forget when looking back on the history of Hollywood cinema is that, in fact, a large portion of the audience seems to have been in favor of the Code. Donald Crafton points out Gregory Black's discussion of Will Hays' article in the July 1930 issue of *Ladies Home Journal* in which the Code was discussed by Hays (for whom the office and the Code have been named) as a set of rules which were "responding to the new moral problems of the sound picture. 'The work of reflecting social and community values in the production of motion-picture entertainment,' [Hays] wrote, 'has constantly progressed.' It was the 'constructive criticism' of women's clubs and similar groups that had impressed the producers with the desirability of revising the Code."[24] That this would continue to be an issue for audiences well into the twentieth century would be demonstrated even more effectively some thirty-seven years later by a survey published in May 1967 in *McCall's*, a similar publication to *Ladies Home Journal*. "Over and over again in the *McCall's* article [titled "What Women Think of the Movies"], references are made to the discomfort, shock, anger, and even

23 Richard Maltby, *Hollywood Cinema: Second Edition* (Oxford: Blackwell Publishing, 2003), p. 61.

24 Donald Crafton, *The Talkies: American Cinema's Transition to Sound, 1926-1931* (London: University of California Press, 1999), pp. 475-476.

embarrassment which movie-goers felt when viewing much of Hollywood's output at that time. When stars are mentioned by name in the article as being beloved, the tendency is toward the old stars (Cary Grant, Bette Davis, Irene Dunne, Clark Gable, Ginger Rogers, and Fred Astaire were amongst those mentioned, though Paul Newman was also named as a favourite) and praise is predominately aimed at older films (according to Hershey, *Gone With the Wind*, 1939, was repeatedly mentioned)."[25]

So for Disney, complying with the Code continued to be necessary even as other studios began to turn a blind eye and allow their directors and producers to challenge and chip away at the various tenants of the Code; otherwise Disney would have alienated its key audience. As I discuss in *Good Girls & Wicked Witches*, one of the issues which comes up repeatedly in the *McCall's* survey is the worry expressed by many respondents about "What's going to happen [to the movies] now that Walt Disney is dead?"[26] That such a worry could be expressed demonstrates that Disney movies – both live-action and animated, presumably, given that, by the end of 1966, the Disney studio had released eighteen animated features and sixty-three live-action features – had become linked with the concept of "safe" entertainment for the whole family in an era which had yet to see the advent of the "Family Film" as a designated movie genre in the United States. This is an important issue for both the Disney film brand *and* for its audience: it must be remembered that, when Walt Disney died in December 1966, the Production Code was suffering its final death throes; the ratings system was adopted by Hollywood in November 1968, and in the year preceding that, approximately sixty percent of films released by the major Hollywood studios were released without a Code seal, which thereby classified them as being for "mature audiences".[27] The "G" (General Audiences) designation came to stand in, essentially, for the basic conception of the Code (namely, that all films be acceptable and inoffensive for watching by all members of the audience). Disney – by this time so heavily identifiable as being family friendly – would also have been seen by a large part of the American movie audience as being not just safe, but also as a reliable, familiar entertainment brand. Moreover, Disney by this stage had produced with synergies across film, television, toys, games, books, two vacation destinations (Disneyland in Anaheim, California, which had opened in July 1955, and Walt Disney World near Orlando & Kissimmee, Florida, which would open in October 1971), and even items to be found in supermarkets across the United States (Donald Duck grapefruit juice, for example, began as a brand in 1941).[28]

25 Davis, p. 134.

26 Davis, p. 134.

27 Maltby, p. 177.

28 Robert Tieman, *The Disney Treasures* (London: Carlton Books Limited, 2003), pp. 14-15.

Unfortunately for the studio, however, as audiences eventually became used to the ratings system and more films within the G and PG ratings bands came into cinemas, Disney's importance as a maker of "safe" films began to decline. Even more unfortunately, much of Disney's reputation for being a maker of "Quality" cinema had also declined by the 1970s and 1980s. This is *not* because the studio no longer made good movies – a number of the films produced during this period have gone on to become classics which are loved by both the original audience who saw them as children in the 1960s and '70s and by younger generations who have come to know these films from their video and DVD releases. A few of the films from the 1960s and 1970s, perhaps most notably *The Parent Trap* (1961, 1998) and *Freaky Friday* (1976, 1995, 2003), have even been remade successfully. But the difficult culture within the studio's hierarchy in the 1970s and 1980s, as well as their failure in some cases to market their films broadly enough to catch the larger audiences they deserved (Leonard Maltin has noted this in the case of the original *Freaky Friday*, for example[29]), meant that, for many years, the Disney studio's output and reputation suffered such that, far from being associated with "Quality", Disney films instead became desperately un-cool; that association with predominately "G" ratings, according to Maltin, was quite probably a part of that.[30] For the Disney studio, the situation had become so dire by the mid-1970s that Kay Stone, in her paper on fairy tales and Disney films, could, in 1975, describe those who were under the age of fifteen as "the post-Disney generation".[31] It would take a new generation of leadership, a new focus on both Disney animation as an art form, and a revamp of Walt Disney Productions as an entertainment brand beginning in the mid-1980s, to revitalise the company and bring it and its films back to prominence. In doing so, individuals such as Roy E. Disney, Michael Eisner, Frank Wells, and Jeffrey Katzenberg would find ways of turning what had become the "negative" of the studio's association with the "G" rating by aligning it with the emerging "Family Film" genre of the late 1980s and early 1990s.[32] It was a lucky coincidence that these two events would coincide for Disney. In the early 1950s, the emergence of the baby boom generation alongside the rise of television had allowed the company to rebuild itself after the financial setbacks they had suffered largely as a result of World War II. In the late 1980s and early 1990s, another baby boom, the "echo boom", would coincide fortuitously with the rise of the VCR.[33] This combination of a demographic change and a new home entertainment medium which was positioned perfectly to be snapped up by the echo boom's parents would help restore

29 Leonard Maltin, *The Disney Films (Fourth Edition)* (New York: Disney Editions, 2000), p. 271.

30 Maltin, p. 270.

31 Kay Stone, "Things Walt Disney Never Told Us", in *The Journal of American Folklore*, Vol. 88, No. 347 (Jan.-March 1975), p. 49.

32 For a discussion on how those inside the company would come to understand – and re-think – the concept of Disney as a brand, see Michael Eisner, with Tony Schwartz, *Work in Progress* (New York: Random House, 1998), "Chapter 9: Broadening the Brand".

33 Robert C. Allen, "Home Alone Together: Hollywood and the 'Family Film'", in Melvyn Stokes and Richard Maltby (Eds.), *Identifying Hollywood's Audiences: Cultural Identity and the Movies* (London: BFI, 1999), p. 113.

Disney's fortunes once again, bringing them the revenue they needed to rebuild the Disney reputation for "Quality" alongside, and as part of, its traditional role within "family entertainment".

The Story So Far ...

In my first book, *Good Girls & Wicked Witches: Women in Disney's Feature Animation*, I began a project which continues here in *Handsome Heroes & Vile Villains*.[34] Part one of the project looked at depictions of gender in human female characters because, first of all, no single-authored monograph had done so. Secondly, in those instances where scholars, journalists, and pundits had touched upon the topic of femininity in Disney animation, it seemed to be based upon generalised assumptions, written for biased political reasons rather than as a true scholarly endeavour. More often than not, such commentaries have been written as part of a knee-jerk reaction, and almost always (and I say "almost" because my academic training compels me to do so; I cannot at this time think of any examples where this was not the case) without the author having the benefit of a thorough – or even fairly thorough – understanding of the history of American animation generally or of Disney studio history specifically. Some even seemed to lack an understanding of the history of American popular culture and depictions of women and femininity within it. When I began the project that eventually led to the publication of *Good Girls & Wicked Witches*, animation studies was still in its infancy within the academy. When I first began my research, I owned every academic book that came anywhere close to the topic, and they occupied not more than two feet of space on my book shelf. All these years later, I am delighted to say that I can no longer claim to own every academic book on the topic of animation history and/or the Disney studio, as their number has grown substantially over the last ten to fifteen years (my personal collection now takes up 4 long shelves of books); there is now even an academic journal devoted to the subject. Yet during this time, *Good Girls & Wicked Witches* has continued to be the only single-authored monograph to examine representations of human femininity in Disney animated features. Surprisingly – but happily for me – no one has bothered to examine men and masculinity in Disney animation, either. For many, "Gender Studies" means studying women and femininity. Women, after all, remain – despite ludicrous claims to the contrary in some reactionary quarters – the subordinate hegemonic group in Western society (and, really, in every major society on the planet). I wish that these claims, made by some, that we can think of ourselves as being "post-feminist" were true; I would love for us

34 There is also a third book planned, and this will complete a project which I always conceived to be a trilogy. Hopefully, this will make some of the background history chapters in *Good Girls & Wicked Witches* make sense to those who wondered about their presence.

– as both a culture and as a species – to have reached the stage when someone's sex and gender (not to mention their race, their sexuality, their religion, their national and/or ethnic origin, or any other such category) did not limit and circumscribe them to very specific roles, paths, and potentials. Sadly, this is not the case. "Feminist" has even become something of a dirty word in many quarters; in an "experiment" of sorts conducted recently by a colleague and me in our separate first-year modules, only one student out of the two groups (numbering approximately sixty students in total) was willing to raise their hand when asked "Who in here considers themselves to be a feminist?" ... and the one hand that *did* go up was raised with obvious hesitation and reluctance. Scholars such as Susan J. Douglas have argued recently (and convincingly) that the West is in the midst of a *very* long anti-feminist backlash, to the point where, as the title of her book implies, feminism has been replaced by a pseudo-feminist form of "enlightened sexism" which has maintained male hegemony and kept women from achieving true equality by pretending (amongst other things) that they *have* achieved it, but then realised that it wasn't worth having after all.[35] Similar books have emerged in the last few years: Ariel Levy's *Female Chauvinist Pigs: Women and the Rise of Raunch Culture* (2005), Angela McRobbie's *The Aftermath of Feminism: Gender, Culture and Social Change* (2009), Catherine Redfern and Kristin Aune's *Reclaiming the F Word: The New Feminist Movement* (2010), Natasha Walter's *Living Dolls: The Return of Sexism* (2010), and Kat Banyard's *The Equality Illusion: The Truth about Women and Men Today* (2011) all examine what has happened to not just the feminist movement, but feminism itself, and present, collectively, the observation that the feminist movement has been derailed, and that unless it is brought back on track, not only will true gender equality never be achieved, but also there is a clear and present danger that many of the gains made by feminists in the 1960s, '70s, and '80s in particular will be lost.

What, you may be wondering, does all of this have to do with a book on representations of men and boys in the animated feature films of the Disney studio? The short answer is: quite a lot, actually. Disney's male characters have been affected and shaped by the discourse surrounding feminism and "post-feminism" just as much as their female characters. To go back to the gender analysis of the films' titles, the idea such comments imply is that it is somehow only natural that boys would prefer *not* to see films about girls – and therefore that you should change the films and their titles, *not* the boys' (and/or their parents') attitudes. Making such a claim, however, forgets that one could argue that boys

35   Susan J. Douglas, *Enlightened Sexism: The Seductive Message that Feminism's Work is Done* (New York: Henry Holt and Company, 2010).

13

learn from one or both of their parents – and society as a whole – to avoid "feminine" stories so as not to be demeaned and diminished – tainted by association – by their enjoyment of a story about a girl or a woman. The other side of the coin is that being interested in stories focused on men and boys should *not* a problem for girls: to enjoy stories for/about boys and men is to look *up* to the dominate hegemonic group and learn how to behave in relation to them. Furthermore, it teaches girls (and women) to learn to admire men and learn what is masculine so that girls and women will know better how to pattern their own performance of "femininity", and thereby avoid seeming too masculine. Disney's merchandising, as has been discussed earlier in this chapter, primarily – though of course not solely – is focused on girls; certainly the focus on merchandise in relation to the *Cars* films (2006, 2011) from Pixar has been an important one for the Disney company in recent years, as has the merchandise coming from its acquisition of Marvel,[36] but these still do not begin to match the size, scale, and scope of the Disney Princess line. But the film titles demonstrate a move very much toward the non-female: since *Mulan* in 1998, of the sixteen animated features released by Disney from 1999 to 2012, there have been seven male names, seven gender-neutral names, and two male+female names. None have been solely female. This would appear to be in line with the strengthening of the anti-Girl Culture movement of recent years, which has seen successful film, television, and literary franchises aimed primarily at girls (both younger girls and teenagers, albeit with a large proportion of women also taking these stories to their hearts) ridiculed and slammed, sometimes (but not always) on supposedly feminist grounds. As Carol Stabile points out in her discussion of the malicious reaction received by late twentieth- and early twenty-first century series such as *Twilight*, "From the Facebook group *TwiHATE*, whose description reads 'Because shirtless guys with abs is all you need for a "great movie" for fat chicks to freak out over,' to the venom aimed at boy singing sensation Justin Bieber, to the Hannah Montana Haters Club, the products of mass-produced girl culture are hated on ad nauseam. Imagine a Facebook group organized around participants' abhorrence of *Halo*'s Master Chief or thousands of antifans devoted to loathing *Lost*'s Sawyer or *Star Wars*' Boba Fett or Michael Jordan and you get some sense of the sexism directed at the mass-produced girl culture so many girls and women love."[37] If it is the case that the popular press can express mock shock that boys will not be interested in films with "Princess" in the title, *and* call for quieter, more introverted Disney and Pixar heroines (and even more

36 The Walt Disney Company: Fiscal Year 2012 Annual Financial Report and Shareholder Letter, Online Version, Published 2013, p. 15.

37 Carol Stabile, "Review Essay: 'First He'll Kill Her then I'll Save Her': Vampires, Feminism, and the *Twilight* Franchise", from *The Journal of Communication*, Vol. 61 (2011), p. E4.

interestingly, in both these cases, these attitudes are being expressed by *female* commentators), and such attitudes can be demonstrated as influencing and affecting Disney's decisions when it comes to the stories they choose, how they shape (or in some cases add new) characters, and even what they choose as the titles for their films, then understanding these films in relation to feminism and feminist theory is entirely relevant.

For looking at representations of men and masculinity in human male characters in Disney's animated feature films, a list of twenty-eight films has been devised. These films are *Snow White and the Seven Dwarfs* (1937), *Pinocchio* (1940), *Make Mine Music* (1946), *Melody Time* (1948), *The Adventures of Ichabod and Mr. Toad* (1949), *Cinderella* (1950), *Peter Pan* (1953), *Sleeping Beauty* (1959), *The Sword in the Stone* (1963), *The Jungle Book* (1967), *The Rescuers* (1977), *The Black Cauldron* (1985), *The Little Mermaid* (1989), *The Rescuers Down Under* (1990), *Beauty and the Beast* (1991), *Aladdin* (1992), *Pocahontas* (1995), *The Hunchback of Notre Dame* (1996), *Hercules* (1997), *Mulan* (1998), *Tarzan* (1999), *The Emperor's New Groove* (2000), *Atlantis: The Lost Empire* (2001), *Treasure Planet* (2002), *Meet the Robinsons* (2007), *The Princess and the Frog* (2009), *Tangled* (2010), and *Wreck-It Ralph* (2012). I have chosen these films because they contain at least one human male character in an important role, and this character receives sufficient narrative focus and/or character development to warrant attention. In the case of the package features, therefore, I am looking at a few characters whose stories are told through music/song (such as Pecos Bill and Johnny Appleseed in *Melody Time*), but will not be looking at characters who are there solely to illustrate a song, such as the boy in the "Once Upon a Wintertime" segment of *Melody Time*. I will also, after careful consideration, be omitting both *The Many Adventures of Winnie the Pooh* (1977) and *Winnie the Pooh* (2011) because, even though they both have the character Christopher Robin, he plays a very distant second fiddle to the animals of the Hundred Acre Wood, and appears very little in these films; his role is not important enough because it receives almost no narrative focus and no character development at all. After having laid out a much more strictly chronological focus for my film analysis in *Good Girls & Wicked Witches*, in this instance I have found it more useful to explore the male characters by focusing on particular character types (i.e. princes, heroes, boys, villains), and then considering their chronological development (contextualised by a relevant theoretical framework) within that thematic analysis.

The purpose of this introduction has been to lay out the theoretical framework and background for the discussion of human male characters, as well as to provide some general historical background. Chapter One looks specifically at boyhood and boys in Disney. It will compare these depictions to those of their female counterparts, and examine the ways (and possible reasons) why these boys tend to be at least somewhat sexualised characters, at least to the extent that the heroine can have a crush on him in a way which seems to encourage younger viewers to form a similar "attachment" to the character. This is an aspect of Disney boys which is very different from the way girls are depicted, and needs examination in its own right. This chapter also examines those films where we see a character grow from boyhood into a fully-adult role. Chapter 2 discusses the non-aristocratic heroes, and Chapter 3 looks at princes. Between them, Chapters 2 and 3 look at the types of men chosen, how their masculinity is confirmed/asserted, and how these depictions change over time. Chapter 4 examines how evil is depicted within male characters.

Though studies of masculinity in the movies are not in and of themselves unusual, studies of masculinity within Disney are. The overwhelming attention has been upon Disney's female characters, more often than not, for political reasons: the reputation of the passive Disney princess (a reputation which, previously, I have argued against, at least in part) has become such a fashionable "whipping girl" that the male characters in Disney, in comparison, have been forgotten. Why look at them? Overwhelmingly, they represent western society's dominate hegemonic group (white adult males), so thinking about the forms they take and the roles they serve in their stories, presumably, has felt less worrisome. But to look at the female characters only and ignore the men in their lives is to miss half the picture. After all, *none* of the characters – male or female – goes through his or her narrative completely in isolation from characters of the opposite gender. Briar Rose may live alone in the woods with the three good fairies, but eventually she meets Prince Phillip and falls in love. Hercules may spend a good chunk of his film training to be a hero with Philoctetes and doing battle with male villains, but one day he meets Megara, and his focus and life change forever. Even when the male characters are in roles which can be described as supporting at best, they nonetheless are there to serve as motivation and reward for the heroine, as well as functioning in some cases as the catalyst for the narrative. They are also the friends, true loves, brothers, and companions of the heroines. In a number of cases, they are the main character of the film. In most of these, they are also "front men" for the story, their name appearing in the title as a signifier of their centrality to their films. Understanding Disney's animated feature films is impossible without examining and understanding the male characters who play such important parts in these stories. Furthermore, understanding how these depictions – and the fact that Disney films have a titular emphasis on male characters but a merchandising focus on female characters – means that a greater understanding of the world in which Disney's films are watched, understood, and interpreted becomes possible.

1

On Wooden Boys and Assistant Pig Keepers

In 2011, a huge "controversy" (in some people's minds, anyway), arose in the United States. A e-mail-formatted mailer, sent out on 5 April of that year, featured a photograph of a mother (J. Crew president and creative director Jenna Lyons) painting – with bright *pink* nail polish, no less – the toe nails of her cherubic, tousled-haired son, Beckett. Both are laughing and smiling, clearing enjoying both each other's company *and* the pedicure. On the mailer, there are two small blurbs of text. To the left of the photo, it says, "Saturday With Jenna – See how she and son Beckett go off duty in style". Below the photo (and to the right of a second photo, this time featuring young Beckett in a medium close up wearing what appears to be eyeglasses, with chunky, black plastic frames, which presumably belong to one of his parents), is the second caption: "quality time – 'Lucky for me, I ended up with a boy whose favorite color is pink. Toenail painting is way more fun in neon.'"[38] Judging from the way some pundits responded to this, you might be forgiven for thinking she was doing something that would permanently harm her son. According to those who found the mailer shocking, that is exactly what she was doing. Some commentators even saw the mailer as "blatant propaganda celebrating transgendered children", going on to claim that "Propaganda pushing the celebration of gender-confused boys wanting to dress and act like girls is a growing trend, seeping into mainstream culture".[39] Others, however, saw this reaction as springing from a very blatant double standard. In an article on these angst-ridden reactions, Dr. Peggy Drexler, the

38 Screenshot of emailed mailer found at http://am.blogs.cnn.com/2011/04/13/shocking-pink-mom-paints-boys-toenails-in-j-crew-ad/

39 Erin R. Brown, "J.CREW Pushes Transgendered Child Propaganda", posted on Friday, April 8, 2011, 12:37pm EDT; found at http://www.mrc.org/articles/jcrew-pushes-transgendered-child-propaganda. Accessed 20 April 2011.

author of *Raising Boys Without Men* (2005) and *Our Fathers, Ourselves: Daughters, Fathers, and the Changing American Family* (2011) – and someone who also happens to know Jenna Lyons and her son – raised a very interesting set of questions in regards to the worries over the "harm" this pink nail polish was going to do to young Beckett:

> Just for the sake of discussion, let's restage the photo shoot. Suppose instead of a mother, it was a father. And instead of a son, it was a daughter. And instead of toenail polish, the father was applying eyeblack to reduce glare on the cheek bones of a little girl, with a backwards baseball cap, who was getting ready for a game.
>
> Would the world be having this conversation?[40]

It is, indeed, a good question. Though feminism, unfortunately, is a very long way from being declared "post-" (to paraphrase Winston Churchill's comment on the D-Day invasion of Normandy, the feminist movement has, perhaps, reached the end of the beginning), nonetheless the idea of a girl dressing "boyishly" or engaging in play activities which, traditionally, have been associated with boys (competitive sports, for example) has become normalised in many western countries, even though some sports continue to have specific gender associations in various countries. Generally, though, thanks in large part to second-wave feminism, girls – without challenging perceptions of "appropriate" or "normal" behaviour – can enjoy being more active and rough-and-tumble than was once the case. But the reverse is not true for boys, at least not to the same extent. In his 1997 best-selling book *Raising Boys*, Steve Biddulph sought to allay fears in this regard:

> Under six years of age, gender isn't a big deal, and it shouldn't be made so. Mothers are usually the primary parent, but a father can take this place. What matters is that one or two key people love this child and make him central for these few years. That way, he develops inner security for life, and his brain acquires the skills of intimate communication and a love of learning and interaction.
>
> These years are soon over. Enjoy your little boy while you can![41]

Yet fourteen years later, the idea that boys might be harmed by engaging in – and engaging with – "feminine" activities like painting their toe nails was still a cause for concern to some. But not to all: the response to the "pink toe nails" controversy to be found online was, by and large, that those who were worried about it were, frankly, a little silly. Most of the comments to these articles pointed out that, sometimes, boys like to do things like have their nails painted (after all, it feels pleasurable!), and it has no impact on them whatsoever; it's not even some kind of "early indication" that they are homosexual, let alone that they are transgender. Typically, it just means that they like having their

40 Peggy Drexler, "Do Painted Toes Make the Man?" posted 16 April 2011, 5:42 ET, found at http://www.huffingtonpost.com/peggy-drexler/do-painted-toes-make-the_b_850104.html . Accessed 20 April 2011.

41 Steve Biddulph, *Raising Boys* (London: Thorsons, 1998), p. 11.

nails painted, and probably also that they enjoy the attention that comes with having their nails painted, as well as enjoying the way it looks and/or feels. To paraphrase Freud, sometimes nail polish is just nail polish. Most of the reactions made by the general public can be summed up by a comment posted on 13 April 2011, to an article about the furore, which was published on Yahoo! News.com: "Isn't criticizing happy little kids ... simply for being uninhibited ... exactly how you create bitter, angry and repressed adults who take out their internal fears and frustrations by making nasty comments about happy, uninhibited, little kids ...?"[42] Even an article on the very conservative foxnews.com, which highlighted two articles criticising – in fairly emotional language and with obvious homophobic agendas – the idea of painting a boy's toenails (the same article mentioned only briefly just one commentator who saw it as a non-issue), admitted that the majority of responses it had to a twitter poll it conducted agreed that the whole episode was no big deal.[43]

What does all of this have to do with human boys in Disney's animated films? The short answer is, quite a lot, actually. As was discussed in the introductory chapter to this book, the perceptions about the real boys who may (or may not) go to Disney films have come to shape, at a very minimum, the titles of some films; how the films depict male and (especially) female characters has been an issue for even longer. Putting likeable, positive boy characters on screen means that the films are more likely to attract boys to the film; making sure that the boys on screen are relatable to the boys in the audience ensures the film's success. Furthermore, putting boys on screen who conform to cultural ideas and expectations about what is suitable as a construction of "appropriate" boyhood means that the films are deemed by parents, child advocacy groups, educators, and society at large to be "safe" and "family-friendly" entertainment which is suitable for a general audience: filmmakers who have catered to these groups, both during and after the Hays Code era, would be foolish to court too much controversy in their characters and their narratives. This chapter, in looking at how boys are depicted within Disney's animated features, considers the various depictions of boys and boyhood, and seeks to link these depictions with ideas about boyhood and childhood that were contemporary to each of the films. The films included in this discussion are *Pinocchio* (1940), *Make Mine Music* (1946: the "Peter and the Wolf" segment), *Peter Pan* (1953), *The Sword in the Stone* (1963), *The Jungle Book* (1967), *The Black Cauldron* (1985), *The Rescuers Down Under* (1990), and *Treasure Planet* (2002). Following the sections looking at different types of boy characters is a section looking at what these charac-

42 Brett Michael Dykes, "Hot pink-toenailed boy in J. Crew ad sparks controversy", found at http://news.yahoo.com/blogs/lookout/hot-pink-toenailed-boy-j-crew-ad-sparks-20110413-085113-688.html.

43 Diane Macedo, "J. Crew Ad Showing Boy With Pink Nail Polish Sparks Debate on Gender Identity", published 11 April 2011, http://www.foxnews.com/us/2011/04/11/jcrew-ad-showing-boy-pink-nail-polish-sparks-debate-gender-identity/.

ters have in common across their depictions. In particular, there is analysis of how the depiction of attraction to a member of the opposite sex (both when the boy experiences it and when the boy is an object of it) can serve as a sign of the character being "ready to grow up", as Wendy Darling describes it in *Peter Pan*. This linking of romance and boyhood is an important and complicated one, and so is worth exploring as a section in its own right.

Not all of the boys in this chapter experience it, however; some are too young, and some are too busy. Our first character under the microscope is one of the busy ones: he's too busy trying to become a real boy to worry about love. Towards the end of the chapter, there is a specific examination of those characters who begin the films as boys, but whom we get to see grow to manhood over the course of the narrative. This theme, until very recently, was unique to the male characters: five characters in four films spend a substantial chunk of their narratives at more than one age; in three of those films, an important thematic concern is an examination of what kind of man a character grows to be, and what forces shape each of them as they grow. Only three female characters are shown as both women and girls in their films: two of the characters are in the same film (Tiana and Charlotte in *The Princess and the Frog*, 2009), and for neither them nor for Rapunzel (*Tangled*, 2010) does their narrative examine too deeply how their childhoods affected their adulthoods; yes, childhood is shown to shape them, but it is more of a narrative device to explain their adult selves and lives than it is an examination of growing up and what makes a woman a woman. What makes a man a man, however, is very much at the hearts of three of the four films where boys become men. The films which will be discussed in this section are *Melody Time* (1948: the "Pecos Bill" segment), *Hercules* (1997), *Tarzan* (1999), and *Meet the Robinsons* (2007).

Little Boys

Generally speaking this group of characters (who are grouped together for discussion because they all are boys throughout their narratives) have certain basic traits in common that can be thought about and borne in mind when reading each character's individual analysis. Generally speaking, the boys in Disney's feature films – or the boys who fulfil major or main roles within their films, anyway – tend to be fairly selfish or self-centred, though not in a mean way. They don't act selfishly because they are bad, but instead because they have never had to think about others, even in those cases (such as in *Peter Pan*) when they have others around them from their own peer group with whom they must interact. They are typically very curious about the world around them, and it is this curiosity, coupled with their disregard for considering how others might be affected by their attempts to satisfy their curiosity through undertaking some sort of adventure or quest, which is usually what leads them into trouble (though, of course, without the "trouble" they get into, we don't get a story). All of the boys in these films are intelligent. Even Pinocchio, despite his ignorance about fairly basic things, is intelligent; it's simply that, in his case, he is only hours/days old, and so has yet to learn and experience a great many things that a real boy of roughly his physical stage would have experienced. Given how new to the world he is, he does very well (though, thankfully, even though he doesn't always listen, he does have Jiminy Cricket to help him when he doesn't understand what is happening). Pinocchio is also naïve, unsurprisingly, but so too are most of the boys in these films. They are just boys, so this is not terribly unexpected, but we do see a few boys (such as Lampwick in *Pinocchio*, as well as Peter Pan, by and large) who are a little more worldly than most other boys. All of the boys, however, tend to be a bit headstrong but, naturally, some are more obstinate than others. Overall, though, they are basically good kids, and are trying to do the right thing. Sometimes they don't know what the right thing is, but that is excused by their youth; when they know what is right and what is wrong, they do the right thing. Again, Pinocchio is the slowest to do this (he may have Jiminy Cricket assigned to him to be his conscience, but – and this is part of how he learns the moral lesson of his narrative – he doesn't *always* listen at first). But even when the boys in Disney's animated features make mistakes, they always try hard to make up for those mistakes, and always do their best to set things right.

Pinocchio certainly tries hard, even if it takes him a long time to do the right thing and redress the harm he has done through his selfishness and gullibility earlier in the film. Pinocchio, overall, is a good boy, but – of course – he's not real. Brought to life by the Blue Fairy in answer to Geppetto's wish and given a friendly, intelligent, practical cricket – named Jiminy Cricket by the Disney adaptation – to serve as his conscience (presumably until he can gain one of his own), Pinocchio is presented from the beginning of his life as a happy, cheerful, innocent child. But early on in the story, his innocence and naivety are presented as the reasons why he gets into trouble; in that sense, he must overcome these qualities – despite their traditional association with childhood – in order to become a "real" boy, rather than remaining a wooden puppet.

It has been claimed that Walt Disney cast child actor Dickie Jones to be Pinocchio's voice because the boy had "a typical nice boy's voice".[44] This is important to bear in mind when understanding how Pinocchio is depicted in the film: he gets into a *lot* of trouble, he often ignores his conscience, he is led away from the right path very often, and (initially, at least) is very self-centred, but he is never mean or bad, something which that "nice boy's voice" helps us remember, especially when, the very first morning of his life, he gets into trouble. He starts the morning eager to be good, excited about going to school. He is on his way to school when he is spied by Honest John and Gideon. Ignoring Jiminy Cricket's warning that Honest John offers nothing but temptation, and should therefore be resisted, Pinocchio is swayed by Honest John's stories of "the easy road to success – the theatre!" despite the fact that Pinocchio has never heard of the theatre and doesn't know what it is. Unbeknownst to Pinocchio until much later, Honest John then sells Pinocchio to Stromboli, who puts Pinocchio on stage with a collection of marionettes and has him to sing the song "I Got No Strings" to the audience, who love the performance. But, of course, Stromboli isn't the honest man Pinocchio believes him to be (being only a few hours old at this stage, Pinocchio has yet to comprehend dishonesty), and so Pinocchio is shocked when he is imprisoned by Stromboli. Originally, it had been Pinocchio's plan to go home to Geppetto and give him the money he had earned from his performance. Instead, he finds himself being held prisoner and carried off into the unknown.

Even here, Pinocchio's basic goodness is emphasised: his plan for his earnings is *not* to treat himself, but to go home to his "father", Geppetto, and give him his earnings. Being locked up by Stromboli is a shock, but of course it is not the full lesson Pinocchio learns from the episode. While locked into a cage in Stromboli's wagon, Jiminy Cricket and the Blue Fairy find him and plan to rescue him. But when questioned, Pinocchio – who has now been the victim of dishonesty himself – begins one of the most iconic lie-telling sessions in the history of telling lies; each time he adds more untruths to his story, his nose grows. Admonished by the Blue Fairy that "A boy who won't be good might just as well be made of wood", he promises that he has learned his lesson, declaring "I'm going to school! I'd rather be smart than be an actor!" Nonetheless, she frees him, and Pinocchio and Jiminy Cricket set off toward home. Yet before the pair can make it back to Geppetto's house, Honest John and Gideon find them again, and fool Pinocchio with a phoney medical examination in which he is diagnosed with being "allergic" (to what, exactly, is

44 "Factoid", from *Walt Disney Pictures Presents Pinocchio, Special Edition – Platinum Edition* (Region 2/PAL, © Disney, DVD release date 9 March 2009).

not specified; it is enough, as a demonstration of Pinocchio's continuing gullibility, to show him falling for such a "diagnosis") and told that "There's only one thing for it – a vacation! On Pleasure Island!" Though reluctant to go with them this time, Pinocchio is nonetheless carried away by them, and this time is sold off to the coachman in a scene replete with Satanic imagery and symbolism: the coachman himself bears a resemblance to the Devil; Pinocchio is to meet the coachman in the liminal (and therefore dangerous) space and time of the crossroads at midnight; his "ticket" to ride the coach is an Ace of Spades from a deck of cards. Indeed, once he reaches Pleasure Island, the visual theme of a kind of Hell on Earth continues: it is dark, apart from the light of various torches, and is full of enactments of sin and vice and depravity; these images are followed not long after by the extreme punishment of transformation into a beast of burden (donkeys, or jackasses, as they are called in the film, "jackass" of course also being a pejorative term for someone who acts idiotically and/or badly) and a life of continuous enslavement and misery in chains. But before Pinocchio realises the penalty of entering into this world of sin, he is taken in hand by another boy, Lampwick, who is shown to be a very worldly, corrupt boy, familiar with smoking, drinking beer, and playing pool; Lampwick's back-alley roughness is further emphasised by his lower East Side twang.

His influence on Pinocchio is strong enough that, at one stage, Pinocchio is seen engaging in wanton destruction just for the fun of it, smashing furniture with an axe and declaring to Lampwick that "Being bad's fun, ain't it!" Yet even here, Pinocchio's innate goodness reveals itself in the fact that, for him, being bad is fun because it is a novelty. Lampwick's reply to Pinocchio, a bored "Yeah ... uh-huh", shows that, for him, being bad isn't fun – it's just normal, unremarkable behaviour. Lampwick shows Pinocchio how to smoke properly, laughing when it makes Pinocchio sick (Lampwick seems to be an experienced smoker). Again, showing Pinocchio's first proper drag on his cigar as something that makes him sick and dizzy shows that he is not *naturally* bad, the way Lampwick is, and that Pinocchio must *learn* bad behaviour, even though he cannot follow through on it fully. This is important, symbolically, this demonstration that some boys, like Lampwick, are naturally bad, but others, like Pinocchio, at best only mimic bad behaviour and do so fairly unsuccessfully. Even when, angry that Pinocchio is ignoring him, Jiminy Cricket storms away, our allegiance to and sympathy for Pinocchio is preserved very carefully. Soon after walking out of the pool room where Pinocchio and Lampwick are hanging out (loitering being another "bad boy" behaviour), Jiminy Cricket discovers that the boys on Pleasure Island are being turned into jackasses to be sold off to the mines. Horrified, Jiminy runs back to Pinocchio to warn him, but it is too late. Because he is the genuinely bad boy, Lampwick is the first to begin turning into a jackass, transforming before Pinocchio's horrified eyes. As soon as Lampwick's change is complete, Pinocchio's begins, a pair of donkey ears suddenly shooting out of his head, then a tail thrusting itself out of his shorts. Realising the danger he is in, Pinocchio begins not only listening to, but following (literally, at this stage) Jiminy Cricket's lead, and the two manage to escape from Pleasure Island. By listening to and following his "conscience", Pinocchio's transformation into a jackass is halted, but it is not reversed: until he is finally transformed into a real boy at the end of the film, he retains his donkey ears and tail.

After this episode on Pleasure Island, Pinocchio and Jiminy Cricket finally make it home to Geppetto's house, only to discover that Geppetto, Figaro the cat, and Cleo the goldfish have gone out looking for him. Jiminy and Pinocchio also learn (from a note sent to them by the Blue Fairy) that Geppetto, Figaro and Cleo have been swallowed alive by Monstro the Whale, that they are trapped within the whale's belly, and that Monstro is on the bottom of the sea. Horrified, Pinocchio becomes determined to save Geppetto and the others, and sets off to find them; he even puts his tail to use, tying a rock to it to use as a weight so that he won't keep floating up to the surface of the water but can instead search the ocean floor for the whale. Pinocchio manages to get to Geppetto when Monstro opens his mouth, swallowing a great deal of water and fish, with Pinocchio riding the wave into the whale's mouth. Reunited with Geppetto, his father is aghast at Pinocchio's donkey ears and tail, but quickly decides that "Old Geppetto has his little wooden head – nothing else matters", and embraces Pinocchio affectionately so that the two touch noses. His love for Pinocchio – and his acceptance of his son, warts and all – is plain to see, and shows that being good and deserving of love does *not* mean having to be perfect. Pinocchio has his faults, but he is still loving and worthy of love and forgiveness. But Pinocchio is shown in this scene to be even more than simply good – he is demonstrably brave, and furthermore has learned resourcefulness during his adventures. When Geppetto suggests starting a fire to cook some of the fish he and Figaro have caught, Pinocchio is inspired: he insists that they build a huge fire that will make Monstro sneeze, and has his little family board a raft so that, when the whale sneezes, they can ride the force of the sneeze out of Monstro's mouth and escape him. The plan works;

they are propelled from Monstro's belly, clinging to the raft for dear life. Monstro is furious, and immediately is in pursuit of them. They manage to evade him, but the raft is destroyed in the process. Geppetto exhorts Pinocchio to save himself, but Pinocchio is selfless and brave, choosing instead to save his father, Figaro, Cleo, and Jiminy and get them to safety by pulling them through a small hole in the rocks that Monstro won't fit through. The waves carry them to shore; but when Geppetto regains consciousness, he sees Pinocchio lying face down – and totally still – in a pool of water. In the scene that follows – and its mise-en-scène is very reminiscent of Snow White's wake in *Snow White and the Seven Dwarfs* – Pinocchio's body is laid out on his bed in Geppetto's house while his family mourns him, Geppetto kneeling at Pinocchio's bedside saying quietly, over and over, "My boy. My brave little boy". We then hear the Blue Fairy, repeating what she told Pinocchio at the beginning: "Prove yourself brave, truthful, and unselfish, and someday you will be a real boy". She then adds, "Awake, Pinocchio. Awake", and her magic transforms the wooden puppet into a human child. He wakes up, and becomes aware that he is now flesh and blood, not wood. It takes Geppetto a little longer to grasp the truth that Pinocchio is both alive and fully human, but when it sinks in, he and Pinocchio, Jiminy Cricket, Figaro and Cleo rejoice, the scene fading out to the reprise of "When You Wish Upon a Star", picking up here with the lines "When your heart is in your dream/No request is too extreme".

It's an interesting note for the film to end on; after all, the reason Pinocchio comes to life in the first place is because Geppetto wishes for it on a star, and the Blue Fairy grants Geppetto's wish because he is such a good, kindly old man. But the Blue Fairy does *not* make Pinocchio a real boy right away – she instructs him that he must show himself to be "brave, truthful, and unselfish" in order to earn his humanity. Pinocchio, in other words, must be the one to fulfil Geppetto's wish. The Blue Fairy does make Jiminy Cricket Pinocchio's "conscience", giving Pinocchio the best tool he will need, and she shows up to help Pinocchio learn to be truthful (allowing him to suffer the penalty for his lying to her – his nose growing – before restoring it when he has learned not only not to tell lies, but actively to be truthful). But being alive – and being basically good but untested – is demonstrated repeatedly by the film as not being enough. It is easy to be good, after all, when no one tries to tempt us into badness. That this is a key theme in the film is emphasised by the song Jiminy sings (which Pinocchio joins in with in places), "Give a Little Whistle":

When you get in trouble
And you don't know right from wrong
Give a little whistle –
Give a little whistle!

When you meet temptation
And the urge is very strong
Give a little whistle –
Give a little whistle!

Not just a little squeak – pucker up and blow!
And if your whistle's weak, yell!
Jiminy Cricket?
Right!

Take the straight and narrow path
And if you start to slide
Give a little whistle –
Give a little whistle!
And always let your conscience be your guide!

It is very soon after this song that Pinocchio first encounters temptation in the form of Honest John and Gideon; but if he always listens completely to his conscience – and, of course, Pinocchio does not – Pinocchio will not learn about the world. In order to understand what is wrong, it seems, a boy must experience it. What marks him out as "good" or "bad", then, is whether he sinks into vice and depravity, or whether he learns that it does him only harm and rejects it. These aspects do mark the Disney version of *Pinocchio* as being different from Carlo Collodi's book, first published in Italy in 1883, which shows a character who *is* more inherently "bad" and gullible: the literary Pinocchio doesn't just ignore the Talking Cricket (he became "Jiminy Cricket" in the Disney version), he crushes and kills him, and is later haunted (and advised) by the cricket's ghost. As Frank Thomas would say to camera on the subject in a documentary on the making of the film, "He [the literary Pinocchio] was brash, and he was cocky he was kinda unlikeable. He was a trouble maker. Walt didn't like that as he was shaping up, so he changed him."[45]

In other words, Pinocchio – the first Disney boy, and the first human male character to carry a leading role a Disney animated feature film – was shaped very carefully by Walt and his artists into a character who could be naughty, but not bad. We like Pinocchio because, ultimately, we know that he is basically good, and that what he goes through is helping to build his character because, for each sin he commits (playing hooky, looking for easy money, telling lies, destroying property, smoking), he is punished very swiftly and thoroughly. He may do wrong, but he learns his lesson and does not repeat his mistakes. But simply

45 "The Making of *Pinocchio*: No Strings Attached." Disc 2, Backstage, from *Walt Disney Pictures Presents Pinocchio, Special Edition – Platinum Edition* (Region 2/PAL, © Disney, DVD release date 9 March 2009).

learning not to do bad is not enough; even though Pinocchio has learned to be good and to listen to his conscience, he returns home to learn that the ultimate outcome of his behaviour is that his family – Geppetto, Figaro, and Cleo – has been endangered in their efforts to find him. It is the fact that, upon learning this, Pinocchio goes back out into the world and single-mindedly seeks out and rescues his family, putting the needs of others ahead of his own, whereby he proves that he deserves to be a "real" boy, and it is this that earns him his humanity – and his chance to grow up, one must presume, and be a true son to Geppetto. Simultaneously, the pattern for boys in Disney animated films is set: in order to be ready for adulthood, a boy must be tested, and experience something of the world, to show that he is worthy: he must, as the Blue Fairy insists, prove himself brave, trustworthy, and unselfish. As we shall see when we look at other boys in other Disney films, how – and how fully – each boy does this depends on the character and the film.

It was six years later that another Disney boy would play a central role in a narrative, even though it is a shorter story, as "Peter and the Wolf" is a fifteen-minute segment in the 1946 package feature *Make Mine Music*. "Peter and the Wolf" is, of course, the story told in music by the composer Sergei Prokofiev,[46] and in the Disney version is narrated by Sterling Holloway. As he is depicted in this version, Peter is a rather headstrong boy whose bravery – and he is brave – comes initially from his innocence. He knows that there is a wolf in the forest, but he believes himself more than capable of hunting down and capturing the wolf. Even when his grandfather intervenes, makes him come back into the house, and takes away Peter's pop gun, Peter is angry, not chastened, and ultimately defiant: he day dreams that he has captured the wolf, who, in Peter's fantasy, walks (bi-pedally) in front of Peter, a rope around his neck and manacles on his "wrists". Determined (in spite of his grandfather's scolding) to catch the wolf, Peter waits until his grandfather has dozed off in front of the fire, steals back his gun (his grandfather is holding it, but falls deeply enough into sleep that he doesn't notice that Peter has retrieved it), and sets off with his pets (Sasha the bird, Sonia the duck, and Ivan the cat) to go and hunt the wolf. Sure enough, the friends come upon the wolf, but it does not go well: Peter, Sasha, and Ivan are terrified and chased up a tree, and it appears that Sonia has been eaten by the wolf. Peter and Ivan are stirred into action when Sasha is nearly eaten by the wolf; they manage to tie a rope around the wolf's tail, which saves Sasha but puts Peter and Ivan in even greater danger, as the wolf is able to scramble up the tree and corner the pair on a branch. Somehow (and we never learn how),

46 In the film's credits, his name is spelled "Serge Prokofieff"; here, however, I have opted for what is now the standard anglicised spelling of his name.

29

Peter and Ivan managed to tie the wolf to the branch by his ankles, and three hunters (Misha, Yasha, and Vladimir) help carry the wolf into the village, Peter leading the parade in triumph as the narrator declares, "Oh, Peter! What a hero! You too, Ivan! Everybody's happy ... except the wolf". We then learn that Sonia is not dead after all, but has been hiding (or possibly just unconscious) in the trunk of a hollow tree. Sasha (who has been crying over the death of his friend) rejoices to see that Sonia is still alive, and the two race back to the village to join Peter.

It is interesting that Peter defies his grandfather – and over something which could, potentially, endanger not only Peter's life but also the lives of his pets – yet he is in no way punished by the narrative. He is proclaimed to be brave and a hero, and the villagers celebrate him and his capturing of the wolf: a triumphal march playing, the villagers dance wildly as Peter and Ivan, followed by the three hunters carrying the wolf, stride past proudly. Even Sonia the duck, who in the 1936 version (as written by Prokofiev) is in fact killed by the wolf, in this version survives: she is portrayed as a rather slow, dim-witted character, so her possibly having been hiding in the tree is characterised not as cowardice, but simply as her being a bit out of it. Particularly when one considers that Pinocchio was punished for far lesser offenses – smoking and lying – but Peter is rewarded for putting his own and his pets' lives at risk, it raises the interesting question of *why* Peter is rewarded, both by the characters on screen (to include the voice-over narration) and by the tone of the story.

It is believed that "Peter and the Wolf" was intended originally as one of the segments that would form part of the larger group of segments for *Fantasia* (1940) that would take turns with one another in various screenings of the film. After the commercially-unsuccessful 1941 road-show run of *Fantasia*, however, this highly experimental idea was shelved; the segments which had been completed (and in some cases partially completed) but which did not appear in the original theatrical run for the film ended up being included – usually with popular (as opposed to classical) musical accompaniment – in the various package features which were released in the mid- to late-1940s. In his book *Walt Disney and Europe*, Robin Allan implies that work had begun on the segment sometime after Prokofiev himself visited the Disney studio in 1938.[47] Michael Barrier writes that the Disney studio signed a contract with Prokofiev in February 1941 to create an animated version of his composition, and imply that work had at least begun on the segment, and was possibly completed, before the United States' entry into WWII in December 1941.[48]

47 Allan, p. 192.

48 Michael Barrier, *Hollywood Cartoons: American Animation in its Golden Age* (New York: Oxford University Press, 1999), p. 388.

Otherwise, very little information on the segment and its history seem to be available within the public domain. What is known, of course, is that it was never used for *Fantasia*, and was not released until its inclusion in *Make Mine Music* in 1946. 1946 was a time not only of instability (it was, after all, the earliest days of the Cold War), but also of a shift in official US attitudes towards the USSR from what they had been during WWII, when the Soviet Union, as one of the Allied nations, was portrayed as a friend. This alliance – purely one of convenience and necessity to defeat the Third Reich – was crumbling even before the end of the war, as the armies of the eastern and western fronts converged on Berlin in the spring of 1945. Yet the film contains numerous and pointed examples of "Russian-ness" throughout. When the title for the segment first appears, it appears in Russian – "Петя и Волк" – before transforming into English. Though Peter is referred to throughout as "Peter" rather than as "Petya" (Петя), many of the other characters are given names for the first time in the Disney version (and they are given Russian names: Sasha, Sonia, Ivan, Misha, Yasha, Vladimir). We also know that a real emphasis was placed in the original planning and sketches for the segment on its having a strong feel of Russian folk art.[49] While just before – or even during – the bulk of World War II it is possible to see such imagery as being not only acceptable, but even encouraged in a film-making climate which was working hard to cast the Soviets as friends and allies with the releases of such films as MGM's *Song of Russia* (Gregory Ratoff, 1944), the fact that it retained these overtly Russian touches by the time that it was released in 1946 is a little surprising. It would have taken very little work to have removed them, and would not have harmed or changed the overall story. Yet they remain. In light of this, therefore, it becomes possible to interpret this celebration of Peter's risk taking – and his defiance of his grandfather's order to stay at home – by looking at it within this larger historical context for the segment. There is a 1941 discussion of child-rearing which links different approaches to discipline and behavioural expectations as analogous to ideals of democratic and totalitarian states which seems to support Peter's defiance of his grandfather: "In a totalitarian state, individuals are told what to do and how to think; in a democracy, they are expected, within the social framework, to think and act for themselves".[50] In this context, it is possible to argue that Peter is rewarded – even celebrated – by the segment precisely *because* he disobeys his grandfather, who stands in for that totalitarian rule which limits its citizens. But Peter, by using his initiative, proves himself resourceful and independently-minded, yet able to work well

49 Ollie Johnston and Frank Thomas. *The Illusion of Life: Disney Animation* (New York: Hyperion, 1981), p. 511.

50 Elizabeth F. Boettiger, "Families and the World Outside (1941)", in Henry Jenkins (Ed.), *The Children's Culture Reader* (London: New York University Press, 1998), p. 499.

with others, as well as (in the words of the Blue Fairy in *Pinocchio*) being brave, trustworthy (not for his grandfather, perhaps, but for his friends, who trust Peter with their lives; and in the Disney version, of course, all of the characters survive) and unselfish (after all, he shares the credit for capturing the wolf with Ivan, who helped him tie up the wolf, and the hunters, who helped him carry the wolf to the village).

While defiance of the grandfather is never explicitly characterised in the segment as a defiance of Soviet authority (which *would* have been surprising if part of the original thinking behind the segment had been to support the US's wartime alliance with the USSR), the tone of the segment overall, by the time of its 1946 release within *Make Mine Music*, is heavily Americanized by Holloway's narration. It is not possible (at least at present, without access to the Disney archives) to determine whether Holloway's voice-over narration was part of the segment as it was originally devised for inclusion in *Fantasia*; likewise the title card which fades from Russian to English. Of the segments included in the original theatrical run of *Fantasia*, none have either narration or title cards; instead, all are introduced by Deems Taylor, who gives a (usually) very brief lecture on each musical selection, and the piece is then played by the orchestra, accompanied on screen by its bespoke animation. If the making of the segment originally took place during Hollywood's supporting the US government's alliance with the Soviets against the Nazis, then the "Russianness" of the look of the animation would fit neatly within that as accompaniment for a modern Soviet composer's work. Yet, in the post-war breakdown of the USA/USSR alliance and the beginnings of the Cold War, the fact that the setting of the story is in what appears to be the past (and therefore pre-Soviet) period of Russia's history, means the segment could, in this context, be seen as enjoying traditional Russian folk culture, but not in such a way as to be friendly towards the Soviet Union. If, therefore, the Russian/English title card and Holloway's narration were added for the 1946 release, then it could be seen as symbolically significant that the Cyrillic version of the title throws off the narrator – who pauses and ums and ahs, unable to make it out – until it changes into English letters and language, when it is finally able to be read – interpreted and understood, in other words – by the strongly American-accented Holloway.[51] Since Peter/Petya himself never speaks in the segment, Holloway's voice stands in for Peter's, and therefore could be seen to lend him an American identity, therefore positioning him as an "All-American" boy.

51 It would be interesting to speculate on whether, at least in part, Walt Disney's motivation for testifying before HUAC in 1947, the year following the release of *Make Mine Music*, was connected to an effort to mitigate/minimise the possible perception that the "Peter and the Wolf" segment could be characterised as being in any way pro-Communist and/or pro-Soviet. An exploration of such a topic, however, must be left to a later date and in a more appropriate context.

Our next "All-American" boy – despite having been born and raised in Australia by an Australian mother – is the lead in one of Disney's least successful animated films. He is Cody, the boy who is at the centre of the narrative of *The Rescuers Down Under* (1990). This film, which Don Hahn says was the first Hollywood film to be produced digitally, was also the first film of any length at Disney to be done entirely using what was then the new CAPS system.[52] Yet, arguably, it is the forgotten film of the Disney renaissance, coming as it does between 1989's *The Little Mermaid* and 1991's *Beauty and the Beast*. As Chris Pallant points out, whereas some (such as Byrne and McQuillan) have discussed various factors within the film itself as the reason for its comparative lack of success, there is another – and probably much more likely – reason that *The Rescuers Down Under* failed at the box office: when it was released on 16 November 1990, it went into general release on the same day as *Home Alone* (1990). As Pallant points out, *Home Alone* was "the highest grossing film of 1990, taking over $285 million at the box office ... Also emerging during the Christmas season were *Three Men and a Little Lady* (1990), *Look Who's Talking Too* (1990) and *Kindergarten Cop* (1990), all of which registered higher box-office figures than *The Rescuers Down Under*."[53] Further adding to its troubles was the decision, made at the company's executive level, to stop advertising the film once it became evident that it was performing below the studio's expectations. As Tom Schumacher, one of the producers for *The Rescuers Down Under*, says to camera in the documentary *Waking Sleeping Beauty* (2009),

> Jeffrey [Katzenberger] pulled all the TV advertising. And I said, "Jeffrey, I just can't believe that. You've pulled it? There's no advertising, nothing?" And he said, "Tom, the movie doesn't work. It's over." And I started to cry on the telephone. And then he said, "It's okay. We're gonna move forward and we'll do something else." He said, "Are you okay?" I said, "I'm all right". He goes, "Okay. We'll start again tomorrow." And then he hung up the phone.[54]

So while the film is not without its faults, its difficult release history in its initial run means that the film has come to be seen as a failure when, in reality, it has aspects which could be said to redeem it. Amongst those is the depiction of boyhood as noble and strong in its lead character, Cody.

That Cody is still a very young boy is denoted by devices other than his physical appearance, which is still small and rounded in the manner of a pre-pubescent child, and by his voice, which has yet to begin to change. It is also shown by his ability to speak with animals, as well as by the ways in which he engages with play.[55] But Cody is no ordinary boy. He is shown to be very sensitive

52 CAPS – or "Computer Aided Post-production System" – is a method whereby traditionally hand-drawn cels are fed into a computer, and the computer is used to colour and layer the cel and background, thereby creating the finished frame on a computer rather than photographing the layers using a camera (multiplane or otherwise) to combine the various cels and background into a single image.

53 Chris Pallant, *Demystifying Disney: A History of Disney Feature Animation* (London: Bloomsbury, 2013), p. 93.

54 Tom Schumacher interview in *Waking Sleeping Beauty*. Written by and interviews conducted by Patrick Pacheco. Produced by Peter Schneider and Don Hahn. Directed by Don Hahn.

55 Direct linguistic communication between humans is something which happens only very rarely in Disney's animated features, contrary to popular myth; this will be discussed at greater length in one of my future monographs.

and tender by the way he can communicate with animals and the way that he will do anything to be their friend and champion: after rescuing a female golden eagle from a poacher's trap, she takes Cody to her nest, and he gently lays his head on one of her eggs to listen to the eaglet inside. He sees one of her feathers – a beautiful golden colour – and it is obvious that he would like to have it for himself, enjoying for a moment its softness when he rubs it across his cheek. But he then lays it tenderly on top of her eggs to help keep them warm; the mother eagle gives him the feather to keep, however, as thanks for rescuing her, as well as in an offer of friendship. During the rescue and in this scene in her nest, the two are shown to form a close bond, even though, unlike other animals Cody encounters in the outback, he and the eagle do not converse with one another (though they communicate nonetheless, he in words, she with her eyes and body language).

Shortly after his rescue of the eagle, he comes upon a mouse tied up in a trap. He frees it (despite its protestations), and immediately falls into a deep hole – a poacher's trap, as he recognises immediately. The mouse tries to help him out of the trap, but before it has the chance, the poacher, McLeach, arrives on the scene. He frees Cody from the hole (claiming it to be a "lizard hole" dug by Joanna, a goanna lizard who is his sidekick), but when he realises that Cody will not be dissuaded that the hole is anything other than a poacher's trap, and also sees that Cody is intent on alerting the authorities, McLeach fakes Cody's death (he throws the boy's backpack into a river full of crocodiles) and kidnaps him. The same mouse whom Cody rescued, but who failed to rescue Cody in return, immediately sets off a chain of communications which send word to the Rescue Aid Society that a boy is in danger and needs their help. The heroes of the Rescue Aid Society – Bernard and Miss Bianca (mice from America and Hungary, respectively, voiced by Bob Newhart and Eva Gabor) – are enjoying a romantic dinner together when word reaches New York (in fact, we learn that Bernard intends to propose to Miss Bianca during dinner, but never gets the chance thanks to the call to rescue Cody). The two address the Rescue Aid Society briefly, then set off immediately for Australia.

Later, we see Cody being taken to McLeach's home, and there McLeach attempts first to intimidate the boy, then bribe him, into telling where the golden eagle's nest is. Cody, however, cannot be frightened or bought: he stands up to McLeach at every turn, and will not be cowered. McLeach throws him into a cage in a separate part of the cave (we are led to think it's an abandoned opal mine, a notion that further links McLeach with the stripping of natural resources from an environment). The room is full of other animals from the outback – koalas, kangaroos, kookaburras, wallabies, and so forth – who have been trapped by McLeach to be skinned and made into leather goods. Unlike the eagle, these animals can converse with Cody, and so he is able to devise a plan with them to try and escape, but they are thwarted by Joanna. An Australian frilled-neck lizard named Frank, however, with whom Cody is sharing a cage, later manages to pick the lock using his tail, and though chased by Joanna, nonetheless manages to get the keys to Cody, who nearly manages to free the other animals before being caught by McLeach. He then takes Cody outside, and lies to him, telling him that the eagle was shot by someone else, and saying to Joanna that it's too bad that the eggs will die. Cody immediately sets off to rescue the eggs, with McLeach (back in his vehicle) following behind. Cody finds the eggs, and settles into the nest to protect them just as Bernard, Bianca, and Jake, the kangaroo mouse who has served as their guide through the outback, reach him to warn him of McLeach's trick. They warn him that McLeach is on the cliff, and he begins screaming a warning to the eagle, Marahute, to turn back. It's too late, however: Cody's innocence and naivety – for which he is not to blame; after all, he is still a fairly-young child – have led McLeach straight to the eagle, and have allowed him to capture her in a net in mid-air. But Cody is too brave and devoted to his friend to let her be taken without a fight. He jumps onto the sack and begins cutting the ropes that bind her, the mice doing what they can to help and protect him.

From here on in, Cody's fate is up to others. Again, this is never denoted as a sign of weakness on his part; in fact, it is a lack of power and control that almost all young children experience, given that they are at least materially dependent on adults for their survival. Captured by McLeach, he nearly dies when he is dropped into crocodile-infested waters, but Bernard's heroism, McLeach's and Joanna's stupidity, Bianca's and Jake's cleverness, pluckiness, and determination, and the eagle's bravery and strength (she flies into the waterfall to grab him before he can be crushed to death on the rocks) are what save his life. But, ultimately, he has earned his rescue: his youth, innocence, good-ness, and kindness have brought the Rescue Aid Society to his aid, and his friendship and bond with the eagle have led to her saving his life from not only a horrific death, but also the same death as the evil McLeach. In many ways, Cody is shown to be the antithesis of McLeach: he helps and befriends animals when McLeach would trap and kill them; Cody understands and can talk with animals, rather than seeing them as mere things and possessions; Cody is brave, and will do anything to rescue those in trouble regardless of the cost to himself, rather than behaving in the ruthless, selfish way that McLeach prefers.

But despite these key differences, Cody and McLeach are linked: they are both very determined and strong willed, they both rely on animals to help them (McLeach has Joanna as his companion, though her loyalty only goes so far, as we see on several occasions), and they are both very familiar with the world of the outback. But whereas McLeach exploits the environment around him, Cody protects it. It is a kind of environmentalist message – one specifically of animal conservation – which was very much an important one in the 1970s, 1980s, and 1990s, and fits with American interests in the conservation of Bald Eagles and Golden Eagles within the United States.[56] While the film may well be set in the Australian outback, it is important to note that – once more incongruously – our lead character, Cody, speaks with an American accent, as does McLeach, the poacher (whose voice is provided by George C. Scott). Even some (though not all) of the Australian animals have American accents. Why Cody, an Australian boy with an Australian mother (though we see and hear very little of her, she nonetheless does speak her few lines with an Australian accent) has an American accent is never explained by the film. So his attempts to protect the golden eagle he has befriended, and his particular efforts to protect her eggs, could be said to link him to American conservation efforts for Golden Eagles and Bald Eagles within the United States. To show a child to be taking the lead in such efforts could be said to carry the further message that it is up to future generations to carry on those efforts, which have been shown to be successful in taking Bald Eagles, at least, off the endangered species list (and moving them to the "Threatened Species List", so still bad but improving) in 1995. Indeed, in 1995, Disney would bring an environmentalist message very strongly into another of their films, *Pocahontas* (1995), so the idea of incorporating such messages into Disney animation does happen from time to time. *The Rescuers Down Under*, arguably, is the first film in the Disney renaissance era to convey such themes, but it could be argued very easily that a similarly conservationist focus is present in *Bambi* (1942), where Man is shown to be a threat to the world of the animals, both through hunting and through the humans' carelessness with fire. Though it is true that there are not many animated examples of such messages in Disney films between 1942 and 1990, Disney's *True Life Adventure Series* (1948-1960), by its very existence, provides precedent in Disney films as a whole for stories which

56 Michael N. Kochert and Karen Steenhof, "Golden Eagles in the U.S. and Canada: Status, Trends, and Conservation Challenges", in *Journal of Raptor Research*, Vol. 36, No. 1, Supplemental (March 2002), p. 32 and table 1, p. 33.

incorporate conservationist messages. Cody, no doubt, would be a fan of the series.

Beginning to Grow Up

The two boys in this next section, Mowgli and Taran, begin their stories in what, it turns out, are the final days of their childhoods. We never see them grow up, but by the time we leave them, they are ready to head into adulthood. What gets them to that point is a combination of experience and their first glimmers of sexual awakening. Very little (if any) of that beginning of romantic desire is explored by the film, but it is pivotal – particularly in Mowgli's case – in terms of persuading the character that, really, growing up might not be such a bad thing after all. As they make their way to that point, we watch these two boys learn more about life, death, good, and evil. Each is on a journey – both literal and figural – that is still underway when we leave them, but it is obvious that they will reach their final destination – adulthood – in the not-too-distant future.

The first to be discussed in this section is Mowgli, the boy whose story is told in the 1967 film *The Jungle Book*, the last animated film made at Disney in which Walt had any direct input before his death on 15 December 1966. For this film, perhaps Walt's most important influence may have been his injunction to his story men and animators that they should ignore, by and large, Kipling's stories, and tell whatever stories they saw fit.[57] Indeed, even the credits for *The Jungle Book* list four Disney artists as the authors of the story (Larry Clemmons, Ralph Wright, Ken Anderson, and Vance Gerry), placing underneath their names, in smaller letters, "Inspired by the Rudyard Kipling 'Mowgli' Stories". In this film, Mowgli (voiced by one of Woolie Reitherman's sons, Bruce Reitherman) is depicted as a sweet, innocent, plucky, lively boy who wants nothing more than to remain with his friends in the jungle. Partially, this could be explained by the fact that Mowgli has no memory of life with humans – Bagheera finds him alone in the jungle, a helpless infant in a basket sitting in a broken boat. Mowgli is taken to live with a family of wolves, and spends ten years amongst them. He is shown to be beloved by those around him, but they recognise more than he that Mowgli can never really be one of them; he is differentiated from them by their referring to him as "Man cub", and the decision is made to take him to the nearest "man village" because Shere Kahn, the man-hating tiger, has returned to the part of the jungle where Mowgli lives, and the wolves who have adopted him into their pack fear that they will not be able to protect him, let alone the

57 Allan, p. 243.

rest of the pack, should Shere Kahn attack. So Bagheera volun-
teers to take Mowgli to the man village, and off they go into the
jungle. It is this event which is the real start of our story, since it
will be Mowgli's experiences during this journey which, ultimately, will prepare him for his return to life amongst humans.

The jungle, therefore, stands out as a place which represents
childhood; when Mowgli insists that he could survive in the
jungle, Bagheera calmly replies, "Why, you wouldn't last a day",
and even has to help him to climb a tree to have a relatively safe
place to sleep that night. Bagheera then has to chase off Kaa, the
python who comes down out of the branches above them, hyp-
notises Mowgli, and tries to eat him. That the jungle is the realm
of childhood is emphasised in particular once Baloo comes into
the story; the lyrics to his song "The Bare Necessities" depict a
world in which one is free of responsibilities, and where the
things which are needed for survival – food in particular, but all
of life's necessities, it is implied – are simply provided without
the need for work. Childhood is about freedom, joy, and play:
adventure, lessons, love, and danger are parts of this which will
continue into adulthood, but the kinds of experiences – and the
ways in which they are experienced – will not be the same in adult
life as they are during childhood. This idea is emphasised in
particular when Mowgli finally stumbles upon the man village;
his first encounter with a human – a girl of his own age – is an
encounter with a human who is working; the song she sings is
one in which work is seen as the natural activity, and though the
type of work one does may change when one reaches adulthood,
work and responsibility will continue nonetheless:

> Father's hunting in the forest,
> Mother's cooking in the home,
> I must go to fetch the water
> Till the day that I am grown.
>
> …
>
> Then I will have a handsome husband
> And a daughter of my own,
> And I'll send her to fetch the water –
> I'll be cooking in the home.

Even the style of her song differentiates her from what Mowgli
has known with his jungle friends and enemies; whereas most of
the music in the jungle is done to a jazz or a swing beat (with a
little bit of jazz-influenced barbershop quartet sung by vultures
thrown in!), the girl's song is one with a much more traditional
beat and style: like the pull of desire and the inevitability of
growing up, her song's style is timeless. When Mowgli follows
the girl – in the grip of a very adult attraction to her – he shoulders

her burden – the jug of water – to carry it home for her. With a backward look, then a shrug of "oh well!" to his friends Bagheera and Baloo, who look on from the edge of the jungle, he follows the girl into the village, and into the life of adult work and responsibility. In contrast, Baloo and Bagheera walk together into the jungle, arms around each other's shoulders, singing "The Bare Necessities". They, as denizens of the jungle, can continue to be sustained by it, and therefore function symbolically as its children.

The idea that animals should be linked to childhood is one which dates back at least to the romantic period, as Richard deCordova discusses in his article "The Mickey in Macy's Window". In an exploration of early Disney merchandising and the ways in which it fit into early twentieth-century ideas about marketing to children as consumers (ideas and trends that, it should be noted, pre-date the Disney studio's foray into merchandising), deCordova talks about the linking of children and childhood with animals and the natural world, a trend that stretches back to the Romantic movement, which constituted a rejection of the early stages of the Industrial Revolution in the late eighteenth and early nineteenth centuries. Noting that "... nature was a way of establishing childhood innocence", he goes on to argue that "The child's relationship with nature and its association with innocence on the one hand and primitivist vitality on the other could be effectively concretized through symbolic procedures that linked the child to animals".[58] While in this article deCordova is focusing on merchandising as his subject, the fact is that this idea – which predates film merchandising, given its origins within Romanticism – is applied easily to an understanding of *The Jungle Book*, both in Kipling's original (first published in serial form in magazines in 1893-94, then published as a book in 1894) and in Disney's cinematic adaptation, which appeared seventy-three years later. Certainly within the Disney version, because it is an animated film which can bring to life the story's animal characters just as easily as it can Mowgli (indeed, in many ways anthropomorphised animals tend to be seen as easier to animate than humans because there are fewer concerns about achieving the same level of accuracy, given that the animals are already behaving less like actual animals and more like humans), there can be an even more direct linkage made between the animals, the jungle, and childhood, since we can hear directly from the animals themselves, and Mowgli can interact with them in a way not dissimilar to how children pretend to interact with their stuffed animals.[59] It is a story which, therefore, works best in animated form, and the Disney artists took full advantage of that fact. We

58 Richard deCordova, "The Mickey in Macy's Window: Childhood, Consumerism, and Disney Animation", in Eric Smoodin (Ed.), *Disney Discourse: Producing the Magic Kingdom* (London: Routledge, 1994), p. 211.

59 As Walt Disney once noted in a 1941 Inter-Office memo to Lee Blair, "I think we should find legends and stories that can be done with animals – animating humans is no cinch". Inter-Office Communication from Walt Disney to Lee Blair, 25 July 1941. From *Walt Disney: An Intimate History of the Man and his Magic*. CD-ROM. Found at: Library/Animation (Memo about animating animals).

are treated to fully-developed personas in the animal characters to at least the same extent (and, arguably, to a greater extent) as we have in Mowgli. We get to know all of them very well, and understand what behaviours are "typical" for their characters.

It is thanks to this fact that it is important to note that Mowgli's encounter with the girl from the village is very uncharacteristic of the Mowgli we have come to know over the course of the film. For most of movie, Mowgli is very talkative: he questions the decisions and authority of those around him, he chatters happily with Baloo, and he engages everyone he meets, to include animals with whom he has had no prior dealings, in some form of conversation. Once he sees the girl, however, apart from asking, in fairly hushed tones, what she is, and commenting that he's never seen one before, it is as if – ironically, given that he is about to re-join the human world – he loses his ability to talk: he remains silent from that point on, not even saying "good-bye" to Bagheera and Baloo as he passes through the gate into the man village. He is simply too overwhelmed by the girl, and caught in the force of his sudden attraction to her (and she shows unmistakably that she, too, is attracted to him). His leaving the jungle for the man village is itself potentially symbolic of the fact that he is leaving behind childhood. That he is entering adulthood is reinforced by this awakening of Mowgli's first sexual desire as he follows an attractive female of his own age into the village.

Likewise, it seems that this notion that an attraction to a pretty girl – even if the boy experiencing it doesn't understand it as such – can serve as a signifier of the passage between boyhood and manhood. This notion is evident in the depiction of Taran in *The Black Cauldron*. I have discussed in *Good Girls & Wicked Witches* the history of this film as an adaptation of part of *The Chronicles of Prydain* by Lloyd Alexander, as well as offering a fairly substantial analysis of Princess Eilonwy, and so will refrain from repeating that discussion here.[60] Instead, drawing upon it when necessary, I will turn my attention upon the other main character of the film, Taran, the Assistant Pig-Keeper who must go on a quest to rescue Hen Wen, the Oracular Pig who belongs to Dallben, his master. During this adventure, he meets Princess Eilonwy; the pair bond during their escape from the Horned King's dungeon and subsequent journey to find the Black Cauldron. Readers of *The Chronicles of Prydain* will know that, amongst the many things that are to be part of Taran's and Eilonwy's destinies, they will fall in love and, once they are adults, will be married. No mention of this is made in the Disney adaptation, but we are given hints that, when the pair are a little older, the

60 For this discussion, see Davis, *Good Girls & Wicked Witches*, pp. 154-161.

bond of friendship between them will grow to include a deeply-felt romantic love.

When we first meet Taran, just two minutes into the film, we encounter a young adolescent boy. The first shot of him is of him gazing out of a window, thinking, unaware that the pot of food he should be tending to is beginning to boil over. It transpires that the food is for Hen Wen, a pig, for whom Taran is responsible. Taran is not unruly toward his master or unkind to Hen Wen – quite the opposite – but we learn very quickly that Taran is decidedly unhappy with his lot as Dallben's assistant pig-keeper, and that he wishes to go out into the world and enjoy some sort of adventure. In fact, his first line in the film is, "Oh, Dallben, I was just thinking: what if the war's over, and I never have the chance to fight!" Shortly afterward, he complains to Hen Wen, "I'm a warrior! Not a pig keeper!" Unbeknownst to Taran, however, Hen Wen has the ability to predict the future by gazing into a pool of water after an incantation is spoken; Taren learns this when Hen Wen becomes distraught when her senses alert her to danger, and Dallben has her use her gift in order to find out what is wrong. Dallben, a very kindly old man who has something of a fatherly role with Taran, realises that the evil Horned King has learned about Hen Wen's ability and is looking for her so that he may use her gift of foresight for his own gain. Immediately, Dallben packs up some food and tells Taran to take Hen Wen to the hidden cottage on the edge of the Forbidden Forest so that she will be safe from the Horned King. Somewhat more impressed with Hen Wen, and clearly glad to be getting a chance for an adventure, Taran sets out with Hen Wen.

In the beginning of the film, we see Taran imagining himself as a great warrior: the first time, he is playing about in the farmyard, using a stick as a sword; later, after beginning his journey to take Hen Wen into hiding, we are given a glimpse into Taran's mind, seeing his fantasy on screen as he imagines himself in a golden suit of armour, being declared "Taran of Caer Dallben, the greatest warrior in all Prydain! A true hero!" protecting the "suddenly" (at least in Taran's eyes) valuable and important Hen Wen. It is interesting to note that this "vision" of himself as a noble hero is seen by Taran (and the audience) as coming out of the ripples of a pool of water, not unlike the vision of the Horned King that Hen Wen produced earlier. Those who have read the books know that Taran is destined to become King of Prydain, so this "vision" might be considered, at least partially, a kind of foreshadowing of Taran's destiny, rather than as simply a boyish fantasy. He is jolted out of his imaginings, however, by his sudden realisation that Hen Wen has wandered off, and he has no idea where she's gone.

It is upon Hen Wen's disappearance – just as he is jolted out of this heroic vision of himself – that Taran's adventures really begin. Panicked, he walks a few steps into the forest, calling for Hen Wen and offering her an apple as an enticement, when he encounters the first of those who will form his band: Gurgi, a strange, hairy creature of no fixed species. He speaks like a human, but in a kind of patois rather than normal speech; he is much smaller than Taran – who himself is not a full-grown man – and has an agility and climbing ability similar to that of a monkey or a squirrel; his behaviour and attitude, most of the time, are very childlike in their simplicity and non-malicious selfishness; one of his most distinguishing characteristics is his greediness for food, and his constant search for and demanding of "munchings and crunchings". Shortly after encountering Gurgi, Taran hears Hen Wen, but fails to rescue her from a dragon which swoops down, grabs her, and – much to Taran's horror – flies her off to the Horned King's castle. It is at this point that Gurgi seems to slip into the role of representing the childish side of Taran's personality (and/or Taran's id) just as Taran himself must reject this and move toward manhood and adult responsibilities. Gurgi, sounding like the voice of Taran's fears, urges him, "Oh no, Great Lord. Not go in there [the Horned King's castle]. Forget the piggy." Gurgi says he is there to be Taran's friend, but refuses, initially, to accompany Taran into the castle to rescue Hen Wen. Taran walks off angrily, and Gurgi says to himself, "If Great Lord go into evil castle, poor Gurgi will never see his friend again". Taran goes into the castle alone, his determination to rescue Hen Wen over-ruling the fears (as embodied by Gurgi) that he leaves behind.

Once Taran has managed to scale the walls into the Horned King's castle, we see depicted a combination of the modern notions of a medieval great hall (the long trestle tables with men eating lots of meat and drinking heavily, being entertained by music and a dancing woman) and the stereotypical gang of thugs who are there to support an evil, powerful villain while simultaneously enacting their own strict hierarchies. The Horned King's arrival in the hall – complete with electrical beams and menacing music – is frightening both to those in the hall and to Taran, who watches from a window overlooking the hall. It is in this scene that we are first introduced to another strange creature, Creeper, who looks like a gargoyle come to life, complete with green skin and obeisant attitude. In fact, it can be argued that Creeper is to the Horned King what Gurgi will become to Taran – a loyal friend who will do anything to protect and serve his master, whom he loves deeply (though, in Creeper's case, that love is as much about fear as it is about affection, and Creeper's loyalty will survive only for as long as his master lives). The presence of such a companion for each of these two characters serves in the narrative as a link between Taran and the Horned King: their fates are linked by the battle that must be fought between them later in the narrative, and by the fact that, just as the Horned King rules Prydain at the time of the story, so will Taran someday rule Prydain, though as a good, high-minded, noble leader who wishes to do right by and serve his people, rather than terrorise his kingdom as an evil, calculating monster who uses his people to achieve his own ends.

Taran sees Hen Wen brought forth to the Horned King in chains and ordered to show, through her visions, where the Black Cauldron can be found. She refuses, and Creeper begins to threaten to burn her with a hot coal. At this point, Taran cries out "No!" and jumps down to rescue her, even though the only "weapon" he finds is a broom. He is thrown to the foot of the steps of the Horned King's throne, but his immediate reaction is relief at being reunited with Hen Wen, rather than terror. It is only when the Horned King speaks that Taran shows any fear. He initially refuses to compel Hen Wen to use her visions, but then when the Horned King nearly has her decapitated because, without her visions, she is of no use to him (other than as food, presumably), Taran agrees to call forth one of her visions in order to save her life. She produces the vision, and the Horned King, overcome with his need to find the Black Cauldron, comes to hover over Taran. He uses this opportunity to startle the Horned King, grab Hen Wen, and flee – it is Taran in the role of rescuer, and shown as particularly brave as he has no weapons, only bravery and intelligence. He is able to get Hen Wen out of the castle by helping her jump into the moat to swim away, but Taran himself is caught and thrown into the dungeon. He taunts himself with his memories of his promises to keep Hen Wen from the cauldron and his earlier over-confidence, when he is startled first by the appearance of a magical, floating bauble, then by the appearance of a young girl, Princess Eilonwy. He follows her out of his cell and down through the trap door through which she had entered his cell; she is disappointed that he isn't a lord or a warrior, but is happy for him to come with her. Soon after they meet, they come upon – and accidentally break down the wall and enter into – a secret, forgotten burial chamber; Eilonwy says she thinks it may be that of the great king who built the castle.

She tells Taran to help her look around, and he soon spots a sword resting on top of the King's coffin. We learn soon afterward, when one of the Horned King's henchmen comes after him with an axe, that the sword Taran has found is magical; the second the axe comes into contact with it, a red electrical beam and strange green mist comes from the sword, the axe blade is destroyed, and the thug is so frightened that, begging for mercy, he runs away. Taran is astounded, but delighted: he brandishes the sword happily, and immediately sets out to "save" Princess Eilonwy from the castle; they use the sword's power to thwart their pursuers, finally cutting the chains that will allow them to lower the drawbridge and escape; they are followed by a minstrel they stumbled upon in the dungeon, Fflewddur Fflam, who himself has a magical harp whose strings break when he lies (not dissimilar to Pinocchio's nose as a device whose functions are both didactic and comedic). When we see them next, recovering from their escape, we come upon a shot of them which, in gender role and psychoanalytic terms, is very interesting: Fflewddur Fflam is singing to them while hiding his lower half behind a bush, Eilonwy is sewing the hole in Fflewddur Fflam's trousers, and Taran is polishing the blade of the magical sword, which lays across his lap. Taran's being linked – both in the book and in the film – with a huge sword with great power is of obvious symbolic value. As James W. Maertens points out in his paper on masculinity in Disney's live-action film *20,000 Leagues Under the Sea* (1954), "In his revision of Freud, Jacques Lacan interprets the phallus not merely as a sign of the physical penis, but as a symbol of male social power and the mystery that surrounds it in patriarchal cultures. ... It [the cylindrical object functioning as phallic symbol] operates as a symbol of individual power only as it signifies membership in the hierarchical order of men in a patriarchy."[61]

This idea, of course, is nothing new. But its inclusion in a family/children's film (itself an adaptation of a series of children's books) is somewhat unusual. Taran – unknowingly the future king of Prydain – thinks of himself as a boy, a role that is a hierarchal position within society as a whole as much as it is a description of his age and gender. That a boy is subordinate to a man – an *adult* male – is emphasised further by his description of himself as an *assistant* pig-keeper. The moment he realises the power of the large sword he has acquired, however, Taran's attitude changes. Though, at one point, he does seem to need Eilonwy to remind him to use the sword (to cut the chains which will lower the drawbridge and allow their final escape from the castle), Taran immediately experiences a change in his self-per-

61 James W. Maertens, "Between Jules Verne and Walt Disney: Brains, Brawn, and Masculine Desire in *20,000 Leagues Under the Sea*", in *Science Fiction Studies*, Vol. 22, No. 2 (July 1995), p. 211.

ception once he realises how much power and advantage the sword gives him. He cares for it, protects it, and guards it carefully. In this scene when he is polishing it, sitting on the same log as Eilonwy, who is sewing, one cannot help but compare Taran's sword to the needle Eilonwy is using; sewing – especially this kind of mending – is an activity which has long been associated with women, and seen as an important skill for a wife and mother (and therefore important for a future wife and mother to perfect). Eilonwy isn't just *any* girl, however, she is a princess; those who have read the books will know that she is not only the future Queen of Prydain – Taran's queen – but also that she is the scion of a long line of powerful sorceresses. But here, in this scene, without that knowledge, what we see is an adolescent girl – a young princess who has been a prisoner in the Horned King's dungeon – and therefore someone with only potential power which is meaningless next to the potential hegemonic power Taran has begun to wield, as symbolised by his newly-acquired sword. So Eilonwy's actual power is symbolised by the needle she holds up: obviously, it is significantly smaller than Taran's sword, and holds a very different – and much more domestic – function. Yet it is in this same scene that Taran and Eilonwy argue about who saved whom and who performed the lead role. Taran claims not to have been frightened during their escape; when Eilonwy expresses surprise at this, he argues that it was he who got them out of the castle.

> Eilonwy: You? *I'd* say it was the sword's magic.
>
> Taran: But it takes a great *warrior* to handle a sword like this!
>
> Eilonwy: [laughing] But still, it *is* a magic sword.
>
> Taran: Ha! What does a *girl* know about swords anyway?
>
> Eilonwy: [angrily] Girl? *Girl?* If it weren't for this "girl", *you* would still be in the Horned King's dungeon!

Fflewddur Fflam tries to intervene in the argument, but the two stalk off in opposite directions, Taran referring to her as a "Silly girl" and Eilonwy admonishing Fflewddur Fflam for taking Taran's side. Though they resolve the argument very soon afterward (each acknowledging that they needed the other to escape), it is an interesting argument in light of the scene's symbolism, particularly Taran's retort "What does a girl know about swords anyway?" The symbolic implications are obvious: girls cannot be expected to understand swords because they do not have penises; as sexually immature and unmarried, they do not even have access to one. But this older notion of masculine hegemony is mitigated in the narrative by the way in which Taran and Eilonwy resolve their quarrel: their agreement that each of them played an *equally*-important part in their escape. Such a combination of traditional symbolism, on the one hand, and acknowledgement of sexual equality, on the other, is an excellent example of the many tensions and contradictions to be found in feminism's on-going dialogue with western culture generally. But in the era of second-wave feminism in particular, women's gains in legal, financial, and educational equality were undermined by the persistence of much older images and representations of Woman as the embodiment of domesticity and Woman as sexual object. In the symbolism of Taran's sword, in particular, it is important to remember that this young man has come to possess a sword which once belonged to a past king of Prydain, and therefore is a particularly potent symbol of male authority and social hierarchy. It is even gold, just as was the suit of armour he envisioned in his earlier imagining of himself as the greatest warrior in Prydain. But we see, too, that Taran will not use his sword – his power – indiscriminately. As Taran and Eilonwy are resolving their argument, they hear shouts coming from a distressed Fflewddur Fflam: they run to his aid; Taran has the sword half-way out of its scabbard when he sees that Fflewddur Fflam's attacker is Gurgi, who is trying to steal Fflam's hat and harp. He puts up the sword, but Gurgi nonetheless ceases his attempted theft, even quickly helping/urging Fflam to stand up and pretending to be Fflam's friend. Later, when they find the witches who have the Black Cauldron and the witches threaten to turn them into frogs and eat them, he not only unsheathes the sword, but points it at them threateningly, demanding to know the whereabouts of the cauldron. The witches think, at first, that they can use their magic and cleverness to trick the little group, but the sword – Taran clinging to the hilt for dear life – destroys the various cauldrons, skillets, and so forth which are flying around Taran, and the witches determine to have the sword, offering to trade the Black Cauldron for it. To the witches, it's another trick. they know that Taran and Eilonwy can do nothing with the cauldron, and so assume that the cauldron will be returned to them at some stage, thereby giving the witches ownership of both the sword and the cauldron. Taran refuses, initially, to trade the sword, but soon decides that it is their only choice (even though Eilonwy begs him not to, and even though the witches remind him that this sword could make him the greatest warrior ever). They then take the sword and hand over the cauldron. But it is then that the band of heroes learns that the cauldron can be stopped only if someone willingly climbs into it and sacrifices himself. The group are distraught, with Taran declaring, "Without my sword, I'm nothing – just an assistant pig-keeper". It confirms the sword as a symbol of masculine hegemony since, without it, Taran loses access to real power, at least for now, while he is still a boy.

It is interesting that, when Eilonwy comforts Taran in this scene, reminding him that he *is* somebody and telling him that she believes in him, it is a sign of the pair's growing attraction to one another. The close-up of Eilonwy's face, as well as the close proximity of her face to Taran's, and her wide, soft eyes and gentle voice as she speaks to him are such that, when he stands and clasps her hands in his, the growing sexual attraction between them is obvious, and a delighted Fflewddur Fflam and Gurgi look on at the romantic scene unfolding before them, before an overcome Gurgi gives Fflam a big, loud kiss on the cheek. This breaks the tension in a comical, innocent way; Taran and Eilonwy may be starting to feel something for each other which is very grown up, but they themselves are not yet adults, either physically or in terms of life experience. They are still some way off from knowing what to do with their feelings, and the situation they are in is such that they do not yet have time to deal with them.

It is shortly after this moment that Taran, Eilonwy, and Fflewddur Fflam are recaptured by the Horned King's minions (Gurgi manages to evade capture), this time with the Black Cauldron also coming into the Horned King's possession. They are all taken back to his castle, where the Horned King begins using the cauldron to create his army of "cauldron born", warriors made from the corpses of the dead warriors of centuries past. But just as the Horned King is declaring himself on the verge of victory, Gurgi finds his way into the castle and unties the prisoners. Taran resolves to jump into the cauldron to stop its powers, but Gurgi stops him and jumps into the cauldron himself, much to Taran's horror. Gurgi's sacrifice works, and the power of the Black Cauldron is broken forever. Taran continues to urge Eilonwy and Fflam to escape, and still hopes to save Gurgi. The Horned King confronts him, but in the cauldron's final death throws, it sucks the Horned King into it, bit by bit, destroying him at last. It then sinks into the floor, beginning the destruction of the castle as it does so; the three surviving heroes only just manage to escape with their lives. They make it to the shore, and the cauldron comes up from the water, floating toward them. The witches appear in a cloud, and when they refer to Taran as "our little hero", he declares that it was Gurgi who was the real hero. The witches are about to take the cauldron (pointing out that it's of no use to Taran), when Fflam steps up, repeating the witches' earlier words that "We never give *anything* away – we bargain; we trade". They offer Taran the sword in exchange for the cauldron, and he is tempted, but then replies, mournfully, "I'm not a warrior, I'm a pig boy. What would I do with a sword?" Instead, he offers to trade them the cauldron for Gurgi. The witches agree, and Gurgi appears on the shore, appearing to be lifeless, but shortly afterward return to life. Instantly, the scene changes from dark to light, and, in this last second, Gurgi tricks Taran and Eilonwy into kissing. Laughing, they all set off for home, hand in hand, as Dallben looks on from Hen Wen's vision, declaring, "You did well, my boy!" This last shot of the film gives no hint to the future which awaits Taran and Eilonwy; the closest we get is the foreshadowing that comes with their brief kiss. But it is interesting and important that, ultimately, Taran is willing to give up the sword, and all that it represents, to save his friend – a friend whom he initially distrusted and rejected, but learned at the last minute was good and honourable. If, as discussed earlier, Gurgi serves as a kind of embodiment of Taran's own childish tendencies, it is interesting that this first hint of physical adulthood comes after not just the adventures and battles which have forced Taran into a leadership role of responsibility and caregiving – forced him, in a very real sense, to begin to grow up – but also after Gurgi's self-sacrifice. Even though Gurgi is revived, in the end (after all, Taran still has some growing up ahead of him, so to kill off his inner child would be too drastic, as well as not being in keeping with a studio – and company as a whole – which has always targeted the inner child[62]), nonetheless Gurgi's willingness to sacrifice himself functions as the symbolic death of Taran's childhood. That he is on the brink of manhood is shown further by his kissing Eilonwy, as well as by the pleasure that both take from the kiss, even if the kiss itself is brief and a surprise.

On the Brink of Manhood (More or Less ...)

The boys in this next section, whether or not they realise it (or even like it), are each in their own ways on the brink of adulthood. They may be frozen there, as is Peter Pan; frightened of future responsibility but coming to terms with it, as is Wart/Arthur; or ready, by the end of their story, to embrace their new role fully, as is the case with Jim Hawkins. This is treated with different signifiers in each of their films: their levels of responsibility (for themselves and others), their ability to understand (and even share) mature emotional connections, and their understanding of the inherent complexities of the world. At the ends of each of their stories, these three characters are all at different levels of readiness, but they are all nonetheless on the verge of adulthood.

62 In a studio memo during the production of *Snow White and the Seven Dwarfs*, Walt Disney wrote "We don't cater to the child but to the child in the adult – what we all imagined as kids is what we'd like to see pictured". He would express the same idea on numerous occasions. Memo quoted in Allan, *Walt Disney and Europe*, pp. 42-43.

For the two who will embrace adulthood and leave their child-hoods behind, it is possible to imagine a bright future. Peter Pan, presumably, is still out there in Neverland, revelling in the heady, liminal landscape that separates these two life stages.

Peter Pan's opening narration sets out to make the story timeless and universal; with a first line which paraphrases Ecclesiastes 1:9,[63] the narration implies that the film's depiction of children and childhood is eternal, and that the story we will be enjoying is just one of the many episodes of this eternal theme: "All this has happened before, and it will all happen again. But this time it happened in London. It happened on a quiet street in Bloomsbury. ... And Peter Pan chose this particular house be-cause there were people here who believed in him." Even as we are being introduced to the Darling family, we are learning about Peter Pan, whose story seems entwined with the family's own. Yet this strong link between the Darlings and Peter Pan still manages to keep Peter separate from them. Even though we learn that Michael and John believe in his actual existence (unlike their parents) and that Wendy is "the supreme authority" on Peter Pan, it must be remembered that there would be no need for belief in his existence, let alone a kind of academic expertise of him (as it is said that Wendy has), if Peter were an actual member of the family. Even at the end of the film, when his existence is proven (even to Mr. and Mrs. Darling) beyond all doubt, Peter is still someone apart: proof that Peter Pan is real comes to the Darling parents when they and Wendy watch him as he steers Captain Hook's ship (which has been sprinkled with pixie dust so that it could be flown to London to return Wendy, Michael and John to their own home) through the clouds and away from Bloomsbury, back to Neverland. He is well known to the Dar-lings – and beloved by them – but, ultimately, he is not one of them because, unlike them, he will never grow up or grow old, and therefore will retain his youthful focus on adventure and freedom, potentially forever.

It could be argued that the way in which Peter is depicted marks him out very strongly as an "All-American" boy: his accent and his speech patterns, his strongly-independent attitudes, and his willingness to "show off" for Wendy and the others all contrast sharply with Michael and John Darling, who are shown to be much more cautious, circumspect, regimented, and polite in a formal way. One article about the film from the 1953 Dis-ney/RKO press pack explicitly mentions his voice (though not his accent) as being "... as he must have been in Barrie's mind ... a precise speaking voice".[64] Given that the same article mentions

63   "What has happened before will happen again, What has been done before will be done again. There is nothing new in the whole world." Ecclesiastes 1:9.

64   "Disney Presents Famed Play in Cartoon-Feature", from *Peter Pan*'s Press Pack, Library of Congress (File C-3), p. 5.

in its first paragraph that the role of Peter Pan is "articulated by Bobby Driscoll", however, there can have been little doubt that Peter would be heard speaking in an American accent; Driscoll's own American (ever so slightly Californian) accent is there in his portrayal of Jim Hawkins in *Treasure Island* (1950), after all. As for the Darling children, little mention of their "English-ness" is made in the press pack articles. Even so, Michael and John are proper little English gentlemen, and Wendy is a proper little English lady, characteristics of which, while depicted in the film as endearing (since, for an American audience, such accents might well have been deemed charming *because* of their difference), nonetheless mark them as different – even Othered – within Neverland, just as Peter is very much an outsider in the Darlings' Bloomsbury nursery, no matter how much they love and admire him. No evidence seems to exist for this, at least not in what is available outside the still-closed Disney archives. Yet it is entirely possible that, as Hollywood film makers who had been making films in the UK for a few years by the time *Peter Pan* was made, it might well have been deemed to be a good idea to endow Peter Pan with an American accent. Surprisingly, this addition to the character may have helped make him seem more enjoyable and identifiable to British audiences than might have been the case had Peter Pan spoken with a British accent of some description, English (in one of its variations along regional and class lines) or otherwise (indeed, an interesting choice might have been to have given Peter Pan a mild Scottish accent in tribute to his creator, the Scotsman J.M. Barrie). However, as Mark Glancy notes in an essay on the reception of Hitchcock's film *Blackmail* (1929), while it may not always have been noted/considered by those who wrote film reviews in the UK, it would seem that, for many British filmgoers, a standard American accent, though initially perceived (and commented on) by some in very negative (even xenophobic) terms, eventually came to be seen as "... a neutral one, or at least one free of the regional and class characteristics that divided British accents".[65] While, certainly, the American audience undoubtedly would have been the Disney studio's primary target audience, nonetheless it would have had an eye on foreign audiences such as the British audience. An accent choice for the title character that would have been identifiable to American audiences as "one of us" and, simultaneously, satisfactory to British audiences as "neutral" (unlike the accents of the Darling family) and therefore acceptable, would have had obvious benefits in bringing such an iconic piece of British children's literature to the screen; this is something which likely would have been of particular concern in 1953, given the rather

65 Mark Glancy, "*Blackmail* (1929), Hitchcock, and Film Nationalism", in James Chapman, Mark Glancy, and Sue Harper (Eds.), *The New Film History: Sources, Methods, Approaches* (Basingstoke: Palgrave MacMillan, 2007), p. 197.

lukewarm reception received by *Alice in Wonderland* when it had been released in 1951.

It could also be argued that this Americanisation of Peter Pan himself, as well as of the Lost Boys (all of whom speak with mainstream American accents and even engage in American slang in a way that Peter does not) extends to Neverland as a whole. Almost everyone who lives in Neverland, from the Mermaids to the Indians to many of the pirates have American accents (we hear most of all from Captain Hook and Smee, and Smee's accent is definitely American, even if Hook's accent – voiced by Hans Conried, the same actor as the one doing Mr. Darling's voice, in accordance with the narrative's theatrical tradition – is rendered as English, albeit by an American actor). The presence of the Native Americans who live there (and, it is implied, are native to the island), and with whom we spend a great deal of screen time while in Neverland, could be said to further emphasise this, despite the racist and stereotyped depiction found in the film (and, indeed, within the traditions of the play), linking as they do to some fairly similar depictions of Native Americans to be found elsewhere in cinema and television in the 1950s, a decade still remembered for its fondness for Westerns. Whether this is done to "explain" or "naturalise" Peter's accent (in much the same way that, a few years later, Hayley Mills' English accent would be explained away when she made her American film debut in *Pollyanna,* 1960, by having Pollyanna's aunt in the film tell another character that Pollyanna's late father had been a missionary in the British West Indies) is hard to say with any certainty. Likewise, it can only be supposed that Neverland was "Americanised" to foster the sense of Peter Pan as an "all-American" boy. Regardless of whether this was (or was not) done intentionally by the Disney studio, it certainly seems to have produced that effect.

Additionally, it is interesting that one of the things about their version of *Peter Pan* that the Disney studio seems to have been keen to emphasise at the time of the film's 1953 release was the fact that this was the first time in the character's history that he was to be played by a boy. In the 1953 press pack created by Disney and RKO to accompany the film's distribution, numerous ready-made newspaper articles included in the pack emphasise that the role had been voiced by Bobby Driscoll. A number of those point out that, in the (professional) theatrical productions of *Peter Pan* since its first production in 1904, the role had always been played by women. But here – thanks to the magic of animation, it is implied – the role has finally been brought to life as Barrie himself must have intended originally – as male. One article in particular is keen to emphasise the character's masculinisation. Beginning with the sentence – hovering over top of the article in such a way as to make it stand out – "Peter Pan is a boy at last!" – the article goes to great lengths to talk about the greater authenticity of the Disney studio's rendering of Peter Pan as a character. The last part of the article is worth repeating in full:

> Since its initial performance in London in 1904, the play has paraded an array of brilliant actresses as *Pan* including Maude Adams, Cissie Loftus and most recently Glynis Johns and Jean Arthur. Children adored them and their elders applauded them and were warmed under the spell of their individual charm. But they were always feminine.
>
> Disney has lost none of that magic power of illusion in his *Pan* character. He is kept anonymous and positively masculine in feature and gesture with the voice roughly boyish, as Bobby Driscoll, a Disney made star, speaks through the cartoon.
>
> Peter's masculinity, in addition to giving character to the role, also provides elbowroom for the uproarious comedy-in-action with which Disney showers the most humorous and exciting fantasy he has ever made.[66]

Driscoll, who had appeared in live-action roles in four previous Disney films, was only arguably a "Disney made" star, contrary to what the article suggests; in fact, Driscoll had appeared in nine roles prior to his first Disney role as Johnny, the lead male character (besides Uncle Remus) in *Song of the South* (1946). In 1950, he won an Academy Award for Outstanding Juvenile Actor of 1949 for playing the lead role in the 1949 film noir *The Window*, and later in 1950 would return to Disney to star as Jim Hawkins in the first completely live-action film produced by Disney, *Treasure Island*. Peter Pan was Driscoll's fifth role for Disney, and by this stage his credentials as a charming, loveable, but nonetheless rough-and-tumble, intelligent, adventurous and very "boyish" boy had been well established through his previous roles, and he was a well-known (and well-respected) child actor amongst Hollywood audiences for his work at Disney and elsewhere. Therefore, by making reference to him in the way that several of the press pack's articles do, this idea of the importance of the "authentic" boy becomes an essential one: as the quote above points out in its final paragraph, it is "Peter's masculinity" in the Disney version – as opposed to the "always feminine" depictions of the character in previous productions – which allows the film to show Neverland to its best advantage *and* allows for the narrative to be (according to the article) funnier and more exciting (an "uproarious comedy-in-action") than all other ver-

66 "Beloved Stage Play Translated to Screen in Walt Disney's Lavish Film, 'Peter Pan,'" from *Peter Pan*'s Press Pack, p. 2.

67 In fact, there is some evidence that the Disney studio – and Walt Disney personally – had attempted on several occasions to contact Maud Adams to discuss her interpretation of the role of Peter Pan on the stage. However, in a studio memo dated 17 March 1941 written by Walt Disney to Kay Kamen, Walt instructs him "Please don't do anything further about Miss Maude Adams and Stephens College, insofar as concerns our version of *Peter Pan*. ... I got nowhere with her at all. She wouldn't even give me the courtesy of looking at our [leica] reel [of some early ideas the studio had about producing a version of *Peter Pan*] – her reasons, as expressed to me through President Wood of the college, were to the effect 'that the Peter whom she created was to her real life and blood, while another's creation of this character would be only a ghost to her'. To me, it's all pretty silly and from my point of view I would say that Miss Adams is simply living in the past." From *Walt Disney: An Intimate History of the Man and his Magic*. CD-ROM. Found at: Library/Peter Pan/ Peter Pan (To Kay Kamen).

68 "Disney Restores Peter Pan to

sions of the play. In other words – and in common with an important theme in the film (and much to Wendy's dismay in the story) – boys are allowed to have more fun than girls; or as Wendy is admonished by one of the inhabitants of the Indian encampment, "Squaw no dance. Squaw get some firewood." As can be seen in the quote from the article, it is more than implied that Disney's version can be more enjoyable than previous versions because having an *actual* boy in the role (even if it is only the *voice* of a real boy, albeit a voice which is combined with the animated drawings of a boy to give a visual dimension to Driscoll's performance) means that the story can engage in more excitement and adventure. It is implied as well that Peter himself is more enjoyable and interesting than was ever possible when Peter was played by an actress, however "brilliant" and well-received those actresses may have been.[67] The articles in the press pack imply that it is Driscoll's maleness that is "giving character to the role", even if his contribution is simply his voice (albeit mediated through the audience's knowledge of him from his live-action roles) rather than a performance which incorporates both his voice *and* his body, as would happen in a live-action performance. The use of a boy's voice is enough to make the character "authentically" real and male, even though his bodily representation is created through animation. In fact, Disney and RKO seem to be at pains in some articles to emphasise that having Driscoll in the role brings an authenticity to the role which, previously, it had been lacking: "By using Bobby as the voice and inspiration in the title role, Walt Disney has returned to the character of Barrie's imagination – the real *Peter Pan*".[68] In any event, audiences responded well to *Peter Pan*, and it was one of the studio's most financially-successful animated feature films of the 1950s; its version of the boy who never grew up would become *the* version of Peter Pan seen by generations of animation fans for many decades following.

Another incongruously American-accented British character is the next boy to lead a Disney animated feature, Wart, who we know will grow up to be King Arthur, in the 1963 film *The Sword in the Stone*. Sadly, little attention – scholarly or otherwise – has been paid to this film, despite the fact that it did reasonably well at the box office. According to Robin Allan, the rights to T.H. White's book of the same name were purchased in 1939, not long after the book's 1938 publication, but an adaptation of the film was delayed, at least in part, because Walt felt that the narrative "... was too English, too localised as a property for a cartoon film"; he changed his mind about this after the 1959 success of *Camelot*, however, and work began on the film.[69] In their classic book *The*

Illusion of Life, Frank Thomas and Ollie Johnston do make numerous references to the film, but only in specific instances where they can use the artwork from the film's production as an example of the craft of animation, such as their discussion of what it took to render Wart and Merlin in the form of squirrels who, while still being believably squirrels, would still be recognisable as Wart and Merlin.[70] Indeed, Robin Allan comments that, when he would mention the film when interviewing Disney artists from the early 1960s, "The artists had difficulty recalling *The Sword in the Stone* and made few comments in interview".[71] The film seems to be overlooked in academic discussion, too. Maureen Fries examines Madame Mim as part of a larger chapter on depictions of the character of Morgana in various films, though there is nothing in the film which would imply that Madame Mim and the traditional Arthurian character of Morgana are one and the same.[72] In an article specifically on various adaptations of the Arthurian legends as the basis for a relatively early course/module on film adaptations of the Arthurian legends (a kind of "fiction to film"-type class which would have been common in English departments in American colleges and universities during the 1980s and early 1990s), Bruce A. Beatie trivialises the film entirely, claiming first that "Disney's *Sword in the Stone* (1963) is too childish to be of use in a college-level course" (this was his "derogative" description of an adaptation of a children's book!), and adding a few pages later – just in case the reader missed it the first time – that the film "... is not worth serious consideration".[73] In neither case does he offer any explanation for such a stridently dismissive opinion; apparently, its designation as a Disney adaptation, at least in his mind, is evidence enough of its worthlessness as a focus of study. Such an attitude is typical of early film studies scholarship, sadly, and even a little over two decades later is still not wholly unknown.

Yet despite such unusually-limited academic discussion of the film, overall it is a sweet, charming narrative told in an amusing, engaging way: as constructed for the Disney version, it is simultaneously the story of Merlin, who finds and educates the boy destined to be England's once and future king, and the story of young Arthur, known as Wart (or the Wart), who must learn the importance of education and intelligence in a world where neither of these is as valued as brute strength and military prowess. Over the course of the film, Merlin teaches Wart to use his reason and intellect to solve problems, and Wart also learns about responsibility, self-worth, and love through a series of "adventures" which come about as the result of Merlin using his magic to teach Arthur lessons about the world (some of which, as a joke, involve

J.M.B.'s Original Idea", from *Peter Pan*'s Press Pack, p. 2.

69 Allan, p. 240.

70 Thomas and Johnston, *Illusion*, pp. 331-332.

71 Allan, p. 241.

72 Maureen Fries, "How to Handle a Woman, or Morgan at the Movies", in Kevin J. Harty (Ed.), *King Arthur on Film: New Essays on Arthurian Cinema* (Jefferson, NC: McFarland & Company, Inc., 1999), pp. 73-74.

73 Bruce A. Beatie, "Arthurian Films and Arthurian Texts: Problems of Reception and Comprehension", in *Arthurian Interpretations*, Vol. 2, No. 2 (Spring 1988), pp. 71, 76.

Merlin teaching Arthur about things which either were unknown or did not exist at all during the Dark Ages, such as a working knowledge of the force of gravity and the fact that someday humans will invent steam engines and flying machines). But Arthur, who is (and, indeed, has to be) more practical than Merlin, recognises that he must live in the times in which he has been born, and so is thrilled when Sir Ector, his guardian, makes him squire to his foster brother, Sir Kay. Merlin is furious and disappointed at Wart's assertion that he is lucky to be Kay's squire, given his position within his society; exclaiming "Blow me to Bermuda!" Merlin takes off like a rocket (literally) and flies from the castle into the distance, leaving Wart alone with Archimedes (Merlin's familiar, a talking owl). Unavoidably in a story about the young King Arthur, the next lesson young Wart will learn is about destiny, when he becomes the one who can pull the sword (Excalibur) from the stone, and thereby show himself to be the rightful and pre-destined king of England. But the implication, when his foster brother, the adult, muscular Sir Kay, tries to re-draw the sword after Wart and finds it impossible, is that it is Arthur's special qualities – his difference, which comes largely from his intelligence and sensitivity – that make him best suited to be England's king. Those who witness Arthur's pulling out the sword hail it as a miracle, and Arthur is put upon the throne of England. But Wart is still very much a boy, and frightened of being king. He decides to escape, but each door he opens leads to his being greeted with shouts of "Long live King Arthur!" so that he slams the door and runs the other way. He stands in the middle of the throne room, confused and panicked, and says to Archimedes, "Oh, Archimedes, I wish Merlin was here!" Suddenly, Merlin appears, flying through a window into the throne room as a cluster of multi-coloured sparkling lights resembling a comet's tail. As his feet touch down in the throne room, he returns to human form – only now he is dressed in red sneakers, yellow Bermuda shorts, a striped shirt, a baseball cap, and sunglasses, and proclaims that he is "Back from Bermuda and the twentieth century! And believe me, you can have it! One big modern mess."[74] He then taps himself on the head with his staff, and resumes the more "traditional" (for Merlin) robe and pointed wizard's hat that he had worn earlier in the movie. He comforts Wart, remembering that it was Arthur's destiny to become "King Arthur and his Knights of the Round Table", assuring him that he'll be a legend, and that they someday will even make a motion picture about him (when Arthur asks, "Motion picture?" Merlin responds "Well, that's something like television – without commercials".). The last shot of the film is

74 Previously in the film, Merlin has made reference to his and Arthur's world as "One big medieval mess".

of young Arthur dressed in his royal robe and crown, seated on the throne, Merlin and Archimedes at his side.

Though in many ways it possible to argue that Wart is the main character, and though he is a sympathetic, likeable character, ultimately he is overshadowed both by the eccentric, dynamic Merlin, and by the knowledge that the audience has of the larger story of King Arthur; like Merlin, we know about not only the changes, discoveries, and inventions which will come about over the centuries between Wart's time and our own, but we know too about this boy's future – its triumphs and its ultimate tragedy. In many ways, it is too large a burden for the character to carry successfully: he is never as well-developed as he might have been, perhaps in part because the role of his voice was shared between three different individuals (Rickie Sorenson, Richard Reitherman, and Robert Reitherman; the Reitherman boys were both sons of the film's director, Wolfgang "Woolie" Reitherman, one of Disney's legendary "Nine Old Men"), so that not even a single actor was given the chance to cultivate more fully the character's persona through the voice performance. He is also overshadowed by a much livelier Merlin, who steals each scene in which they appear together (and most scenes featuring Arthur include Merlin). But in a discussion of boyhood as it is depicted by Disney animated features, it should be noted that it is very much the character's boyishness – his youth, inexperience, naivety, and enthusiasm – which are integral to this version of the story of King Arthur, even though we never get any kind of glimpse or foreshadowing of his time as ruler of Camelot (Camelot is never mentioned by name; the closest we get is to the single, brief reference from Merlin to the Knights of the Round Table). There is no chance meeting with a young Guinevere or any of his future knights, no allusion to the island of Avalon. Instead, this is solely Arthur's youth, when his greatest aspiration must be nothing more than to be squire to his foster brother, and where his destiny becomes known to him only by accident, and only in the final fifteen minutes of the film. But it is possible to argue that it is *how* he is depicted as a boy that hints at his future greatness: Wart is a conscientious and hard worker, honest, honourable, intelligent, enthusiastic, resourceful, respectful, mentally flexible, and able to empathise with those around him. He stands up for himself when he must, but never seeks trouble or discord, and certainly he is no bully, nor is he broken or cowed by the somewhat bullying treatment he receives from Kay and, to a lesser extent, his guardian, Sir Ector. When he first becomes king, he is frightened, and still young enough to think that it might be possible to run away, but after a few words from Merlin, we see him sitting on the throne – his legs still too short for his feet to reach the ground – ready to face his destiny and become the great king we – the audience, who are aware of the Arthurian legends – know he will be. This, ultimately, seems to be the depiction of boyhood as a time of waiting: what the boy will be and what his life will be like cannot be known to him even if it is known to the audience, but we can, occasionally, be given brief glimpses of the nature of the man he will become, and thereby receive some assurance that, ultimately, all will be well. It is not, however, boyhood as transitional phase; if anything, the film shows that boyhood is valuable in and of itself, and worthy of attention and celebration. It is in his boyhood, after all, that Wart gets some of his most colourful experiences (experiencing life in the bodies of a fish, then a squirrel, then a bird, thereby taking him beyond his human body and human perspectives), and where the idea of his potential – of what he *might* be – is explored most explicitly. Once he has become king, and has accepted this role, the film ends: we know what awaits him, and the comparative lack of freedom to enjoy adventures – especially fantastical ones – means that, in this case, it is a story with which, the narrative implies, it is not really worth bothering.

Our final boy in this section, Jim Hawkins, is the boy who finds the treasure map and sets forth in a ship to find not only riches, but also his best path through life. But unlike in Robert Louis Stevenson's novel, or even in Disney's first-ever live-action feature film, the Jim Hawkins we're discussing here sets forth in a galleon-shaped spaceship called the R.L.S.[75] Legacy in the 2002 film *Treasure Planet*. In this version, which is set in a time and place which is a (rather odd, admittedly) combination of the eighteenth-century setting of *Treasure Island* and some futuristic world (or possibly the setting is meant to be a long time ago in a different galaxy far, far away …), we meet a Jim Hawkins who is being raised by a single mother (who works hard to run their inn, the Benbow, while still being a good and devoted mother who loves her son dearly). We learn during the film that Jim's father walked out on him and his mother several years previously. Jim, despite being intelligent and good at heart, is nonetheless constantly in trouble with the law for getting up to mischief of all sorts, to include racing around on a kind of futuristic, solar-powered flying skateboard/surfboard. Only a few minutes into the film, young Jim rescues an elderly seaman, Billy Bones, and acquires Bones' map to Treasure Planet, which in the film is considered by the characters to be a legendary place that the supposedly mythological Captain Flint used to store the "treasure of a thousand worlds". Jim asks his mother to be allowed to go

75 R.L.S. is, presumably a tribute to the author of the source/inspiration novel, Robert Louis Stevenson.

57

in search of the treasure, but she is reluctant; she believes that the stories of Flint and Treasure Planet are fictional, plus she is worried about letting her son go so far away, no doubt fearing that he will get into trouble of some kind, and possibly end up injured or killed. Finally, she is persuaded by their family friend, Dr. Delbert Doppler, an eccentric astrophysicist, to allow Jim to undertake the journey (under Doppler's supervision), arguing that "There are much worse remedies than a few character-building months in space". It is clear that Sarah is afraid for her son and for his future, but decides to trust in her son and hope for the best.

Despite Sarah's reluctance to let Jim go, Doppler's advice proves to be sound: Jim benefits enormously from his time on the Legacy, despite – and because of – the fact that he finds himself under the charge of John Silver, a cyborg who, by day, serves as the ship's cook, but who in fact is plotting an insurrection in which he will lead the crew to take over the ship and steal the map once they have reached Treasure Planet. Silver's plan is that he will work Jim so hard that he'll be too tired to notice the plotting going on around him. To Jim, the fact that Captain Amelia has put the cook in charge of him is infuriating, and he seems in danger of slipping into his usual pattern of rebellion, seeking out excitement rather than accepting responsibility. Though initially suspicious of Jim, Silver begins to feel sorry for the boy, and takes Jim under his wing: this combination of hard work and love – coming as it does in the form of a father figure of sorts – is just what Jim needs, and he begins to thrive, enjoying the responsibility and excitement of the voyage, as well as the chance to bond with someone whose dreams and enjoyments are similar to Jim's own (presumably, this is why Doppler never fulfilled such a role in Jim's life, as he is too bookish and cerebral to serve as a role model for Jim). Though the film never comments explicitly on it, nonetheless it is worth noting that neither his mother – even though they seem close – nor Captain Amelia are able to set Jim on the straight and narrow; it seems it takes a man – and a rugged, tough man at that – to reach Jim. Whether this is a comment on single mothers and women as role models to boys is hard to say, however, as there are men in Jim's life – Doppler, the police – who try to help him but equally are unable. So perhaps the implication is that traditional authority figures are the issue, since each of them give him either too much understanding (Sarah, Jim's mother) or too little love (the police, Doppler, Amelia). Silver, however, employs his own brand of tough love, and it is thanks to this balance of affection and discipline that Jim is able to mature.

Despite the hard physical chores (scrubbing the decks, cleaning the mountains of dishes and cookware from the galley) which, at least initially, Silver makes him do in order to wear him out (arguing that the boy will be too tired to notice that mischief is afoot on the ship), Jim *does* begin to suspect that something is going on, though it is some time before he knows for certain that Silver is connected to it. He does, however, suspect that all is not quite right with Silver soon after meeting him. As his bond with Silver grows, however, he seems to forget about this. As we learn from a montage that begins not long after Jim reveals to Silver that his father walked out on him and Sarah several years earlier, we see that his initial anger at being made to serve as Silver's cabin boy – and all of the hard work that role entails – transforms in the face of Silver's growing respect for his hard work. The two bond, and Jim finds in Silver a substitute father. This means that when one of the crew, Scroop, unbeknownst to all but Silver, cuts one of the lifelines that it was Jim's responsibility to secure and the first mate, Mr. Arrow, is lost during their escape from the field of a dying star that had devolved into a black hole, it falls to Silver to help Jim deal with his guilt. Though Jim is certain that he secured the lifelines properly, nonetheless he is devastated to think that he might be responsible for Mr. Arrow's death, unaware that he has been framed deliberately. Jim feels deeply upset, but is comforted by Silver's assertion that, "You've got the makings of greatness in you, but you gotta take the helm and chart your own course! Stick to it, no matter the squalls, and when the time comes and you get the chance to really test the cut of your sails and show what you're made of ... well ... I hope I'm there – catching some of the light coming off ya that day." Jim lets down his guard at last, turning to Silver for comfort, and Silver hugs the boy, consoling him as best he can.

The next morning, however, Jim, who has chased Morph into the galley and ended up in a barrel with him, overhears the pirates confronting Silver, both about their wish to begin the insurrection and about Silver's relationship with Jim. To his horror, Jim hears Silver first reveal himself as the leader of an insurrection intent on stealing the treasure, then hears Silver deny that he cares about Jim when Silver tells the angry pirates, "I care about one thing and one thing only – Flint's trove. You think I'd risk it all for the sake of some nose-wiping little whelp? ... I cozied up to that kid to keep him off our scent. But I ain't gone soft." There is a cry of "Land-ho!" but Jim cannot bring himself to react; he sits in the barrel, devastated by what he has just overheard as, in effect, he is abandoned by a second father. He pulls himself together and is about to climb the steps up to the deck when Silver appears, and realises that Jim must have heard everything. We see his cyborg hand, hidden behind his back, transform from a mechanical hand into a pistol; Jim, no longer trusting Silver, realises that he is in danger, and reaches on the table behind him for a weapon. He manages to duck under Silver, stabbing the hydraulics in Silver's leg so that he can't catch him, and runs up on deck to retrieve his map, a gold mechanical sphere hidden in the captain's state room. Silver announces that the time to begin the mutiny has come. But Jim has secured the cabin door and reached Doppler and Amelia in time to warn them. They arm themselves, and managed to escape the captain's stateroom just as the pirates break down the door. Morph gets the map from Jim – not to steal it, but to play a game with it – and once again Jim must rely on his youthful agility and speed to beat Silver to it. He gets to the longboat just in time, and the trio make it to the surface of Treasure Planet. The captain has been hurt, however, and so she sends Jim to find a place where they might take shelter and better defend themselves. Determined to find such a place – and angry that he has just realised that what he thought was the map was in fact Morph (who had assumed the map's form), and that the map sphere is still on the Legacy – Jim sets off into the planet's strange forest. Almost immediately, he encounters B.E.N. (a reference to Ben Gunn, from the novel; in this case, B.E.N. stands for Bio-Electronic Navigator), a hyperactive robot (voiced by Martin Short) with a missing primary memory circuit who has been marooned on Treasure Planet for many years. Jim realises that B.E.N. has some connection with Captain Flint, but B.E.N.'s missing memory circuit means that he cannot make sense of the fragments he recalls. B.E.N. allows Jim and the others to take refuge in his home (an easily-defensible spot), and they set about determining what they need to do.

The pirates find them, and Jim agrees to meet Silver halfway and "palaver" with him; Jim realises that Silver believes that he has the map. His distrust for Silver is evident, as is his hurt; when Silver tells him that he didn't mean what he said about Jim, and that he's willing to make a deal with Jim to split the treasure evenly, Jim pretends to play along, before confronting Silver, throwing Silver's words back in his face and swearing that Silver won't get a single piece of the treasure. In his anger, he even mimics Silver's accent derisively back at him. But rather than be hurt or mournful, as he was when his real father left, this time he is fully determined to hold his own. It is worth noting that an important difference between the Jim Hawkins of *Treasure Island* and the Jim Hawkins of *Treasure Planet* is that the Jim being discussed here is several years older. Whereas, in *Treasure Island*, he is a boy of probably no more than ten or eleven years of age (an estimate based on the fact that his voice has yet to change from a child's into a man's), the Jim of *Treasure Planet* is well into his teens – probably around the age of sixteen – and so is on the cusp of manhood. His reaction to Silver is indicative of this, too, as he shows himself to be able to move quickly past the hurt he feels at Silver's betrayal, and instead embrace a steely determination to beat Silver at his own game. That night, he muses that, without the map, there's nothing they can do to save themselves, when B.E.N. happens to mention that his home has a backdoor. Realising that it will allow him to slip past the pirates, Jim goes with B.E.N. and Morph back to the Legacy to retrieve the map. He is forced into a fight with Scroop, but kills him (it is very much a case of kill or be killed) by letting him fly out into space, and still manages to retrieve the map, get the laser cannons disconnected and return to B.E.N.'s hideout. Unfortunately, the pirates have taken over B.E.N.'s hideout, and they get the map from Jim. Silver is unable to figure out how to work the map, however, and forces Jim to do it. Jim refuses to hand it over, however, telling Silver that, if he wants the map, he (Jim) is coming with them.

They follow the map's trail, then realise that the map opens a portal which functions as a giant door, allowing instant access to any point in the universe. While Silver and the others are mesmerised by the enormity of Flint's treasure, Jim determines to find a way to escape, vowing that he won't go home empty-handed. Unfortunately for all, a booby trap has been tripped, and the planet begins to fall apart. Jim begins trying to hotwire Flint's craft (which sits amongst the treasure, Flint's remains sitting on a throne on deck) and sends B.E.N. to find Doppler and Amelia. He manages to get the ship working just as Silver makes his way onto the deck. He tries to cosy up to Jim, but Jim refuses to be taken in this time; he pulls a machete on Silver, but before they can do anything, the ship is hit by a falling piece of the planet and the two are knocked overboard. Silver manages to save himself, but realises that Jim is in trouble. He knows that he can't hang onto both the ship (which is full of treasure) and rescue Jim, so he lets the ship go and saves Jim instead. It restores Jim's faith in the pirate, and the two work together to save the few survivors before the planet is destroyed. Amelia and Doppler have managed to retrieve the Legacy, and they pick up Jim and Silver (B.E.N. is safely aboard already, and a handful of pirates are imprisoned below). When the ship's thrusters are damaged, Silver and Jim work together to change the portal so that it opens onto their home port: Jim uses his "surfing" skills (which had landed him in trouble at home) to change the portal door so that the Legacy can fly through it and they can escape the destruction of Treasure Planet, ending up back at Montressor. Amelia promises to recommend Jim to the Interstellar Academy, and Doppler enthuses, "Just wait until your mother hears about this! Of course, we may downplay the life-threatening parts." B.E.N. and Morph celebrate, too, but it is to Silver that Jim looks, only to realise that Silver has disappeared. He follows Silver into the hold, seeing that Silver is about to escape (knowing that he faces prison for leading an insurrection). Jim opens the hull, acknowledging that he is happy to turn a blind eye and let Silver get away. Silver asks Jim to come with him, promising excitement and freedom. Jim's reply, however, shows how much he has grown: "You know, when I got on this boat, I would've taken you up on that offer in a second. But I met this old cyborg, and he taught me I could chart my own course. That's what I'm gonna do." When Silver asks him, "And what do you see, off that bow of yours?" Jim replies, simply, "A future". The very best of Jim's and Silver's affection for one another is revived, and they part on the best of terms, but they do so with Jim knowing exactly who – and what – Silver is. There is still a father-son bond between them, but it is no longer adult-child. Instead, it is two equals. That Jim has grown up during his adventure in further shown when he is greeted by his mother at the docks. Before he left home, he was still a boy, and still a little shorter than her; he also tended to stoop. Upon his return, he has grown to be slightly taller, has acquired the proportions of a young man, and most importantly (and symbolically) of all, has learned to stand up straight. In the final scene, the celebration of the reopening of the Benbow Inn, Jim arrives escorted by the police, mirroring an earlier scene in the film. This time, however, he is dressed in a white navel uniform, and the police shake his hand. He joins his mother briefly in the dancing, but our last shot of him is of Jim gazing through the window up to the sky; in the clouds, he sees the shape of John Silver, smiling down at him. He may have become a man to be proud of through his own hard work, but Jim will never forget who helped him onto that road in the first place.

Becoming (Like) Real Boys

Each of the boys we have examined – with the possible exception of Peter Pan – has undergone an adventure which has served him as a voyage of self-discovery and maturation. Though some of the boys we have discussed travel further than others (Peter goes into the forest near his home to capture the wolf, whereas Jim Hawkins travels deep into the galaxy to another planet), all experience their ultimate self-discovery when they leave home – or at least their daily routine – and experience something of the world beyond what they know already. Interestingly, it is the one who experiences the least amount of growth – Peter Pan – who sticks closest to his routine. True, he voyages between the Darlings' Bloomsbury nursery and Neverland, but it is a journey which we know he has made on many occasions (since he likes to listen in at the nursery window to Wendy's stories about him). For our other characters – Pinocchio, Peter/Петя, Wart, Mowgli, Taran, Cody, and Jim – the story which unfolds around them, ultimately, is one in which they learn about the things which western society deems to be unsuitable for children: they learn about suffering, fear, danger, betrayal, death ... and in some cases, also have their first experience of physical desire. As James R. Keller notes in his examination of the boys of *South Park* (1997-present),

> "Often the end of so-called innocence is signalled by the attainment of carnal knowledge or, alternatively, knowledge of the cruel, violent, and vulgar world that awaits the child at the end of its pre- and post-pubescent repose. To contemporary sensibilities, the opposite of innocence is ... Knowledge – the symbolic – and knowledge subsequently recodes innocence as ignorance or emptiness. The process of maturation is of course the filling up that emptiness with content, of learning to suture the gap between the reality of fragmentation and the imaginary unification of ego."[76]

Though Keller's subjects – the boys of South Park – inhabit a very different (and much more graphic, chaotic) world, nonetheless the idea rings true for Disney. Yes, part of what it means to grow up is to reach certain landmark ages. These can vary, however, between different cultures and time periods. These milestones automatically – and one might argue, arbitrarily – grant an individual with certain adult rights and privileges, such as being allowed to apply for a driver's license, the right to vote, being allowed to buy cigarettes and alcohol, to join the military, to engage in sexual relationships, to marry, and so forth. But it is widely recognised that some individuals can seem "mature" even before he or she has reached these landmark ages, whereas others are deemed to be "immature" (as opposed to "young at heart") sometimes long after they have passed into middle or even old age. As Keller describes it, and as the boys discussed in this chapter have experienced it, what moves these characters forward in their lives, and shows that they will become responsible, respectable, and successful adults is that, over the course of his story, each of these characters loses at least a piece of his innocence – his ignorance – about some part of his world's reality, and replaces that innocence with knowledge which has been gained

76 James R. Keller, "'Among School Children': Lacan and the *South Park* Felt Board Lesson Set", from Leslie Stratyner and James R. Keller (eds.), *The Deep End of South Park: Critical Essays on TV's Shocking Cartoon Series* (Jefferson, N.C.: McFarland & Company, Inc., 2009), p. 168.

63

by experience. Pinocchio, Peter/Петя, Cody and Jim learn primarily about violence and the love shared by family and friends. Peter Pan, Wart, Mowgli, and Taran also experience violence to greater and lesser degrees, but they each seem to experience the most personal growth when they each have their first experiences of sexual attraction, as object and/or personally.

Wendy's (& Tinker Bell's, and Tiger Lily's) attraction to Peter are important plot points and catalysts within *Peter Pan*, but Peter's role in these scenarios is partially – but not entirely – that of the object of affection. Nonetheless, he brings Wendy back to Neverland to be a "mother" to the Lost Boys; given his paternal role amongst the group, this means that, ultimately, he and Wendy begin to function as a couple, "co-parenting" the boys in Neverland (not only the Lost Boys, but also Michael and John, Wendy's younger brothers). In some of these scenes, it is striking that Peter wants to keep Wendy to himself, and even exhibits signs of jealousy – mainly because he isn't at that moment the sole object of her attention – when Wendy sings a song about mothers to the boys as a kind of lullaby for them. It is also clear that Peter enjoys the attention he receives from the Mermaids, Tiger Lily, and Tinker Bell, but seems to take particular delight in showing off in front of Wendy, especially in the scene when, during their tour of Neverland, Peter torments Captain Hook when they find him threatening to drown Tiger Lily; Peter does eventually save Tiger Lily, but not before he has had sufficient fun – *and* a reminder from Wendy, just in the nick of time, that he needs to rescue Tiger Lily from drowning. Earlier in the film, while in the Darlings' nursery, he doesn't know what a kiss is when Wendy says she's going to give him one, but later, he and Tiger Lily rub noses (what is sometimes called an "Eskimo kiss"), after which he crows triumphantly, flying into the air in a stiff-legged pose reminiscent of an aroused and excited Tex Avery character. The "chemistry" between Wendy and Peter is never resolved; it cannot be, because Peter is the boy who never grows up. But it seems that this, as much as Wendy's irritation with the childish games that comprise daily life in Wonderland, are part of her motivation for wanting to return home and "begin" to grow up.

As with Peter Pan, Wart/Arthur is likewise the object of affection and desire when Merlin is changing the two of them into different species so that Wart will learn to use his brain (and the importance of brain over brawn) and how to be mentally flexible and adaptable. After experiencing what it is like to be a fish, Merlin transforms the two of them into squirrels. It is during this sequence that Wart (in squirrel form) attracts the attention of a female squirrel, who falls for him and wants him to be her mate. Wart doesn't understand entirely, asking Merlin why she likes him, to which Merlin replies that he doesn't have time to explain, laughingly telling Wart that he'll have to fix it for himself, and that it's simply a fact of nature. Indeed, this first experience of love and desire – albeit in rather unusual circumstances – is deemed important enough that the sequence earns a song:

> It's a state of being, a frame of mind
> It's a most befuddling thing
> And to every being of every kind
> It is discomboomerating
> You're wasting time resisting
> You'll find the more you do
> The more she'll keep insisting
> Her "him" has got to be you
>
> It's a rough game, anyone knows
> There are no rules – anything goes!
> There's no logical explanation
> For this discomboomeration
> It's a most bemuddling, most befuddling thing!

In the third stanza of the song, an older female squirrel takes a shine to Merlin, who previously had been taking much amusement from watching Wart's efforts to get away from the young female squirrel (interestingly, it seems that Wart's main reason for wanting to evade her is, as he says, "But I won't be a squirrel tomorrow!"). Indeed, Merlin, despite his greater age, wisdom and experience, is less capable of handling the experience than is Wart, growing angry and indignant and confused by the attentions he is receiving. Merlin is distracted enough that, when Wart becomes imperilled, it is the young female squirrel who must save him. But whereas, when Merlin transforms both himself and Wart back into humans, the older female becomes furious that Merlin has deceived her, the young female – who has received more sympathetic treatment from Wart even as he has tried to evade her – is heartbroken; she runs into a hole in a nearby tree, and we hear her sobbing as a concerned Wart reaches toward the hole, overcome by a wish to comfort her. He joins Merlin, who comments, "You know, lad, that love business is a powerful thing". Wart looks back, and sees the female looking out at him, still crying, but then, because he must, he and Merlin walk away. The scene ends on a fairly sombre note, complete with a fade to black, bleak mise-en-scène, and melancholy music, as the young female runs to the top of the tree to watch Wart walk away, as Wart comes to terms with his first experience of the power of love. Wart has been shown to be a sensitive, caring boy, so it is not surprising that he feels sorry for the squirrel. But the emphasis the scene receives in the film, and the length of the scene, seem to indicate that this experience is of particular importance for Wart. Simultaneously, it highlights that, despite the fact that Merlin is many years older and much more educated, Wart is more mature, and better capable of handling the complexity and heartbreak involved in his first experience of romance. Of course, most of the audience is aware that another love awaits Arthur, his future queen, Guinevere; in most versions, that relationship, too, leads to heartbreak. That relationship's complexities would be too much to hint at in a film aimed predominately at children, however, so this unnamed squirrel gives us a glimpse into Wart's romantic development and allows him to learn valuable lessons for his future.

Of all of our characters, this awakening of desire is most profound for Mowgli. It is erotic attraction, after all, that is shown to be the one thing powerful enough to persuade Mowgli to return to the "man village" and leave behind the animals who have been his family and friends for as long as he can remember; all it takes is a pretty girl making eyes at him and walking away from him with a suggestive sway to her hips and a backward gaze, and Mowgli follows her willingly, drawn less by her humanity than he is by her sexuality and his attraction to her. In doing so, he leaves behind everything and everyone from the life he has always known, and begins again in a completely new way of life. The scene is a very short one – only a few minutes – yet it provides the climax for the film. Death couldn't come between Mowgli and Baloo – at one point, he thinks Baloo has been killed by Shere Kahn, but then Baloo regains consciousness, and he and Mowgli are reunited joyfully. But when he falls for the human girl, all it takes is for her to draw him out (she pretends to drop her water vessel, compelling Mowgli to pick it up, refill it, and carry it for her back to the village), and he abandons Baloo without apology or explanation. Clearly, Mowgli feels the need to give neither.

Taran's attraction to Eilonwy does not bring about a change in his routine, per se: the first portion of the end credits for *The Black Cauldron* is a shot (meant to resemble an illustration from a medieval manuscript) in which we see Taran, Eilonwy, Gurgi, and Fflewddur Fflam arriving at Caer Dallben, Taran, Hen Wen, and Dallben's home and where we first meet Taran. For Taran, who is the oldest of the characters in this chapter to experience first love, his relationship with Eilonwy is shown to be the thing which enables him to reach full maturity, even to the point whereby he can relinquish the magical sword he had found in the Horned King's dungeon, yet do so without fearing any real loss of status or power. In his growing relationship with Eilonwy, and therefore in a larger sense, Taran has begun to take on a masculine heterosexual role; we see other signs of this before their kiss, such as when Taran comforts Eilonwy, and when he uses his body to shield hers when the witches destroy their house and bring the Black Cauldron to the surface (it had been buried under the witches' house). It is a reminder, perhaps, that Taran no longer *needs* the sword to stand in as a symbol of his hegemonic power; his power comes from his hetero-normative fulfilment of a traditional adult masculine role/responsibility: the finding of a mate and the creation of a family (albeit one in which Gurgi fulfils the role of the family's child). That he will achieve a more traditional family union with Eilonwy is implied (though readers of the Lloyd Alexander books will recall that Taran and Eilonwy's marriage did not produce children). The sword, therefore, becomes redundant for Taran; he is (or soon will be) man enough without it.

The Boy is the Father of the Man

One small but very interesting group of characters is those whose boyhood and adulthood we get to examine, watching as they grow up. In these characters, we are able to see exactly how those childhood experiences have contributed to their adult lives and selves. As was mentioned (quite some time ago!) at the start of this chapter, this may be only a small number of adult male characters, but it is relatively unique to the male Disney characters. We see only three Disney heroines as both children and adults, but we only see their childhoods relatively briefly: Tiana and Charlotte in *The Princess and the Frog* (2009) and Rapunzel in *Tangled* (2010). As can be seen by the dates, these films are both very recent, and were made very close together. Five male characters, however, in four films, are seen as both children and as adults for significant portions of their stories. Particularly interestingly, one of the five characters whom we see as both child and adult functions as his film's villain: Goob, in *Meet the Robinsons* (2007): he is Lewis' roommate in the orphanage.[77]

The oldest of these narratives comes from the 1948 film *Melody Time*, one of the package features produced by Disney during one of the studio's most difficult financial periods. The segment of the film which is being examined here is the final section of the film, and concerns the tall tale of Pecos Bill, described as being the greatest cowboy on Earth by the segment's narrator, Will Rogers (accompanied in the singing and in the live-action scenes which bookend this segment by the Sons of the Pioneers, as well

[77] Goob will be examined in detail in the chapter on villains.

as by child stars Luana Patten and Bobby Driscoll). The segment's narrative is somewhat fragmented, bringing together as it does several episodes from Pecos Bill's story; likewise, each section is told to comic, exaggerated effect, as is the tradition of the American tall tale. But one-third of the narrative looks at events from Bill's childhood: his falling off the wagon that was carrying his (very large) family out west and being left behind in the Pecos desert, his being adopted by a mother coyote, of his growing up amongst the animals of the desert (where he learns to "out loped the antelope, out jumped the jack rabbit – Bill even out hissed the rattle snake!"), and of his rescuing and befriending a colt who will grow up to be his horse (and best friend), Widowmaker. His childhood is shown in these episodes to be the time when Bill became extraordinary; when we first see him as an adult, he is already a legend, and can be described in the narration/accompanying song which introduces the adult Bill as "the roughest, toughest critter/Never known to be a quitter/'Cause he never had no fear of man nor beast!" His adult exploits are no less extraordinary, and as in his childhood, he is just as capable of taming nature as he is of dealing with his foes. Some of his accomplishments in adulthood are that he rides a tornado and tames it to a breeze, brings rain from "Californy" to create the Gulf of Mexico and alleviate a drought, digs the Rio Grande, and – in the main part of the narrative – inspiring the coyotes to howl at the moon.

It is this part of Bill's story that is the focus of the segment, and is about when Bill fell in love with, and then lost, Slue Foot Sue. Described as "the first female woman Bill'd ever seen", her effect on Bill is profound. The narrator switches from speech to song, describing Bill's reaction in this way:

> Give him a right peculiar feelin' –
> Set his senses plum a-reelin' –
> With a pounding sound inside his ears
> Like the galloping hooves of a thousand steers –
> Inside his chest was a-seethin' and burnin' –
> His blood was a-boilin', his brain was a-burnin' –
> A-burnin' with a fire that could only be cooled
> In the beckoning depths of two blue limpid pools ...

The images accompanying this sung narration are of Bill beginning to combust, until he literally turns red and his body takes off like a rocket in a way which seems to have been inspired by Tex Avery's Wolf character. It is the most profound event in Bill's life, and he is physically, mentally, and emotionally overwhelmed by his attraction to Sue. Though – again – the episode is played for laughs and therefore is treated in an exaggerated manner, nonetheless the transformation this first encounter with a human female brings to Bill's life is the same as the one brought to the other wild child we have discussed in this chapter, Mowgli. Like Bill, he is raised around animals (wolves adopt Mowgli, but coyotes – more appropriate to the American southwest – adopt the infant Bill). The two see their first human female several years into their lives: Mowgli at an earlier stage, just as he is reaching adolescence, Bill only after he has reached full physical adulthood. With Bill, we are able to get a more in-depth exploration of his courtship with this first object of desire, and it is through this that Bill's immaturity is highlighted. He may have "never had no fear of man nor beast", but his earlier life has allowed him to maintain his childishness. His exploits are more like games and adventures than anything Bill does out of a sense of responsibility or a drive for creativity. He enjoys being top dog, and is shown to delight in the physical action of defeating cattle rustlers and warring Indians and tornados. He digs the Rio Grande not because he wants to help the animals or improve where he lives; he and Widowmaker get lost in the desert and are thirsty, so he grabs a stick, spurs Widowmaker to a gallop, and digs the river simply to satisfy his own thirst. Likewise, his relationship with Widowmaker bears most of the hallmarks of a child's association with animals and the natural world: the pair bond so tightly that the narration describes them as being "like warts on a toad, like birds of a feather", implying that they are almost one being: we even see Bill give Widowmaker a big, loud kiss on the mouth. When Sue enters Bill's life, Widowmaker becomes jealous to the point of insanity, and is the ultimate reason why, at the end of the story, Sue will be stranded on the moon and out of Bill's life forever: Widowmaker has been pushed into second place in Bill's heart, and it makes him livid, again in a childish, selfish way. But it is Bill and Sue's courtship that shows Bill's innocence – his immaturity – to its greatest effect. Whereas the narrator sings of all that Bill does to court Sue ("He arranged for the moon to rise just right and flood the land with a silvery light/Ordered the stars in Heaven above to form a token of undying love"), the imagery on screen shows that Bill – the "Western Superman" – is rendered helpless and passive, so that it is Sue who must take the lead in their relationship, moving it forward at each step, and even leaning over him, placing his arms around her waist, and tilting his head up so that they can experience their first kiss.

The scene cuts to their wedding day, and by this stage, Bill is shown to be a bit more confident, but fearful – and with good reason – because Sue insists on being married while sitting on Widowmaker, who is beyond infuriated and does everything he can to buck her off. In the end – because Sue is Bill's equal in terms of her confidence and prowess as a cowpoke – what defeats her isn't Widowmaker, but rather the bustle she wears under her wedding dress, which begins to bounce thanks to Widowmaker's bucking, and which causes her to bounce higher and higher. But rather than be frightened by Sue's peril, Bill is described as – and shown to be – "calm, confident. He built his loop with careless ease, he judged his distance, tested the breeze. Then a whirl and a twirl and a twist of the wrist, he let her [the lasso] go! But the champion missed." Bill, who is said to have been "never knowed [sic] to miss", is not to blame: unbeknownst to all but the audience, Widowmaker has stepped on the end of the rope – deliberately – and caused Bill to miss. Given Widowmaker's function as symbolic of Bill's inner childishness, and combined with the fact that Bill isn't shown to make a second attempt to try and save Sue, it would seem that, for all his incredible prowess and skill, Bill cannot – or perhaps will not – grow up. Sue's bustle bounces her to the moon, where she becomes stranded forever, and Bill returns to the coyotes (and therefore to the world of his childhood). On screen, we see his and Widowmaker's tracks heading away from the town and off into the desert – initially tracks made by boots and horseshoes, but then we see a pile of clothes, saddle, boots and horseshoes, and the pair of tracks becomes bare human footprints and unshod horse hooves. We learn that, from then on, Bill would look up when the moon was out and howl at it (again, in Bill's case, this is a return to the language of his childhood), mourning his lost love. We are told that "so painful was his grief to see, the varmints joined in, out of sympathy. And that's how come, to this very day, coyotes howl at the moon that way." The segment's end – and the segment's end is *Melody Time*'s end – is quite a sorrowful one, with Roy Rogers and the Sons of the Pioneers singing the end of "Blue Shadows on the Trail", as the formerly dynamic Bill is left alone (with Widowmaker, who has become an extension of Bill – we see their silhouette, and they appear to be a single being) to mourn Sue. The implication of the story is clear, and in many ways strengthens the assertion made previously that, in these films, it is the attainment of a mate which signals that a character has reached manhood, more so than any other trait. The loss of his mate before the relationship can (presumably) be consum-mated fully means that Bill cannot grow up, and so he retreats into childhood, regressing not just to the level at which he was when he met Sue, but even further back, to the time when, as a youngster, he first became a part of the desert world.

It is romantic love which brings out the strongest and best in a man – that is the implication of the narratives of these films, and certainly that is true of both Hercules and Tarzan, whose stories have many strong parallels. Both are raised by foster families of different, and "lower" species from themselves (Hercules, an Olympic god, is raised by humans; Tarzan, a human, is raised by gorillas) from very young ages; both, in essence, are foundlings. Both are opposed by an evil, ruthless man who comes from the world into which the hero was born (Hercules is endangered by Hades, God of the Underworld; Tarzan by Clayton, an English hunter and guide who has come to the jungle where Tarzan lives). Both become strong and heroic as they grow to manhood, and famed in the worlds where they live. But it is love for a woman which, ultimately, elevates them, making them accept the power and responsibility of manhood and rounds each out as a character. And in both cases, when forced to choose between a life which would return them to the level of their births and life with the woman they love, both choose love, bringing together their foster homes – their childhoods – and their fully-adult selves: it is a choice that the narrative celebrates. It is doubtful that these two films – released only two years apart (*Hercules* in 1997, *Tarzan* in 1999) and both part of the Disney renaissance period (albeit toward the end of the era) – have so much in common simply by mere coincidence. Given the length of time that these films were in production, it is likely that at least some of their production periods overlap, and certainly the two teams who worked on the films would have been aware of what the others were doing. Equally, however, the common characteristics described above are far from unique to these two films; in fact, similar narratives are to be found throughout folklore and literature going back centuries; indeed, Pecos Bill, Hercules, and Tarzan all have much in common with the boys who have been described earlier in this chapter, and the heroes who will be described in chapter two: their stories emphasise romantic love, and love is shown to be the one experience which will compel them, whatever their strengths and weaknesses, to be their very best selves. The only thematic difference between the films described in this section of the chapter, those whose discussions proceeded and those that will follow, is that we are given a better understanding of who the main character is by being given a privileged look at his childhood, and seeing how the experience of love taps into – and/or contradicts – what has made him the man he is.

We learn from the Muses, who are the narrators (a "Greek chorus" à la Motown), that Hercules, though rendered mortal by a potion Hades creates, retains his superhuman strength because he never drank the last drop. He is raised by an older, childless couple who find him as an infant, and he becomes the child they had longed for: they raise him as their own, and they love him dearly. But when we meet Hercules again, he is a gawky, awkward teenager whose unusual strength is more of a liability than an asset. He is clumsy, and so his strength tends to cause destruction (accidentally, of course). When he encounters a group of boys his own age and asks whether he can join them in their game, they tell him that they've already got enough guys. As they run off, we – and Hercules – overhear them saying, "What a geek!" "Destructo-boy", and "Maybe we should call him Jerk-ules!" Indeed, when he catches the discus they throw – Frisbee-like – into the centre of the marketplace, Hercules catches it, but stumbles back and causes the destruction of the entire marketplace, to include most of the goods that have been brought there for sale. The angry people say that he is too dangerous to be around them and call him a freak, though his father defends him, and tries hard to comfort him. Hercules cannot be comforted, however, and says that he feels that he doesn't belong. Finally, his parents tell him that they found him and raised him, and show him the medallion they found with him, a medallion which shows that he has some link to the Gods. He sets out to the temple of Zeus to see whether he can get answers, and the statue comes to life and tells Hercules his origins. Zeus also tells him that becoming a true hero on Earth will allow his godhood to be restored. He is reunited with Pegasus, and sets out to become a hero. Determined to re-join the gods of Olympus, he seeks out and finds Phil (Philoctetes), whom Zeus has proclaimed a trainer of heroes. Phil, a satyr, is reluctant, initially, to train Hercules (he has trained many in the past, some of whom – Jason, Odysseus, Achilles – came close, but all failed, ultimately, and so he has retired as a trainer), but is convinced when Zeus hits him with a lightening bold. We then get a training montage (full of comedy and intertextual references to Hollywood films generally as well as Disney films, theme parks, and the Disney Store), by the end of which Hercules is bronzed, not just "filled out" but muscular and brawny, and highly skilled in the arts of a warrior and hero. Hoisting Pegasus over his head, Hercules proclaims, "Next stop, Olympus!" and he, Pegasus and Phil set out to Thebes so that Hercules can prove himself. But on the way, they hear a woman's scream, and encounter what they believe – assume – to be a damsel in distress who is in need of saving. The damsel is Meg (Megara), who wants nothing to do with Hercules, retorting rather sarcastically to his confusion as he tries to intervene, "I'm a damsel, I'm in distress – I can handle this. Have a nice day!"

Hercules refuses to desist; with a bit of coaching from the sidelines from Phil, he defeats the centaur who was harassing Meg (in a fight played very much for laughs). Phil does berate him for the mistakes he made during the fight, but Hercules pays him little attention: after all, he did win. But even more of a distraction from Phil is the sight of Meg: Hercules is captivated by her beauty and falls for her instantly. Phil – and especially Pegasus – are both *very* irritated at his obvious attraction to Meg. After some flirtatious banter from Meg (and a few tongue-tied responses from Hercules), they part, and Hercules, Pegasus and Phil continue on to Thebes, a town which is linked to New York by being described as the "Big Olive", and of which Phil says, "If you can make it there, you can make it anywhere". The townsfolk are sceptical at first, but then Meg bursts upon the scene saying that two children have been trapped in a rockslide (really Hades' two minions, Pain and Panic, in human form). He rescues the "children", but is attacked by a dragon-like creature (rendered particularly otherworldly by being created through CG animation) who grows multiple heads (first he has one, then three, then dozens) every time one is cut off. The people of Thebes watch in horror (Hades, who has sent the creature, watches excitedly). A rockslide occurs, and seems to have killed both the dragon and Hercules, when Hercules emerges from the dead dragon's claw. The people of Thebes are ecstatic, and Hercules is proclaimed a hero (or, as one of the muses says, "He was so hot, he made steam look cool!"). He becomes a heart-throb, the centre of a merchandising bonanza which makes him rich, and continues enjoying himself as he defeats a succession of creatures. The muses sing the song "Zero to Hero" as we see a montage depicting Hercules' success, and break into a gospel-inspired section of the song where they sing:

> Who put the glad in gladiator?
> Hercules!
> Whose daring deeds are great theatre?
> Hercules!
> Isn't he bold?
> No one braver!
> Isn't he sweet?
> Our favourite flavour!
>
> …
>
> Bless my soul, Herc was on a roll –
> Undefeated, riding high – and the nicest guy! – not conceited!
> He was a nothing – zero, zero
> Now he's a honcho – he's our hero!
> He hit the heights at break-neck speed –
> From zero to hero
> Now he's a hero – yes indeed!

But though Hercules is shown to be a huge success as a hero, very little has changed about him; he retains the sweetness and innocence which characterised him as a teenager.[78] He may not become arrogant with his many victories, wealth, and adulation, but neither has he been invited to re-join the gods on Olympus. We learn that it has been Hades who has sent the various creatures to defeat Hercules; frustrated that none of the monsters have worked, Hades hits upon a new plan: he sends a reluctant Meg to stop him, hoping that Hercules will become too distracted by his attraction for Meg to be able to fight. Meg rescues him from a mob of adoring girls, and convinces him to "play hooky" from his schedule, serving as a kind of honey trap to try to learn his weaknesses. Over the course of their romantic day and evening, however, she finds herself falling for his kindness and open-hearted innocence. They nearly kiss, but Phil and Pegasus swoop in and stop him. Meg finally comes to terms with her growing love for Hercules (and in the process loses some of her cynicism about men – she had been wounded badly in her last relationship and "sworn off man-handling" as a result), and begins to oppose Hades in his efforts to destroy Hercules. Phil, however, over-hears and misinterprets her confrontation with Hades, and tells Hercules that Meg has betrayed him. Meanwhile, Hades realises that Hercules does indeed have a weakness: Meg. At this stage, however, his love makes him act out childishly, playing and teasing and leaping around in joy. When Phil tries to warn him, Hercules lashes out and Phil leaves. Just then, Hades shows up, telling Hercules that he has captured Meg and that, if Hercules will give up his strength for twenty-four hours, he will release Meg: Hercules makes Hades swear that Meg can come to no harm during that period, and – off-handedly – Hades promises that Hercules will get his strength back instantly if Meg is hurt. She implores him not to listen to Hades, but his love compels him. They shake on the deal, and Hercules' godlike strength is removed. Hades also tells him that Meg was working for him, only pretending to be falling in love with Hercules. Weakened and heart-broken, he sinks to the ground, dejected. Hades goes off to free the Titans and begin his assault on Olympus, which he plans to retake from Zeus. He also sends the Cyclops to destroy Thebes; as its champion, Hercules sets out to fight him, even though he now has only ordinary mortal strength. Meg tries to stop him, but Hercules is too dejected by his loss of love to be worried about being killed in a battle. Meg and Pegasus go to find Phil to try to help Hercules, arriving just in time to see him accept defeat. Phil gives him a pep talk, however, and Hercules finds a way to defeat the Cyclops. A column is about to fall on Hercules,

78 Andreas Deja, the lead animator on Hercules as a character, notes that Tate Donovan's voice for the adult Hercules has an "energy and a sort of naïve quality in Hercules which we found through time". Spoken to camera in "The Making of Hercules", *Hercules* (Region 2/PAL, © Disney, DVD release date 12 August 2002).

but Meg pushes him out of the way and is crushed herself. Instantly, because Hades' deal has been broken, Hercules' strength is restored, and he realises that Meg loves him genuinely. He heads off to Olympus to defeat Hades and leads the gods to victory, destroying the Titans, but then realises that Hades is about to capture Meg's soul. He tries to reach her, but arrives just after she has died from her injuries. It is at this instant that Hercules experiences an internal change: love inspires him to true heroism, and he goes to sacrifice himself to save Meg. It is his willingness to die for someone he loves that allows his status as a god to be restored, and becoming a god again is what enables him to save Meg's soul from Hades' river of death. He carries it back to her body and brings her back to life, healed of her wounds. They are about to kiss when – once more – they are interrupted, this time to be carried on a cloud to Olympus, where Hercules is reunited with his parents and praised by the other gods. As Zeus tells him, "A true hero isn't measured by the size of his strength, but by the strength of his heart". It is the ultimate validation of the notion that true love ennobles a man most. Simultaneously, it is this love which inspires him to reject his status as a god, since accepting it means that he would be parted from Meg forever. His immortality is taken from him as he and Meg kiss – a kiss that becomes more intense once his mortality is restored. He is now shown to be a true, fully actualised man, and returns home with Meg to his foster parents, celebrated in the stars and sur-rounded on Earth by a family of whom he is the centre.

Tarzan, too, becomes the centre of the world into which he was adopted, a family of silverback gorillas who adopt him after one of the females, Kala, finds the infant Tarzan in the home his shipwrecked parents built, and where they soon after were killed by Sabor, the same leopard who killed Kala's baby. Having lost her own child, she saves Tarzan from the leopard and brings him back to the troop to be mother to him. Though Kerchak, the dominant male, allows Kala to keep him, he will not accept Tarzan as his son, and is displeased about the human's inclusion in the family. Tarzan has to work hard to earn his position, and spends most of his childhood trying to prove himself.

This is a film whose analysis is somewhat problematized by the heavily anthropomorphised animals around him; like Mowgli, being raised amongst animals means that he can converse and communicate with them freely. Equally, this is a story which is rather heavily weighted by its messages about tolerance and acceptance. Tarzan must battle Kerchak's prejudice against him, but wins over the other gorillas and the animals around him. By the time a teenage Tarzan emerges in the film (twenty-three minutes into the story), he looks gangly, but can fly through the trees (swinging on the vines, of course) with grace and agility. His appearance indicates that he is almost fully grown, yet his playing with his friends – especially his wrestling with Terk – and the way this is tolerated by the adults of the troop – suggest that he is still situated, by and large, within an adolescent role. Yet when Sabor shows up and attacks the troop, Tarzan finds himself having to take over the fight from Kerchak. Tarzan, as a human, is not as strong as a gorilla, but he is incredibly strong (for a human) from a lifetime in the jungle; his being human gives him the advantage of being able to create weapons, and the stone-tipped spear he has made allows him to kill Sabor at last. The others crowd around him, celebrating, but Kerchak is displeased because of the threat this poses to his position as dominate male; Tarzan realises this, and brings Sabor's body to him, offering it as a tribute and assuming a subordinate pose. We don't have a chance to see Kerchak's response, however, because at this moment a gunshot is heard echoing through the jungle: humans have arrived. Kerchak orders the troop to move out, but Tarzan's curiosity compels him to go and find out what it was.

It is interesting that his first contact with humans makes Tarzan appear more animal than human: he sniffs the tracks and broken plants where they have passed, sniffing and then tasting the shell casing he finds. He follows the noise they are making, and hides in the undergrowth, watching them. Clayton, the film's villain, senses something is there and shoots at it, and Tarzan gets out of the bullet's path with an agility rarely seen in humans. When Professor Porter and his daughter, Jane, realise that they have stumbled across a gorilla's nest and decide to explore the area, Tarzan swings down from a vine behind Clayton's back (the scene is treated rather comically at this point), sniffing him as he tries to figure out what is lurking around them. Shortly after this, Tarzan will rescue Jane from a troop of baboons, and with her, he will have his first encounter with another human since infancy; soon after, he will also meet Jane's father and Clayton. In his first encounters with humans, two things become obvious: he is incredibly intelligent and curious, and he is in love with Jane. Even when Kerchak forbids the troop from having anything to do with the humans, Tarzan cannot keep away, and continues to visit their camp in secret. It is clear that he increasingly is fascinated by Jane, and she by him: just as she begins to introduce him to the human world, he introduces her to the wonders of the jungle. The more each learns about the other, the more their attraction deepens. Once again, this developing romance is a source of displeasure to the hero's animal friends: Kala is concerned, but Terk is angry, harrumphing, "I give it a week". Tarzan returns to the Porters' camp just as sailors are packing it up and loading everything onto a ship which is there to pick up Jane and her father to take them back to England. Jane asks Tarzan whether he would like to come to England with them; when he realises that it would mean he might never return to the jungle, he asks Jane to stay there with him. They realise that one must give up everything to stay with the other. Jane runs off, crying, and Clayton seizes the opportunity to trick Tarzan into bringing the humans to see the gorilla encampment. Tarzan persuades his friends to lead Kerchak away, then brings Jane, her father, and Clayton to see the encampment. The first gorilla they see is Kala, who is very wary of the humans, even when Tarzan tries to explain to her who they are. The other gorillas approach slowly, and Jane and the professor are delighted to meet the troop. Clayton, however, marks the encampment on his map; his reason for wanting to see the gorillas has nothing to do with science.

Jane asks Tarzan to teach her to speak gorilla, and the phrase he teaches her, we learn, is "Jane stays with Tarzan". Just as Jane realises what she has said, Terk and Tantor (their elephant friend) accidentally lead Kerchak back into the encampment: Kerchak is furious, and when he sees Clayton about to shoot one of the gorillas, he charges at him. Tarzan fights Kerchak, however, yelling at the humans to go while he stops Kerchak from harming them. Realising that he has challenged the dominant male, Tarzan is horrified. He runs away, and soon is followed by Kala. She takes him to see the tree house his parents built – where she found him – for the first time, and he realises that the world of the Porters was the world into which he was born. She leaves him in the house, gazing at the photograph of himself (as an infant) with his parents, and sits on the balcony. A few moments later we hear footsteps, and Tarzan walks out of the house, fully upright (rather than knuckle-walking, as he tends to do around the gorillas), and wearing his father's suit and shoes. He goes to her, though, telling her that no matter where he goes, she will always be his mother, and the two embrace: in this moment, Tarzan is rejecting almost completely the gorilla side of his upbringing, deciding to become fully human. Finally, he walks away, and finds the Porters and Clayton on the shore, getting into a boat to head out for the ship. When he boards the ship, however, he realises that the Porters and some of the sailors have been taken prisoner. He evades capture momentarily, but is caught. It is then that he learns that Clayton intends to capture the gorillas and sell them back in England, and cries out; he is heard by Tantor, and together with

Terk they go to Tarzan's aid. Freed, Tarzan rushes off to warn the troop of Clayton's intention, but Clayton and the sailors get there first, capturing as many gorillas as they can. Just as Clayton is about to shoot Kerchak, Tarzan's famous yodel is heard and he reappears, stripped of his clothes, and leading a herd of elephants (and the Porters and good sailors). Tarzan has come home (as he tells Kerchak), and he goes on the offensive against Clayton; he gets Clayton's rifle and Clayton taunts, "Go ahead – shoot me. Be a man." Tarzan mimics perfectly the sound of the rifle, terrifying Clayton. He throws away the gun, saying angrily, "I'm not a man like you!"[79] Moments later, Clayton becomes entangled in the vines; Tarzan realises that he's about to be injured and warns him, but Clayton refuses to listen, and accidentally hangs himself.

The battle is over, but Tarzan realises that Kerchak is dying from a gunshot wound. He goes to him, and for the first time, Kerchak calls Tarzan his son, bidding him to take care of and lead the troop. He mourns for a moment, but then sees the other gorillas watching him. He assumes the dominate pose and gestures of the alpha male, and leads the troop away. Tarzan cannot go with Jane to England now, as he has the responsibility to lead his family as the dominate male. Though planning to return to England, Jane changes her mind at the last minute, running into Tarzan's arms and kissing him. Tarzan doesn't know what kissing is, and is too startled at first to react; it embarrasses Jane, and she begins rambling when, realising that what Jane had done felt good and natural, Tarzan takes her face in his hands and kisses her. They walk toward the gorillas, who are watching them, and Jane tells them in gorilla language, using the phrase Tarzan taught her earlier, "Jane stays with Tarzan". It is here that we see that Tarzan's journey is complete: he and Jane are seen flying through the jungle, sliding on tree branches and swinging from vines (her father following along behind, having decided that he, too, preferred the jungle), and the pair come to a stop on a high branch overlooking a clearing. With Jane now at his side (and wearing her own loincloth and matching top!), he gives the iconic yell (made famous in the 1930s and 1940s Tarzan movies featuring Johnny Weissmuller), and the film ends. It is interesting that, just four years earlier in the film *Pocahontas* (1995), Pocahontas, like Tarzan, finds that she cannot follow her heart as she must take up her duties as a leader for her tribe, but the film still sends John Smith away (on the ridiculous grounds that the only way for him to survive a gunshot wound is to make what, in 1607/8, would be a voyage of around three months to get back to England to receive medical treatment). Yet when faced with the same dilemma – stay

79 This is an interesting moment to readers of the novel by Edgar Rice Burroughs, who will recall that Tarzan's birth name was John Clayton, and that in England he held the title of Viscount Greystoke. This will be discussed further in the chapter on Villains in the discussion of the Disney character Cecil Clayton, the name no doubt borrowed from William Cecil Clayton, Tarzan's cousin in Burroughs' novel.

in an uncharted land to be with her true love or return to her life in England – Jane chooses to stay, and Tarzan gets to keep his love. Both films end with a shot of the title character high up, gazing into the distance: but whereas Pocahontas must watch her true love sail away and leave her behind, her face turned away from the audience, Jane is at Tarzan's side, and he practically faces the camera. Admittedly, there are narrative justifications for this: Tarzan and Jane must stay together because they were together in the Weissmuller films, and have become an iconic screen couple (though, in the novel, Jane leaves Tarzan behind to return to her home in Baltimore, and it is later that Tarzan will go there to seek her). Pocahontas, we know from the few reliable historical accounts, did not have a romance with John Smith, and so he must leave her life so that, eventually, she can meet and marry John Rolfe (though Rolfe plays almost no part in the many folkloric versions of Pocahontas' story).[80] Instead, what is interesting about these two endings is that both John Smith's choice to return to England and Jane Porter's choice to stay with Tarzan are made to seem *natural*. It fits well with the traditional notion that a woman must be willing to give up her home and family to be with her husband – an idea symbolised (and in many ways actualised) by the custom of a wife taking her husband's last name. But the man who stays in a foreign place to be with his wife becomes, at least to a degree, subordinated to her, in cultural terms, because he will, initially, be dependent on her for entry into the society/culture to which she has brought him. For Tarzan, staying in the jungle means, in effect, that he becomes king of it. That it is a white male who assumes hegemonic authority of the jungle – again – cannot be laid at Disney's feet: it is part of Edgar Rice Burroughs' 1914 novel, and was cemented (and increasingly altered and embroidered upon) in over eighty other films. In fact, apart from when Kerchak dies and Tarzan assumes the mantle of leadership, his role as alpha is downplayed somewhat by the Disney film, and are limited to two brief moments. Rather, the focus seems to be on his incorporation of his humanity into his self-image, and this reinforces his adult status: he now stands tall and upright, like a human, and has taken a human mate. We also know that he has assumed the role of leader and protector of his troop and of the jungle as a whole, an exercising of male hegemony that carries enormous responsibility. These demonstrate that, along with his now very muscular, fully-grown physique, he has, by the end of the film, achieved full adulthood. This renders the whole story a coming-of-age drama, and therefore makes it more in keeping with an important

80 For a longer discussion of the Disney version of the story of Pocahontas, see Davis, "Borrowing the Earth: Saving the Planet and Disney's *Pocahontas*", in Reynold Humphries, Gilles Ménégaldo, and Melvyn Stokes, Eds., *Cinéma et Mythes*, University of Poitiers, 2002, pp. 77-89.

theme for Disney movies as a whole – both animated and live-action.

It is interesting that Danton Burroughs, the grandson of Edgar Rice Burroughs and the director of Edgar Rice Burroughs, Inc., says of the Disney adaptation that, "Finally, we were able to portray my grandfather's characters as he truly wrote them. It just shows you the magical ability of animation and what you can do with it."[81] It must be the case that Burroughs is referring solely to Tarzan's physicality in the film: in fact, there are significant omissions in the Disney adaptation, to include Tarzan's aristocratic heritage and the fact that Cecil Clayton is his cousin, who is engaged to the *American* woman Jane Porter (in the Disney adaptation, Jane, voiced by Minnie Driver, is every inch the proper English Edwardian lady). Also missing is the fact that it was Kerchak who killed Tarzan's father, and that many years later, jealous of Tarzan's physical prowess and natural leadership abilities, Kerchak challenges Tarzan and Tarzan kills Kerchak, assuming the role of alpha. The downplaying of these aspects of the novel mean that the Disney version of Tarzan is about growing up, about the harm caused by intolerance, and – through the portrayal of Clayton – about environmentalism and wildlife preservation. It is worth noting, in connection to this, that Disney's Animal Kingdom, the Walt Disney World theme park dedicated to animal conservation, opened on 22 April 1998, a little over a year before *Tarzan*'s release (but while it was in production). Animal Kingdom – as emphasised by its linked hotel, the Animal Kingdom Lodge, has a decidedly African orientation.

Someone else who grows up to be a leader – the last boy in our study[82] – is Lewis. When we first get to know him, Lewis is twelve years old and living in an orphanage in a large city. He is shown to be unusually intelligent and creative, inspired by science and the dream of becoming a great inventor. His head is so full of ideas that he has to write them all down in a notebook, and despite his youth, he already has about him the aura of a scientific genius – his wild, messy, standing-up hair, his glasses, and his forgetful, distractible nature (his roommate has to use an air horn to get Lewis' attention). Lewis is also shown to be a misfit: we learn that he has had 124 adoption interviews, yet no one has wanted him for their family. We first start getting to know Lewis during the 124th interview, when a very nice – but very ordinary – couple are unable to relate to him and his far-out ideas for inventions; when the husband asks what Lewis' favourite sport is, Lewis replies, "Is inventing a sport?" The interview goes horribly awry

81 Backstage Disney/The Characters of Tarzan/Tarzan/ "Creating Tarzan". Disc 2, from *Tarzan: 2-Disc Special Edition* (Region 2/PAL, © Edgar Rice Burroughs, Inc., and Disney Enterprises, Inc., DVD release date 8 February 2013).

82 You'll be pleased to hear!

when Lewis accidentally sprays peanut butter on them and the husband has an anaphylactic reaction to the peanuts. Later, during his conversation with Mildred, the kind woman who runs the orphanage, Lewis becomes determined to find his birth mother, whose identity is unknown. He begins working on an invention which he hopes will allow him to access the memory, which he is sure is buried in his brain, of seeing his mother when she left him on the orphanage's doorstep as an infant. He works obsessively to create a memory machine: he keeps his roommate, Goob, up all night as he works, causing Goob, the next day, to fall asleep during a baseball game and miss an important catch, losing the game for his team. Lewis also begins skipping subsequent interviews with potential adoptive parents. The one person who seems to enjoy Lewis' tenacious curiosity is his science teacher, Mr. Willerstein, who gives him a flyer for the science fair and allows Lewis to demonstrate the latest versions of his machine in class (despite their tendency to explode).

Lewis arrives at the science fair and finds that he is being stalked by a thirteen-year-old boy. The boy identifies himself as Wilbur Robinson, saying he is there to protect Lewis from a tall man in a bowler hat. Wilbur goes off to patrol the gym where the science fair is taking place, and becomes distracted when he accidentally causes a young girl to spill a box full of frogs. While he's helping her to pick them up, the man in the bowler hat appears – a strange, sinister, rather grey-skinned figure. The hat flies off his head and across the room, sprouts mechanical legs (giving it a spidery appearance), and flies up under the blanket covering Lewis' project. The hat removes some of the bolts so that the machine – a memory scanner – begins to fly apart, creating havoc in the gym. Lewis, distraught, runs out of the gym, Wilbur running after him. The bowler hat then mends the broken machine as the strange man watches. He then steels Lewis' machine and disappears.

Lewis is torn between wanting to know why his machine didn't work and frustration that he's still unable to find his mother. He becomes upset, but Wilbur reappears, urging him to go back and fix the machine, reminding Lewis that he's from the future and so should be taken seriously. Lewis doesn't believe him, so Wilbur throws him into his time machine and takes him to Wilbur's present – Lewis' future – to prove to him that it is real. To Lewis, however, there's no longer any point in fixing the memory scanner; he can use the time machine to go back and see his mom. When Wilbur refuses, Lewis accidentally crashes the time machine. Wilbur demands that he fix it; until he does, there is no way to return to his own time. They go back to Wilbur's house; Wilbur doesn't want Lewis to leave the garage, insists that he wear a big hat that looks like a fruit bowl (saying, cryptically, that Lewis' hair is a "dead giveaway"), and tells him to get to work on the time machine. Nonetheless, sucked into a giant tube and propelled into the garden, Lewis ends up on a tour of the house (given by an old man wearing his clothes backwards), and meets all kinds of strange relatives and characters everywhere he goes (though he does not encounter Wilbur's father, Cornelius) in what turns out to be an enormous mansion.

Lewis is unable to fix the machine, and ends up staying for supper. The family finds themselves very drawn to Lewis, and after a wild dinner, an invention going awry, and a wild dinosaur chase through the garden, they tell him that, since he's an orphan and they love having him there, they would like to adopt him. Lewis agrees and all celebrate until Lewis' hat gets knocked off and they see his hair. He admits that he is from the past, but the family berate Wilbur for bringing him there, and tell him that he has to go back to his own time: it is obvious they recognise Lewis, but they don't tell him why. Lewis runs off, crying, when Bowler Hat Guy shows up and says that he will take Lewis to see his mother if he'll fix the memory scanner. Lewis agrees. He fixes the machine, but the Man breaks his promise. When Lewis says that he doesn't understand why the Man is so angry, the Man reveals that Lewis is Wilbur's dad, and grows up to be a famous inventor and hero; the Man also reveals himself to be Goob, whose life is "ruined" by missing the ball which lost his little league team their baseball game (a failure that he has stewed over ever since). Lewis is horrified and apologises immediately, but Goob (as we now know him to be) isn't interested in apologies; he wants revenge. Wilbur and his robot, Carl, rescue Lewis and the scanner, but the bowler hat, named Doris, gets it back and she and Goob take off for the past, this time to be able to sell the machine successfully. It becomes clear that the plan has worked as first Wilbur, then the Robinson family and household, disappear. The memory scanner comes to life, and Lewis watches in horror as he sees how Goob has altered the future far beyond what he intended, as his passing off Doris as his machine – and getting thousands of replicas of her made – has enabled her to cause havoc and take out her revenge on humanity generally. Terrified but determined to set things right, Lewis climbs into the still-broken time machine, manages to fix it, and sets off to put things right.

Because this narrative involves time travel, Lewis (along with the audience) is able to see what his future holds and know what sort of man he will grow up to be and what his life as an adult will be like. His future self – who has taken the name Cornelius Robinson – has created the life Lewis longs for as a child: an orphan, his future has him at the centre of a huge, extraordinary family. Obsessed with science and inventing, he becomes one of the greatest inventors of all time, and can spend his days experimenting and creating. In learning this, he also learns to be self-confident, and comes to understand the motto, shared with him for the first time by Wilbur – his son – "Keep moving forward". For Lewis, it means never giving up, and seeing failure as a chance to learn an incredibly valuable lesson – a much bigger lesson than can be learned from success. Once he embraces this, he finds the confidence he needs to stop Goob (and Doris; mainly Doris) from destroying the future. When Doris threatens him, he looks her squarely in the "eye" and says, "Doris, I am *never* going to invent you". She hesitates for a moment, and then disappears. He then brings Goob to see what happened to the future, because of Doris, and the two watch as their stopping Doris restores the future to what it should be, to include bringing Wilbur back to life. He tries to get Goob to join the future Robinson family, but Goob disappears; Lewis doesn't seem him again. But he does see himself – his adult self – who has returned home and discovered that both the time machines are missing. The two Lewises – Lewis the child and Cornelius the man – stare at one another in amazement, but then Cornelius takes Lewis to see their lab. There, Cornelius shows him the invention of which he's most proud: the memory scanner: it was his first successful invention, and the one that started it all. But Cornelius tells Lewis nothing more about his future, other than that he must go back to the science fair. Before he gets into the machine, Cornelius' wife gives him one last piece of advice: "I am always right. Even when I'm wrong, I'm right." Wilbur, in returning Lewis to his own time, makes one detour: he takes Lewis back to see his mother leave him at the orphanage, and he sees her hugging his infant self; he almost reaches out to touch her, but then stops himself. He sees now that she did love him and did want him, but for whatever reason, couldn't keep him. He knocks on the orphanage door, and Mildred comes out, picks him up, and brings him inside. He doesn't need to know his birth mother because, as he tells Wilbur, "I already have a family". It is a wonderful image: in this, we have a character who can look upon his future life and be delighted with it: it is a rare thing indeed, and serves as a lesson to be true to oneself. Wanting a similarly happy life for poor Goob, he stops on his way to the science fair to wake up Goob, who is dosing in the outfield, just in time for Goob to catch the ball he'd missed in the original time stream. The team celebrates, and we know that Goob, too, will have a very happy future. Lewis can now begin to build his future, confident that it will be exactly right for him.

Conclusion

It is interesting that, in an examination of twelve very different characters (Pinocchio, Peter/Petya, Peter Pan, Wart/Arthur, Mowgli, Taran, Cody, Jim Hawkins, Pecos Bill, Hercules, Tarzan, and Lewis/Cornelius) who span sixty-seven years of Disney animation history, there are so many traits that the characters have in common. First of all, all of the boys are innocents, and the telling of their story leads to at least a partial loss of their innocence, replacing it with experience. All of the characters have had to leave home; each character's journey involves very different destinations, and some (such as Peter/Petya's and Tarzan's) are very limited indeed, going only to a different part of the forest or jungle where he lives. But whether they travel only a few miles, to the end of the galaxy, or thirty years into the future, what is important is that they go, and that they go without a parent to protect them. Most of the boys lose their parents very early on (Peter/Petya, Wart/Arthur, Mowgli, Taran, Pecos Bill, Hercules, Tarzan and Lewis/Cornelius); one has his mother but has lost his father (Jim Hawkins), and two of the boys – Pinocchio and Peter Pan – never have parents (as such) in the first place. Nine of them experience their first love and/or meet their future wives (granted, we cannot say that Lewis falls in love or even feels his first stirring of attraction, even though he is of the right age to do so; his trip to the future, however, does include his meeting his wife and son, and receiving some advice from his wife on how to get along with her; upon returning to his own time, he knows that the girl in front of him will be his wife someday, though she does not, so there is no need for him to experience the surprise of attraction when he meets her). For these boys, what is important is that each is beginning to fulfil – or at least knows with certainty that he will one day fulfil – this most adult step: the finding of a mate and the creation of a family. This is the thing that offers him the most profound catalysts and lessons.

Love is the most important point in all of these stories. Peter Pan's experience of romance is the most limited of those who do experience it, but it makes him selfless enough to take Wendy and her brothers home to Bloomsbury when he would rather she stayed in Neverland and took care of him. It teaches Wart about pain and compassion and desire. It draws Mowgli into the man village when no force could compel him to leave the jungle. It gives Taran self-confidence and authority, and prepares him for his great destiny. It civilizes Pecos Bill, and its loss causes Bill to regress to a state of being which is both primitive and childlike. It makes Hercules a god, makes Tarzan the lord of the apes and king of the jungle, and brings Lewis the fulfilment of his dreams of having a family, allowing him to use his creativity and brilliance to make the world a better place for all. The three of the four boys who experience no romantic love at all – Pinocchio, Peter/Petya, and Cody – are physically and emotionally not ready for romance. Yet love is still the force which makes them be their best selves: it urges Pinocchio to risk everything to save Geppetto, gives Peter/Petya the courage to capture the wolf who threatens his pets, and drives Cody to be willing to do whatever it takes to protect his beloved friend Marahute's eggs. Jim Hawkins is old enough physically to experience romantic love, but we are made to understand through montages that, emotionally, he is still the small boy whose father abandoned him. Only by learning what it means to have a father's love – even the love of an imperfect father like John Silver, the cyborg pirate – can Jim finish growing up and be ready to face his future.

But why pin such themes onto the stories of young boys? As James R. Keller points out, "The construction of childhood is not even the child's idea of self, but the adult's and one created from a position of maturity, and since the adult can never merge with or become the child, s/he can only project an idealized self-image – regret, desire, melancholy, or anxiety – onto the empty child".[83] In other words, the children we are watching grow up are not real children: they are constructs, created by adults, and therefore carry the same hopes, fears, and desires for wish fulfilment that their adult creators possess. Indeed, many films about childhood receive ratings/certificates which place them outside of what is considered suitable for children: films as diverse as *Fanny and Alexander* (Bergman, 1982), *Billy Elliot* (Daldry, 2000), *Pan's Labyrinth* (del Toro, 2006), and *Let the Right One In* (Alfredson, 2008) all tell the stories of children, yet none are recommended for children under the age of fifteen. While it is no surprise that the animated Disney features discussed in this chapter are all deemed suitable for children (bearing in mind that *The Black Cauldron* was the first Disney animated feature to receive a PG rating at the time of its release), the fact remains that the children we see in these films are the creations of adults. Judith Armstrong points out that "Children's writers often say they are writing for the

83 Keller, pp. 168-169.   child they once were, or the child they might have been, or the

child they still are deep down ... .".[84] The same is true for film makers: by creating images of children – and stories about children – which resonate with themselves, they tap into ideas about childhood – to include, particularly for the animator, ideas about what a child should look like – which, while personal to themselves, are understood by their society as a whole.

[84] Judith Armstrong, "Ghosts as Rhetorical Devices in Children's Fiction", *Children's Literature in Education* Vol. 9, No. 2 (June 1978), p. 64.

2

Dashing Heroes

The heroes of Disney's animated features are a varied lot: they range from shy, bookish sorts, to soldiers, to street-smart thieves who reform. Most function alone (or alongside a female romantic interest), but a small number find themselves teaming up – sometimes with the greatest reluctance – with another hero for whom, at least initially, they feel rivalry and jealousy. What all have in common is their importance to the narrative: either they are at the centre of the plot, or else they are essential for moving it along.

It is interesting that most of the non-aristocratic adult male characters in leading roles come significantly later in Disney studio history. Until Bernard (an unusual character in and of himself) comes along in 1977's *The Rescuers*, Disney's twenty-third animated feature, the main characters of the sixteen single-narrative films produced up to that time tended to be either young adult females (Snow White, Cinderella, Aurora), children (Pinocchio, Alice, Peter Pan and Wendy, Wart, Mowgli), or animals (Dumbo, Bambi, Lady and Tramp, Pongo and Perdita and their puppies, Duchess, Thomas O'Malley and the kittens, Robin Hood, Winnie the Pooh). Adult male characters in leading roles featured only rarely, and when they did, they – with the exception of the seven dwarfs – were either princes (the Prince, Prince Charming, Prince Phillip) or were in shorter narratives in the package features: Johnny Appleseed and Pecos Bill in *Melody Time* (1948), Ichabod Crane and Brom Bones in *The Adventures of Ichabod and Mr. Toad*. Bernard appears in two films: *The Rescuers* and *The Rescuers Down Under* (1990). But beginning in the 1990s, more non-aristocratic male characters begin to appear with greater frequency: Aladdin in *Aladdin* (1992), John Smith in *Pocahontas* (1995), Quasimodo and Phoebus in *The Hunchback of Notre Dame* (1996), Hercules in *Hercules* (1997), Li Shang in

Mulan (1998), Tarzan in *Tarzan* (1999), Pacha in *The Emperor's New Groove* (2000), Milo Thatch in *Atlantis: The Lost Empire* (2001), Dr. Delbert Doppler in *Treasure Planet* (2003), Flynn Rider in *Tangled* (2010), and Wreck-It Ralph and Fix-It Felix in *Wreck-It Ralph* (2012).

As to why there is a comparative increase in leading male characters in Disney's animated films, it is hard to say: no access to the archives means that any studio memos or story meeting notes which might suggest why, in the first forty years of Disney's animated feature production (1937-1977) there are only eight male leads plus the seven dwarfs (who function more as a unit than as seven individual characters), yet from 1977 to 2013 (the year in which this study was completed) – a period of thirty-six years – there have been a further sixteen male leads (both royalty and commoners), with fifteen of those appearing in the twenty-three years between 1989 (Prince Eric) and 2012 (Wreck-It Ralph and Fix-It Felix, the most recent characters at the time of the publication of this book). However, a number of trends in the larger context of Hollywood cinema suggest several possible explanations for this increase in Disney's male leads generally, and non-aristocratic leads especially. For a start, there seems to have been a shift, beginning the in the 1960s and 1970s, in which Hollywood moved away from targeting primarily the female audience to aiming mainly at the male audience (specifically young white men aged sixteen to twenty-five years). Jackie Stacey writes in her study of female audiences that "... it has been argued that the cinema industry (linked as it was with other consumer industries) has always addressed its female spectators as consumers more generally".[85] However, as Robert C. Allen, writing around the same time as Stacey, points out, "Since the late 1960s, if not before, films had been marketed at what Hollywood with empirical reason regarded as its 'primary' box-office audience: young people between the ages of thirteen and twenty-five (particularly while males within that age group)".[86] This change in audience demographics, whether it is real or perceived, means that, very likely, Disney – in much the same thinking as I discussed in the introductory chapter of this book regarding the preference for film titles which were either gender neutral or at least included a male character's name – is acknowledging this shift by increasing both the number of male leading characters *and* by making them more prominent.

Richard Sparks, writing in 1996 about that decade's representations of men in Hollywood cinema, offers an interesting possible explanation for that decade's fascination with action

85 Jackie Stacey, *Star Gazing: Hollywood Cinema and Female Spectatorship* (London: Routledge, 1998), p. 85.

86 Robert C. Allen, "Home Alone Together: Hollywood and the 'Family Film,'" in Melvyn Stokes and Richard Maltby (Eds.), *Identifying Hollywood's Audiences: Cultural Identity and the Movies* (London: BFI, 1999), p. 117.

heroes: "It has often been suggested that heroic fictions presuppose some sort of failure of social arrangements – or their violent disruption by a figuratively or literally alien force – in a way that makes redemptive intervention from without necessary. ... Arguably what we see in some recent Hollywood cinema is a magnification of these antique starting points."[87] Though for the last decade many scholars and pundits have talked about American society in particular, but the west in general, as being either pre-9/11 or post-9/11 – and in certain respects, they are right to do so – the fact is that there have been continuities within American society and politics: an increasingly polarised political climate with particular distrust (by one side or another) of the US president has been one constant since the early 1990s. Between 1993 and 2013, there have been three two-term US presidents whose time in office has generated controversies (both real and imagined) which have been fed by, and in turn contributed to, the feeling that American society was fundamentally flawed and in need of saving. Bill Clinton (President from 1993 to 2001) was beset by a variety of scandals (Gennifer Flowers, the Whitewater Controversy, Monica Lewinsky) and became only the second president in US history to be impeached.[88] George W. Bush (2001-2009) began his presidency in the wake of his technical, Electoral College-based victory in which he lost the popular vote but carried enough states' Electoral College representatives to become president (even his re-election in November 2004 was marred by voting issues, but did not go to the courts, unlike in the 2000 "hanging chad" controversy, because his rival in 2004, Democrat John Kerry, conceded). His presidency included the September 11 attacks and the subsequent – and highly controversial – "War on Terror" in Iraq and Afghanistan, as well as the establishment of the politically-divisive detainee camp at Guantanamo Bay, Cuba, in January 2002. Barack Obama's presidency (2009 to 2017, expected), though elected and re-elected with majorities in both the Electoral College and the popular vote, has faced problems including thinly-veiled racist claims that he is not a US citizen by birth (the so-called "birther" movement), the continued existence of Guantanamo Bay Detention Camp (despite his efforts to close it), the on-going war in Afghanistan, and the on-going Wikileaks controversy. Likewise, 1937, the year in which *Snow White and the Seven Dwarfs* was released, was during a difficult period of the Great Depression as well as a difficult year politically: the Spanish Civil war raged, the Sino-Japanese war began, Stalin launched a major phase of the Great Purge, the Hindenburg disaster occurred, Amelia Earhart disappeared, and the Nazi party contin-

87   Richard Sparks, "Masculinity and Heroism in the Hollywood Blockbuster", from *The British Journal of Criminology*, Vol. 36, No. 3: Special Issue (1996), p. 357.

88   The first US president to be impeached was Andrew Johnson, president from 1865 to 1869, impeached in 1868.

ued to grow more dangerous, edging the world ever closer to war. 1948 and 1949 – the years in which *Melody Time* and *The Adventures of Ichabod and Mr. Toad* were released – were also years whose turbulence and uncertainty are reflected in Hollywood's films: the movement later dubbed *Film Noir* would be in its heyday in this period, science fiction would begin depicting wave upon wave of alien invasion as it began to take on elements of the (at this period) nearly defunct horror genre, and melodrama would enter (arguably) a golden era with the films of Douglas Sirk and Vincente Minnelli. Signs of this unease can be found in the stories of Pecos Bill (discussed in the previous chapter), and in the character who features at the start of the second section of adult leading male non-aristocratic heroes: Johnny Appleseed. Johnny Appleseed, however, is a friend to all he meets, and is our least confrontational, most pacifist hero in all of Disney's animated films. He will be discussed along with three other characters with whom he shares the trait of being an unlikely hero owing to his quiet, gentle nature. This first group of characters never seek out heroism, but when they find themselves called upon to act, they do so bravely and selflessly. Following their section, discussion will continue to examine, thematically, our other heroes: the street-smart thieves who reform, the men of action and adventure, the pairs of men – whom I've dubbed "Frienemies", using popular recent vernacular – who find themselves thrown together by circumstance and, despite being competitors, find that, ultimately, they are on the same side ... more or less. But to begin our discussion of Disney's non-aristocratic heroes, we can go right to the beginning of the history of Disney's animated feature films – *Snow White and the Seven Dwarfs* – to look at a group who are amongst the most iconic of the Disney characters: the dwarfs themselves.

Team Work: The Seven Dwarfs

So ... can *you* name all seven off the top of your head? Being asked to do so is a popular trivia question, arguably separating the "real" Disney fans from the rest of the herd. They are, of course: Doc, Happy, Bashful, Sleepy, Sneezy, Grumpy and Dopey. They live together in a little cottage, built by their own labour, deep in the forest, and together they spend their days mining in the Seven Jewelled Hills. Returning home from work one evening, they are amazed to discover, after a bit of confusion, that Princess Snow White is asleep in their beds. When she awakens, she begs them to let her stay with them (and in return, she will contribute to the household by looking after the cottage and doing the cooking), and they agree (Grumpy reluctantly, the others enthusiastically). They all grow to love Snow White, and she comes to love them, too; they become one big, happy family. Of course her step-mother, the Queen, finds the cottage and tries to kill Snow White, but the dwarfs, with the help of the forest animals, chase her off and she ends up falling off a cliff as it is struck by lightning; she is crushed by the boulder she had intended to roll down the mountain onto the dwarfs. The dwarfs cannot revive Snow White, so they protect her body and keep vigil by her until, one day, the Prince, who had fallen in love with Snow White just before her stepmother ordered her murder, finds the dwarfs and Snow White. He kisses her, she awakens, and they go away, saying good-bye to the kindly, faithful dwarfs.

That is the basic plot of the Disney version of an ancient folk tale, a version of which was recorded by Jacob and Wilhelm Grimm in 1812 in the first edition of their *Kinder- und Hausmärchen*.[89] Numerous changes to the tale have occurred over time, to include in different editions of the Grimms' collections. For example, D.L. Ashliman notes that, "Beginning with the edition of 1819, the Grimms add the statement that Snow-White's mother died during childbirth, and that her father remarried. Note that in the first edition, presumably the version closest to its oral sources, Snow-White's jealous antagonist is her own mother, not a stepmother." He goes on to add that "Beginning with the edition of 1819, the poisoned apple is dislodged when a servant accidentally stumbles while carrying the coffin to the prince's castle".[90] Of course, one of the changes most associated with the Disney version is their giving individual names to each of the seven dwarfs. But Disney is not the first to do this. He is not even the first to do this on film. The 1916 live-action silent film version of the tale, *Snow White*, starring Marguerite Clark and directed by J. Searle Dawley, establishes the dwarfs as having individual names: Blick, Flick, Click, Snick, Plick, Whick, and Quee. Walt Disney claimed that he attended a screening of this film as a young boy in Kansas City, so it may have influenced him in some respects. However, it is important to note that the idea of having seven leading characters appear in a film who do not have names of any sort (not even a generic one like "The Prince") would have been unusual for a film maker. There is evidence that names were considered for the dwarfs early in the film's production, with a list of possible names appearing in the story meeting notes from 9 October 1934. Some of the names appearing – Happy, Doc, Sleepy, and Dopey – would survive and be used in the finished film. Others, such as Hickey (because he hiccups frequently), Gabby, Nifty, Sniffy, Lazy, Puffy, Stuffy, Shorty,

89   It should be noted that there existed prior to this other versions of the story, both within the German-speaking regions of Europe and elsewhere, to include "Gold-Tree and Silver-Tree", from Scotland, and "The Young Slave", "Maria, the Wicked Stepmother, and the Seven Robbers", and "The Crystal Casket", all from Italy. For more information, see http://www.pitt.edu/~dash/type0709.html, which gives the texts of these versions of the tale in English.

90   D.L. Ashliman, "Snow-White and other tales of Aarne-Thompson-Uther type 709", found at http://www.pitt.edu/~dash/type0709.html.

Wheezy, Burpy, Dizzy and Tubby, did not.[91] In a much later story meeting (22 December 1936[92]) for *Snow White*, Walt would claim that,

> When I was in Europe, I went to the various book stores and purchased copies of the story and brought them back with me. In our version of the story we followed the story very closely. We have put in certain twists to make it more logical, more convincing and easy to swallow. We have taken the characters and haven't added any. The only thing we have built onto the story is the animals who are friends of Snow. This wasn't in the original fairy tale. We have developed a personality in the mirror and comic personalities for the dwarfs.[93]

When asked by Fred Moore, "Is the mirror a hand mirror or a mirror on the wall?" Walt's reply is that "Different versions vary in this". It implies that he has read multiple versions, and that he and his staff have researched the tale to the point whereby they feel comfortable in describing it as a close adaptation. David R. Williams, who transcribed the extracts from the notes which were given to the British Film Institute's Library, records, "26 July 1934. First dated sheets in file give synopsis of Grimm's [*sic*] Fairy tale version of Snow White, and the Snowdrop story by Marion Florence Lansing Also Snow White from *Europa's Fairy Tales* by Jacobs".[94] Again, this indicates that multiple versions of "Snow White" were consulted, with aspects of them that seemed most appropriate for a cinematic rendering of the story making the cut.

Likewise, there is ample evidence from the Williams recording of the story meeting notes that an enormous amount of time was spent on the dwarfs, with Walt himself writing notes by hand on guides which would likely have been handed out to the team working on the film. One of these notes, on a guide dated 15 December 1936, sees Walt writing the following:

> All dwarfs have definite characteristics except when called upon for unity of action. Then all are capable of moving or exerting with equal activity. For example in the scrum over the bed in sequence 5A. Also when a certain mood involving all characters is to be put across [all] can act with the same ability in getting across the mood; for example the walk into Grumpy in Sequence 6A where all the dwarfs approach the same action in the walk and stand around the barrel with the same body movements.[95]

While this is not the most articulate description ever given of the dwarfs, it is important to note that Walt's idea of them was that they act as individuals when in normal situations, but in key moments that they should lose some of that individuality and act as a unit. This, by and large, is what happens in the finished film. When individual personalities are emphasised, some receive more attention than others, presumably because these personalities can contribute more to the narrative's progression. Though

91 Extracts from Story Conference Notes Relating to *Snow White and the Seven Dwarfs* in the Disney Archives, Burbank, California, copied by David R. Williams, August 1987, p. 1.

92 This is almost exactly one year before the film's premiere, which was on 21 December 1937.

93 Extracts from Story Conference Notes Relating to *Snow White and the Seven Dwarfs* in the Disney Archives, Burbank, California, copied by David R. Williams, August 1987, p. 21.

94 Extracts from Story Conference Notes Relating to *Snow White and the Seven Dwarfs* in the Disney Archives, Burbank, California, copied by David R. Williams, August 1987, p. 1.

95 Extracts from Story Conference Notes Relating to *Snow White and the Seven Dwarfs* in the Disney Archives, Burbank, California, copied by David R. Williams, August 1987, p. 15.

much is made of Dopey – even Walt emphasised him in the film's publicity, pushing forward Dopey's clay model in the newsreel "How Walt Disney Cartoons Are Made" in such a way as to privilege the character[96] – in fact it is Grumpy who plays one of the key roles amongst the dwarfs. He is reluctant to allow Snow White to stay with them, warning the others that the Queen will "swoop down and wreak her vengeance on us" for sheltering the girl. The next day, when the dwarfs leave for their work in the mine, while Doc may warn her that, "The old Queen's a sly one, full of witchcraft, so beware of strangers", and the others beg her to be careful, it is Grumpy who takes a firm tone, saying, "Now, I'm warnin' ya. Don't let nobody or nothin' in the house." His advice is far more practical, and his coming to care for Snow White is made out to be a bigger deal, given his initial reluctance to let her stay. After the Queen (disguised as a pedlar woman) shows up to poison Snow White and the animals come to warn the dwarfs and get their help to rescue Snow White, as soon as the dwarfs realise what is happening, the other dwarfs fly into a panic, asking "What'll we do?!" It is Grumpy who jumps into action, yelling "Come on!" to his brothers and, hopping onto the back of a deer, cries out "Giddap!" as he leads the way back to the cottage, riding at full speed, fearless and determined. The others follow his example, and they race back to their cottage. Spotting the Queen, Grumpy leads them in the chase, spurring the others on as they climb up the mountain after her. He is fearless, and proves himself to be a true leader, giving the others courage and direction. Even though they are too late to save Snow White, Grumpy's actions show him to be the true hero of the film. He is also, incidentally, the first one we see break down and sob when they gather around Snow White's lifeless body.

Yet in other respects, the dwarfs function as a unit: they work together, eat together, sing together (introducing, in their first scene in the film, one of the most famous work songs of all time, "Heigh Ho"), sleep in the same room, and when instructed by Snow White, all wash together at the same trough (except Grumpy, who heckles them throughout the scene and declares, "I'd like to see anybody make *me* wash, if I didn't wanna".). They are depicted as old men (apart from Dopey, who seems to be younger), and because they are dwarfs, their bodies are proportioned differently than those of Snow White, the Evil Queen, and the Prince. But as Perce Pearce notes in the story meeting notes from 3 November 1936,

96 "How Walt Disney Cartoons Are Made", produced by RKO, 1938.

Walt feels very strongly the point that we have got to keep these little fellows cute – mustn't get grotesque. In some cases you want to see how far it has developed in the early stages from the first reel. The head size has a definite bearing on it. We are playing with figures with bulgy noses and features. Walt points out that the animators must always try to feel the cuteness in the personal treatment of all these characters. This is a hard thing to catch.[97]

This cuteness, it seems, is what the animators and Walt Disney believed would make the dwarfs seem likeable and familiar, rather than strange or uncanny. They spent months discussing the dwarfs in terms of their design and general "cuteness", as the story meeting notes show, and often discuss them in terms of various screen personalities, in particular the comedians of the silent era (or, when they liken Dopey to Harpo Marx, they reference silent comedians in the most literal sense). At one point, during a meeting on 17 November 1936, Perce Pearce says of Dopey that "Dopey has some Harpo in him, and Walt says that he's made up of Harry Langdon, and a little bit of Buster Keaton and a little trace of Chaplin in the fellow".[98] A few weeks later, on 9 December 1936, Walt asks his staff whether they can obtain and run some of Harry Langdon's films to study his movements, presumably to incorporate some of them into Dopey's actions. The drive towards realism at the studio was an essential part of the Disney studio's animation in the 1930s, and it was felt very strongly that *Snow White* should incorporate this realist aesthetic. Yet it was understood that to make the characters appear *too* realistic would render them strange, even (potentially) off-putting to the audience. This incorporation of the principle of cuteness and roundness into the dwarfs, in particular, makes them entirely sympathetic as soon as we see them.[99] Their personalities add edge and humour, and their strong work ethic and close familial bond makes them admirable. Though they take a great deal of time to discuss each individual dwarf's physical characteristics, voice and personality, they also show that they need the dwarfs to function as a unit. This strengthens their appearance as a family, and therefore makes their welcoming of Snow White into their family come across as entirely innocent and wholesome. She is simultaneously a mother and a daughter to them, and they likewise function as both her fathers and as her children.

Interestingly, D.L. Ashliman notes that there is a brief folktale from Switzerland, "Death of the Seven Dwarfs" ("Tod der sieben Zwerge"). In this, the dwarfs get into a great deal of trouble when, once more, they open their home to a lost young girl, this time a peasant girl. They have only seven beds, but offer her one nonetheless. A peasant woman then shows up, but the girl tells her that there is no more room, that the dwarfs only have seven

97 Extracts from Story Conference Notes Relating to *Snow White and the Seven Dwarfs* in the Disney Archives, Burbank, California, copied by David R. Williams, August 1987, p. 6.

98 Extracts from Story Conference Notes Relating to *Snow White and the Seven Dwarfs* in the Disney Archives, Burbank, California, copied by David R. Williams, August 1987, p. 10.

99 Thomas and Johnston, *The Illusion of Life*, pp. 68-69, 244-245.

beds. The woman accuses the girl of sleeping with all of the dwarfs, and vows to put a stop to it. She goes away, and brings back two men who break into the house, kill all seven of the dwarfs, bury them in the garden, and burn down their cottage. The peasant girl's fate is unknown.[100] It is a gruesome end for the kindly dwarfs. Happily, it is a story which never makes it into the world of Disney. They are a happy group of brothers when they bid good-bye to Snow White in their final shot (Doc and Grumpy even have their arms companionably around each other's shoulders), and it is nicer to think of them still living in their comfortable cottage and digging in their mine the whole day through.

Meek and Mild

Johnny Appleseed, whose story is narrated and sung by Dennis Day in a segment of *Melody Time*, is a very atypical hero. He is introduced in his segment as defying the stereotypical hero, and yet it implies that these differences are what make him a truly-exceptional hero:

> On the pages of American folklore, a legion of mighty men have left the symbols of their greatness: there was Paul Bunyon's axe, John Henry's hammer, Davy Crockett's rifle, and then, quite unexpectedly, one comes upon a tin pot hat, a bag of apple seed, and a holy book. And strangely enough, these are the symbols of one of the mightiest men of all: John Chapman – a real-life pioneer.

At the beginning of his story, Johnny is living on a farm in Pennsylvania, and he watches with longing as settlers begin heading out to settle the newly-acquired territories of what, in the early nineteenth century, would have been the West. Johnny, however, considers himself too "puny" to be a settler, even though he dreams of going. Suddenly, his guardian angel appears to him, and berates him for denying his dreams. Dismissing Johnny's worries that he is unsuited to be a pioneer, the angel points out that Johnny has an invaluable skill: he can grow apple trees. Johnny scoffs at this; what good are apple trees to the cause of westward expansion? The angel is shocked – of course apple trees are vital! They are a nutritious, versatile fruit, can grow in many different climates, and are delicious, too. The angel also persuades Johnny that he needs very little equipment for his journey: his bag of apple seeds, a cooking pot (that he can also wear as a hat), and his Bible. Singing a refrain that will run throughout the segment, the angel's pep talk concludes with his singing, "So pack your stuff and get a-goin'/Get them apple trees a-growin'/There's a lot of work out there to do!/Oh, there's a lot of work to do!" Another oft-repeated phrase – this one spoken, rather than sung – is that Johnny undertakes his mission "With-

100 D.L. Ashliman, "Death of the Seven Dwarfs: A Legend from Switzerland", found at http://www.pitt.edu/~dash/dwarfs.html

out no knife, without no gun". When he begins to plant his first clearing with apples, he amazes the wild animals there: they have never seen a human before who didn't try to kill them, yet Johnny is so peaceful and good-willed that he even pets the skunk who approaches him. From that moment on, the animals of the forests trust him and are his companions, and though he never seems to adopt any particular one as a pet, he nonetheless is friendly, sharing his apples with them and showing them kindness and love. Throughout the segment, the only interaction we see him enjoy is with the animals; though he never is shown interacting directly with other people, it is made clear that he is planting his trees to benefit those who live in this new territory (and this is true of *all* of the people: in one scene, Johnny comes upon a harvest dance, and watches from afar with pleasure as the white settlers and Native Americans dance and celebrate together, all sharing equally in a feast which features a preponderance of apple-based foods and drinks, of course!). This theme carries on throughout the remainder of Johnny's life. At the end, we see him as an old man, asleep under a tree, when his guardian angel returns to fetch him. Johnny looks back and realises that his body (or his "mortal husk", as the angel calls it) is still sitting under the tree, and that he has died. Johnny is furious: he cannot die, he insists, because he still has so many trees to plant. The angel, however, informs Johnny that he is needed in Heaven; it seems Heaven is running very low on apple trees! Happy once more, Johnny and the angel march off toward Heaven, singing once more that "There's a lot of work to do". Johnny will go on to plant apple trees all over Heaven, which leads to the creation of "apple blossom skies".

To say that Johnny Appleseed is not an action hero is an understatement: he may travel on foot all over the western territories of the young United States, planting thousands and thousands (it is implied) of apple trees over the course of his life, yet neither his arms nor his legs ever show any sign of muscle development. Johnny also refrains throughout from even possessing, let alone using, any defensive weapons. The refrain of "Without no knife, without no gun" reinforces a particularly-heightened form of pacifism: after all, a knife is not always a weapon, and can just as easily (and in many cases, more easily) function as a tool. Johnny seems not to carry even basic farming equipment: when we see him planting his first apple trees at the start of his mission, he finds a stick, breaks off a few superfluous branches, and uses it as a plough (in what must be unusually soft ground!) to create furrows for planting apple seeds. His role as a creator is stressed to an unusually-high degree by characterising him in this way.

Admittedly – and as the beginning of the segment points out – the story of Johnny Appleseed is based upon the life of a real individual, John Chapman.[101] But the fact is that the choice to tell this story – let alone to craft it in this way – is important. 1948, the year in which the film was released, was not an easy one. The United States would enter a relatively brief recession in late 1948 which would last well into 1949. The Cold War was in its early days, and Hollywood was still reeling, to a degree, from the HUAC investigation into the possibility that communists might be working within its studios, using Hollywood films to spread propaganda all across the United States and to its allies abroad. Walt Disney himself testified before HUAC in this period, infamously appearing before the committee as a "friendly" witness who not only named names, but even spelled one of them out.[102] So why tell the story of someone like Johnny Appleseed? After all, there is nothing about him which suggests that he could function, as Pecos Bill does at the end of the same package feature, as a superhero who could save the day (as Bill is shown to do on many occasions). But Johnny is, in his own way, a hero, not least because he embodies many rare, important traits, most significantly humility and selflessness. His story, at least as it has been mythologized – and certainly as it is told in the Disney version (which, it must be said, adheres fairly closely to the surviving version of the legend) – brings to mind the final lines of Abraham Lincoln's inaugural speech, given in March 1865:

> With malice toward none, with charity for all, with firmness in the right as God gives us to see the right, let us strive on to finish the work we are in, to bind up the nation's wounds, to care for him who shall have borne the battle and for his widow and his orphan, to do all which may achieve and cherish a just and lasting peace among ourselves and with all nations.[103]

Melody Time – and therefore the Johnny Appleseed segment – came to cinema screens at a time when the Allied Nations of World War II were still engaged in dealing with the aftermath of the war. In Europe, programmes of deNazification, which had been taking place (as a matter of US and Allied foreign policy) since Allied occupation had begun was, by 1948, becoming controversial in terms of its effectiveness, and genuine anger can be found in discussions of the policy in the final years it was in place.[104] Johnny, who roams (what was in his era) the western frontier – now the Mid-West – bringing people together and nourishing them through the planting of apples – apples which the people harvest for themselves, as Johnny only plants the seeds and tends the young trees – could be said to serve as an exemplar.

101 John Chapman, a.k.a Johnny Appleseed, 1774-1845. For more on the history of the real individual upon whom the legend of Johnny Appleseed is based, see David Skarbek, "Alertness, Local Knowledge, and Johnny Appleseed", from *The Review of Austrian Economics*, Vol. 22, No. 4 (December 2009), pp. 415-424.

102 The Testimony of Walter E. Disney Before the House Committee on Un-American Activities, 24 October 1947. Found at http://eserver.org/filmtv/disney-huac-testimony.txt.

103 Second Inaugural Speech, President Abraham Lincoln, delivered 4 March 1865. Speech found at http://avalon.law.yale.edu/19th_century/lincoln2.asp.

104 An example of this can be found in John H. Hertz, "The Fiasco of Denazification in Germany", from *Political Science Quarterly*, Vol. 64, No. 4 (December 1948), pp. 569-594.

He embodies the spirit of peace and togetherness which, in the late 1940s, was sorely missing from world politics. Further, Johnny, by participating in such a positive way in the nation's westward expansion, is engaged in a very political form of nation-building. As the narrator of the segment says, "Johnny was planting hope". It is a concept which would have been very meaningful to audiences in 1948.

Our next retiring soul to be discussed also made his cinematic debut in another difficult era, this time in the second half of the 1970s. Bernard, the mouse from the Rescue Aid Society who, along with Miss Bianca, is called upon to save young children in terrible circumstances, was first brought to life in the 1977 film *The Rescuers*; unusually, he is the only one of the characters being discussed in this book to appear in two separate films. *The Rescuers Down Under* is considered by some to be a sequel, but given that the only aspect of the original story to carry over is the relationship between Bernard and Bianca, I would argue that it is no more a sequel than were any of the twenty-three James Bond films which followed *Dr. No* (1962). Another aspect of Bernard as a character which separates him from others discussed in this book is that he is the only one who is not physically human (or at least humanoid, as is the case with Delbert Doppler from *Treasure Planet*). As I note in *Good Girls & Wicked Witches*, Bernard and Bianca are exceptional animal characters in Disney, given the fact that they can communicate directly with humans in clear, intelligible English.[105] It is on the grounds that Bernard is so unusually heavily anthropomorphised that he should be included in a discussion of human characters: he functions more like a human than like an animal, and his (and Bianca's) proven ability to communicate and interact with humans justifies his inclusion in this discussion. Bernard is an interesting character. He appears in two films, *The Rescuers* (1977) and its sequel, *The Rescuers Down Under* (1990), and is shown to be simultaneously a very timid, cautious figure as well as a very brave one. His partner in the films – a work partner who becomes his romantic partner – is Miss Bianca, an exotic, glamorous Hungarian mouse voiced by Eva Gabor. Bernard, at the beginning of *The Rescuers*, works as a janitor at the Rescue Aid Society, which is located in the basement of the United Nations and which serves to rescue children in need all over the word. The two meet when Bianca chooses Bernard to work with her to save Penny, even though he is a janitor for the society, rather than an actual agent. He is reluctant – after all, there are official delegates who are volunteering to go – but Miss Bianca's calm assertion that he is the right mouse for the job is all it takes: from then on, he and Miss Bianca will work

105 Davis, *Good Girls & Wicked Witches*, pp. 147-48.

98

together. Their first case is the rescue of Penny, an orphan girl who has been kidnapped and taken to a swamp, Devil's Bayou, to help Madame Medusa and her sidekick, Mr. Snoops, find the Devil's Eye, the largest diamond in the world. Over the course of their working together to save Penny, Bernard and Bianca grow increasingly close, despite their very different personalities; by the time their mission is completed and they have returned to New York, the pair are in love.

Bernard and Bianca, because they are so different from one another, balance each other perfectly: whereas Miss Bianca is glamorous, sophisticated, and loves travel and excitement, Bernard is a retiring, rather meek individual who prefers a quiet, predictable life. His cautious nature is further underscored by the persona of Bob Newhart, the actor who provides his voice in both films, and who was a popular American television and film star of the 1960s-2000s. In fact, at the time of each of the *Rescuers* films, Newhart was involved in two of his more iconic series, *The Bob Newhart Show* (1972-78), in which he played a neurotic psychiatrist, Dr. Bob Hartley, and later, *Newhart* (1982-1990), in which he played Dick Loudon, a neurotic "How-To" book writer and owner of an inn in a quirky town in Vermont. Like most of Newhart's trademark characters, Bernard is neurotic; but though he may be fearful and therefore tread cautiously into a dangerous situation, he is brave nonetheless, and will work his hardest and do his best to fulfil the latest mission he and Miss Bianca have undertaken. Furthermore, with his plainer appearance and introverted ways, he is a perfect foil to Miss Bianca, whose elegant, cultured personality is shown to be daring, bold, extroverted, and fond of adventure and action.

On the surface, such a representation of manhood is very unusual: though Bernard is brave, he is not an obviously heroic figure. He is frightened of excitement and danger, and clearly is someone who would be happiest with a more settled life, were it not for his attachment to Miss Bianca and the work he feels compelled to do with her on behalf of the Rescue Aid Society. He never seeks adventure – in fact, he seeks to avoid it whenever possible – and even shows himself to be frightened of air travel (though, admittedly, this is probably sensible, given that air travel for Bernard and Bianca involves riding in a sardine can strapped to the back of an albatross). In *The Rescuers Down Under*, when he and Miss Bianca meet Jake, the mouse in charge of the runway where they land in Australia, he feels himself to be overshadowed by (and forced into competition with) Jake, a ruggedly handsome Australian kangaroo mouse who shows himself to be very like

Miss Bianca when it comes to enjoying adventure, and also proves himself knowledgeable of the part of the outback where they must rescue Cody. Jake, who accompanies Bernard and Bianca as a guide through the outback, even interrupts Bernard's second attempt at proposing to Miss Bianca when he is nearly eaten by, but then ties up and masters, a huge snake named Twister, whom he uses to carry himself, Bianca and Bernard to McLeach's hiding place so that they can rescue Cody, the boy at the centre of the narrative.

When the trio arrive, they do so just as McLeach, the film's villain, is tricking Cody into believing that the mother eagle, Marahute, is dead so that Cody will go and find Marahute's eggs to protect them. The mice manage to hide in McLeach's vehicle, then get to Cody and warn him of McLeach's trick. Unfortunately, they are unable to warn him in time, and Cody, the eagle, Miss Bianca, and Jake end up caught in McLeach's cage. But it is here, just when things look their worst, that Bernard comes into his own. He hides the eagle's eggs and replaces them in the nest with stones; this prevents Joanna, McLeach's goanna lizard sidekick, from eating them. Once Joanna is gone, he then returns the eggs to their nest, and enlists Wilbur (the albatross who got them to Australia) to help him protect the eggs while he himself goes after Cody, Bianca, Jake, and the eagle. Miss Bianca certainly believes that Bernard can help them, and tells Cody so; Jake, who sees Bernard's timidity as a sign of incompetence and even cowardice, pretends to agree, but admits privately to her that he thinks Bianca is bluffing to make Cody feel better. But, of course, Bianca is right. Bernard will stop at nothing to rescue them, no matter how frightened he is. He even approaches a razorback, insisting that it help him reach McLeach's vehicle. The next time we see him is just after he has shut off McLeach's vehicle just as McLeach is about to use its crane to lower Cody to his death in a crocodile-infested river. Bernard steals the keys, then throws them to Miss Bianca and Jake so that they can free themselves from the cage, and leads Joanna away when she realises that he's trying to stop McLeach. When Bernard sees McLeach trying to shoot the rope that is suspending Cody over the crocodiles, Bernard goads Joanna into chasing him, then runs up McLeach's trouser leg so that Joanna will chase him onto McLeach. Bernard jumps away from McLeach just as Joanna knocks herself and McLeach into the water; Bernard then goes after Cody, whose rope has snapped and dropped him into the water (though, by this time, the crocodiles are following McLeach and Joanna, who are floating downstream on the current). Bernard then dives into the water and tows Cody to the surface, using the rope with which Cody has been bound to try and haul Cody out of the water. They are pulled into the water by the strength of the current, however, and go over the waterfall, but are rescued in time by the Golden Eagle, Marahute; with Cody, Jake, and Bianca on her back (and Bernard still clinging, petrified, to the end of Cody's rope), she flies above the clouds and into the moonlit sky. Cody takes Bernard into his hand and thanks him before placing him on Marahute's back, next to Bianca. Bernard performs his final act of bravery for the film, seizing the moment and proposing to Miss Bianca at last. She accepts, and they all fly off to take Cody home before, presumably, returning to Marahute's nest (where Wilbur is tending her eggs for her) before Wilbur, Bernard, and Bianca set off for their return to New York.

In a documentary short on the making of *The Rescuers Down Under*, the film's director, Mike Gabriel, says of Bernard that he is "… the underdog. He's really our little link with the audience in this story. Bianca is the leader of the little duo – the rescue team – but Bernard's the one you link with because you know that he's been trying to propose to Bianca and he keeps getting put off for some reason or another, so you're rooting for him."[106] In many ways, at least at first glance, Bernard's personality traits have more in common with the sidekick of a film, the character whose role is to make the hero look good. But given the bravery and strength Bernard shows when he must rescue single-handedly Cody, Marahute the eagle, Bianca, and Jake, Bernard demonstrates that being brave is about doing what one must despite being afraid. It is an important lesson, and one which can be overlooked in characters who are stronger physically, not to mention much larger – we are talking, of course, about a heavily-anthropomorphised mouse operating in a human world. Sadly for Bernard, his efforts in this film are sometimes forgotten, overwhelmed as *The Rescuers Down Under* is by the enormous success of the Disney animated features released on either side of it, as well as by the film's limited box office success. Nonetheless, he *is* remembered from *The Rescuers* as a likeable, sympathetic character.

Another unlikely hero is Milo Thatch, the main character of *Atlantis: The Lost Empire*. Milo is a scholar, an expert in ancient and modern Linguistics with a wide range of degrees and academic interests.[107] It becomes apparent early on in the film, however, that despite his brilliance, his career has been marred by his interest – practically an obsession – with finding the lost city of Atlantis, which he is certain was a real place, and not the myth it is assumed to be. At the start of the film, which is set in

---

106 "The Making of *The Rescuers Down Under*", Bonus Features, from *The Rescuers Down Under* (Region 2/PAL, © Disney Enterprises, DVD release date 28 January 2002).

107 According to the "Dossier" on Milo Thatch on disc two of the *Atlantis* dvd set, Milo was "Educated at Oxford University (1896-1903) [and] holds a double Doctorate in the fields of Linguistic Theory … and Dead Languages … . Minor Degrees in Chemistry, Literature … Art History, Sociology and Anthropology." At age 32, he is by far the most educated and accomplished Disney character, male or female. Found at Disc 2/Files/Milo, page 3/8. From *Atlantis: The Lost Empire*, Disc 2, *Atlantis: The Lost Empire, 2-Disc Collector's Edition* (Region 1/NTSC, © Disney Enterprises, Inc., DVD release date January 29, 2002).

1914,[108] he is working in the Cartography and Linguistics department of a Museum (presumably the Smithsonian, though it remains unnamed) in Washington, D.C., but seems to be based in the boiler room, rather than having an actual office. He is practicing a speech to give to a committee in the hope of receiving funding to further his research, when he finds that the committee has tricked him: they send him a letter informing him that his presentation to an earlier time (at a little after 4pm, they tell him that his 4:30 meeting has been moved to 3:30) and then, in a letter which follows the first one by only seconds, tell him that, because he missed the re-scheduled meeting, his application for funding has been denied. Milo runs immediately to catch up with the board, and angrily resigns. He returns home to find a mysterious woman, Helga Sinclair, waiting to take him to meet Mr. Whitmore. It turns out that Whitmore was an old friend of his grandfather (also an academic and also obsessed with Atlantis), and that Whitmore is now prepared (thanks to his team finding the last piece of the puzzle) to launch an expedition to find and explore Atlantis, hopefully retrieving lost knowledge, proving its existence, and bringing back a mysterious power source which, according to legend, gave the people of Atlantis access to technology and capability far beyond that of not only the ancient world, but of the twentieth century, too. Whitmore has assembled a crack team, which he describes as "the best of the best", and now wishes to add Milo to it, both because he is the best with dead languages and knowledge of Atlantis, and also because of Whitmore's friendship with Milo's late grandfather.[109] Milo is overwhelmed, but excited beyond belief that he is being taken seriously *and* is about to set out to find Atlantis.

Upon joining the expedition's crew, Milo finds himself a little bit excluded (they seem to think him too bookish – too much of a geek/nerd, in modern parlance – to be worth paying attention to; one of the characters, Audrey, comments dismissively that "I used to take lunch money from guys like this!"), but Milo is too obsessed with studying *The Shepherd's Journal* to notice much. The crew starts to warm to him, however, and gradually he is welcomed into the group, especially when his knowledge proves to be invaluable to the mission. But it is when they encounter – very unexpectedly – living people in Atlantis that Milo comes into his own. Initially, he is the only one who can communicate with them (at least until it is realised that the Atlantean language is a root of most modern ones, and this (rather magically) enables the Atlanteans to be able to communicate, with a little adjustment, in English, French, German (the languages we hear them speaking to the various members of the team) and so forth. Milo soon

108 Mention is made at the start of the film that winter is on its way, and we see the Washington D.C.-based characters wearing overcoats. No mention at all is made of WWI, however, which would have begun a few months earlier in Europe. America was not involved, but it is interesting that the war plays no part even in their planning their sea voyage to find Atlantis.

109 The final key the team has acquired is a book, *The Shepherd's Journal*, which is written in a language that Milo is one of the last people alive who can read; this means that they need him to translate what it says in order to get past the obstacles between them and Atlantis.

forms a friendship with Kida, one of the warriors they meet when they first encounter people in Atlantis. Kida is also a princess, and the heir to her father's throne. She is shown to be highly intelligent, and also terribly worried. She is very aware that Atlantis is in trouble: its culture is dying (not even she can read their written language), the city is falling apart, and though the people are not yet suffering, she fears that it is only a matter of time. Realising that Milo's ability to read her language might mean that she can help her people, she turns to him, and as they work to piece together the lost knowledge of Atlantis, the two form a bond. When, at one stage, Kida removes her skirt so that they might swim to see an underwater ruin of a mural (which has writing on it she is sure will help them uncover more knowledge), he is shown by his reaction to the sight of her (she is wearing something equivalent to a modern bikini) to be both embarrassed and attracted to her. There is no time to explore their attraction, however, before the expedition's leader, Rourke, reveals his true colours and takes Kida hostage, forcing Milo to help him find and retrieve the Heart of Atlantis to take home with them to sell.[110]

Milo is torn: he has no desire to help Rourke steal the Heart of Atlantis, not least because it will lead to the destruction of the city and its people, but he is even more unwilling to allow Kida to be hurt. Reluctantly, he helps Rourke find the Heart of Atlantis; to his horror, Milo then must bear witness as Kida is lifted up by the Heart and bonded with it. She is transformed, and becomes the vessel for the Heart. From here on out, it will become Milo's mission to save Kida/the Heart, yet he is aware that he lacks the weapons and the physical strength to oppose the team. However, it is made very apparent that he has more than enough love, integrity, and moral strength to defeat Rourke, and this endows him with (or perhaps brings out in him) the abilities of a leader. By pointing out the immorality of what they are doing, Milo is able to persuade most of the expedition's crew, apart from Helga and Rourke, that what they are doing is wrong, and that they should stand together to save Atlantis and Kida. He then shows the Atlanteans how to use the flying machines which had belonged to their ancestors (but which, because they could no longer read, they could not figure out how to work). Together, and under Milo's leadership, they are able to defeat Rourke and Helga, rescue Kida, and restore the Heart of Atlantis to its rightful place, freeing Kida from its bond so that she can assume her role as queen (her father, the King, died shortly after the Heart was taken from Atlantis). The rest of the expedition returns home (bringing with them a huge amount of treasure given to them by the grateful Atlanteans), but Milo stays behind, saying that Atlan-

110 Rourke is analysed in detail in Chapter 4, in the section "Enemies of the Earth".

tis needs someone who can "read Gibberish", as the ancient language – and his ability to read multiple dead languages – had been disparaged earlier in the film. The crew leaves (and later, we see them all with Whitmore, settling on a story which will not reveal Atlantis' whereabouts yet will explain why Milo, Rourke, and Helga are no longer around). We also see as the old king – Kida's father – is memorialised and Kida, with Milo as her consort, rules over a revitalised Atlantis as its queen.

When she is released from the Heart, Kida falls into Milo's arms and they embrace tenderly; later, as they bid farewell to the expedition team, we see a close up shot of their hands, which move to clasp each other in the way that only couples hold hands. We can also see that it is Kida's hand which is on top, in a way that body language experts often cite shows who is the "dominate" member of the couple.[111] Shortly after this, during the memorial service to the late king, we see Milo, now dressed as an Atlantean, standing by Queen Kida's side, in the role of her consort. Otherwise, very little "courtship" is shown between the couple, at least in the traditional sense of the idea. Milo never seeks to woo Kida: depicted in many ways as the typical scholar, his head either in a book or in the clouds, he cannot even drive a car (one could make much psychoanalytic meaning out of the fact that he fumbles briefly with the gear shift before admitting that he does not know what it's for), let alone know what to do when a pretty girl lets him know that she is interested in him (and, indeed, Kida does exhibit mildly flirtatious behaviour when she prepares to swim with Milo to the sunken mural). But Milo *is* shown to be someone who knows how to fix things and solve problems: when we first meet Milo, working down in the boiler room, he knows how to fix the temperamental boiler when it malfunctions; he later uses the same technique to fix the expedition's malfunctioning digging machine. Because he can read Atlantean, he is able to show first Kida, then the others, how to use the flying machines, and it is he who manages to turn the tide in his favour when he persuades the majority of the crew to switch their allegiance from Rourke to him. Milo is sweet, unaffected, enthusiastic, upright, and kind. He is very much an intellectual and a scholar, and it is in these pursuits where the determination that is part of his character first exhibits itself. But his greatest strength seems to be his moral integrity: when Kida, the Heart of Atlantis, and the people of Atlantis are all under threat, Milo will stop at nothing to save them. It does not matter that most of the others are shown to be stronger and more athletic than he (Kida, when she first meets him, comments, "You are a scholar, are you not? Judging from your diminished physique

111 For a discussion on the body language of handholding, see Judi James, *The Body Language Bible: The Hidden Meaning Behind People's Gestures and Expressions* (London: Vermilion, 2008), pp. 170-173.

and large forehead, you are suited for nothing else."). But Milo has heart, and he has brains. These triumph over the brawn exhibited by Rourke. In many ways, Rourke is depicted as the hard-bodied action man and Milo the sensitive "new man" of the 1990s. For this reason, neither the narrative nor the characters ever question what Kida sees in Milo or why they are a good match: both are shown to be strong willed, intelligent, and willing to stand up for what they hold dear. They become friends, then their friendship deepens into something more. It may happen quickly, but it is not the classic "love at first sight" which is so often thought to characterise love in the movies. When the chips are down, it will fall to Milo to save the day, and he does. We are shown that he would have done anything to stop Rourke's theft whether or not he had fallen in love with Kida. He wins despite the superior physical and military strength of the villain he opposes, and it is his goodness and strength of character which allows him to triumph. In the following chapter, on the princes, I will discuss this notion much more in relation to the Beast (from *Beauty and the Beast*), as he is the Disney hero who most embodies (and does so simultaneously) the rejection of the hard-bodied action hero of Reaganite cinema and the rise in mainstream depictions of a "kinder, gentler" action hero. For now, it is enough to say, in relation to Milo, that his unquestioned status as hero of the film shows that, by the time the film was released in June 2001, this particular type of masculinity had become very much the mainstream. Big, over-developed action heroes had become dated; geek chic was in.

Not quite a chic geek – and in no other way a typical dashing hero – is one way to describe our final character in this section, Dr. Delbert Doppler, the dog-eared (literally) astrophysicist who accompanies young Jim Hawkins into space in the 2002 film *Treasure Planet*.[112] Though in some ways Doppler functions as a sidekick for Jim, he nonetheless plays an important function in the plot, as it is Doppler who convinces Sarah Hawkins, Jim's mother, to allow Jim to go into space. He finances the expedition to find Treasure Planet, and he accompanies Jim on the journey. When we first meet Doppler, dining at the Benbow Inn (owned by Sarah Hawkins), we see that he and Jim's mother are old, close friends (albeit with no hint of anything other than a close, supportive friendship between them). Though it is clear that he has known Jim, too, for years, we are shown that he is not comfortable with young children; we also find that he is somewhat impressed with himself (albeit in an inoffensive way) when he intervenes, briefly, when the police bring Jim home after being arrested for yet another scrape. Doppler's persona is informed a

112 Doppler's name seems to be a reference to the mathematician, physicist, and astronomer Christian Doppler (1803-1853).

great deal by the fact that his voice is provided by David Hyde Pierce, best known for playing Dr. Niles Crane on the television series *Frasier* (1993-2004); in his performance as Doppler, he plays very much on Niles' tendencies towards fussiness, on the one hand, and unbridled enthusiasm for pursuing his goals on the other. When they realise that Jim has obtained a map which will lead them to Treasure Planet, Doppler is ecstatic. He rushes around his home gathering what he needs to take on the journey, enthusing that he will finance the voyage and accompany Jim. Having pointed out to Sarah that such a trip might be good for the troubled boy, Sarah asks him, "Are you saying this because it's the right thing, or because *you* really want to go?" Doppler's reply sums up his character well: "I really, really, *really* want to go – *and* it's the right thing".

Of course, Doppler's enthusiasm in no way means that he actually knows what he is about to undertake. When he and Jim go to board the ship, Doppler shows up wearing a huge, elaborate "spacesuit" (albeit one which looks rather like a nineteenth-century diving suit) which makes him seem very naïve and out of place, and renders him something of a laughing stock (the scene has parallels with Niles Crane, in an episode where he promises to take his father ice fishing and arrives decked out in an elaborate hunting/fishing ensemble, commenting that he never realised how much he liked fishing until he knew how much shopping it involved[113]). Captain Amelia seems particularly amused by Doppler, smirking at him, poking fun at his ineptitude by adjusting his ridiculous costume so that he at least is wearing it correctly, and shortly after they come on board and Doppler nearly lets slip in front of the crew that Jim has a treasure map, the captain expresses her poor opinion of him in no uncertain terms; speaking slowing and enunciating her words in a way which implies her doubt that he will understand her if she speaks normally (and her normal speech is fairly fast, clipped, and precise), "Doctor, to muse and blabber about a treasure map in front of this particular crew demonstrates a level of ineptitude that borders on the imbecilic ... and I mean that in a very caring way". Doppler is insulted by her attitude toward him and tries to retort, but Amelia never gives him the chance. He storms off, fuming "That woman! That feline! *Who* does she think is working for *whom*?" Doppler proves his worth to Amelia and the ship later, though, when a star they are sailing near begins to go supernova, but then implodes upon itself, transforming into a black hole. The ship is in danger of being sucked into the black hole, but it is Doppler's knowledge of mathematics, physics, and astronomy which enables him to see that there is a chance for them to save themselves

113 *Frasier*, Season 2, Episode 20, "Breaking the Ice", Original US Air Date 18 April 1995.

if they can ride the star's last explosive wave out of range of the black hole that is forming. In essence, his knowledge and quick thinking, combined with Amelia's knowledge as a sailor and a captain, work together to save the ship, with only one man lost (and that happens when one of the evil crew cuts Mr. Arrow's lifeline when the first mate has fallen overboard, not as a result of Doppler's actions).

It is at this moment that Doppler and Captain Amelia begin to see one another differently, and in much more favourable terms. This change in their relationship will become of great importance later, when they and Jim are forced to flee the ship when the pirates mutiny. Captain Amelia throws Doppler a pistol, but (unsurprisingly) he has no experience with them. When they are forced to shoot at the pirates while freeing their longboat from its moorings in the Legacy's hull, Doppler is just as amazed as Amelia when he manages to hit a small target which saves them, and begins firing back at the pirates with greater confidence. One of the pirates fires the ship's cannon at the boat, and though they avoid taking a direct hit, the longboat is clipped nonetheless and Amelia is hurt. She lands the ship successfully, but is injured enough that she must send Jim to look for a safer place for them to hide, and Doppler sets about tending to her wound. Once Jim has found a place for them to take shelter (B.E.N.'s home, where they can defend themselves while Amelia recovers from her wound), we next see Doppler carrying Amelia in his arms as she is still in a bad way (though we see that he has done his best to bandage her wound). When B.E.N. sees Doppler carrying Amelia and then gently laying her down, he comments, "Isn't that sweet! I find old-fashioned romance so touching, don't you? How about drinks for the happy couple?" It is the second time in the film that Doppler has been paired mistakenly with a female character: the first time was when Jim is brought home by the police and they ask whether he is Jim's father. In that scene, when he and Sarah Hawkins deny this and confirm that he is just an old family friend, we hear Sarah accidentally let slip, "Eew!" at the thought of being married to Doppler (and certainly he is no one's idea of handsome, given that he seems to be a somewhat canine-inspired humanoid: he has long, floppy ears and a large, brown dog nose). But in this instance, rather than look repulsed or irritated, Amelia looks at him fondly, with soft eyes, just as Doppler tells B.E.N. that they're not a couple. The realisation that Amelia is not repulsed by him seems to catch Doppler off guard, and he turns his attention to the markings on the walls and ceiling of B.E.N.'s home. The diversion works only for a moment; Amelia sits up to tell Jim to keep a lookout, but when she winces from the pain, Doppler tells her to lay back down and stop giving orders. Rather than take offense, she looks at him, and says, almost flirtatiously, "Very forceful, doctor. Go on – say something else." The shot cuts back to Doppler, who is looking at her with great affection; the two are beginning to realise that they are falling for one another. A short while later, when Amelia, losing her train of thought, comments, "Doctor, you have wonderful eyes", Doppler cannot help but cry out, "She's lost her mind!" When Jim implores him to help Amelia, we are treated to another comic moment: a brief *Star Trek* reference ("Dang it, Jim, I'm an astronomer, not a doctor!"), then a dissembling ("I mean I *am* a doctor, but not *that* kind of doctor. I mean, I have a doctorate, it's not the same thing – you can't *help* people with a doctorate, you just sit there, and you're useless …"). Later, after Doppler, Amelia, Jim, and B.E.N. have been captured by Silver, he and Amelia sit in a boat, tied back to back, while the pirates revel in the treasure. Doppler laments to Amelia, "All my life I dreamed of an adventure like this. I'm just sorry I couldn't have been more helpful to you." It is at this moment that he realises that his wrists are too thin to be bound up properly, and he is able to get his hands free. He then taunts the pirate standing guard over them, takes his gun, and rescues himself and Amelia. They retrieve the Legacy and come to the rescue of Jim and Silver, having already picked up B.E.N. and the surviving pirates (whom they secure in the hold). Once they are free of Treasure Planet and safely home, Doppler and Amelia embrace. They don't kiss, but they look at each other in such a way as to imply that they now recognise that they are a couple. How do we know it all works out for the couple? In the final scene, at the party celebrating the opening of the rebuilt Benbow inn, we see that Doppler is holding three infants who look like Amelia, while she cradles one who looks like Doppler. They have found love, started a family, and – it is heavily implied – will live happily ever after.

It is interesting, given Jim Hawkins' age, that a romantic element was displaced onto Doppler, elevating him from mere sidekick or secondary character to a level almost equal with Jim, and equal to that of John Silver in terms of character development. It is not a plotline which is original to the novel or found in Disney's 1950 adaptation; Doppler seems to be fulfilling the role of Squire Trelawney (and to a lesser extent, Dr. Livesy), and the captain in the original, Captain Smollett, is male (and particularly given the 1950s, and especially the late Victorian era, when Stevenson's 1883 novel was published, a romance between two male characters would be unthinkable). Disney seems to have decided that the film needed a romance, but rather than alter the storyline further and provide a romantic partner for Jim, instead the characters of Doppler and Amelia were created. Perhaps the thinking was that a romantic interest for Jim would create too many tensions with and distractions from the father-son relationship he creates with Silver; as it is, very little of the romance is shown on screen, only a few loving looks and, later, a litter of babies (litter being the appropriate word, given Doppler's canine aspects and Amelia's feline traits). So while Doppler may not be the most dashing of our heroes, nonetheless he provides the narrative with the means to get Jim off on his adventure, with a strong degree of comic relief, and with a figure to use to allow for the obligatory romantic subplot to be developed. Interestingly, he also helps to mitigate the incredibly strong, independent character of Captain Amelia: he feminizes her and softens her, and by creating a heteronormative relationship with her, then creating a family with her, he domesticates her in a very real, tangible way. Nonetheless, in our final shots of the couple, Amelia is still dressed in a captain's uniform: becoming a mother has not meant giving up her career, and presumably Doppler supports her in this.

Street Smart Scamps

Our next two heroes have in common the fact that, at the start of each character's narrative, he makes his living as a thief. Not only that, he is good at it. He is charming, intelligent, quick-witted, and fast, which makes him able avoid capture by the authorities. Neither is a thief because he is "bad", however. Both are orphans, both have found themselves in difficult situations, and both have turned to stealing out of necessity. It is when they each find love – and this love inspires them to find a better way of living – that the two will become their best selves, each finding strengths they had been unaware of, and each stopping a villain who targets the woman he loves. In the process, each will be elevated to the role of prince: but true love with a good woman and finding the best in themselves – not the princesses they each help – is their real reward.

Aladdin is introduced to us in an opening monologue by a market trader as "a diamond in the rough": he is called a "street rat" and a "thief". When we first meet him, Aladdin is working the marketplace, fleeing from the guards after stealing a loaf of bread (and marvelling that such a small theft is getting such attention). The fact is that this is far from Aladdin's first brush with the law: as he says in the song "One Jump Ahead", the number he sings during this scene, "Gotta steal to eat/Gotta eat to live". He (and his monkey, Abu) are highly-skilled thieves with an enormous amount of practice. Yet at the conclusion of the scene, when Aladdin and Abu have managed to elude the guards and find a safe place to eat they see two small children scavenging in the rubbish and finding nothing. Aladdin has worked hard to steal the loaf of bread, and definitely is hungry, but he cannot resist giving his entire portion of the loaf to the children (he then persuades the much more reluctant Abu to give them his portion, too). The impression we are given is that here is a young boy, alone in the world (we learn in the song "One Jump Ahead" that he has no parents), doing what he must to survive but never letting go of his more noble instincts. He dreams of being more than he is – of being better – but at the start of the film, it is clear that he confuses being "better" with being rich. This, presumably, is because he is shown to be conflicted about having to be a thief; being rich and living in the palace would mean that he would never have to steal again.

When he first sees Princess Jasmine (who has disguised herself so that she might explore the marketplace for the first time), Aladdin is overwhelmed by her beauty. He watches her, and sees when she gets in trouble for stealing when she gives an apple to a child but has no money to pay for it (having never been outside the palace before, she was unaware that she needed to carry money to pay for things). The vender grabs her arm to cut off her hand (as punishment for thievery), when Aladdin comes to her rescue, pretending that she is his insane sister. He brings her back to his home, and the two bond over the fact that each feels trapped in his/her life. They may come from different worlds, but they are the same in spirit.

Meanwhile, Jafar, the Sultan's evil advisor, has realised that Aladdin is the "diamond in the rough" who can retrieve a magic lamp from the Cave of Wonders. Jafar kidnaps Aladdin, tells Jasmine that he has been beheaded for kidnapping her, and sends him into the cave. After a series of mishaps (caused mostly by Abu, who is tempted by the treasure around them, tries to take a jewel, and brings about the destruction of the magical cave), Aladdin finds himself trapped in the cave, his only company Abu and a sentient magic carpet they have found and befriended. It is then that Aladdin realises that Abu has the lamp: he takes it and tries to polish off some dirt to read the inscription, and ends up releasing Genie. Aladdin demonstrates his cleverness by tricking Genie into getting everyone out of the cave but not using one of his three wishes to do it. He promises to free Genie using his third wish, but uses his first to be turned into a prince – Prince

Ali Ababwa – so that he might be eligible to court Jasmine (by law, we are told, a princess can only marry a prince).

Initially, Aladdin works hard to seem like a "true" prince, arriving at the palace with overwhelming pomp and speaking with a kind of macho bravado that he thinks shows his power and wealth. But it is only when (as Genie keeps telling him) he lets down his guard and is himself with Jasmine (mostly; he still lies and tells her that he was a prince in disguise in the marketplace, rather than admit that he is a street rat disguised as a prince) that Jasmine lets down her guard. As they ride together on the magic carpet, singing "A Whole New World" as they fly over foreign, exotic lands, the two fall in love. An hour into the film, with nearly thirty minutes left of the narrative, the two share a kiss – a very unusual move in this genre, given that the couple typically share their first kiss as the film draws to a close.

Unfortunately, the elation of falling in love is quickly shattered for Aladdin when he is kidnapped (again) by Jafar (only this time, Jafar believes he is kidnapping a prince who will ruin his chance to marry Jasmine and become sultan himself; he believes Aladdin to have been killed in the collapse of the Cave of Wonders). Jafar's thugs tie him up and throw him over a cliff into the water to drown, but fortunately Genie's lamp was hidden under his turban, and so Genie is able to save his life and return Aladdin to the palace. He arrives just as the Sultan, under Jafar's hypnotic control, tells Jasmine that she must marry Jafar. Realising what is happening, Aladdin accuses Jafar of trying to have him killed, and breaks Jafar's magical staff, thereby breaking his hold on the Sultan. They have the guards arrest him, but Jafar manages to escape and disappears. The Sultan realises that Aladdin (or Prince Ali, as he thinks he is) and Jasmine are in love, and he declares that they will be married at once, telling Aladdin that someday he will become Sultan. Aladdin's reaction here is key: intrigued and excited at the idea of being sultan, he is shown to have doubts as he hears the Sultan tell him, "A fine, upstanding youth such as yourself, a person of your unimpeachable moral character, is exactly what this kingdom needs". As the sultan speaks, Aladdin's face falls: he cannot help but be aware of the deception he is committing, and what it says about his character. When we see him next, he is trying to figure out a way to tell the sultan the truth; when the Genie congratulates Aladdin on his success, Aladdin becomes angry: Genie reminds Aladdin that he had promised to use his third wish to set Genie free (his first wish was to become prince; the second – which Genie claimed Aladdin had assented to – was to rescue Aladdin from drowning when

Jafar's men threw him over a cliff), but Aladdin refuses:

> Aladdin: Look, I'm sorry, I really am. But they wanna make me sultan. No – they wanna make "Prince Ali" sultan. Without you, I'm just Aladdin
>
> Genie: Al, you *won*!
>
> Aladdin: Because of *you*! The only reason anyone thinks I'm worth anything is because of you. What if they find out I'm not really a prince? What if Jasmine finds out? I'd lose her. Genie, I can't keep this up on my own. I can't wish you free.
>
> Genie: Fine. I understand. After all, you've lied to everyone else. Hey, I was beginning to feel left out. Now if you'll excuse me ... "master" ... [With a mock bow, Genie vanishes into the lamp.]

Aladdin speaks in an angry tone, but it is plain from his facial and body language that he is upset, and that he hates having to lie, feels terrible about having to go back on his promise to Genie, and is scared of losing Jasmine, whom he loves genuinely. He tries to apologise, but Genie will not accept it. Realising he has done wrong, he decides to tell Jasmine the truth.

When Aladdin goes to find Jasmine, Iago sneaks into his room and steals the lamp, bringing it to Jafar. Jafar rubs the lamp, bringing Genie under his command. Jafar makes his first wish to become sultan, and his second to become the most powerful sorcerer in the world. He then reveals to Jasmine that "Prince Ali" is the street urchin Aladdin, throws the boy into one of the palace's towers, and fires it off like a rocket. It comes to land in a far off, snow-covered place. Aladdin survives the journey, and finds himself alone in a frozen wasteland with Abu. He had been prepared to tell Jasmine the truth, and realises that, had he kept his promise to Genie and set him free, none of this would have happened. Vowing to set things right, Aladdin begins to make his way out. He discovers that the carpet is also with them, and so Aladdin and Abu hop aboard and they head back to Agrabah. When they arrive, they see that Jafar is abusing the sultan and Jasmine. He has just ordered Genie to make Jasmine fall in love with him; the genie tries to remind him that he cannot grant such a wish, and Jafar begins bullying Genie, ordering him to grant the wish. Jasmine then sees Aladdin and the others, but they signal to her not to reveal that they've returned, and so she pretends that Genie has granted Jafar's wish and, in a moment played very much for laughs, begins complementing Jafar on his most unattractive traits. Just then, Genie, too, realises that Aladdin has returned. He is thrilled to see Aladdin, but warns him that he can do nothing to help Aladdin so long as he is under Jafar's command. Aladdin, however, has regained his self-confidence. He reminds Genie that, as a street rat, he is a good improviser, and very nearly manages to grab hold of Genie's lamp, but Jafar sees Aladdin's reflection in Jasmine's crown and stops him with his sorcerer's power. Nonetheless, each of the characters continues trying to get hold of the lamp, but Jafar stops them at every turn, laughing manically. Aladdin calls him out, daring Jafar to fight him directly rather than using his powers, but Jafar transforms himself into a giant cobra and tries to kill Aladdin.

As a street rat, one of Aladdin's greatest resources is his cleverness and his ability to con people by using their own foibles against them (we saw this earlier, when he tricks Genie into getting them safely out of the Cave of Wonders without using one of his wishes). He reminds Jafar that, while he may be an all-powerful sorcerer, it was Genie who gave him that power, and therefore Genie could take it away. This goads Jafar into wishing to become a genie himself, just as Aladdin had wished. The others are horrified, and it is with the greatest reluctance that Genie grants the wish. But just as Aladdin remembered, being a genie may come with "Phenomenal cosmic powers", but it also comes with "itty bitty living space". In other words, by tricking Jafar into becoming a genie, Aladdin has made Jafar become a slave trapped inside a tiny lamp, unable to use his powers except at someone else's command, and only if they call him forth from the lamp. Genie proclaims Aladdin a genus, and order is restored.

But the restoration of order means that Aladdin is no longer Ali the prince, and therefore means that, by law, he and Jasmine cannot marry. Not at all angry that Aladdin pretended to be a prince to get close to her (since she knows that he did it because of his true feelings for her rather than as a ploy for wealth and power), Jasmine laments the law that keeps them apart. Genie reminds Aladdin that he has one wish left and can wish to be made a prince again, but Aladdin reminds him that he had promised to free Genie with his third wish. Aladdin gently refuses. He tells Jasmine that he loves her, but "I got to stop pretending to be something I'm not". He then wishes Genie free. It is a selfless and noble action, and also a kind of sacrifice, since Aladdin believes that honouring his promise to Genie means that he will never be able to be with the woman he loves. Genie is exultant, and Aladdin is truly happy for him, even if his happiness is bittersweet since it means giving up Jasmine; it also means giving up his friend Genie, since now Genie, no longer enslaved to whomever possesses the lamp, can go wherever he wishes. Genie hugs Aladdin, saying that no matter what, Aladdin will always be a prince to him. The sultan, who has stood by quietly throughout the scene, suddenly speaks up. Telling Aladdin, that "You've certainly proven your worth as far as I'm concerned", he declares that the old law is dead, and that the princess may marry whomever she deems worthy. Jasmine choses Aladdin, and the film ends with a brief reprise of "A Whole New World" as the two – now officially a married couple – fly off into the moonlight on the magic carpet.

Essentially, Aladdin cannot win – he cannot make his dreams of success come true and be with the woman he loves – so long as hides his true nature. What is interesting is that his pretending to be Prince Ali is not the first deception we witness Aladdin commit in the film: the first is when he pretends to be *nothing more than* a thief and a conman. Aladdin is a noble, kind, generous, and honest young man, but feels that he has no choice but to use his intelligence and cleverness – his "street smarts" – to steal. He tries to justify this, mostly to himself, when he says in the song "One Jump Ahead" that "I steal only what I can't afford – and that's everything!" He leads the guards on a merry chase through the marketplace and surrounding houses, at one point singing to them, "Gotta eat to live/Gotta steal to eat/Otherwise we'd get along!" The line could be said to be an acknowledgement that his thievery is the one wrong he is committing, and it is an arguable wrong, given that he steals only what he needs to be able to survive, not to profit. This point is further emphasised later, when Aladdin gives the loaf to the pair of orphan children, then defends them further when a prince on his way to the palace to woo Jasmine nearly whips them for being in his path. Aladdin jumps in front of the whip, letting it curl around his arm and yanking it out of the prince's hand, lambasting him that "If I were as rich as you, I could afford some manners!" before throwing the whip back at him. The prince pushes Aladdin into the mud and Aladdin jeers him, saying, "Look at that, Abu – it's not every day you see a horse with *two* rear ends!" The prince turns on him angrily: "*You* are a worthless street rat. You were born a street rat, you'll die a street rat, and only your fleas will mourn you." He rides through the gates, which slam shut in Aladdin's face. *This* wounds Aladdin, and he sings the song "Street Urchins":

> Riff raff – street rat –
> I don't buy that.
> If only they'd look closer.
> Would they see a poor boy?
> No, siree –
> They'd find out there's so much more to me!

It indicates that Aladdin is deceiving everyone around him by being a thief, and in many ways he is deceiving himself, too. He is better than the life he leads, but he tells himself that he has no alternative, just as later he tells himself that there is no other way to be with Jasmine than to pretend to be a prince and ask Genie to transform him into one. Aladdin achieves success only when he uses the clever intelligence he has gained from his life on the streets and combines it with the noble part of his character that only drew notice when he pretended to be Prince Ali. It is similar to the scenario in *Mulan*, which I discussed at length in *Good Girls & Wicked Witches*, in which Mulan achieves the final victory over the Hun not in her disguise as Ping, but rather as the Mulan who has revealed that she is also Ping, the "boy" who thwarted the Hun and defeated them in battle by causing them to be buried under an avalanche.[114] Whereas Mulan cross-dresses in her film because she finds herself in a desperate situation and must disguise herself in order to save her father's life, Aladdin, by dressing as a prince, cross dresses not across gender, but across class, and does so because he, too, is in a desperate situation: he is an orphan, stealing to live, being pursued by the palace guards, and unable to be with his true love because she significantly outranks him and is forbidden by the laws of the kingdom from being with a man who is not a prince. Yes, there is a strong element of social climbing in his cross-class dressing, but his situation makes it more than something he does simply to make his life better materially. It is also about him achieving the opportunity to be the man he truly is. When he is Aladdin the street rat, then Prince Ali, he is still a diamond in the rough. Once he proves that he is willing to sacrifice all that is most precious to him so that he can remain true to himself and keep his promises, it is then that his best self can be revealed. This is shown, symbolically, by the final costume we see him wear in the film. His rags as an urchin included a fez-type hat and a vest with no shirt, and were ragged and patched. His Prince Ali costume was exaggeratedly blousy and full, and he was covered almost completely, so that even his turban had a long piece of fabric that concealed his neck. He struggled constantly to keep his turban from flying off, demonstrating that it was not his natural costume. But when he is Aladdin, the consort of Jasmine, he wears a nicer version of his street urchin rags, though with touches of the embellishments of his Prince Ali costume: long sleeves and large gold-coloured, exaggerated shoulder pieces (a cross between wings and epaulettes) but an open jacket with no shirt and a larger, nicer fez-type hat. It is like the finery of a nobleman, but understated, and worn as if it is as comfortable as the rags he wore at the film's

114 Davis, *Good Girls & Wicked Witches*, pp. 197-200.

beginning. It is emblematic of the true Aladdin, and it is in this that he can fly away with Jasmine into the whole new world of their life together.

Flynn Rider, our other thief who reforms himself when inspired by his love for a good woman, likewise must learn to be his true self – his best self – in order to live happily ever after with the film's heroine, Rapunzel. Flynn and Rapunzel balance one another well. They could be described accurately as the co-stars of *Tangled* (2010). Rapunzel, who has spent her life in a tall tower hidden away in the woods, has grown up knowing only her "mother" (really her kidnapper), Mother Gothel, and Pascal, her pet chameleon. She has no idea of her true identity, knows nothing of the world outside, and dreams of someday journeying to see the mysterious lights that float up into the sky every year on her birthday. Flynn, on the other hand, grew up in an orphanage and is now a thief who roams the kingdom, conceals his true identity behind the name and persona of a character called Flynn Rider (about whom he used to tell stories to the other children in the orphanage), and dreams only of being very rich. In this version of the tale, Rapunzel has magical hair. When her mother was pregnant, she became very ill and nearly died, but was saved by drinking a brew made from a magical flower which had grown from a drop of sunlight. For many centuries, this flower had been guarded jealously by Mother Gothel, who would perform a spell with it in which she would sing to the flower and it would restore her youth. The queen is healed by the flower, and soon gives birth to Rapunzel. Mother Gothel sneaks into the royal family's bedroom not long after Rapunzel is born, intending to steal a lock of the child's golden hair, knowing that it contains the flower's magic properties. But when she cuts the lock of hair, it turns brown and loses its magic. Mother Gothel kidnaps Rapunzel so that she may continue to restore her own youth, and raises Rapunzel as her daughter. Though she expresses love to Rapunzel through a charming back-and-forth ("I love you. I love you more. I love you most."), she constantly belittles the girl, too, weakening her self-confidence so that she will be too fearful ever to leave the tower.

Interestingly, all of this is told to us at the start of the film, mostly in voice-over narration, by Flynn Rider himself. It is an unusual touch that a character would narrate his own film. Up until *Tangled*, the closest any other films come to this is the "Legend of Sleepy Hollow" segment of *The Adventures of Ichabod and Mr. Toad* (1949), and even here it is only that all of the voices and narration are done by Bing Crosby.[115] Having Flynn to begin the

115 In 2012, however, Wreck-It Ralph would, like Flynn, narrate his film's opening and conclusion.

telling of the story – and especially to have him tell Rapunzel's story – is a particularly interesting touch. Though we see his version of her life confirmed by the animation (rather than contradicted, as in the disparity between what "Don Lockwood", played by Gene Kelly, tells us about his life, which is false, and the images we see, which are true, in the opening scene of *Singin' in the Rain*, 1952), it still privileges Flynn's position in the narration. His framing of the story further privileges him since, rather than begin by telling us about the little girl we are watching grow up, then introducing himself, his opening line for the film, as the camera moves forward and comes to focus on a wanted poster of Flynn hanging on a tree, is, "This is the story of how I died". It certainly grabs the audience's attention. Of course, he quickly follows this line, in a much lighter tone, by saying, "But don't worry, this is a fun story, and the truth is, it isn't even mine. This is the story of a girl named Rapunzel." Nonetheless, Flynn's claim that it is his story, yet not his story, is distracting. Of course, as it turns out, both his statements are true: Rapunzel's story *is* also the story of how he dies, not least because he dies to free her from Mother Gothal's clutches. As was said above, they are equally the narrative's focus, and have roughly equal screen time, most of it spent in each other's presence. Each learns from the other and grows to be a stronger, better person with greater self-knowledge and strength, and it is thanks to each other that they both find their roles in the world as well as their love for each other.

We get to meet Rapunzel first, visually: we see her childhood as part of the film's prologue, and then meet her properly a few days before her eighteenth birthday in a scene in which she sings about how she fills her days with a million activities, trying to stave off boredom as she asks, "When will my life begin?" We also learn of her fascination with the lights she sees every year on her birthday, and how she longs to go and see them up close someday. As the scene ends, we then move to much more dynamic action as we see three men scuttling about on the roof of a castle. We quickly learn that one of them is Flynn, a handsome, rather rakish young man with a sense of humour and a cocky but charming demeanour. It turns out that the three are there to steal something from the castle's throne room, which they do. The film then cuts back to Rapunzel as she plans to ask Mother Gothel to let her go and see the floating lights for her eighteenth birthday. In a song befitting a Broadway diva in which she recounts the terrible things out in the world, Mother Gothel sings "Mother Knows Best", then warns menacingly that Rapunzel must never again ask to leave the tower. Mother Gothel then departs, and Rapunzel is left on her own. This sets us up for Flynn's attempt (along with the Stabbington brothers) to escape the pursuing palace guards. He tricks the brothers and gets away from them with the loot, but the guards catch up to him. He manages to knock one of the guards off his horse and jump on its back, but the horse, Maximus, screeches to a halt: an unusually intelligent horse with a strong sense of justice, the horse continues the attempt to capture Flynn, knocking the bag with the loot out onto a tree limb. Both Flynn and Maximus climb out onto the limb after it, but the branch breaks and they fall deep into a canyon. Miraculously, neither is hurt, but they are separated. Maximus, sniffing the ground like a dog, continues to pursue Flynn, who has managed to hide behind some vines. It is then that he stumbles into the valley and spots Rapunzel's tower. He climbs up it, hops into a window, closes the shutters, and gazes into the bag, saying, "Alone at last!" He is then knocked out by Rapunzel, who hits him in the head with a cast iron frying pan. She has never seen a man before, and he is not nearly as horrific as she had been led to believe men are, but she is still frightened of him, so as he comes to, she knocks him out again and bundles him into her closet. It is then that she comes across his loot, a bejewelled crown which, it turns out suits her perfectly. Mother Gothel returns, and Rapunzel is about to tell her about this strange man in her closet, when Mother Gothel flies into a rage. Realising that her only hope of seeing the outside world is to keep secret what she has found, she sends Mother Gothel to bring her some special white paint for her birthday – paint that it will take Mother Gothel three days' journey to get. She then ties up Flynn and waits for him to regain consciousness. Flynn tries to charm her: it is clear that this technique has worked on other women he has met, and he assumes that Rapunzel will be no different. But just because she has never seen a man before does not mean that she is overwhelmed by him. Whereas the male characters who had been raised in isolation from other humans (which we discussed in the previous chapter) – Pecos Bill, Mowgli, and Tarzan – are overcome the first time they encounter a human female, Rapunzel's first encounter with a human male is very different. She finds him strange, and it takes some convincing before she believes that he has not come to steal her hair. When he tries to "smoulder" at her, she is unmoved and unimpressed. For her, meeting Flynn is not the cause of her first stirrings of desire or the awakening of passion: he is an unknown quantity, and she decides to trust him only up to a point, and only because she needs someone to guide her in the strange world outside her tower. She makes a deal with him: he will take her to see the lanterns and bring her back home safely, and she will return his satchel. Eventually, he agrees.

Instead, what overwhelms her is her first experience of the world outside her tower: the first time her bare foot touches the grass, the first time she experiences freedom. It sets her on an emotional rollercoaster where she goes between exhilaration and guilt, Flynn waiting patiently for her to settle down. Initially, he tries to manipulate her into returning early, but it backfires. He then tries taking her to a tavern which is the hangout of murderers and thieves (with the incongruous and comic name of "The Snuggly Duckling"), but though frightened initially by the men she meets, she soon has them all charmed, as they sing together about each of their life-long dreams (in the song "I've Got a Dream"). The ruffians then help Rapunzel and Flynn escape when the palace guard shows up. It is in this scene, as they escape the guard, and in particular when they become trapped in a cave that is filling up with water, that they begin to share with each other – and with us – what has led them to this point. It is in this scene that we learn that Flynn's real name is Eugene Fitzherbert, and it is at this point that Rapunzel reveals to Flynn that her hair is magical and glows when she sings. She uses it soon after they escape to heal his injured hand. She begs him, "Don't freak out", but of course he does, comically trying to act nonchalant as he asks her questions about it, his tense body language and his voice (which sounds like it is on the edge of a scream) betraying just how thrown off he is by this revelation about Rapunzel. His shock changes quickly to sympathy, though, when he realises that, because of her hair and Mother Gothel's "protection", she has never before left her tower. It is the first open, honest conversation the two have, and their relationship – as well as Flynn's motivations and intentions – change as a result. He admits that he took his name from a book, *The Tales of Flynnagan Rider*, and talks about how Flynnagan had enough money to do whatever he wanted to do, saying that, "For a kid with nothing, I don't know, I ... Just seemed like the better option". For Flynn, his dream of enormous wealth is not a selfish or stupid dream, as it turns out; it is a dream which equates wealth with freedom, something he has never really had. It is this lack of freedom – this being trapped in a life from which they can see no means of permanent escape (after all, Rapunzel feels as though she will have to return to her tower once she has seen up close the mysterious lights) – that unites them and helps them realise that they are the same, even if the forms their entrapments have taken have been very different. They have come to care for one another, however, and it is within their growing feelings for one another that the two are able to find freedom, symbolised by the song that we hear sung by Rapunzel and Flynn in duet, first as voice-over narration/internal monolog, then out loud to each other, "I See the Light". Initially, Rapunzel is mesmerized by the lights; she then turns to Flynn, and he gives her a lantern, too, so that each has one, and they release them. They then begin singing to one another as they fall in love. In terms of its narrative importance, and in touches of its mise-en-scène, it is reminiscent of Aladdin's and Jasmine's duet, "A Whole New World". As in that film, the realisation of their love leads to a moment of crisis: in this case, Rapunzel is tricked into believing that Flynn has abandoned her (really, he has been knocked unconscious and tied to the wheel of a ship so that it looks as though he is sailing away intentionally), and so she returns to the waiting arms of Mother Gothel, who has used the Stabbington brothers to get Rapunzel back. Flynn crashes into the side of the castle, where he is captured and, guilty of stealing the crown, he is about to be executed. Back home, it is then that Rapunzel realises that she is the lost princess (since she finally is able to put together various clues that have presented themselves to her during her day in the kingdom). Likewise, as he is being led to his execution, Flynn realises that Rapunzel, back with Mother Gothel, is in danger. Flynn is rescued by the ruffians from the Snuggly Duckling; they reunite him with Maximus (who has helped him help Rapunzel get to the kingdom to see the lanterns), who gets him safely from the castle and to Rapunzel's tower. He goes to rescuer her, and is tricked into the tower by Mother Gothel; having bound and gagged Rapunzel, she mortally stabs Flynn as soon as he enters the tower. Mother Gothel then prepares to take Rapunzel away, vowing that they will go somewhere that they can never be found. Rapunzel makes a deal with her, however, to save Flynn's life:

> Mother Gothel: Rapunzel, really – enough already! Stop fighting me!
>
> Rapunzel: No! I won't stop! For every minute of the rest of my life, I will fight! I will never stop trying to get away from you! But if you let me save him, I will go with you.
>
> Flynn: (Weakly) No! No, Rapunzel.
>
> Rapunzel: I'll never run. I'll never try to escape. Just let me heal him, and you and I will be together – forever, just like you want. Everything will be the way it was. I promise. Just like you want. Just let me heal him.

Mother Gothel relents, and Rapunzel goes to him to heal his wound. He begs her not to, saying that healing him would mean her (metaphorical) death. He leans in as if he is about to kiss her, but gathers up her hair in his hand and uses a shard from a broken mirror to cut it off. It turns dark brown and loses its magic. Mother Gothel instantly begins to age rapidly; she falls backward out of the tower window, but is dust before she hits the ground. Rapunzel tries desperately to heal him, but he stops her, telling her that she was his new dream. She replies that he was hers. He smiles weakly, then dies. She sings faintly the old song that made her hair's magical powers activate, and a tear drops from her eye onto his cheek. It sends a light through him which fills him and the room with golden threads, healing his wound and restoring him to life. They embrace and kiss. Shortly afterward, they journey back to the castle, and Rapunzel is reunited with her parents, the king and queen. They embrace, and pull Flynn into their family hug. The lost Princess Rapunzel is home, and the orphan Eugene has a family who loves him.

The film closes with voice-over from Flynn/Eugene again, describing the kingdom's celebration of Rapunzel's return. We learn what came next for various characters, to include Flynn, who says of himself, "I started going by Eugene again, stopped thieving and, basically, turned it all around. But I know what the big question is: did Rapunzel and I ever get married? Well I'm pleased to tell you that, after years and years of asking and asking and asking ... I finally said yes." We hear Rapunzel chastise him indulgently, and he admits that he asked her. The two agree that they are living happily ever after. Flynn still gets the last word, but we do hear briefly from Rapunzel in the final narration, presumably implying that they are equals within their relationship. We are informed, however, that it is Rapunzel who would rule the kingdom after her parents: no mention is made of Eugene ruling, even alongside her. This is not commented on in any way by the narrative, however: they are simply shown to be in love, happy, teasing one another and enjoying each other's company as friends, as well as being deeply in love with one another and passionate about each other. In this respect, they differ greatly from Aladdin and Jasmine: like Jasmine, Rapunzel is the daughter of the ruler of the kingdom. Unlike Jasmine, no law requires her to marry (she marries solely because she has fallen in love), and Rapunzel can rule her kingdom in her own right; Aladdin may become Sultan because he marries Jasmine, but Flynn/Eugene does not become King because he marries Rapunzel. Though the eighteen years that separate these two films may, in many respects, have seen feminism lose ground in the real world for real women, things have become better for Disney's heroines ... or at least for the princesses who marry thieves.

Action Men

John Smith, the hero of *Pocahontas* (1995) is introduced early on in the film as a dynamic action man. When he arrives at the dock to board the ship bound for Virginia, Smith strides confidently forward, his back to the camera. We see a long rifle slung across his back, and a small amount of gear, but very little else: Smith travels light, and he travels fast. When he arrives, the sailors all know him by reputation if not personally, and they are impressed and pleased that he is joining them. One says proudly, "You can't fight Indians without John Smith!" and Smith replies, "That's right! I'm not about to let you boys have all the fun!" It is easy, light-hearted banter, and shows Smith to be at ease with the sailors under his command (he is *Captain* Smith, after all, and so is in charge of the ship). Rather than walk up the gangplank, Smith stands on one of the cannons being hoisted onto the deck: he looks comfortable in that position, as if this is neither showing off nor playing around, but simply an expression of his athletic and adventuresome nature. This immediately contrasts him with Governor Ratcliffe, who arrives just after we see Smith board the ship. He is brought to the ship in a stately carriage with plumes adorning the roof, and walks along a carpet with an honour guard saluting him on either side. Whereas Ratcliffe is pampered, pompous, and aloof, Smith mixes well with the men on the ship, working alongside them and leading them in particular during a terrible storm, when a young crewman, Thomas, is washed overboard but saved by Smith, who ties a lifeline around his waist and dives in after the boy. It is a heroic rescue that only a true action man could have achieved, and ties in with the persona at that time of Mel Gibson, who provided the voice for Smith, and with the various action heroes he had played up to that time, including Max in the *Mad Max* trilogy (1979, 1981, 1985), Martin Riggs in the *Lethal Weapon* films (1987, 1989, 1992), and, a little less than a month before *Pocahontas'* debut, as William Wallace in *Braveheart* (1995). Though he played other sorts of characters, too, these were amongst the roles with which he was most associated in the mid-1990s, and he was a popular, respected Hollywood actor, an earthy, heroic type more than willing to roll up his sleeves and get to work.

Yet even with his hands-on approach and adventurous spirit, Smith is shown to be unprepared for what awaits him in Virginia, especially his meeting with Pocahontas. She and her tribe, the Powhatan, are shown to live in complete harmony with nature, tending their crops, hunting and fishing, the men and women working together happily and living a good life. Of course, we learn that they do not live in paradise: our introduction to the Powhatan tribe and its chief (who is called Powhatan because he is the leader of the people) includes the community and its leaders celebrating their victory over the Masawomecs, another tribe, who has threatened the Powhatan villages. In particular, the warrior Kocoum is singled out for praise of his role in the day-long battle. Kocoum is an important contrast to Smith, at least for Pocahontas. Her father wants her to marry Kocoum, but Pocahontas is reluctant: she finds him too serious, commenting sarcastically about the intense, stern young man, "I especially like his smile". She is drawn to Smith, however, because, while he can be serious, he also has a ready smile and enjoys laughter. He is a contrast to Kocoum, but very similar to Pocahontas: they make a loving, very compatible couple. While Smith's role within the Jamestown colony may well position him in a similar role as Kocoum – an accomplished fighter who can lead his people in battle if necessary – Smith would rather maintain peace and friendly relations, while Kocoum's first instinct is to fight. It is this instinct which will get him killed: seeing Pocahontas and Smith kissing passionately, his jealousy of Smith overpowers him and he attacks Smith, since he regards Pocahontas as his intended. Thomas, the young sailor Smith saved during the storm at sea, sees the attack and shoots Kocoum in order to defend Smith. This event – and Smith's assuming responsibility for it – will set in motion an important chain of events which will lead, ultimately, to Pocahontas saving Smith and bringing peace to the Powhatan and the British. It will allow the lessons Smith has learned from her to be shared with the British as a whole.

Of course, very little about this event changes John Smith: it is Smith's initial meeting with Pocahontas that changes his life irrevocably. When he first arrives in Virginia, he sees the "New World" as an adventure and a challenge, someplace he can explore and map. When he first begins to talk with Pocahontas, he tells her patronisingly that he and the English can instruct her people to "use this land properly – how to make the most of it", adding that the British will "build roads and decent houses". Pocahontas, however, is unimpressed with his attitude, and in the song "Colors of the Wind" she educates Smith, teaching him to empathise with and respect other groups and cultures, and to recognise that his way is not necessarily the better way, not least because he thinks of the land and animals as things that can be used and claimed and possessed, whereas she is aware of them as living things, asking in the song's prelude, "How can there be so much that you don't know you don't know?" To his credit, inspired by his growing feelings for Pocahontas and by his generally open-minded approach to life, he listens to what she has to say and begins to recognise the environment as an organism that is in balance and needs to be respected and protected. He also realises that the British have much to learn from the Powhatan. These themes of environmentalism and ecology, which are core parts of the narrative, are the most obviously didactic aspects of *Pocahontas*, and it is in the song "Colors of the Wind" that they are most apparent. But these messages are found elsewhere in the film, such as in the negative way that the narrative treats Ratcliffe's efforts to dig until gold is found, and to fell as many trees as possible, robbing the landscape of its real treasures.

Smith falls in love with Pocahontas – and she with him – fairly quickly, and it is their love which inspires them, at least in part, to try and find a way for their two peoples to get along. Eventually, each will perform a heroic act which will inspire others to do what is right: Pocahontas will throw herself over Smith to stop her father from executing him, and a few moments later Smith will throw himself in front of Chief Powhatan, taking the bullet (fired by Ratcliffe) that was meant to kill the chief. Pocahontas' bravery will stop a war from breaking out, and Smith's self-sacrifice (in which he is badly wounded but does not die) will lead to the British men's overthrow of the corrupt Governor Ratcliffe. It is by following Smith's journey – both his physical journey to and around Virginia, and his spiritual journey toward becoming in touch with the environment and learning to respect other cultures and ways of life – that the film is able to convey its messages championing environmentalism as part of a larger drive in some of its films in the 1990s.[116] From the perspective of a gender study focusing on masculinity, Smith functions as an example of the action man with an intelligent and open mind. He is strong and athletic, but Smith is not an example of the exaggerated hyper-masculinity of 1980s action films. He is Man as active and adventurous. Initially, he seems to be fulfilling the role of man as invader: after all, he is a leader amongst a group of men who intend to colonize and claim Virginia for their own. Naturally, the end of the film implies the historically-accurate fact, known to all watching the film, that of course the Jamestown settlement was an important step in the British gaining a foothold on North America, eventually conquering, renaming and claiming thousands of square miles of it along the eastern seaboard in what became known as the thirteen colonies, leading eventually to the founding states of the United States of America by the time of the American Revolution (1775-1783). But by following Smith's example, these first colonists learn to get along with the Powhatan (who consider the land to be theirs and initially see the

116 A more in-depth discussion of this trend in Disney's animated films during the 1990s may be found in chapter four of this book in the section entitled "Enemies of the Earth".

British as a dangerous invasion ... again, not a wholly inaccurate interpretation, given the consequences of European settlement for the Native American peoples), allowing the film, at least, to end on a hopeful note.

But the film cannot end on a romantic note. There are no known versions of the myth of Pocahontas and John Smith in which the two marry (in only some of the versions do they have any kind of romantic interaction), and many, at least amongst the American target audience for the film, would have been aware both of that fact and of the historical fact that Pocahontas would marry a different Englishman, John Rolfe. Therefore, narratively, there needed to be a reason to keep this couple apart, despite the fact that much of the film is spent showing how perfect they are for each other and how much they love one another. Though the idea of sending Smith back to England to receive treatment for a gunshot wound is preposterous in the extreme for many reasons (the nature of sea voyages in the early seventeenth century, the idea that the Virginia Company would have sent a group of people to found a settlement in Virginia and *not* have sent a doctor of some sort with them ... the list goes on), it is an effective way of separating the pair. She cannot leave her people because of her leadership responsibilities, but he does not lose face as a man who cannot form a solid, loving adult relationship. Their separation comes about in the story as a result of his great heroism when he saves her father's life, as well as her sacrificing her own longing and wishes out of her duty to the Powhatan and her new role with the British settlers, who respect her as a figure of wisdom and authority. Smith and Pocahontas are an example of an idealised, egalitarian, heterosexual couple. Given the erosion of feminism that was taking place in the 1990s, perhaps the separation of the couple – narratively crucial to comply with the traditional story – also served to preserve the illusion that, had they married, they would have continued to maintain their perfectly balanced, equal relationship. It is a way to highlight the possibility of a truly equitable marriage which avoids exploring the implications this would have for gender roles within the story. Ultimately, given the romantic constraints built into the myth, the most important message for this film was not about gender roles, but instead about environmentalism.

A more obvious choice of narratives in which to discuss gender roles and the representation of masculinity is *Mulan* (1998). What it means to be male and what it means to be female are vital themes, as Mulan herself spends a large section of the film trying to pass as a young man. She disguises herself as a soldier in order to protect her elderly, crippled father so that he will not have to re-join the army when the Huns invade China. It is a fascinating film and very enjoyable to watch, though – in reality – the same issues about how gender restricts our roles in life (and how others react to us) could have been discussed in a setting rather closer to home than medieval China. Many of the issues the film examines – what behaviours are appropriate for each gender, whether one particular gender is more suited for certain activities than the other gender, how much of gender is natural and how much is performative – continue to be discussed and debated, belying the notion, inherent to the misleading concept of Post-Feminism, namely that Feminism has succeeded, creating a society in which men and women are respected as equals in all things. This, of course, is patently (albeit sadly) not true, and does not require a story set in medieval China to illustrate it. Yet for those who cannot recognise that sexism is alive and well, perhaps seeing it depicted in an extreme form, as in *Mulan*, can help them to think about where the modern west still needs to improve.

The story of *Mulan*, essentially, is that a young woman – one who is intelligent, lively, resourceful, loving and brave – who disguises herself as a young man in order to take her elderly father's place in the army when China is under threat from the Hun. She struggles, initially, in her attempts to pass as a man, and is nearly thrown out of the army, but her determination (and desperation) both are such that she passes her army training. In battle, she proves herself again when she uses her brains to thwart the Hun and (initially) stop them. She is injured, however, and found to be a woman. The penalty for pretending to be a man is death, but her (rather dishy – yes, Mulan has noticed) commanding officer, Li Shang, spares her life because of her bravery and because she saved his life during the battle. After the rest of the company has moved on, she realises that the Hun were not killed, and that they are now advancing on the capital. She manages to beat them to the Imperial City and tries to tell her former comrades, but because she deceived them once, they do not believe her, initially. A few finally decide to trust her, however, including Li Shang, and together, under Mulan's leadership, they are able to kill Shan-Yu, the leader of the Hun army, and save China. Mulan returns home, having brought honour to her family. Soon after, Li Shang arrives at Mulan's house; it is obvious that he has fallen for Mulan, and that he respects her as an equal. Though nothing is stated, it is strongly implied that Mulan and Li Shang will be married, and that they will enjoy a marriage of true equals.

Having discussed the symbolic, historical, and cultural implications of Mulan's cross-dressing in *Good Girls & Wicked Witches*, I will only reiterate here that, ultimately, Mulan achieves her greatest triumph when she allows herself to be her *whole* self, utilising equally both her animus (the male side which went by the name Ping when she was in the army) and her anima (the beloved daughter and tomboy we met at the start of the film).[117]

So what of Li Shang, the young captain of the troops who trains and leads Mulan and her fellow soldiers? We meet him when he is made captain and begins leading a unit for the first time. His excitement and eagerness at this surprise promotion come out briefly, but he quickly regains control of himself. For Shang, control and strength are enormously important parts of being a man. This is shown in the first training exercise he sets the men: shooting an arrow into the top of a pole, he has them try to climb up to retrieve the arrow while carrying two weights: one represents discipline, the other strength. One by one the men and Mulan try and fail to reach it; it becomes the ultimate goal for all the men. In the training montage which follows, Shang sings the song "I'll Make a Man Out You", and both taunts the men and teaches them what it means, by his/the army's definition, to be men. The second verse and chorus of the song are particularly instructive in this respect, and echo his focus on discipline/control and strength:

> Tranquil as a forest
> But on fire within
> Once you find your centre
> You are sure to win
> You're a spineless pale, pathetic lot
> And you haven't got a clue –
> Somehow I'll make a man out of you!
>
> (Be a man –) You must be swift as a coursing river
> (Be a man –) With all the force of a great typhoon
> (Be a man –) With all the strength of a raging fire
> Mysterious as the dark side of the moon!

Mulan, of course, is the first to figure out how to use the weights to help her climb the pole (by linking them together around the pole so that they become extensions of her arms) rather than as forces which drag her down, and her success inspires the men to excel in the training programme which, before Mulan retrieved the arrow, had been rather too much for all of them. By the end of the montage, the army is well-trained, strong, and can function as a single unit. Shang has succeeded in moulding them into a strong, cohesive unit who will be able to do battle effectively.

117 See Davis, *Good Girls & Wicked Witches*, pp. 195-202.

Mulan is the main character in the film, so we see things primarily from her point of view. But we also get to know Shang in his more private moments, and are shown that he, too, must struggle with an enormous duty and responsibility while dealing with a detractor who constantly questions his ability – Chi Fu, the emperor's counsel. Shang's – and his troops' – chance to prove their worth comes when they have their first encounter with the Hun. It comes shortly after they stumble upon the burned-out ruins of a village, then a battlefield littered with dead. They discover that Shang's father was amongst the soldiers killed. Horrified by what they have found, their attitude changes from one of excitement – of seeing the war as an adventure – to one of determination to do their part to protect the emperor and save China. Very soon afterward, they are ambushed by the Hun army, who vastly outnumber them. Shang tells his men, "Prepare to fight. If we die, we die with honour". Shang intends to lead his men against the Hun in a straightforward way, but Mulan/Ping has different ideas. She fires a cannonball over the heads of the Hun, striking a snow-covered cliff which causes an avalanche and buries the Hun army deep under the snow. She is struck by Shan-Yu's sword, however, and wounded. Nonetheless, she manages to save herself, her horse, and Shang, but finally collapses from her wound. When the doctor treating her discovers that she is a woman, he informs Shang. Shang's reaction is strong. He is shocked and furious, unable to speak. We see a brief glimmer of understanding when Mulan tells him that she pretended to be a man to protect her father; having just lost his own father, this is clearly meaningful to him. He walks toward Mulan with her sword, seemingly about to execute her, but then tosses her sword on the ground in front of her, saying only, "A life for a life. My debt is repaid." He then orders the rest of his men to move out, and they leave Mulan behind without another word. Yet when all are celebrating the victory parade, Shang and the men are dejected; they have won the battle and (they think) saved China, but they have lost their friend Ping; Shang has also lost his father. When Mulan comes riding up beside him to warn him that Shan-Yu and the Hun army are on the move, he dismisses her, saying he has no reason to trust her. When Shang is presented to the emperor, he offers him Shan-Yu's sword; before the emperor can accept it, however, Shan-Yu's falcon swoops down and takes it, returning it to Shan-Yu, who is crouched nearby on the roof, hiding in the shadows. His men swarm out of nowhere and seize the emperor, dragging him into the palace, Shang and his men hot on their heels, but unable to break down the door. Mulan signals them, saying she has an idea, and her three closest comrades follow her. Shang hesitates, but soon we see him join them, though opting *not* to follow their example and dress like women so that they can sneak past the Hun.

In fact, though Shang plays an instrumental role, saving the emperor from Shan-Yu's initial onslaught, ultimately it is of course Mulan who saves the day. What shows Shang to be worthy of the status of hero is his reaction to this: he is not jealous, angered, or defensive. Very much to the contrary, he defends Mulan against Chi Fu, the emperor's counsel, who demeans Mulan by referring to her as "it" when, in replying to Shang's assertion that Mulan is a hero, replies, "'Tis a woman. She'll never be worth anything." Shang is amazed but proud when Mulan is honoured by the emperor, gracefully and willingly bowing to her, following the emperor's lead. He is proud of her, but feels awkward; we realise that it is because he has begun to feel an attraction to her (one which has grown out of his admiration and respect for her as they rescued the emperor, and combined, no doubt, with what he came to know about her when he though she was a boy). He watches her ride away from the palace when the emperor comes to stand beside him, saying "The flower that blooms in adversity is the most rare and beautiful of all". Shang expresses his confusion, and the emperor gives his advice in a more straight-forward manner: "You don't meet a girl like that every dynasty". Shang smiles to himself; we are given the impression that the emperor's words have helped him to realise that his feelings for Mulan are honourable and good. When he shows up at Mulan's family's home shortly after she has returned, he comes on the pretext that he is returning to her the helmet she left behind, but his nervousness indicates that he has come to court Mulan, and that he will be her perfect match because he accepts her and respects her for her true self.

Both John Smith and Li Shang are the perfect balance of physically strong and emotionally sensitive. Each is a warrior, highly capable and well-trained in the skills of combat, yet each seems to be aware of the fact that fighting is at its most successful when it is avoided. Of course, for Shang, whose homeland has been invaded by a savage army, avoiding a fight is not an option: he knows that, sooner or later, his troops will find themselves in a battle. Therefore, he does everything he can to ensure that they are ready; he does this not only so that they will be able to defeat their enemy, but also so that, hopefully, they will have a chance of survival. Smith, too, is seen teaching those who lack experience (such as the young sailor, Thomas) how to shoot, and making the first attempts to show the British that the Powhatan can help them to survive in their new home. Likewise, neither Shang nor Smith is interested in monetary gain: when Smith learns from Pocahontas that there is no gold in Virginia, he merely shrugs, commenting (with a degree of amusement) that many of the men will be disappointed. Likewise, Shang fights not for glory but out of his sense of honour and duty. He is a soldier, from a distinguished military family, and his country has been invaded by a hostile force. If he must die, he will do so readily. When he has the opportunity (if he wishes) to take credit for Mulan's victory in killing Shan-Yu, he insists that she is the hero and gives her full credit for what she has achieved, even defending her against the emperor's prejudiced, sexist counsel. When they realise that they have fallen in love with the strong, intelligent, capable woman who is at the heart of their narratives, each man is aware that this love – and this woman – is worth fighting for and dying for, and they become better men as a result of their relationships with these women. Shang and Mulan will be able to be together and happy in their love for one another, their film's ending implies. Pocahontas and Smith might have been, but circumstances outside their control have separated them forever. Each has a truly loathsome enemy to defeat, and each works (knowingly or otherwise) in conjunction with his love interest to stop the villains they face. These are action men as whole, balanced men, capable of using reason and intellect, as well as being in touch with his feelings.

Frienemies

Our final section will look at three pairs of heroes who find themselves thrown together, linked by a common love interest (which makes them rivals) or a common goal. At the start of their stories, they are not friends. Though each scenario plays out differently, we see that the better the two men learn to work together, the better the outcome is for all involved. In the case of the first pair, Ichabod Crane and Brom Bones, however, what begins as mild antagonism only escalates; by the end of their story, the fate of Ichabod Crane is a mystery, the possibility hanging over the narrative that he, as the final line of the film suggests, "had been spirited away by the Headless Horseman".

Ichabod Crane and Brom bones are two of the leading characters in the "Legend of Sleepy Hollow", which is the second half of the 1949 package film *The Adventures of Ichabod and Mr. Toad*. It is a much-loved Disney film, and as a segment was for many years shown on American television (independently of the "Wind in the Willows" half of the film) in the lead-up to Halloween. Though in recent years, and in particular outside of the United States and Canada, some may be more familiar with the Tim Burton film *Sleepy Hollow* (1999), in fact Burton's film bears only a marginal resemblance to Washington Irving's novella. The

Disney version, however, follows the story much more closely, with whole sections of Irving's prose (albeit somewhat condensed) comprising the narration performed (wonderfully!) by Bing Crosby. For those unfamiliar with this version, Ichabod Crane, an itinerate schoolteacher, arrives in the little town of Sleepy Hollow to run their schoolhouse. Ichabod is described as "a most unusual man. To see him striding along, one might well mistake him for some scarecrow eloped from a cornfield. ... Altogether, he was such an apparition as is seldom to be seen in broad daylight". In the first song of the segment, which describes the townsfolk's reaction to his arrival (and which is begun in recitative by Brom Bones, who declares, "Odds bodkins! Gadzooks! Look at that old spook of spooks!), Ichabod, though seen as unusual, nonetheless is welcomed into the community. Shortly after we are given Ichabod's description (and just before the song about Ichabod), we are told about Brom Bones: arriving onto the scene in very dynamic fashion, galloping into town on horseback (as contrasted with Ichabod's arrival, on foot, his large nose buried in a book), we are told that Brom, "was a burly, roistering blade, always ready for a fight or a frolic". Both are shown to be popular with the residents of Sleepy Hollow: Brom is introduced to us as he joins a group of friends outside the local tavern, where they meet simply to have a drink and enjoy each other's company (and Brom's generosity is demonstrated when he makes sure that everyone present – even the dogs and his horse – are able to enjoy a beer). Ichabod is described as "the town's ladies' man, [who] gets around like nobody can". So neither is a threat to their community, and both contribute actively to its happiness and well-being. Even before they become rivals for Katrina's heart, we learn that Brom enjoys teasing Ichabod, but not in a harmful way; the narration says that, "To Ichabod, these were trifling matters, for the schoolmaster possessed a most remarkable equanimity that remained quite undisturbed".

Right from the beginning, the two men are contrasted against one another, and a dichotomy is established which, in more modern language and types, can be characterised as "nerd" (Ichabod) versus "jock" (Brom). This notion is supported by the narration and by their visual depictions. The narrator (Bing Crosby) says that "It was inevitable that such a figure as Ichabod should become an object of ridicule to Brom Bones and his gang". Ichabod nonetheless finds a place for himself within the community. In addition to teaching Sleepy Hollow's children at the local schoolhouse, he is also shown teaching singing to a group of young ladies. A glimpse we get of his social calendar reveals that he also attends such gatherings as the Young Ladies Sewing

Circle, the Women's Tatting and Chatting Club, the Ladies Auxiliary, a box social, dinner at the homes of his pupils, and the Ladies of Sleepy Hollow Choral Society. This last is actually shown, and played for laughs, as Bing Crosby's "crooner" style of singing becomes Ichabod's own, much to the delight of the three young ladies who swoon, bobby-soxer style, at his melodic scatting. These associations, however, serve in some ways to feminise Ichabod, and contrast him with the more hyper-masculine Brom. We see Brom often in the company of other men, but typically Ichabod is seen with women. Yet, the narration implies, this is to do with Ichabod being something of a ladies' man: they like him and flatter him and fawn over him, and so he prefers their company. The boisterous Brom, however, prefers the outdoors and is more rough-and-tumble; his friends, therefore, are mostly men. Visually, we see an extremely thin Ichabod: he is tall and long-limbed, but narrow, and has a small, round head. The only things large about Ichabod are his nose (which is exaggeratedly large and beaky) and his appetite. He walks at a leisurely pace, and his worldly goods seem to fit in a handkerchief tied to the end of a stick. The song about him says that he is "Lean and lanky, skin and bones/With clothes a scarecrow would hate to own". However, and in contrast to this, the song goes on to say of Ichabod, "Yet he has a certain air/Debonair and Devil-May-Care". Ichabod is not at all handsome: not to us as the audience, not to those around him. Rather, Ichabod's appeal is his calm, confident sophistication and intelligence. In contrast, Brom is shown to be a man's man, an action man, but rustic. His muscles come, we can assume, from years of farming work; the years of good eating and physical activity have built Brom into a strong, more attractive man, but they have come at the neglect of his developing his manners and his education. It is never implied that Brom is stupid, just that he has never had any need to develop his mind when his strength and sense of humour were enough to gain him friends and admirers throughout his community.

What ties them to one another is their shared attraction for Katrina Van Tassel; she is not the *cause* of their competition with one another – that competition is well established by the narrative before she is introduced to the story – but she is the catalyst which takes it to a whole new level. Before Katrina, they were just two opposites who clashed in a friendly, sparring kind of way. Once she shows up, the gloves are off as they become genuine rivals. Because they are involved in a love triangle, both contenders for the heart of wealthy beauty Katrina, and because Katrina enjoys playing them off against each other, they never have any real incentive to become better people. Unlike the other two pairs of frienemies being examined in this section, Ichabod and Brom have no common enemy, and therefore lack any reason to work together. Neither is a villain, however: Ichabod, for all his faults, never does anything harmful or hateful, nor is he ever really vicious or cruel, even when he takes the opportunity to put Brom in his place (remembering, of course, that Ichabod had taken Brom's teasing good-naturedly for some time); the narration tells us that even Brom was forced to admit (albeit grudgingly) that Ichabod presented "a flawless picture of ease and grace". Ichabod is shown as more cultured and sophisticated than the rustic Brom, and therefore is better at courting and romancing Katrina. Equally, the narration makes a point of saying that, "though Brom was much given to madcap pranks and practical jokes, still there was no malice in his mischief. Indeed, with his waggish humour and prodigious strength, Brom Bones was quite the hero of all the country 'round". We are given to understand that Brom was one of Katrina's many suitors prior to Ichabod's arrival, and that he used his intimidating physical presence to rise to the top. But this irritates Katrina, we are told: "Now the ease with which Brom cleared the field of rivals both piqued and provoked the fair Katrina, and she often wished some champion would appear and for once take the field openly against the boisterous Brom". She welcomes Ichabod's attentions; whether she is genuinely interested in Ichabod is debatable, however, as she makes a bit of a fuss about demonstrating her affection for Ichabod in front of Brom in a way that is designed to make Brom jealous. It is clear, though, that she enjoys Ichabod's more cultivated manners and social skills: we are shown that Ichabod is better read, more of a gentleman, and a much better dancer than Brom. Likewise, Ichabod is seen to be better at flattering Katrina (and her father). It is clear that Brom had assumed that he would win Katrina's hand eventually; Ichabod, unexpectedly, is his first real competition.

Though both are shown to have good qualities, each is shown to have equally despicable traits: Ichabod maybe a good and conscientious school teacher, but he is also shown to be a social-climbing gold-digger. Brom is generous, good-hearted and has a lively sense of humour, but he is rough, rude, cocky, and tends to be a bully. Indeed, as enjoyable as the film and the characters are, it is increasingly hard to like any of them, not least because it is impossible to tell whether any of them actually have feelings for each other. Ichabod finds Katrina attractive, but he seems to find her father's wealth and farm – and the fact that Katrina will inherit the whole of her father's estate – at least as attractive as he does Katrina herself. We are never given the sense that Brom is interested in Katrina's position as an heiress; however, she is shown to be *the* leading beauty of the town, in whom all of the young men are interested. In a way that would be echoed forty-two years later with Gaston in *Beauty and the Beast*, Brom seems interested in Katrina because she is the most beautiful young woman in the town, and that makes her the best. Therefore, he pursues her because capturing the best young woman in town will show that he is the best young man in the town. As for Katrina herself, she is shown to be more interested in Brom's and Ichabod's competition over her than she is in either of them individually, and repeatedly stirs up their rivalry for her own amusement. She does, in the end, marry Brom; after Ichabod's disappearance, we see Katrina kiss Brom enthusiastically at their wedding. Her allowing herself to be courted by Ichabod may have been her way of making sure that Brom "appreciated" her, rather than taking her for granted. Whatever the reasons, the rivalry between the two men only gets more heated as the story goes along.

The climax of the story – and of Brom's and Ichabod's competition – is when Ichabod, riding home from Baltus Van Tassel's Halloween party, is terrorised by the Headless Horseman. We are told the story of the Headless Horseman by Brom Bones at the Van Tassels' Halloween party. Brom knows that Ichabod is very superstitious and a "firm, potent believer in spooks and goblins", and decides to use this to his advantage, telling the story knowing that it will frighten Ichabod, and also knowing that Ichabod will have to ride through the Horseman's territory later that night to get home. Ichabod's fears begin to play upon him during his ride, and he becomes more and more frightened until he realises he has been imagining things. He begins to laugh, nervously but with relief, when he and his horse hear an angry, booming laugh and turn to see the Headless Horseman himself. The Horseman gives chase, Ichabod and his panicked horse trying to flee. The scene is both comic and frightening (in perfect balance), utilizing the multiplane camera in some shots in order to heighten the reality and therefore make the mise-en-scène menacing. The scene culminates with Ichabod crossing the bridge over the brook (according to Brom's story, the boundary past which the ghost cannot go) and the horseman throwing a flaming jack-o-lantern across the bridge at him. The scene fades to black. The story resumes in the light of early morning, on the road just past the bridge. We are told that, "The next morning, Ichabod's hat was found, and close beside it, a shattered pumpkin. But there was no trace of the schoolmaster". What we are *not* told, however, is who the Headless Horseman was. There is a moment during the chase scene when we see Ichabod gaze into the open neck hole of the Horseman's jacket and, to his terror, see no sign of a head. The Horseman is shown to be a very skilled and lively rider, like Brom, and to have a very well-developed physique, also like Brom. But we never know for sure that this was Brom trying to trick Ichabod and drive him away. There is a bit more evidence in Irving's novella which implicates Brom: "Brom Bones, too, who shortly after his rival's disappearance conducted the blooming Katrina in triumph to the altar, was observed to look exceedingly knowing whenever the story of Ichabod was related, and always burst into a hearty laugh at the mention of the pumpkin; which led some to suspect that he knew more about the matter than he chose to tell".[118] But as closely as the Disney adaptation follows Irving's novella, this detail is omitted. We are, however, given evidence that Ichabod did not die: that he in fact (and in a detail which differs from the novella) "was still alive, married to a wealthy widow in a distant county". We are shown Ichabod presiding over a dinner table, surrounded by a woman and seven children (who all have his same large nose and ears and so are undoubtedly his offspring), as he lifts the lid off of a sumptuous roasted turkey as the family prepares to eat dinner. This is described as a rumour, and we are told that the "Good Dutch settlers refused to believe such nonsense, for they knew the schoolmaster had been spirited away by the Headless Horseman".

In other words, the individuals whose story this is – Ichabod Crane and Brom Bones – never have the chance to redeem themselves in the narrative. They start out reasonably likeable, grow increasingly contemptuous of one another, and their competition ends only when one of them, Ichabod, is driven completely from the community. Brom is kept from being the villain of the piece, however, because he is never implicated directly; the Disney adaptation in particular makes no suggestion that Brom went to such lengths to terrify and drive out Ichabod; all he does is tell the story (in a context in which the Van Tassels' guests are invited to tell ghost stories for Halloween), and even says that he himself was chased and threatened by the Horseman a year earlier. So while neither character is particularly bad, neither is particularly good, either. The story can end on a fittingly mysterious note, and thereby allow the viewers to decide what they think really happened. Arguably, such an ambiguous resolution is possible because, ultimately, the section of the film in which this story is told lasts just under thirty-two minutes. We are not encouraged to love or hate the characters, only to watch them and enjoy their antics and scrapes, and we are reminded visually, by being shown, at the start of the segment, a leather-bound book

118 Washington Irving, *The Legend of Sleepy Hollow*, Illustrated Deluxe Edition for Kindle, (Northpointe Classics, 2008), Location 503 of 552.

135

being taken from a shelf and opened to a title page which displays the title of the novella and the author's name prominently; what we are watching is an adaptation of classic literature, and therefore what happens in the film is what happens in the book, it is implied. It is Irving who made them despicable, not the team at Disney.

Our next pairing, Quasimodo and Phoebus from *The Hunchback of Notre Dame* (1996), are also from a literary adaptation. In this film, we find two men who, initially, seem very different, but who transform from rivals into true friends. We meet Quasimodo first, up in his bell tower, encouraging a baby bird from a nest in the bell tower so that it will learn to fly and, therefore, so that it can fly away. He looks out over the square outside the cathedral, but is sad because, as Laverne, one of the gargoyles (who are his friends), says, "What good is watching a party if you never get to go?" For Quasimodo, the gargoyles are alive because he is alone most of the time and needs someone to talk to. Other than ring the bells for the cathedral, all that he has with which to keep himself occupied is the model he has made of the cathedral square: it is an elaborate, beautifully and somewhat whimsically-rendered model, and a source of great comfort to Quasimodo as it gives him a means for pretending to be a part of the ordinary world and interacting with others (amongst the model people is a little miniature of Quasimodo himself). Quasimodo is shown to be kindly, sensitive, and very good-hearted. With the gargoyles' encouragement, he determines to disguise himself and sneak out of the bell tower just for a few hours so that he can experience the festival below – the annual Feast of Fools – for himself. Because he is an innocent, he believes what Frollo has told him: that his deformed appearance makes him a monster, and that others will look upon him as an abomination. But his craving to experience just one day amongst the people he has watched all his life is too much for him to bear anymore, and so he determines to sneak away from the bell tower and experience the Feast of Fools in person.

We are next introduced to Esmeralda, the beautiful Gypsy woman who will befriend Quasimodo, and Phoebus, the new captain of the guards who has just returned to Paris to take up his post. We are shown very quickly that Phoebus does not suffer the same prejudice against Gypsies as Frollo and the city's guards: when two of the guards attempt to arrest Esmeralda and steal the money she has earned as a street performer, he helps her to get away by getting in the path of the guards, only using his authority when they threaten him. We see that he is in no way like Frollo when he arrives at the Palace of Justice to report to the judge; we see that Frollo is overseeing the torture of a prisoner, and that Phoebus disapproves, even though he makes no comment (nor can he, since Frollo is his superior).

The four characters at the heart of the story – Quasimodo, Frollo, Phoebus and Esmeralda – come together when Esmeralda dances as part of the festival and Quasimodo ends up being crowned king of the festival (on the grounds that they were looking for the ugliest face in Paris, and Quasimodo has it). Initially, it seems as though Quasimodo's worst fears are coming to pass: when the people realise that he is not wearing a mask, they are horrified; they are reminded that the King of Fools is supposed to be the ugliest person in Paris, however, and so their horror changes to celebration. Quasimodo is crowned and lifted up on their shoulders. Then the guards start throwing rotten food at him, and the villagers, shocked at first, also begin laughing. Quasimodo's moment of triumph becomes his torture, and he begs Frollo to help him. Phoebus asks persmission to put an end to the cruelty, but Frollo tells him to wait, saying, "A lesson needs to be learned here". Esmeralda, however, steps forward and stops his humiliation, apologising for putting him into such a position. When Frollo forbids her from helping Quasimodo, she ignores him, cutting the ropes that have him bound, and starts to comfort him. Phoebus is shown to be glad; shortly after this, when he sees Esmeralda fight off ten soldiers and escape, he exclaims, "What a woman!" He cannot help but admire her. He follows her into the cathedral, and the two spar, both verbally and physically: they are shown to be equally matched, their cut and thrust demonstrating that they have compatible personalities and temperaments. She realises that he has not followed her into the church to arrest her; when Frollo bursts in and orders her arrest, he whispers to her to claim sanctuary. When she does not, he pretends that she has, reminding Frollo that he cannot arrest her so long as she is in the cathedral. Esmeralda (and Djali, her goat) cannot bear to be inside for too long, and so Quasimodo helps her to escape the cathedral.

Quasimodo and Phoebus meet just as Quasimodo is climbing back into the cathedral. Phoebus is looking for Esmeralda; it is implied that he cannot stop thinking about her, and wants to get to know her better. Quasimodo, too, has fallen for her, because she has shown him kindness and friendship. He quickly realises that Phoebus means her no harm, but still keeps secret that Esmeralda has escaped. Their rivalry for Esmeralda is established when we see that Quasimodo has confused Esmeralda's affectionate friendship for romantic feelings, and he begins to hope that the two of them are falling in love. He is upset, however, when Esmeralda brings a wounded Phoebus to his bell tower to hide him, and sees that she has developed romantic feelings for Phoebus, not him; when Esmeralda and Phoebus kiss, he is heartbroken. But he still protects Esmeralda and Phoebus from Frollo; when Phoebus plans to find the Court of Miracles and warn the Gypsies of Frollo's intention to raid the "Court" and destroy the Gypsies, he shames Quasimodo into helping (Quasimodo hesitates because he has already suffered so much for defying Frollo). Quasimodo is jealous of Phoebus, but he relents, though he says he is doing this only for Esmeralda. They call a truce in order to help Esmeralda: a common enemy and a common friend have united them, and their dislike for one another is put to one side. Unfortunately, Quasimodo has been tricked by Frollo, and inadvertently leads Frollo and his men to the Court of Miracles. The Gypsies, Phoebus, and Quasimodo are arrested, and Esmeralda is declared a witch. Frollo ties her to a stake and sets the pyre alight, a vindictive grin on his face as he watches her begin to burn.

Quasimodo has been chained to a ledge on the cathedral so that he is forced to watch his friends die; finally enraged, he breaks free of his chains, rescues Esmeralda, and sets in motion a chain of events which will allow Phoebus to break free and stir the citizens of Paris to rise up against the evil Frollo. Quasimodo fights from overhead, Phoebus leads the charge from down below, and between them they are able to defeat Frollo and his minions. Quasimodo is distraught, however, when he realises that Esmeralda may be dead. Frollo creeps into Quasimodo's bedroom, where Esmeralda is laid out; we see that he is holding a knife behind his back as he approaches Quasimodo, clearly intending to kill him. Frollo claims that it was his duty to execute Esmeralda and that he hopes he can be forgiven. Quasimodo then sees from the shadows that Frollo is about to stab him, and so overpowers him and grabs the knife. He berates Frollo, saying that "now I see that the only thing dark and cruel about [this world] is people like you". Just then, Esmeralda stirs; Quasimodo grabs her and flees, Frollo close behind them with a sword. Frollo thinks he has Quasimodo trapped, but Quasimodo is able to turn the tables; soon it is Frollo who is dangling from high up on the side of the cathedral, the fire he lit on the pyre now raging out of control. For a moment, Frollo manages to climb onto one of the rainspouts, raising his sword to strike Esmeralda as she holds onto Quasimodo; the rainspout breaks, however, and Frollo plunges to his death. Esmeralda loses her hold on Quasimodo. A few stories below, Phoebus is able to catch him and pull him into the cathedral to safety. At this moment, Quasimodo is able to let go of his jealousy: he hugs Phoebus, then Esmeralda, then brings them together, placing Esmeralda's hand in Phoebus' and blessing the match. This time when Phoebus and Esmeralda kiss, he looks on happily. They lead him out onto the steps of the cathedral so that the people can acknowledge his victory, and a little girl comes forward from the crowd, hugs him, and leads him forward. They cheer him and celebrate him as a hero, this time genuinely. He looks back and waves at his friends: all his jealousy and dislike of Phoebus have been forgotten, and replaced with true respect and admiration.

Wreck-It Ralph and Fix-It Felix are our final pair of "Frienemies", and our last characters to be considered in this chapter. The stars of *Wreck-It Ralph* (2012), the two do not like or trust one another because each has been designed to be pitted against the other. They are characters in a 1980s video arcade game called "Fix-It Felix, Jr.": Felix is the hero who saves the Nicelanders (the people who live in the building), and Ralph is the thug who tries to destroy their apartment building. It is his role in the game, and Ralph accepts this, to a degree. But at night, when the arcade closes and the game's characters relax and celebrate another day's play, Ralph is cast out from them, forced to sleep on the side of a waste dump, where he lays and watches Felix and the Nicelanders through the windows of their apartments. We learn all of this about Ralph during a meeting of a support group for video-game villains, Bad-Anon, and also see that this is a common sentiment amongst the bad guys. As one of them, Zangief, says, in an effort to help Ralph understand the importance of being the bad guy in his game, "If Zangief is good guy, who'll crush man's skull like sparrow's egg between thighs? And I say, 'Zangief, you are bad guy, but that does not mean you are "bad" guy.'" The others applaud, but Ralph does not understand. He sees Felix receiving medals and pies every day to celebrate his accomplishments within the game, and does not understand why his own accomplishments cannot be celebrated, too. He is spurred to attend the meeting because it is the thirtieth anniversary of his game, and therefore is feeling worn down and reflective. He admits that he no longer wants to be a bad guy, much to the horror of the other bad guys: they react with shock, worried that Ralph is about to "go turbo", or leave his game during the hours when the arcade is open (which means that the game will be thought to be broken, and will end up being unplugged and junked). He denies this, however. The Bad-Anon meeting ends with the "Bad Guy Affirmation", and Ralph returns to his game.

139

When he gets home, he sees that the Nicelanders and Felix are having a thirtieth anniversary party, attended by the heroes of other games, like Pac Man. Ralph goes up to join them, much to their horror. Felix goes out to "talk" to him, really to smooth things over and get Ralph to go away, but Felix (voiced by Jack McBrayer, whose Felix character borrows heavily from his sweet, innocent, kindly character Kenneth Parcell from the series *30 Rock*, 2006-2013) finds that he cannot get Felix to go away in a diplomatic fashion. Reluctantly – since he does not trust Ralph not to wreck the party and knows that the other guests do not want Ralph there – he finds himself inviting Ralph in to have a slice of cake. Ralph is made to feel very unwelcome, however, not least because the cake, a depiction of the building and the game's characters, has him standing in a mud-puddle and the other characters celebrating atop the roof. He gets into a confrontation with Gene, one of the Nicelanders, who tells Ralph that he does not deserve a medal and does not belong in the celebration. He taunts Ralph: "Only good guys win medals, and you, sir, are no good guy". When Ralph replies that he could be a good guy and win a medal if he wanted to, Gene is dismissive: "Uh-huh. And when you do, come and talk to us. … If you won a medal, we'd let you live up here in the penthouse! But it will never happen, because you're just the bad guy who wrecks the building." In his fury, Ralph slams down his fist and smashes the cake. Realising what he has done, he vows that he will win a medal and prove himself to the others. He leaves the game, going in search of an opportunity. He soon finds one, and enters into a much more modern game, "Hero's Duty", where he mingles with the ranks of the soldiers in the hopes of winning the medal that is claimed by those who complete the game. Though the game is far more intense and violent than anything he has ever experienced, he is successful and wins a medal. However, his destructive presence causes havoc; the game descends into chaos as he inadvertently unleashes too early a new swarm of Cy-bugs, and Ralph finds himself expelled from the game entirely when he stumbles into an escape pod (accidentally bringing with him one of the Cy-bugs which terrorise the soldiers in "Hero's Duty"), ending up in another modern – and very different – game called "Sugar Rush". It is here where the majority of the film's action will take place.

At this stage, we have only met Felix briefly: we know that he is the hero of the game (and that it is named after him), that he is beloved by the citizens whose apartment house he rebuilds, and that he is a sweet, diplomatic, friendly, warm-hearted guy, but that he, too, does not trust Ralph or want him around. He has spent thirty years fixing the damage Ralph has inflicted, and so when he learns (from Q*bert, who has watched Ralph enter the "Hero's Duty" game), that Ralph has "gone turbo" and that "Fix-It Felix, Jr." is in danger of being turned off by the arcade manager, Felix, too, leaves the game, determined to go find Ralph, bring him back, and thereby fix the damage that has befallen the game as a whole. He tracks Ralph down to "Hero's Duty", where he makes contact with the commander in charge of the troops in "Hero's Duty", a tough, no-nonsense woman named Calhoun; Felix is amazed at the "high definition" of her face, and is instantly smitten. When he and Calhoun realise that Ralph and one of the Cy-bugs have left "Hero's Duty", they are determined to find them and restore order. We learn that Calhoun – whom Felix finds to be very intense – has been programmed to have "the most tragic backstory ever": in a flashback, we are shown Calhoun on her wedding day – "the one day she didn't do a perimeter check" – when a Cy-bug attack kills her groom as they stand before the altar, about to be married. This background has left her bitter and emotionally shut down, intent on destroying the Cy-bugs at all costs. Felix and Calhoun team up: Felix will fix what Ralph wrecks (as per his programming), and Calhoun will hunt down and destroy the Cy-bug.

Much to his displeasure, Ralph finds that the escape pod from "Hero's Duty" has crash-landed in the "Sugar Rush" game, which he describes dismissively as "that candy go-cart game owned by the Whac-A-Mole". He plans to grab his medal and go home, only to realise that it is stuck on a high branch in a candy tree. He starts to climb up after it when he meets a little girl from the game, Vanellope, who teases and annoys him. When she spots his medal, she races up to the top of the tree after it, and manages to get it. She wants it for herself so that she can use it to enter the races. As she walks away, she suddenly glitches; we are told later, by King Candy (who, it turns out, is the game's villain) that she is considered a "glitch" in the game – a programming fault with the potential to destroy it if she is allowed to race and somehow manages to win. Initially, Ralph is angry at Vanellope for stealing his medal, but then he sees her being bullied by the other avatars and his attitude begins change toward her: they make a deal that, if he will help her build a new go-cart (after the other avatars destroyed the one she built herself), she will give him back the medal when she receives her winnings (all of the gold coins paid in by those participating in the race). Likewise, as they journey through the "Sugar Rush" game together looking for Ralph and the Cy-bug, Felix and Calhoun begin to bond and, despite their very different personalities and programming, begin to fall in love

– an attraction of opposites that, at least partially, is humorous because the two are so different in every way, especially physically. Naturally, Felix and Calhoun's romance runs into a few snags, not least his inadvertently referring to her as "a dynamite gal", the same thing her fiancé had called her and which triggers in her a rush of terror that makes her dump Felix and run away. But they are reunited eventually, when, later in the film, Calhoun finds the nest of eggs that the Cy-bug has laid, the eggs hatch and begin destroying "Sugar Rush", and she charges in to evacuate the game's citizens to safety and to try and hold back the Cy-bugs from leaving the game. After this, except when they are in their respective games doing their jobs, they are together; our final scene with the two of them is of their wedding. They have found true love, and will always be together.

At one stage, after helping Vanellope to build a car and learn to drive it, Ralph is convinced by King Candy that allowing Vanellope to win the race could lead to the destruction of the "Sugar Rush" game: if the human gamers see her glitching, King Candy warns, they will assume that something is wrong with the game, it will be shut down, and all will be left homeless. Even worse, because glitches cannot leave their games, Vanellope will be trapped in the empty void forever. Ralph falls for King Candy's lie, and tries to convince Vanellope not to race, even going so far as to destroy the car they built together. It is when he returns to his own game, however, that he begins to doubt King Candy's story. Alone in the Nicelanders' penthouse, gazing out through the screen, he notices a picture of Vanellope on the side of the "Sugar Rush" console – something that would not be there if she was nothing more than faulty programming, as King Candy claims. Ralph begins to uncover the truth, returning to "Sugar Rush" and interrogating Sour Bill, King Candy's lackey. He learns that, in fact, the game's programming has been altered by King Candy, who tried to delete Vanellope from the game completely but was unable; he could only turn her into a glitch. If Vanellope ever completed the race, it would re-set the game and restore order; this is why King Candy is desperate to stop her. Ralph also learns from interrogating Sour Bill that Felix is being held in King Candy's dungeon (or "fungeon", as King Candy likes to call it), and goes immediately to rescue him. The two quarrel (Felix telling-off Ralph), and Felix realises that his terrible experiences – being rejected by Calhoun and then treated like a criminal by King Candy – mirror Ralph's daily life of rejection by the Nicelanders and being forced to live in a dump. They talk, and Ralph explains to Felix what is happening. From that moment on, they begin to work together to help Vanellope and fix

"Sugar Rush", two allies united by a common enemy and in support of a common goal. Felix fixes Vanellope's car, Ralph breaks her out of the dungeon, and they hurry to the race track, where Vanellope is able to join in just after the race has begun. It turns out that, as she suspected, Vanellope is a born racer (or, in the language of the film, racing is in her code). She may have joined the race late, but she forges ahead, soon moving up into number two, hot on the heels of the lead racer, King Candy, whom she soon overtakes. He attacks her, their cars hitched together, and he, too, begins glitching. As Ralph and Felix watch on the monitor from the finish line, they are shocked to realise that King Candy is none other than Turbo, the main racer from "Turbo Time" who, decades earlier, had escaped his game, destroyed both it and another racing game (causing them both to be unplugged), and disappearing: he is the inspiration for the reference "Going Turbo". They realise that Turbo has disguised himself in a new persona and taken over "Sugar Rush". Vanellope, too, realises what is going on; having learned (to a degree) to control her glitching, she uses it to her advantage, glitching intentionally to detach her car from King Candy's and heading off toward the finish line; King Candy/Turbo, however, ends up driving into the open mouth of a Cy-bug (the one that came in with Ralph laid eggs; they have hatched, and now "Sugar Rush" is under attack from a swarm of Cy-bugs, Calhoun doing all she can to protect the game's citizens and defeat the Cy-bugs). It looks, at least at that moment, as though King Candy has died.

A swarm of Cy-bugs destroys the finish line; Calhoun is about to shut down the game to prevent the Cy-bugs from spreading to other games, but of course Vanellope cannot leave the game. It is then that Ralph has a brainwave. He learned in "Hero's Duty" that the only way to stop the Cy-bugs is to create a beacon which destroys them. He races to a part of the game made up of a diet cola hot spring, with Mentos stalactites hanging over it. Knowing that the Mentos will create an explosion with enough light to attract the Cy-bugs, Ralph plans to use his wrecking skills to knock all of the Mentos into the diet cola hot spring. He is nearly stopped by King Candy, who has joined his programming with one of the Cy-bugs and become even more dangerous (he thinks), but ultimately he is too manic. Ralph is able to escape Candy's clutches. Believing himself to be sacrificing his life, Ralph recites the "Bad Guy's Affirmation" – this time with true understanding – as he falls amongst the Mentos. Vanellope is able to use her car to jump through the falling Mentos and catch Ralph, however, and they escape. The beacon draws all of the Cy-bugs, including the King Candy/Cy-bug, and peace is restored. Felix fixes the finish line, and Vanellope finally crosses it. The game is reset; Vanellope is transformed into a princess as the other players remember her true identity. Vanellope, however, is not interested in being a princess. She knows that she is a racer at heart. She will still lead them, but instead declares herself to be President Vanellope von Schweetz. All celebrate the restoration of "Sugar Rush". Ralph, Felix, and Calhoun return to their own games just before the arcade opens; order is restored to all of their games, and peace returns to the arcade. We learn that, back in the "Fix-It Felix, Jr." game, things are much better. Ralph is still the wrecker, but that is only during the day. At night, he joins the Nicelanders in their community activities; they even adopt the homeless Q★bert characters, who help them out in the bonus levels of "Fix-It Felix, Jr." The game becomes more popular than ever, and all within it live happily. Felix and Calhoun are married, with Ralph as their best man and Vanellope as the maid of honour. Ralph tells the support group (Bad-Anon) at the end that, for him, the best part of his job now is when the Nicelanders lift him up to throw him off the roof, because then he is high up enough to look out and see Vanellope racing in the "Sugar Rush" game. As he says, "Turns out I don't need a medal to tell me I'm a good guy. 'Cause if that little kid likes me, how bad can I be?" He, Felix, and the Nicelanders are all friends now, living together happily; Felix even builds Ralph and the Q★bert characters a street of lovely new homes so that they are no longer homeless.

A possible explanation as to why Quasimodo and Phoebus, as well as Ralph and Felix, can unite, ultimately, and work together is that they have a definite common foe. Judge Frollo may be more dangerous than King Candy, but both are equally threatening to the existence of each of the film's heroines, Esmeralda (*Hunchback of Notre Dame*) and Vanellope (*Wreck-It Ralph*). Because Ichabod and Brom have no one who threatens directly either them or Katrina, they have no reason to move beyond the friendly rivalry that exists between them, a factor which causes it to escalate almost out of control; their competition ceases only when Ichabod disappears after the Headless Horseman has attacked; in this sense, it is immaterial whether or not the Horseman was Brom in disguise – something which the characters in the film do not believe, though Irving's novella hints that Brom very likely was involved. Being romantic rivals creates tension between Phoebus and Quasimodo, too, though ultimately their love for Esmeralda – and their need to stop Frollo – unites them and turns them from enemies, to "frienemies", to true friends; Quasimodo can even be happy for Phoebus' and Esmeralda's love for each other. As for Wreck-It Ralph and Fix-It Felix, they are never romantic rivals, only two characters who have been created to work in opposition to one another. They learn to be friends, however, when Felix understands how miserable he and the Nicelanders have made Ralph over the thirty years that their game has run, and when Ralph learns to embrace his destructiveness and use it for the good of others. Ralph and Felix can be friends because they realise that they need each other: if Ralph does not destroy things, Felix will have nothing to fix. They are both parts of the whole, a balance to each other, and – ultimately – brothers.

Conclusion

The characters examined in this chapter – the non-aristocratic leading male characters – come in many forms. If there is anything which unites most of them – Ichabod and Brom, as well as Johnny Appleseed, are the exceptions here – it is their shared sense of justice and their being motivated to be their best possible selves by the love they feel for a woman. This is not to say that this is always a romantic love: the seven dwarfs' love for Snow White is fairly paternal in nature, as is Ralph's for Vanellope. For Bernard, Doppler, Aladdin, Flynn, John Smith, Shang, Quasimodo, Phoebus, and Felix, the love they experience is very much a romantic one. Quasimodo's is unrequited (though Esmeralda loves him, it is only as a friend), but it still helps him to grow and become better than he was. Milo is perhaps given greater energy by his love for Kida to keep fighting against all odds, but it is clear that his since of moral outrage at Rourke's actions is independent of his love for Kida: he would have fought no matter what. Only Johnny Appleseed has no human love interest. However, he is very full of his love of God and his wish to do his best for his fellow man. The only exceptions to the idea that love has made them better are Ichabod Crane and Brom Bones. However, as was said previously, whether they feel actual love for Katrina is debatable. So perhaps the implication is that real love makes us better; desire, however, is too selfish on its own to cause anything but harm.

Though these characters range across the whole of Disney's history of producing animated feature films – we started with the seven dwarfs, from 1937, and finished with Ralph and Felix from 2012 – it is interesting that so many of the non-aristocratic adult male leading characters have arisen since 1990. Prior to 1990, only four of the films in this chapter featured such characters. Since 1990, there have been nine films whose characters warranted inclusion in this discussion. Why this is, as stated at the beginning, may at least in part be linked to changing audience demographics: as Hollywood as a whole began to focus on young men as audiences, more films featuring male leading characters have been created. Though, traditionally, Disney has aimed at the family audience since before that became an official Hollywood designation/genre, it still hopes to attract viewers who are not generally thought of as being part of the family audience. Therefore, producing animated films – at great expense – which have a chance of pulling in boys and men is crucial to a film's financial success, and therefore is important to the health of the studio. Yet it is also important to stress that a large proportion of the films discussed in this chapter – five out of twelve – were made during the 1990s. Before this period, again, we have four films spread out over a forty-year period (1937, 1948, 1949, 1977). After the 1990s, we have another four films spread across eleven years (2001, 2003, 2010, 2012). Expand that to include *all* films with male characters (of any age, both royals and commoners) in leading roles, and you get, in the first fifty-three years, twelve films out of twenty-eight; from 1990 to 1999, eight films out of nine (*The Lion King*, 1994, is the only film in this period not to have a *human* character in a leading role, and of course it still had male leads); and in the thirteen years since, seven films out of fourteen. The remaining films had either animals in leading roles, or else were package films whose segments had no discernible human male leads. Perhaps this shift since the 1990s reflects a shift of the target demographic away from a male focus to one which is roughly equal in terms of male:female. This, of course, is hard to know, particularly as we are still going through the post-1999 period; better analysis of the first two decades of the twenty-first century can only come after they have become firmly ensconced in history.

But beyond that, including such characters in their roster gives Disney the chance to broaden their focus more generally, and to address themes and stories which incorporate a broad range of character types. Including male characters who are not bound by their roles as princes means that the men can enjoy much broader adventures and experience different outcomes – to include, as is the case for the seven dwarfs, Johnny Appleseed, John Smith, Ichabod Crane, Quasimodo, and Wreck-It Ralph, no romantic entanglements at all. Unlike princes, they have no duty to marry and continue the royal line. This means that, while they *can* be romantic leading men, they can be other things, too.

3

Handsome Princes

119 Sheldon Cashdan,
*The Witch Must
Die: The Hidden
Meaning of Fairy
Tales* (New York:
Basic Books,
1999), p. 28.

120 There is a second
Bibbidi-Bobbidi-
Boutique at Walt
Disney World,
located at the
World of Disney
Store in
Downtown Disney
Marketplace.
Much of the
customer feedback
available online,
however, indicates
that, though the
Downtown Disney
branch is good and
gets good
customer reviews,
the boutique in
Cinderella's Castle
in the Magic
Kingdom is the
"main" and
preferred location.

In *The Witch Must Die: The Hidden Meaning of Fairy Tales*, Sheldon Cashdan claims that, "In contrast [to witches, god-mothers, and other female characters], male figures are relatively minor figures in most fairy tales. The prince tends to be a cardboard character, almost an afterthought, who material-izes at the end of the story to ensure a happy ending."[119] Certainly, in terms of public perception of the princes and heroes in Disney animation, there are grounds for thinking this applies. After all, the Hero/Prince is overlooked in many ways by Disney audiences, and one might perceive, when looking at the role which the Hero/Prince figure plays in Disney merchandising schemes, that he is not important as a figure to the Disney studio. There is the hugely-successful (and now relatively long-lived) Disney Princess line of products and placements, ranging from very inexpensive and practical items like notebooks featuring the characters, all the way up to being able to book an appointment at the Bibbidi-Bobbidi-Boutique at Walt Disney World, a session which can cost (as of 2013) nearly $200. By way of backing up my claim that the princess overshadows the prince, one need only look at the "packages" on offer at the boutique, which is located inside Cinderella's castle in the Magic Kingdom.[120] There are four "Princess Packages", each in a different price bracket. De-pending upon the package, they offer hair styling, make up, a dress and accessories to correspond with one of the Disney princesses, as well as photographs of the girl once she has been outfitted fully so as to preserve her memory of the experience. That this is very popular can be attested to by the number of little girls one sees everyday throughout the park who clearly have had a visit to the salon. When I enquired during my visit to Walt Disney World in August 2012, I was told that the next available appointment was not until close to Christmas; that this is the case is easy to believe. Indeed, it is hard to imagine a visitor to Walt Disney World who has not noticed the number of little girls in full princess gear, hair and make-up included, given how ubiquitous they have become. Notable by their absence, however, were boys who had been dressed as the prince (or hero) of their choice. The salon *does* offer a package for boys. One. It is called the "Knight" package, and, according to Walt Disney World's official website, it includes "hair styling as well as a mighty sword and shield for $15.95 plus tax".[121] But in no way is what is offered for boys as big of an experience as the options for girls, nor is there any indication on the Disney website that the boys get to choose to be a particular male character. It is particularly interesting that they are "Knights", not "Princes". The image of the Knight is of a figure who is daring, brave, fierce, and strong, charging into battle or jousting in tournaments. The Prince, however, fulfils potentially a more liminal role – he is potentially a future king, but is not king yet – or else is more of a supporting player: he marries the heroine and lives happily ever after at her side.

But is it just "Disney" audiences who overlook the prince as a character? In an article published in *The Journal of American Folklore* in 1975, the popularity of male versus female hero archetypes in folklore and fairy tales is discussed at some length. In comparing the popularity of the hero in Europe and North America, the author, Kay Stone, found that the presence of heroines in collections of Grimms' fairy tales "jump[s] from twenty percent in the original Grimm collection to as much as seventy-five percent in many children's books. In this sense the fairy tale, a male-oriented genre in Europe (both by tale and by teller), becomes a female-oriented genre in North American children's literature."[122] Whether or not one agrees with Stone's analysis that Europe is more male-archetype oriented and North America more inclined to focus on female archetypes, it is nonetheless true that, in the earlier Disney studio films based on fairy tales, central female characters and supporting male characters would seem, by and large, to have been preferred.

Nameless "Heroes"

In most discussions of the Disney princess, a common, favourite critique is to note their passiveness. Such readings describe Disney's women/princesses as "not only passive and pretty, but also unusually patient, obedient, industrious, and quiet";[123] "In these animated worlds, good women are domesticators and resources".[124] Indeed, such readings have been used as a critique of

121 http://disneyworld. disney.go.com/tours - and-experiences/ bibbidi-bobbidi- boutique/, accessed on 28 February 2013.

122 Kay Stone, "Things Walt Disney Never Told Us", in *The Journal of American Folklore*, Vol. 88, No. 347 (January–March 1975), pp. 43-44.

123 Stone, p. 44.

124 Elizabeth Bell, Lynda Haas, and Laura Sells (eds.). *From Mouse to Mermaid: The Politics of Film, Gender, and Culture* (Indianapolis: Indiana University Press, 1995), p. 11.

Disney itself, and some – whose zealotry overrules their logic – have gone so far as to claim that such representations of women are the *cause* (rather than a symptom) of sexist attitudes amongst the general population. Yet there are hardly any readings of this sort which take into account the character, personality, and activity/passivity of the prince who corresponds to the princess coming under fire. When examined closely, just how well does the average Disney prince fair in terms of *his* levels of activity?

It is interesting to note, first, that – unlike the heroines – the first two Disney princes lack known/actual first names. They are – semi-anonymously – "The Prince" (*Snow White and the Seven Dwarfs*) and "Prince Charming" (*Cinderella*). It is only with the third prince – in *Sleeping Beauty* – that we finally get a first name: Prince Phillip. As we shall see, having a name substantially increases a prince's character development, drive, and narrative contribution.

The fact is that, unlike the heroines at the centres of each film, these two nameless princes never seem to do very much. The Prince functions predominately as a bookending device for *Snow White*: he comes upon Snow White, they fall in love, and the scene serves, narratively speaking, as the final straw for the Queen's jealousy of Snow White. In *Cinderella*, Prince Charming functions as something of a MacGuffin: the King cares deeply that Prince Charming find a wife, settle down, and become a father, and Cinderella earns him as a prize for her hard work, her patience, and her faith. For the audiences of the two films, however, neither prince is a focus, or even terribly important. Having no actual name attributed to them may, in fact, heighten each prince's symbolic value to the narrative in which he belongs. Such an idea is highlighted by Christine Gledhill when discussing another iconic nameless figure who would emerge in later decades, the "Man with No Name" of *High Planes Drifter* (Eastwood, 1972) and *Pale Rider* (1985): "As the 'Man with No Name', he is produced in an imaginary space outside the social structures of patriarchal power which uses violence in support of greed, exploitation, and corruption".[125] In both *Snow White and the Seven Dwarfs* and *Cinderella*, it can be argued that Patriarchy in its most destructive form – that which pits women against each other as competitors for power and wealth – is embodied within the female roles of the Evil Queen (*Snow White*) and the Wicked Stepmother (*Cinderella*). In both cases, the presence of a prince for the heroine to marry means that he functions as what Gledhill describes as a character who "abstracts masculine power as a purifying instrument in the service of an invincible authority".[126]

125 Christine Gledhill, "Women Reading Men", from Pat Kirkham and Janet Thumim (Eds.), *Me Jane: Masculinity, Movies, and Women* (London: Lawrence and Wishart, 1995), p. 86.

126 Gledhill, p. 86.

Such a description of a male character abstracting masculine power is fitting of both princes being discussed here, but in particular fits the character of The Prince from *Snow White*. The Prince is an independent figure who rides into the film at key points – the beginning and the end – where he sparks off the first crisis (inspiring the Queen's jealousy and therefore motivating her to order Snow White's murder), then resolves the second (reviving Snow White from the "Sleeping Death" spell cast by the Queen). The only other character with whom The Prince deals directly is Snow White, and it is his love for her – not hatred of the Evil Queen or gratitude toward the Seven Dwarfs – which motivates all of his actions. When we first see him, it is when he hears Snow White singing; he climbs the wall to the courtyard, sees her singing into the wishing well, and is captivated by her instantly. He appears to Snow White as if she had summoned him by wishing into the well (the song she is singing declares "I'm wishing for the one I love/To find me today", and his first word in the film is to echo Snow White's last word in her song, "Today!"). Initially, Snow White runs away from The Prince, but after a short prelude declaring that "Now that I've found you/Here's what I have to say", he proclaims his love for Snow White immediately and unequivocally:

> One song – I have but one song
> One song only for you.
> One heart tenderly beating, ever entreating, constant and true!
>
> One love that has possessed me –
> One love thrilling me through –
> One song my heart keeps singing
> Of one love only for you!

Presumably before The Prince has a chance to court Snow White in a proper, respectful way, however, she has disappeared, having been forced to flee for her own safety. Since it is Snow White's story – not The Prince's – we then follow Snow White on her journey to the Dwarfs' house and her life in the forest. For the story as it is told in this version, The Prince has no on-screen function again until the end of the film. For most of the story, his role is to serve as a symbolic beacon of hope and love; Snow White knows that they will be together again someday, once she is out of danger. It is implied by the final shot of the film (the castle in the clouds upon which Snow White and The Prince gaze) that The Prince also carries with him the privilege of power: after all, he is a prince, so the likelihood is that, one day, he will rule a kingdom. It should be remember that this gives him equitable royal status to that of Snow White, who is a princess by birth, not by marriage. Her power has been usurped by her evil step-mother, the Queen, but the Queen's death means that Snow White's kingdom will now be restored to her. As for The Prince's own kingdom ... we know nothing. Nor do we know what he has been doing in the off-screen portion of the story until the end of the film, when we learn through a series of inter-titles that "The Prince, who had searched far and wide, heard of the maiden who slept in the glass coffin". He then returns to the screen, reprising "One Song" to show that his love – and his role within the film – have remained constant. He reverently approaches the alter that has been made out of Snow White's tomb, leans down to kiss her farewell, then kneels and weeps at the loss of his love. The kiss that awakens her is powerful, but inadvertently so. He intends to kiss her, of course – it is both him paying his respects to the deceased (it is an ancient custom to kiss the bodies of the recently departed) and his only chance to express his feelings for his true love. But he has no idea that his kiss will awaken her from a spell. From his perspective and hers, that is just miraculous good luck. Symbolically, because the kiss which can reverse the spell (we are told by the Queen's spell book) must be "love's first kiss", we know that each is the other's true love. It does *not* mean, however, that The Prince knows Snow White any better than she knows him. It has been noted that Snow White has idealised and pined after a man who is a stranger to her, for all intents and purposes. The Prince's behaviour, however, implies that he, too, has idealised and pined after her just as much as she has dreamed of and longed for him. Otherwise, there would be no need for him to search far and wide for Snow White in particular; he would have found another nice young woman – maybe even another princess – and married her, and this other young woman could have served as his queen and as the mother of his children just as effectively as Snow White. The fact is, however, that he does *not* look elsewhere for true love – his focus is on Snow White, the beautiful young girl whose singing drew him to her and with whom he fell in love at first sight, only to lose her almost immediately.

Happily, being in possession of a horse and without a death threat forcing him into hiding, he has been able to seek out Snow White. But he plays no active role in rescuing her from danger: he does not defeat the evil Queen who threatened and bewitched Snow White, neither does he provide her with shelter or sustenance during the time she is in hiding. His kisses her good-bye – passively accepting his supposed fate as one who has lost his true love – and then is relieved and overjoyed to realise that she is alive after all, and that they can live together "happily ever after". At least one can say that, when he gets his second chance, The Prince does not let it slip past: he picks her up, puts her on his horse, and journeys by her side to their new kingdom. It is the only real activeness – apart from the wandering he does off screen – that he demonstrates in the narrative. This is nowhere near as active as his true love, who "... flees from danger, and, once she finds the dwarfs' cottage, she takes an active role in earning her keep by doing housework for them", thereby forming for herself a new home and family, one in which she has a position of authority and in which she is respected and loved.[127] But, of course, it is Snow White's story, not The Prince's. His function in the narrative is limited, but vital. His romantic attentions to Snow White inspire the Queen's jealousy and fury. His honourable, true, and undying love breaks the spell of the Sleeping Death in which Snow White is trapped. Between those times, he serves as a symbol of attainment – a goal for Snow White. That was always The Prince's primary function in the story, and makes him an important – but nonetheless supporting – character in Snow White's tale.

The Prince, however little he does in *Snow White*, can be proud of two things: when his second chance comes to be with Snow White, he (literally) grabs hold with both hands and refuses to let go; he also demonstrates the strength of his love by searching far and wide for her, even if he is of no use to her until the final moments of the film. He does come through for Snow White in the end, and they are equally overjoyed to be reunited. This differentiates The Prince greatly from his fellow nameless royal prince, the "hero" of *Cinderella* (and the second prince in Disney feature animation history), Prince Charming.

The first that we hear about Prince Charming implies that he has shown no interest in finding himself a wife and fulfilling his royal duties as heir to his father's throne. We learn this from the King, who is complaining very angrily to his aid, the Grand Duke, that "My son has been avoiding his responsibilities long enough. It's high time he married and settled down!" Determined that finding Prince Charming a wife amounts to nothing more complicated than "arranging the conditions" in which he can meet a girl and fall in love, the King orders the Grand Duke to arrange for a "welcome home" ball to be held in Prince Charming's honour that very evening. The Duke sets about making the ball happen, and the King looks forward to his vision of what he hopes will occur.

Unfortunately, the story of Prince Charming finding Cinderella and living happily ever after does not progress smoothly. Prince Charming is even less of a go-getter than The Prince. When we

127 Amy M. Davis, *Good Girls & Wicked Witches: Women in Disney's Feature Animation* (Eastleigh: John Libbey & Co., 2006), p. 101.

see him on screen for the first time, it is at the royal ball, which his father, the King, is hosting with the express purpose of compelling his son to find a wife and thereby get on with the business of providing the King with grandchildren, and presumably also guaranteeing the line of succession. No mention of the dynastic implications of Prince Charming starting a family is made in the story, however: we hear the King bemoaning the fact that Prince Charming has yet to settle down, and then see the King's daydream of playing happily with his grandchildren. Instead, it is simply a father who wants his son to settle down and make him a grandfather. At the ball, Prince Charming is being introduced to all of the eligible maidens in the kingdom, and his boredom is apparent: bowing to each young woman as she is introduced to him, he stifles a yawn, looking for the most part very detached from the scene until he spies Cinderella as she enters into the crowded ballroom. His attraction for her – at least at that moment – motivates him enough to approach her and dance with her, and later to sit alone with her on the terrace. But when midnight comes, and Cinderella jumps up and flees before her Fairy Godmother's spell is broken, his reaction is minimal, given that she is supposed to be his one, true love (at least according to the tradition of the fairy tale). He, too, does jump up when he realises she is running away, and calls after her "Wait, please! I don't even know your name – how will I find you?" He follows her, but only part of the way; Cinderella runs through the ballroom and out the entrance to the palace, and Prince Charming follows behind, but is stopped by a group of young women from the ball. Why he cannot get away from them to continue his pursuit is not depicted. Instead, it is the Grand Duke – not Prince Charming – who follows her out of the palace and retrieves the glass slipper that came off her foot. In fact, by all appearances, Prince Charming plays no further part in finding Cinderella. The Grand Duke is the one who informs the King that Cinderella has fled the palace, though he does claim (while being threatened with a sword by the irate king, who wildly accuses the Grand Duke of treachery and sabotage and of being "in league with the Prince all along!") that Prince Charming has declared himself to be madly in love with the girl and that "he'll marry none but the girl who fits this slipper". It is his father, the King, declaring "He said *that*, did he?! Ha-ha! We've got him!" who decrees that every house in the kingdom be searched until the young woman in question is found. When the Grand Duke points out, "But Sire, this slipper may fit any number of girls", the King responds "That's *his* problem! He's given his word? *We'll* hold him to it!" The Grand Duke then carries out the actual house-to-house search, trying the shoe on all of the young women of the kingdom (and even here, he almost bungles it; it is Cinderella who produces the mate to the glass slipper which he allows to get broken, an act which, along with allowing the slipper to be placed on her foot and showing that it truly fits, proves that she is its rightful owner and the maiden whom the Grand Duke is seeking on the King's behalf). Yet never, it seems, does Prince Charming play an active role in that search. From the time he is seen being "blocked" from following Cinderella by a group of young women attending the ball, we do not see Prince Charming again until we see him hand-in-hand with Cinderella as they come from their wedding, running down the steps together, hurrying into their carriage, and riding away together. It is interesting that, once again, Cinderella loses her slipper as she runs down the palace steps, yet even this time it is not Prince Charming who retrieves it for her and places it on her foot – it is the King. It seems to confirm that it was the *King's* resolving that Cinderella be found for Prince Charming, rather than the Prince's own declaration (of which we learn only second-hand) that he is determined to marry her, which has brought about their wedding.

Given what seems to be his (at best) half-hearted interest in being with Cinderella beyond the glamour of the ball, it is easy to see how, in the *Saturday Night Live* sketch of 2012, "Real Housewives of Disney", Prince Charming, who is the only Disney prince to be depicted, is very strongly implied to be homosexual, his marriage to Cinderella an unhappy sham which has left her a bitter alcoholic. Here, Prince Charming (played by Taran Killam) is portrayed as bitchy, sarcastic, and camp, the very antithesis of an ideal husband. As Cinderella herself (played by Kristen Wiig) says of the "prince who's not so charming", "Here's some good advice: never marry a guy who's really into *shoes*". Such a portrayal could be said to rest on the passive role that the 1950 Disney Prince Charming plays in finding his bride, and *might* even be said to be hinted at as a presumed subtext to the King's complaints about his son's failure up to that point to find a bride for himself. While, unsurprisingly, the notion that Prince Charming is gay is not emphasised (or even implied in any real sense) in the 1950 Disney film, what *is* in the film is the idea that Prince Charming is not particularly interested in finding a wife, he is bored by all of the young women he meets at the ball (apart from Cinderella, who is depicted as being particularly beautiful and glamorous and eye-catching), and it is his father's refusal to accept defeat that sees Prince Charming and Cinderella reunited and married. We never hear directly from Prince Charming *himself* that he is in love with Cinderella, nor do we see his love demonstrated by his searching for her, or even pursuing her more enthusiastically when she flees the ball at midnight. Once the clock begins to toll the midnight hour, the spell begins to break, and Cinderella flees the palace. Apparently, a healthy young man wearing trousers and two good shoes has no hope of outrunning woman in a cumbersome ball gown wearing only one shoe ... one *glass* shoe. With a high heel.

It is interesting how this depiction of Prince Charming differs from the one which Walt Disney himself directed, the 1922 Laugh-O-Grams version of "Cinderella". In the Laugh-O-Grams short, it is Prince Charming himself, described in the inter-titles as "a fine fellow", who goes himself (accompanied by his dog) to find Cinderella. He takes an active role in seeking her out, and in this way demonstrates his true love. Whether Prince Charming of the 1950 feature version is truly in love – or is marrying Cinderella solely to appease his father – must remain a matter for conjecture, however (modern depictions of Disney's Prince Charming notwithstanding). For scholars such as Cashdan, ideas about the sexual longings of fairy tale characters are not especially important, particularly as it relates to how the characters' actions are understood by audiences (especially younger members of the audience). According to Cashdan:

> While no one will deny that children are sexual beings, and that some fairy tales may tap sexual longings, sex is far from the most pressing concern in the lives of the very young. Children worry more about pleasing their parents, making and keeping friends, and doing well in school than they do about sex. Children worry about their standing in the family, and about whether they are loved as much as their siblings. They wonder whether there is anything they might say or do that could lead to their being abandoned. Many of the concerns that occupy the minds of the very young have less to do with sex than with thoughts and impulses that affect their relationships with significant figures in their lives.[128]

It may seem obvious, but nonetheless it is worth pointing out that the concerns Cashdan attributes to the very young are also important themes within many of the most popular fairy tales. However, whether these stories and portrayals shape our own understandings of gender roles and sexuality is a matter of continuous debate. For Cashdan, this is true particularly when it comes to understanding sexual matters which may (or may not) be part of a fairy tale's underlying themes. Yet it is the case that sex is a motivating factor for all of these stories. The Disney films discussed in this chapter are not chivalric accounts of courtly love, they are romance stories which tend (with very few excep-

128 Cashdan, p. 12.

155

tions) to culminate in marriage (and even when no marriage takes place for the hero, romantic love coupled with sexual longing is very much part of the story). Demonstrations of sexual longing – such as courting/being courted, kissing (i.e. "love's first kiss"), brief touches of self-grooming (which all of our young heroines do at some stage, such as when Snow White hides behind a curtain in the castle when The Prince begins singing to her, then quickly touches up her hair and straightens her ragged skirt before coming onto the balcony to receive The Prince's declaration of love), and so forth – are all depicted in the Disney films as being perfectly normal and acceptable when they are the result of – or culminate in – feelings of romantic love between two characters. But for Disney films – which despite Walt's idea that, in *Snow White*, he was producing a women's film[129] – have been seen since the start as being at least equally (if not predominately) children's entertainment, depictions of the physical side of a character's sexual longings and sexuality had to be kept in careful check. Even after Walt's day, however, in a later fairy tale film about a prince with no actual name, overt sexual overtones had to be depicted only very symbolically and sparingly, with any feelings of lust – sexual desire not accompanied by true love – laid to rest squarely on the shoulders of the story's villain. But the hero of the film – the Beast – eventually conquers his animal nature by finding true love and learning to be selfless.

It is perhaps a little surprising to realise that a prince with no name could be an important character in a film made as late the so-called Disney Renaissance, but the 1991 film *Beauty and the Beast* – the Disney animation studio's fifth fairy tale film – has as its male lead a character whose name we never learn. We are told of a young prince who is cursed. We hear his servants refer to him as "Your Highness", "Your Grace", and "Master", and he is called, simply, "Beast" by Belle in the few instances where she addresses him by "name". Interestingly, a first name *was* found for the heroine. Granted, "Belle" is the French word for "Beauty", but "Belle" is also a first name sometimes given to women, and so functions for the heroine of the film as such in the fullest sense. But rather than call him "Bête" (perhaps it sounded too much like "Bette", a woman's name), some other name could have been found for him in the same way that a name – Eric – had been found for the prince in Disney's adaptation of Anderson's version of "The Little Mermaid". Likewise, the hero in "Rapunzel" is both given a name – Flynn Rider (or Eugene, which he reveals to be his *real* name) – and a substantial back story for his role in *Tangled* (2010). But the Beast remains "the Beast" or "Beast" in his film, much as The Prince and Prince Charming

129 Robin Allan, *Walt Disney and Europe: European Influences on the Animated Feature Films of Walt Disney* (London: John Libbey & Company Ltd., 1999), pp. 42-43.

never received first names. Unlike these two earlier characters, however, the Beast plays a decidedly more important role in Belle's story, sharing not only the title, but also narrative centrality with the heroine. Indeed, some critics have argued that the Beast overtakes Belle, and that Disney's version of *Beauty and the Beast* becomes *his* story, not hers.

According to those involved in the production of *Beauty and the Beast*, which character was the "real" centre of the narrative was a subject of debate for some time. As Don Hahn later remembered the discussion:

> "It's definitely Belle's story", and others said, "Oh, it's definitely the Beast's story". And then Howard [Ashman] came in one day and said, you know, "It's called 'Beauty and the Beast' – why are we even having this discussion? It can be both: Beauty *and* the Beast!"[130]

Admittedly, this contrasts with a quote from Don Hahn from a *Newsweek* article published in 1991 (the year of the film's release), when he says that "It was Ashman who realized, contrary to tradition, that this had to be Beast's story. We didn't agree with him right away. But he was right. The Beast was the guy with the problem."[131] Frankly, it is hard to know which of Hahn's quote is closer to the truth. Indeed, a huge amount of credit for the shaping of *Beauty and the Beast* is given to Howard Ashman, one of the two lead song writers and an executive producer for the film, who died of AIDS eight months before the film's Hollywood premiere. It is interesting that two contradictory quotes about Ashman's shaping of the narrative (making the Beast central versus having him share the spotlight with Belle) have come from Hahn, himself a producer on *Beauty and the Beast*. Regardless of whether the intention was for the Beast to star or co-star with Belle, the fact is that his position within the narrative is crucial. It is the Beast's back story which opens the film (when we learn why and how he and his servants were cursed), it is his character development which is the major theme of the film, and it is his transformation back into a human which is the climax of the narrative. As Kirk Wise, co-director of *Beauty and the Beast* would describe the Beast in a documentary short on the film's characters, "He's the character who goes through the most growth, he's the character who goes through the most change. Therefore he's really kinda the protagonist. We start with him, we end with him, you know. He's literally the one who has to transform from one physical being to another."[132]

It is that transformation which, arguably, is at the heart of *Beauty and the Beast*, though it could also be argued that, just as the Beast

130 Spoken to camera in the documentary short "Strength of Character"/The Characters, Disc 2, "Cogsworth and Lumiere's Library", from *Walt Disney Pictures Presents Beauty and the Beast, Special Edition – Platinum Edition* (Region 1/NTSC, © Disney Enterprises, Inc., DVD release date October 8, 2002.

131 Quoted by June Cummins, "Romancing the Plot: The Real Beast of Disney's *Beauty and the Beast*", from *Children's Literature Association Quarterly*, Vol. 20, No. 1 (Spring 1995), pp. 23-24.

132 Spoken to camera in the documentary short "Strength of Character"/The Characters.

has to transform from a selfish, angry, tormented soul into someone capable of giving and receiving love, equally Belle must transform herself from the role of loner and outsider (her "place" within her village, a point made very clear by the opening musical number of the film, "Belle") into someone who engages with those around her and actually participates in life (in the beginning of the film, we see her reading about romance; by the second half of the film, she is experiencing romance and true love for the first time, an experience which she describes in a sung internal monologue as "New ... and a bit alarming!"). Belle's transformation is more subtle than the Beast's, which may be why scholars such as June Cummins and Susan Jeffords have either failed to notice it or disregarded it. Belle's changes are internal: she learns to experience life first hand and to communicate with those around her – to let them in so that they can get to know the "real" Belle. The Beast's transformation, however, being as much external as internal, is decidedly impossible to overlook, culminating as it does in his physical transformation as the spell is broken and he becomes human once more. For Glen Keane, the supervising animator for the Beast, his animation of the Beast's physical transformation was nothing more or less than a depiction of the Beast's spiritual transformation – an event which he cast in decidedly religious terms.

> And as I started animating it, I realised that, for me, it's really an expression of my spiritual life. There's a verse in the Bible that says, "If any man is in Christ, he is a new creation. Old things have passed away and all things have become new". [*sic*] And I wrote that on my exposure sheet there as I'm drawing this, 'cause it's really about an inner spiritual transformation that's taking place in the Beast. I saw it as a parable of my own life.[133]

Certainly the scene itself is set apart from the rest of the film by the shower of magical sparks which fall upon the Beast, as well as by the particularly dramatic music which scores the image. The Beast's body is lifted into the sky by an unseen force before being brought slowly back to the balcony where he had lain, presumed by Belle (and the audience) to have died from a stab wound inflicted by Gaston, the film's villain. So not only is the Beast transformed in terms of his shape, he is – to a degree – resurrected by the lifting of the curse, and therefore by the power of Belle's love for him as a response to his love for her. The Biblical passage Keane refers to (but misquotes slightly) is 2 Corinthians 5.17: "Therefore if any man be in Christ, he is a new creature: old things passed away; behold, all things are become new".[134] Yet the metaphor is apt, and supports the idea that the Beast's physical transformation can be linked with his being integrated into the

133 Spoken to camera in the documentary short "Transformation: Glen Keane"/Animation, Disc 2, "Cogsworth and Lumiere's Library", from *Walt Disney Pictures Presents Beauty and the Beast, Special Edition – Platinum Edition* (Region 1/NTSC, © Disney Enterprises, Inc., DVD release date October 8, 2002.

134 From the King James Version of the Bible, Kindle Version, Location 67270 of 72316.

society which – as one is given to understand by the story of how he came to be cursed in the first place – he shunned as beneath him. Indeed, the same part of the Bible quoted by Keane goes on to stress this, in 2 Corinthians 5.19: "To wit, that God was in Christ, reconciling the world unto himself, not imputing their trespasses unto them; and hath committed unto us the word of reconciliation". This idea of the reconciliation of those who had sinned against love, and of their becoming new again, is one which it could be argued is to be found in numerous films of the late 1980s and early 1990s.

Susan Jeffords notes in her discussion of masculinity in *Beauty and the Beast* that this transformation of the lead male character through love and family associations is typical of films of the late 1980s and early 1990s, as the Reagan-era's hard bodies and strong men gave way to the figure of the "New Man". This is exemplified for Jeffords in characters such as John Kimball, played by Arnold Schwarzenegger in the 1990 film *Kindergarten Cop*. In this film, Kimball begins as a hard, angry cop and a loner, operating within the law, but only narrowly, and only when the law does not stop him from enacting his own ideas of justice. Over the course of the film, however, Kimball (and, arguably, Schwarzenegger's persona alongside this now iconic Schwarzenegger character) transforms into a beloved and successful kindergarten teacher and family man, a vital part of the community which takes him in, and an upholder of the law.[135] According to Jeffords, "*Kindergarten Cop* anticipates the endings of many 1991 films that are resolved through a man's return to his family. ... In these films, families provide both the motivation for and the resolution of changing masculine heroisms."[136] For Jeffords, *Beauty and the Beast* fits neatly within this larger trend found in live-action films: "The Beast is The New Man, the one who can transform himself from the hardened, muscle-bound, domineering man of the '80s into the considerate, loving, and self-sacrificing man of the '90s. The Beast's external appearance is here more than a horrific guise that repels pretty women, but instead [is] a burden, one that he must carry until he is set free, free to be the man he truly can be."[137]

For Jeffords, the Beast is a beast because his surroundings and his society made him that way. As she puts it, "what men thought they were supposed to be – strong, protective, powerful, commanding – has somehow backfired and become their own evil curse".[138] Indeed, central to her argument is that the film serves as an apologia for 1980s "Hard Men": 1980s American values made them that way, but a post-Reagan America – a "kinder,

135 Susan Jeffords, "The Curse of Masculinity: Disney's *Beauty and the Beast*", in Bell, Elizabeth, Lynda Haas, and Laura Sells (eds.). *From Mouse to Mermaid: The Politics of Film, Gender, and Culture* (Indianapolis: Indiana University Press, 1995), pp. 161-172.

136 Jeffords, p. 163.

137 Jeffords, p. 170.

138 Jeffords, p. 171.

gentler nation" (to quote from George H. W. Bush's 1988 RNC acceptance speech) – will let him overcome those old, hard ways, so that "all things are become new" (2 Cor.5:17). Certainly, it is an interesting notion, and could be said to fit within an America which could begin to hope for a genuine thaw in the Cold War in the late 1980s. This is the mood depicted by George Bush Sr. in his acceptance speech (for becoming the party's presidential candidate) to the Republican National Convention in New Orleans on 18 August 1988. He talks about the United States' "new relationship with the Soviet Union", and in talking about how "weakness and ambivalence lead to war", he makes his stance – at least at that moment – perfectly clear: "My life has been lived in the shadow of war – I almost lost my life in one. I hate war. I love peace. We have peace. And I am not going to let anyone take it away from us."[139] The irony of this, of course, is that just two and a half years later, on 16 January 1991, Bush Sr., in declaring war on Iraq at the start of what would become known as Gulf War 1, became the first US president since FDR officially to declare war on another country. Yet an unintended outcome of the Gulf War period – ranging from the Iraqi invasion of Kuwait on 2 August 1990 until the declaration of a ceasefire and the end of Operation Desert Storm on 28 February 1991, and therefore very much in the background of the period under discussion here – is a theme which mirrors the notion that the Hard Man is transformed by love and acceptance and re-integrated into the family. This is the conscious effort made to apologise for the treatment of Vietnam veterans, whose sacrifices and bravery were first acknowledged publically – and most significantly, popularly – as an outcome of the protests being made against a US-led invasion of Iraq in 1990/91. Anti-war protestors, clearly operating with the cultural and historical memory of the anti-Vietnam protests and their (as it would be seen later) victimization of returning Vietnam veterans very much in the forefront of their minds, were always careful to stress their support for the troops, even if not for the war itself.[140] Love and acceptance, it would seem, were being highlighted in bringing forgotten and abused warriors in from the cold, just as the Beast's spiritual and physical renewal was enabled by his newfound ability to give and receive love.

But *who* causes the Beast's transformation? Does he transform himself, as Jeffords describes, in a way which sideline's Belle's importance to the narrative? Indeed, the angst expressed by some scholars at the idea that the Beast might become central (or even just more central) to the story is interesting in and of itself; why is it so upsetting to them? Is it purely on feminist grounds, as

139 Text from George Herbert Walker Bush's acceptance speech at the Republican National Convention, New Orleans, 18 August 1988. Found at http://www.presidency.ucsb.edu/ws/index.php?pid=25955.

140 For an extended discussion of this, see Thomas D. Beamish et al, "Who Supports the Troops? Vietnam, the Gulf War, and the Making of Collective Memory", from *Social Problems*, Vol. 42, No. 3 (August 1995), pp. 344-360.

some (especially Cummins) have implied? Cummins claims that making the Beast more central to the narrative makes this film "the same old story, a romance plot that robs female characters of self-determination and individuality. Not at all a feminist movie, Disney's *Beauty and the Beast* slips easily into the mold of almost all other popular versions of fairy tales; that is, it encourages young viewers to believe that true happiness for women exists only in the arms of a prince and that their most important quest is finding that prince."[141] Frankly, I think this is a rather odd interpretation of the film – an interpretation that says a great deal more about Cummins' own prejudices against Disney feature animation than it does about the film itself. Belle's choices are limited in her world, which unquestionably is characterised as existing well before the twentieth (and possibly before the nineteenth) century: she lives in a "poor provincial town" where she is described by the other villagers as "odd" and "peculiar" because she goes about the village "With a dreamy, far-off look/And her nose stuck in a book". Belle's worth is seen by those in the village (especially Gaston) as being primarily in her looks; this is also true, arguably, within the Beast's castle. The fact that she is a girl – and a pretty girl at that – causes Cogsworth, Lumiere, Mrs. Potts and the rest immediately to fixate on the idea that she will be the one to break the spell. It does not occur to them to assess her character and her temperament. Yet Belle defies the expectations of those around her: despite the villagers' assessment of her (of which she is aware, as is demonstrated by her asking her father whether he thinks she is "odd"), she refuses to change who she is or what she wants out of life. Far from going on some "quest" to find a prince to marry, she sets out on her own – it never seems even to occur to her to ask for help from the men (or women) in the village – to find her lost father. When she finds him, she trades her freedom for his, and resigns herself to spending the rest of her life in a prison cell in a tower of the Beast's castle; it hardly sounds like someone who is bound and determined to find herself a prince to marry. The fact that, as it turns out, the Beast is a prince under a curse and will one day be her true love ... frankly, according to the narrative, that is luck and/or destiny, but it is most definitely *not* Belle's design, nor does the narrative imply that it was. Instead, Belle is characterised very specifically by the song lyrics of the film's opening number ("Belle") and the mise-en-scène (whereas the village and its inhabitants are dressed in earth tones, Belle wears a blue dress and white apron, marking her as visually different from those around her) as different – and misunderstood – by those around her. They do not seem to know how to understand someone who is beautiful yet is also independent, intelligent and strong willed. As Marina Warner points out,

> This fairytale film is more vividly aware of contemporary sexual politics than any made before; it consciously picked out a strand in the tale's history and deliberately developed it for an audiences of mothers who grew up with Betty Friedan and Gloria Steinem, who had daughters who listened to Madonna and Sinead O'Connor. Linda Woolverton's screenplay put forward a heroine of spirit who finds romance on her own terms. Beyond this prima facie storyline, the interpretation contained many subtexts, both knotty and challenging, about changing concepts of paternal authority and rights, about permitted expressions of male desire, and prevailing notions in the quarrel about nature/nurture. Above all, the film placed before the 1990s audience Hollywood's cunning domestication of feminism itself.[142]

While Warner goes on to talk about how, ultimately the Beast does end up stealing the show, she does not imply that this is necessarily a problem: his becoming a film character – his being represented in a visual medium – in itself is enough of an edge, given that his physical appearance must always be more unusual – more striking – than the human form Belle possesses throughout.

But equally, the Beast's looks overshadow his inner self, and cause all who see him but do not know him to take for granted the notion that he is a danger who threatens their very lives. That his appearance troubles the Beast himself becomes evident when we see the west wing of his castle – the one part of the castle which Belle is immediately and expressly forbidden from exploring. Mirrors are smashed, a portrait of him in his human form (painted prior to his transformation into a beastly form, one assumes) has been slashed and torn so that it no longer is obvious what he once looked like, and a chaos which speaks of a furious, destructive, rampaging animal litters the forbidden wing of the castle. Indeed, that Belle is forbidden to go to the west wing of the castle, but does any way out of pure curiosity, only to be caught and terrorized by the Beast when he discovers her there, hints at the story of Bluebeard. Though this theme is not developed explicitly in the film, traces of the idea do linger about the edges of the narrative. Its inclusion at this stage of the film merely hints at what, at that point in the film, is the Beast's inherent threat against others from both a patriarchal and a class position: he is a prince, and Belle and her father are commoners, and so therefore are under his authority. Likewise, he is male, and so assumes as his "due" a position of authority in relation to Belle. These ideas of superiority and inferiority fade, overall, as the narrative progresses. They must fade, if the Beast can transform spiritually, thereby allowing for his physical transformation. As

142 Marina Warner, *From the Beast to the Blonde: On Fairy Tales and Their Tellers* (London: Vintage, 1995), p. 313.

the Beast learns to love, he lets go of his need to assert his dominance over those around him. This allows them – and especially allows Belle – to recognise her growing feelings for the Beast as something which, far from being "new, and a bit alarming", are in fact integral components to a "tale as old as time". Even more interesting is the similarity noted by Marina Warner between the Beast, as he is depicted by the Disney version, and the North American buffalo, a visual linking which "tightens the Beast's connections to current perceptions of natural good – for the American buffalo, like the grizzly, represents the lost innocence of the plains before man came to plunder. So the celluloid Beast's beastliness thrusts in two contradictory directions; though he is condemned for his 'animal' rages, he also epitomizes the primordial virtues of the wild".[143] This visual link with a real-life beast which is such a deep-rooted American icon carries with it connotations not only of great strength and of what Warner describes as a "lost innocence". It also encourages strong feelings of sympathy for an animal which was hunted piteously and cruelly nearly to the point of extinction by an invading, colonizing movement westward, an uncivilized enforcement of "civilization" and encroachment which is mirrored and enacted in the film by Gaston and the villagers. Just as modern Americans have learned to feel sorrow (and even a degree of shame) for the atrocities committed against the buffalo – and the Native Americans – in the nineteenth century in particular, so too are we moved to align our sympathies and allegiance with the Beast – and with the enchanted servants who look after his castle and fight the invading (white) villagers.

Yet despite all of the sympathy we feel for him, and despite his centrality to the narrative, even when the Beast becomes human again, we never learn his name. He remains, semi-anonymously, "the Beast" in our minds, in a way which, arguably, preserves his symbolic function. Once he is no longer beastly in form, calling him "the Beast" seems inaccurate. Thankfully for our purposes, we see the Beast as a human being for only the last few minutes of the film, and we hear less from him (and almost nothing from Belle). The final lines of the film come from Maurice, Mrs. Potts, and Chip, and are about how Belle and the Beast are going to live happily ever after; the hint in a change in *all* of the characters' previous sleeping arrangements comes from Chip, when he asks Mrs. Potts, in a slightly irritated tone, "Do I still have to sleep in the cupboard?" Interestingly, the film ends not with a marriage, but with a waltz between Belle and the character formerly known as "the Beast". No mention is made of a wedding, just that they

143 Warner, *Beast to Blonde*, p. 315.

are going to live "happily ever after". A wedding may be presumed, but it is not implied.

Phillip, Eric, and Naveen

In 1959, *Sleeping Beauty* would debut to somewhat mixed reviews, many of which, even when they said good things about *Sleeping Beauty*, nonetheless would compare it unfavourably with *Snow White and the Seven Dwarfs*. *Harrison's Reports* claims that "As an entertainment it should go over big with the youngsters, for its ingredients of fantasy, comedy, romance and villainy, all presented in the inimitable Disney style and culminating with good triumphant over evil, undoubtedly will enthral them. It is doubtful, however, if adults will find as much satisfaction in 'Sleeping Beauty' as they did in 'Snow White and the Seven Dwarfs', with which this latest effort will assuredly be compared because both stories are in many respects similar."[144] Bosley Crowther had a similar criticism of the film, saying that it "... is more than a little reminiscent of his first and perhaps most memorable animated feature, 'Snow White and the Seven Dwarfs'. Evidently, Mr. Disney is sentimental in his remembrance of things past."[145] Interestingly, Crowther carries on to claim numerous similarities to *Snow White* (though in such a way as to reflect unfavourably upon *Sleeping Beauty*), perhaps going a bit too far when he claims of the leading ladies of the two films, "The princess looks so much like Snow White they could be a couple of Miss Rheingolds[146] separated by three or four years".[147] (This about a plump brunette and a lithe blond! As for the Miss Rheingolds, they were notable for their ethnic diversity, as was all Rheingold Beer advertising, so – again – it's a strange thing for Crowther to say, unless he is trying very specifically to connect with a particular portion of his readership.) But when he turns his attention to Prince Phillip, however, his tone becomes decidedly more favourable:

> But Mr. Disney has pepped up "Sleeping Beauty" with a chase and a dragon fight that make a patty-cake party of Snow White's famous flight through the woods. When the prince is liberated from the witch's dungeon and is chased by her gibbering guards ... there is plenty of fearful action to make the kiddies cower in their chairs.
>
> And when he has at the witch, turned into a dragon, it will make a few adults groan. Mr. Disney here reaches the apex of his build-up of animated horror.[148]

This early review of *Sleeping Beauty*, published the day after the film's New York City premiere, hints at the fact that, whatever fault some viewers may have found with the film (and it definitely

144 Anonymous, *Harrison's Reports*, Vol. XLI, No. 5 (Saturday, January 31, 1959), p. 18.

145 Bosley Crowther, Film Review of *Sleeping Beauty*, 18 February 1959. From *New York Times Film Reviews, 1913-1968, vol. 5 (1959-68)* (New York: *New York Times* and Arno Press, 1970), p. 3109.

146 "Miss Rheingold" was an annual pageant (spanning 1940 to 1965) which elected one young woman to serve as the spokes model and ambassador for Rheingold Beer, a New York beer which was sold originally from 1883 to 1976.

147 Crowther, p. 3109.

148 Crowther, p. 3110.

was not one of their most successful film releases), Prince Phillip's key scenes are mentioned with praise.[149]

It is very much the case that the third prince to appear in a Disney animated feature film (after The Prince in *Snow White* and Prince Charming in *Cinderella*) brings a great deal more action to the narrative than either of his predecessors. Far from being a book-ending device or a mere prize for the heroine and MacGuffin for the audience, Phillip's personality is much more developed, as was his physicality. As Charles Solomon notes, "Most of the animation of Prince Philip [*sic*] was done by Milt Kahl, who made him a much more dynamic figure than the Princes in 'Snow White' and 'Cinderella.'" He goes on to say, however, of Phillip and Aurora, that "Both human characters seem too close to the live-action reference footage to be very interesting in animation. Although rendered with consummate skill, their waltz in the forest seems dull."[150] Early on, he is shown to have a sense of humour, wrinkling his nose disdainfully at the infant Princess Aurora the first time he sees her when he is a small boy. When we next see him, this time as a young man, again he is shown to have energy and liveliness about him. Even in his first meeting with Briar Rose (Princess Aurora's alias when she believes herself to be a peasant), he uses a light, witty manner with her, teasing her that he isn't a stranger, and that they have in fact met before: "You said so yourself – once upon a dream!" Yet Phillip is shown very quickly to have emotional depth as well; as he waltzes with Briar Rose, it is obvious that he is falling in love with her. Likewise, his brave fight against the evil Maleficent shows him to be a man of strength and honour. Even before this, however, his determination to marry the girl he loves, and not be forced to marry the princess to whom his father betrothed him (at this point, he does not yet realise that Princess Aurora and Briar Rose are the same person) shows a strength of character which is much missing from his princely predecessor, Prince Charming. In fact, his will is so strong that he *almost* exhibits Jedi mind powers twenty-eight years before *Star Wars* (1977)! Having announced to his father that he has fallen in love with a peasant girl and that *she* will be his bride, he has the following conversation with his father, King Hubert, who (unsurprisingly) is adamant that Phillip do his duty and marry Princess Aurora:

Phillip: Now, Father, you're living in the past – this is the fourteenth century! Nowadays ...

Hubert: Nowadays I'm *still* the king! And I command you to come to your senses!

Phillip: And marry the girl I love!

Hubert: Exactly!

149 Charles Solomon, *The History of Animation: Enchanted Drawings* (New York: Wings Books, 1994), p. 200.

150 Solomon, p. 198.

> Phillip: (laughing) Good-bye, Father!
>
> Hubert: Good-bye, Father! Marry the girl you ... No! No!

Happily for all involved, Phillip and Aurora have fallen in love with one another even before they realise who they are to each other, and after Phillip has overcome the curse on Aurora (with the help of the three good fairies who are Aurora's godmothers and raised her for her first sixteen years). His defiance of his father's orders is rendered redundant. Nonetheless, this is a prince who shows a great deal more vivaciousness and activity than the eponymous heroine of the film, so much so that, by the time he has been shackled in Maleficent's dungeon, the story very much becomes his: while the Sleeping Beauty ... well ... sleeps, Prince Phillip battles his way out of the depths of Maleficent's castle, jumps onto his gallant horse, Sampson (a white horse no less!), and does battle with a Maleficent who has transformed herself into a dragon so ferocious that the animation bringing her to life has been described as having "a remarkable, almost primal power, rarely equalled in animation – or live action".[151] He slays Maleficent, then makes his way to Aurora's chamber, where he awakens her with a kiss. After what must have been a very long, tiring day, he nonetheless summons up the energy (and the gallantry) to escort his love downstairs to the throne room, where she is reunited with her parents. Phillip and Aurora then waltz as the film ends, as all look on approvingly.

Though the film in which this prince appears may not have been a success during its first release in 1959, Phillip as a type of prince – active, sharing a large proportion of screen time with the heroine, and with a well-developed personality – would set a new standard for Disney princes. When we come to the fourth Disney prince, Prince Eric in *The Little Mermaid* (1989), we get another action-oriented hero whose relationship with his future bride is hugely important to the narrative of the film.

Again, when we first meet Prince Eric (which we do before Ariel first encounters him), we see a happy, athletic, lively young man. Far from standing on rank and ceremony, Prince Eric is seen not only interacting with the sailors on his ship, but working along-side them amongst the ship's rigging. His dog, Max, a sheepdog with wild, bushy, somewhat unkempt fur and a boisterous, friendly manner, serves as a mirror for the prince's personality: Eric may be more polished looking than his dog, but he is just as friendly and down to earth. This is somewhat bemoaned by Grimsby, Eric's tutor, himself a much more stuffy, aristocratic figure. Nonetheless, he clearly supports and cares about Prince

151 Solomon, p. 200.

Eric, worrying about the fact that their trip (when we see them on the ship, they are returning from a visit to another kingdom where Eric was introduced to a princess it was hoped he might marry) was unsuccessful and wanting the young prince to find a wife and settle down. Later in this same voyage, we see Grimsby present Eric with a birthday present – a magnificent statue of Eric in a heroic, "princely" stance – and though Eric is polite about the gift, it is clear that it is not at all something he would want; in the role of Eric's animus, Max's reaction – to growl at the statue – accompanied by the four-note non-diegetic musical reference to losing (or winning a "booby prize") is a truer reflection of Eric's distaste for such an ostentatious and narcissistic gift. Though once we see him in his castle Eric appears comfortable within the surroundings of his home, he seems to feel equally at ease scaling the riggings of the ship and dancing and playing a flute during a party amongst the sailors. When a hurricane comes up suddenly and puts all in danger, Eric is right in the middle of the action, grabbing the wheel to steer the ship, and when the ship is broken up and sinking, he helps to save the lives of those on board, to include risking his life to save Max from the fire ragging on the ruins that have yet to sink.

He saves Max, but in the process is thrown into the sea when an explosion destroys what is left of the ship. It is at this point that he is rescued by Ariel, who has been watching him surreptitiously throughout the party and the storm. Unconscious from the explosion, Eric is brought to shore by Ariel, who stays with him until he is just beginning to return to consciousness. He sees – and more importantly, hears – her very briefly before she has to scuttle quickly back into the sea before Grimsby and Max find Eric and bring him to his palace. He has not registered her face fully, but he remembers Ariel's beautiful voice, and becomes determined to find and marry the mysterious "girl" who rescued him.

Yet when he first meets Ariel after she has made her deal with Ursula the Sea Witch and traded her voice for a pair of legs, Eric fails to recognise her as the one who saved him. It is clear that it is her voice – emblematic of her personality and her "self" in modern discourse – which Eric remembers best. Walking along the beach with Max, he is playing the melody of "Part of Your World" (which Ariel was singing to him as he regained consciousness) on his flute before remarking to his dog, "That voice – I can't get it out of my head! I've looked everywhere, Max … where could she be?" It is shortly after this that Ariel, still wobbly on her new legs, and dressed in the remnants of a sail tied on with a rope, is discovered by Max, who first encountered her as she clung to the side of the ship during Eric's birthday party, and who recognises her instantly (again, Max stands in for Eric's animus *and* for his intuition; his irritation when Eric does not recognise Ariel is palpable). When Eric first sees her, it seems initially that he recognises her: upon seeing Ariel on the same beach where she left him, he says to her that she seems familiar, asking whether or not they've met. Ariel (who at this stage has no voice) nods enthusiastically; he exclaims, grasping her hands, "I knew it! You're the one! The one I've been looking for! What's your name?!" But when Ariel is unable to speak her name to him, and he realises that she has no voice, his disappointment is evident; his response is "Oh. You couldn't be who I thought". Nonetheless, he brings Ariel back to his palace, where she is bathed, dressed in human clothes, and given her own room. She is his guest, and he treats her well, having her to dine with Grimsby and himself as a member of his household.

His fondness for – and growing attraction to – Ariel becomes increasingly evident. Indeed, had it not been for Ursula's hench "men" (the electric eels Flotsam and Jetsam) intervening directly and capsizing the row boat Ariel and Eric are floating in during the song "Kiss the Girl" (in which, as the song builds to its climax, Eric very nearly does kiss Ariel, which would have made her human permanently), Eric might well have fallen for Ariel without realising that she was the one who had saved him from drowning. But once the mood is broken, he makes no further romantic overture towards her. Later that evening, Grimsby – in a fairly fatherly moment with his student – gives Eric the advice that "far better than any dream girl is one of flesh and blood. One warm, and caring, and right before your eyes." As Grimsby says this last bit, he gestures upward, and as Eric's eyes (and the camera) follow the direction of the gesture, we see Ariel in the window of her room. Eric thinks a moment, throws his flute into the sea (an interesting move from a Freudian perspective, perhaps), and begins to head, we can only presume, to Ariel's room to propose to her. But at that moment he is stopped by the sound of a beautiful voice – Ariel's voice, being used by Ursula, who has disguised herself as a young human woman in order to keep Ariel from being kissed by Eric and becoming permanently human. He falls under the spell of the voice – literally, it seems, given the strange glowing mist that enters his eyes and then shines out of his pupils – and, in a hypnotic trance, we see him the next morning, arm-in-arm with "Vanessa" (Ursula's disguise), ordering an amazed Grimsby (who believes that the young "woman" is the "dream girl" Eric sought) to organise a wedding for that evening. We, Ariel, and her friends think all is lost and that Ariel is doomed, when Scuttle the Seagull realises who Vanessa is. Ariel and her friends immediately go into action to save Eric, and after some effort, Ariel's voice (which is contained in a shell worn around Vanessa's throat) is freed and returned to her, also breaking Eric's trance and allowing him – finally – to recognise that the young woman he has spent the last three days with is indeed the one who had rescued him. He is just about to kiss Ariel when the sun sets, and Ariel is transformed back into a mermaid, grabbed by Ursula (who has now returned to her octopus form), and dragged away from Eric into the sea.

But, of course, all is not lost. Eric has one final chance to prove his love and his heroism, and he does not fail. In the sea battle that ensues once Ursula has managed to capture King Triton's powers, Eric, finding himself on a wrecked ship that Ursula has brought to the surface, uses its broken bowsprit to stab and kill Ursula, breaking her spell, returning Triton's powers to him, and freeing all of the cursed merpeople who had languished in Ursula's "garden" for years. He nearly drowns again, however, and Ariel returns him to the beach once more, and sits watching him on a rock. Triton, realising that Ariel and Eric truly love one another – and that Eric is worthy of Ariel's love – transforms Ariel back into a human (this time making sure to give her a glamorous, sparkling, periwinkle evening gown so that she will not make her way onto the beach nearly naked, as she did when Ursula transformed her), where she and Eric immediately run to one another and embrace, finally sharing their first kiss. The scene transforms so that, as the camera pulls back from the close up of their faces, we see that they are in their wedding clothes and that they have just been married. Both the humans and merpeople celebrate, and Ariel bids her father (Triton) farewell and goes to be with Eric, who bows to Triton before Ariel takes his arm and they wave to Triton and the merfolk once more before sharing a final kiss as the film ends.

Eric's role in the narrative, clearly, is a significant one. It may officially be Ariel's story, but it is Eric – and his love as expressed by a first kiss – which has huge potential (if ultimately unrealised) power in the narrative since it is this which will allow Ariel to become human permanently. For some, the film's "message" struggles to attain feminist credentials, and this is a highly problematic aspect for them.[152] That Sells' critique of the feminist symbolic value of the voice in *The Little Mermaid* is problematic is something which I have argued already in my book *Good Girls & Wicked Witches*.[153] Building upon this (and addressing the issue

152 For more on this, see Laura Sells, "'Where Do the Mermaids Stand?': Voice and Body in the Little Mermaid", in Bell, Haas, and Sells, *From Mouse to Mermaid*, pp. 175-192.

153 Davis, pp. 179-181.

of Eric's role in the narrative more closely), it is interesting to note that it is Ursula – the villain of the film – who assigns Eric with the power to make Ariel permanently human by bestowing a kiss – an act which can be seen as (and in a wedding ceremony certainly is the symbolic representation of) a sexual act (Eric's kiss – a kiss of romantic love – will be motivated as much by his sexual desire for Ariel as it is by his emotional connection with her). If one is not paying attention, ascribing Eric such power means that it is Ariel's role as a sexual object which must be exploited for her to become fully human. But – and this is important – this is *not* what happens: just as Eric is *about* to kiss her, the sun sets and Ariel becomes a mermaid once more. Eric, therefore, is *not* the one to bestow permanent humanity upon Ariel. Subsequently, throughout the battle with Ursula, Ariel remains a mermaid, and separated from Eric by the ocean waves stirred up by Ursula, who has taken King Triton's crown and trident and is now ruler of the oceans. It is later in the narrative, after having worked hard, regained her voice, and suffered for her love, that Ariel's father, King Triton, uses his power (which Ariel and Eric have battled to return to him) to grant Ariel her dearest wish. Rather than owe Eric her humanity, she has earned it from her father, who not only bestows it as a reward, but himself sees it as his act of letting Ariel go – of recognising her as an adult, no longer his little girl to be protected. Admittedly, that humanity is given to her by her father, the god of the sea, does have potentially strong patriarchal overtones. But, at least this way, she is able to begin her marriage to Eric on an equal footing ... figuratively and literally. So, ultimately, Eric's role is still, like the first two Disney princes, that of a prize bequeathed to the heroine by dent of her determination, steadfastness, and faith that all will turn out well. But he is a much stronger, better prize than The Prince or Prince Charming: he has come to know his princess gradually, and both Eric and Ariel have had to fight to be with each other. His role is not that merely of a catalyst or MacGuffin, either; Ariel's desire to be human – expressed most explicitly in the song "Part of Your World", comes before she has ever seen Eric. Her decision to go to the Sea Witch for help is motivated partially out of her specific desire to be with Eric, but also by her older desire to be human. But her decision's most decisive catalyst is the destruction of her collection of human artefacts by her father, and her fury that he could do this to her; going to the Sea Witch to become human, ultimately (at least at this stage of the narrative) is Ariel's rejection of her father (and this could have been played by the narrative as a petulant act, but is not; Ariel's behaviour is dignified and determined, not bratty or childish). Eric has very little to do with it. His role initially *is* that of a prize, but it evolves during the film into that of a partner: in the final shots of the two of them together, Eric and Ariel stand side by side as equals, before equally sharing a passionate kiss.

Kisses in fairy tales are very important, powerful magic, and the need for a kiss – either the first kiss of true love or a kiss from a specific person – can have the weight of life and death for the one who needs to be kissed. A kiss awoke Snow White and Sleeping Beauty from coma-like trances ("sleeping death" and all that), and had it been administered in time, a kiss from her prince would have made the Little Mermaid permanently human. But in the case of our final prince, it is *he* who needs a kiss, not the heroine. But it does *not* have to be the kiss of true love; for him, it just has to be given by a princess. As the narrative makes clear, *any* princess – even a temporary, Mardi Gras princess – will be good enough to transform Prince Naveen from a frog back into a human.

The 2009 film *The Princess and the Frog* drew most of its attention due to the fact that the film's heroine, Tiana, is a black woman from 1920s New Orleans. Some criticized her various name changes (from Maddy to Tiana; some said Maddy sounded too much like "Mammy"; others had no problem with Maddy – short for Madeline – but thought Tiana sounded weird and made up). Others had no problem with that, but were opposed to her original occupation: chambermaid to a New Orleans debutant. Her occupation was changed to that of a waitress. Even the title came under scrutiny, since the original title, *The Frog Princess*, was thought possibly to be insulting to the French (!).[154] Clearly, such alterations to the original version of the character were inspired by a sensitivity (arguably a hypersensitivity) to racial stereotyping in the film.[155] Finally, it was pointed out by some critics that the first African-American Disney princess spends most of her time on screen not as a black woman, but as a green frog.[156] Neal A. Lester writes that, "Many noted that the first and only African-American princess, unlike other Disney princesses, is not a princess by birth but rather becomes a princess through marriage to a prince".[157] This, of course, is untrue: Cinderella, though from what seems to be the gentry, was nonetheless not a princess until she married Prince Charming; Belle was (at best) a middle-class girl from a "poor, provincial town" until she married the Beast (something we never actually see happen in the film, though, so – unlike Tiana – she never *actually* achieves the rank of princess on screen). Admittedly, princesses by birth (six prior to the 2009 release of *The Princess and the Frog*, plus Rapunzel in *Tangled* the

154 Anonymous, "Protests Come Early to Disney's 'Princess,'" *Studio Briefing*, 11 May 2007. Article found at http://www.imdb.com/news/sb/2007-05-11/#film3.

155 Sarita McCoy Gregory, "Disney's Second Line: New Orleans, Racial Masquerade, and the Reproduction of Whiteness in *The Princess and the Frog*, from *The Journal of African American Studies*, Vol. 14 (2010), p. 442.

156 Ajay Gehlawat, "The Strange Case of *The Princess and the Frog*: Passing and the Elision of Race", in *The Journal of African American Studies*, Vol. 14 (2010), p. 417.

157 Neal A. Lester, "Disney's *The Princess and the Frog*: The Pride, the Pressure, and the Politics of Being a First", in *The Journal of American Culture*, Vol. 33, No. 4 (December 2010), p. 297.

following year) outnumber those who become princesses when they marry (Tiana is the third to marry into royalty). But it is her *lack* of royal status the first time she kisses Naveen that leads to the unfolding of their love story.

According to the story as it is laid out in the Disney version, in order to be restored to his human form, the frog prince must be kissed by a princess. When Naveen (in frog form) sees Tiana (in human form), she is dressed as a princess (in finery borrowed from her friend Charlotte) for the La Bouffs' masquerade ball (at which Tiana is serving beignets, and accidentally gets food spilled all over her original costume, more obviously a costume because she is dressed as more of a medieval princess). Naveen believes that she is dressed as a princess because she really is one, though, and so persuades her to kiss him (promising her the money to begin her restaurant as a reward) in order to restore him to human form (presumably she believes him because he is a talking frog). But because Tiana is *not* a princess – in fact she is from a lower-middle-class (at best) black family in pre-Civil Rights New Orleans – the spell backfires; rather than her kiss breaking the spell, it drags her into it, and she, too, becomes a frog. Forced to team up initially for safety and to find help in breaking the spell, the two begin to learn about each other, growing to like and care about each other. Naveen, who has never worked a day in his life (and in fact seems to have gone to such lengths to avoid responsibility that his parents have disinherited him so as to force him out into the world to learn to survive) learns from Tiana the value of a strong work ethic, some self-sufficiency, and the good side of roots and responsibility. Tiana, who works day and night in two different waitressing jobs, saves as much of her earnings as she can (to put toward a down payment on a restaurant of her own), foregoes time off with her friends, and even, we learn later, has never danced before. She learns from him to enjoy life, to relax, and that there is more to life than work; work is good, and important, but the most important thing is love. While still frogs, Naveen and Tiana realise that they have fallen in love with each other.

Initially, they are given by Mama Odie the hope that Tiana's friend Charlotte – who is Mardi Gras princess that year (since her father, "Big Daddy" La Bouff, has been declared Mardi Gras King) – is princess enough to kiss Naveen and restore both Naveen and Tiana to human form. The catch is that it must be done by midnight, because once Mardi Gras is over, Charlotte will no longer be a "princess". Realising the situation – and that Tiana and Naveen are in love – Charlotte is happy to help them, no strings attached. Unfortunately, just as she picks up Naveen to kiss him, the clock strikes midnight; as of that second, she is no longer princess enough to kiss him and break the spell (though, apparently, she is still princess enough to be protected from the spell; unlike Tiana, she does not turn into a frog when she kisses Naveen; and she kisses him several times to try and break the spell, as the lipstick marks left all over Naveen's frog mouth comically attest). Though a bit disappointed, Tiana and Naveen are okay: as they tell Ray (their Cajun firefly friend):

> Tiana: "We're staying frogs, Ray".
> Naveen: "And we're staying together".

We see them shortly afterward (once Ray, who has died, is laid to rest), in a bayou-set wedding, surrounded by all of the swamp animals who have become their friends, being married by Mama Odie. She pronounces them "frog and wife", and they kiss. Instantly, they are restored to human form: now that they are married, Tiana is a *true* princess, and so her kiss to Naveen breaks the spell for them both. That this is *especially* empowering for Tiana is something which seems to have gone unnoticed, by and large, by those writing about the film: Naveen may make Tiana a princess, but Tiana – and her kiss – is what makes them both human again. But by this stage, their transformation is just a bonus: they are so consumed with their kiss that it is only after it is finished that they realise that they are both human again (and are visibly startled). They realise why the spell was broken, but they're too busy being in love to focus on it too much:

> Tiana: "You just kissed yourself a princess!"
> Naveen: (humorously seductive) "And I'm about to kiss her again!"

The scene then fades into a very similar mise-en-scene, but this time within a church, where the couple, watched by their family and friends, are married once more in a human ceremony. Shortly afterward, we see that the lessons each has learned from the other – and that they are a team – have continued. For the first time, we actually get a glimpse of the couple's life *after* the wedding, and it is exactly as one would wish. We see them in "normal" clothes in the Fenner Brothers' real estate office, where Tiana gives them the money to buy the mill she has hoped all along to transform into her restaurant. Clearly – in a detail which evidently has been missed by some commentators[158] – it is *her* money (not money from Naveen or his parents) that she is using, as it is still in the collection of red Bissman's coffee cans that we

158 Gehlawat, p. 426, footnote 21.

first saw in her dresser drawer at the beginning of the film, no doubt intended to show that Tiana is still a strong, self-support-ing, independent woman even within her marriage to Naveen. What "persuades" the Fenner brothers, this time, to accept Tiana's down payment is not Naveen, but rather Louis, the jazz trumpet-playing alligator they befriended in the bayou, who stands next to the brothers, his "arms" folded across his chest, and growls menacingly at them. The brothers quickly accept Tiana's payment and hand her the key. As the montage continues, we see Tiana and Naveen standing outside the mill they now own; Tiana lifts a hammer, Naveen rolls up his sleeves, and the two set to work transforming the broken-down old building into the restaurant of her dreams; the only change is that, instead of the sign out front saying "Tiana's Place", it now reads "Tiana's Palace" (no doubt a nod to her new status as a princess). But inside, the menus still say "Tiana's Place": the front cover is the picture Tiana has cherished all these years, and the back cover is a photo from her childhood of Tiana with her parents, her father at the centre of the shot. The symbolism enacted by the building is clear: outside, it may be a princess' palace, but inside, it is still the same Tiana. Only now, thanks to Naveen, she's able to laugh and dance and enjoy her success. And thanks to Tiana, Naveen can enjoy both working in the restaurant (we see him presenting with a flourish a covered platter at the table where Tiana's mother and Naveen's parents are sitting). Not only are Tiana and Naveen happy in their work in the restaurant, but Louis the alligator is, too: we see him on stage with (presumably his) band, "The Firefly Five Plus Lou" (a reference to the "Firehouse Five Plus Two", the famous Dixieland jazz band born from the Disney animation studio's staff, mainly from the story and animation departments), living out his dream of playing trumpet in a real jazz band. Naveen and Tiana join him on stage, and then are seen dancing on the roof of their restaurant, where they enjoy a kiss. The camera pulls back, showing their restaurant at the "centre" of New Orleans, pans upward to the sky, where we see Ray and "Evangeline" (the evening star, which Ray had believed was his true love; after his death, a second star appears next to "Evan-geline", however, lending credence to his belief and showing him to be united forever with his true love, just as Tiana and Naveen are), and then the film ends.

As for Naveen (since we are here to talk about princes), he, too, came under criticism as a character, mainly because of his ethnic and racial ambiguity.[159] Ajay Gehlawat points out that "While it is clear that Naveen is a foreigner, it is, again, unclear exactly where he is from. While sporting an Indian name (in Hindi,

[159] For more on this, see Lester, p. 300.

'Naveen' means new, which would technically make him Disney's 'new prince'), his accent and diction seem more European – 'Is beautiful, no?' – and he clearly understands French, translating the French lyrics of the Creole firefly Raymond's song for Tiana. Similarly, his term for the frog prince – 'fraggiputo' – seems to invoke a European-esque lexicon."[160] Gehlawat also argues more than once that Naveen's mother is wearing an Indian sari in the two shots we have of her and Naveen's father.[161] However, if one looks closely, it is evident that both of Naveen's parents are wearing identical crowns and turquoise-blue sashes across their chests – Naveen is wearing one too at the start of the film, before he pulls off his princely clothes to reveal his more dapper "jazz" togs. It seems, upon careful examination, that, instead, she is wearing a darker turquoise dress underneath, just as Naveen's father is wearing a royal blue military-type jacket with gold buttons and epaulettes; Naveen's six and a half year old brother is seen wearing the same sash, too, in a later shot, dancing with Charlotte. When Naveen is discussed at all (and his role in the film seems to take a back seat to Tiana's, despite the amount of screen time they share and despite the fact that they are both noted in the film's title), most commentators seems very keen to discuss Naveen's race (or lack thereof), choosing to judge him by the colour of his skin rather than by the content of his character (to paraphrase Martin Luther King, Jr.). What this does is distract us from the fact that, for a prince, the Naveen we get to know, initially at least, is not terribly noble.

While he would not be the first Disney prince to eschew royal garb and aloofness to make music and dance with the common people (Prince Eric did this too, of course), it is clear that his mixing with commoners is *not* because he is down to earth. Instead, we learn soon after meeting him that his parents have cut him off from his inheritance and royal income because he lacks both seriousness and an appreciation for the value of work. This is made clear in a rather distasteful way when, after gregariously pledging to buy a round of drinks for everyone on the street around him, his servant, Lawrence, reminds him that he lacks the funds for such a gesture. "You have two choices", Lawrence tells him, "marry a rich young lady, or *get a job*!" As Lawrence says this, he indicates a man whose job is shovelling horse dung from the streets. Naveen sees this specific occupation – and clearly the idea of *any* work – as repugnant, and grimaces in disgust. It becomes evident very quickly – and is repeated several times in the first half of the film – that Naveen's ultimate goal is to "marry well", as the expression goes. Tiana (by this time in frog form) points out to him that marrying for money will tie him down and take

160 Gehlawat, p. 423.
161 Gehlawat, p. 425.

away the freedom he so loves, but Naveen seems resigned to that. It is also apparent very quickly that the "rich young woman" who has become Naveen's goal is Charlotte La Bouff, the charming, warm-hearted, funny, lively, but incredibly spoiled daughter of one of the city's richest men, "Big Daddy" La Bouff, as well as one of Tiana's oldest friends (they are first seen in the film together, in Charlotte's bedroom, listening to Tiana's mother, Eudora, reading to them the story of "The Frog Prince" while, in her capacity as a professional seamstress, she creates yet another elaborate princess outfit for Charlotte; from the first, it is made clear that Tiana and Charlotte – who refer to each other as Tia and Lotte – are close, loving friends). We are given to understand as well, however, that just as he would be marrying Charlotte for her money, she would be marrying him to fulfil her lifelong ambition of becoming a real princess; in a sense, they are two healthy, intelligent, spoiled, attractive young people choosing to pursue each other not out of love but because each has something – wealth for one, status for the other – that the other desires. They are hurting no one, and so the narrative condemns neither character for such calculated marriage plans. When Naveen has explained to Charlotte that her kiss will free both Tiana and himself from the curse, he initially does so agreeing to marry her (as her reward) so long as she gives Tiana the money she needs for the restaurant, even though he is now in love with Tiana. When Charlotte realises that Naveen and Tiana are in love, she immediately waves her demand: "I'll kiss him, for you, Honey – no marriage required!" When we see the human wedding ceremony, she is there, smiling and happy, celebrating, and later, in the restaurant, she dances with Naveen's baby brother, declaring, "Well, I've waited this long ...!" implying (humorously) that she can wait for this other prince to get old enough to marry.

This later decision Naveen makes, to marry Charlotte even though he is in love with Tiana, is interesting: it is done not out of selfish greed, but because he thinks it is the only way to make Tiana's dream come true. The only thing that stops him is Tiana telling him that her dream would be incomplete without him. It is the first time we see Naveen make a truly unselfish gesture. We can be certain that he would have seen through his promise to marry Charlotte, too, out of a sense of honour (something he also seemed to lack initially, as was implied by his willingness to be a gold digger). Happily, he does not have to do this, and it only makes him that much better. Learning to love – to think first and foremost of someone else – is seen in *The Princess and the Frog*, just as it was seen in *Beauty and the Beast*, to be what truly makes a prince into a man. In both of these cases, love has the power to transform bestial men into *real* men. Yes, in Naveen's case, it does also require a kiss from a princess (the Beast did not need to be kissed; all it took in his case were Belle's whispered words, "I love him"). But Naveen's princess is a princess because he fell so in love with her that he was willing to do anything to stay with her, to include remain a lowly frog. In a sense, the kiss comes off as a mere technicality: Naveen had already become a better man through his willingness to sacrifice for Tiana, and because he had learned to see the importance and value of honest work. In an earlier scene in the bayou, when Tiana sets to work making gumbo for herself, Naveen, and Louis, and teaches Naveen to mince mushrooms (the first work he has done in his life), he reflects upon his life so far:

> When you live in a castle, everything is done for you ... all the time. They dress you. They feed you. Drive you! Brush your teeth! I admit it was a charmed life until the day my parents cut me off. And suddenly, I realised; I don't know how to do *anything*.

The implication is clear: Naveen is the way he is because he has never learned to work. He avoids work because it seems distasteful to him at first, but also because he has no idea how to go about it. It is not that he is lazy; if anything, he is going to great lengths to find himself a rich wife so that he can continue to live the high life. Likewise, when he is dancing and playing his ukulele earlier in the film, and when he and Tiana are trying to survive the predators they face in the swamp (alligators and a trio of frog hunters seem to be their biggest threats), he shows great energy in fighting to protect both Tiana and himself. But it becomes evident that work – and his growing love for Tiana – give him a sense of purpose. As the overall narrative makes clear, through the inner transformations we see in both Tiana and Naveen, it is only through achieving a balance between work and life that we find true happiness. Once we do that, we are set to achieve our greatest dreams – and most of all, once we achieve them, we'll be able to enjoy them.

Emperor Kuzko

So far, we have looked at the Disney princes, and the idea of the prince. But in this final royal character, we have someone who has gone past the stage of "prince" and achieved full royal power: Emperor Kuzco of *The Emperor's New Groove* (2000). Once again, we see a royal brought low: transformed into a llama by an evil sorceress' potion, Kuzco is then spirited away from his palace by Kronk, the (sweet but rather dumb) henchman of the sorceress (and Kuzco's political rival), Yzma. Fortunately for Kuzco, Kronk bungles his attempt to dispose of him; unconscious and tied up in a sack, Kuzco ends up on the back of Pacha's cart and many miles away from the palace, back in Pacha's village. Pacha, himself at odds with Kuzco over the Emperor's plans to demolish Pacha's village and build a summer home there, agrees to help Kuzco the llama return to the palace (provided he promises to build his summer palace somewhere else), a journey which becomes longer than expected and fraught with dangers for them both. Over the course of their journey, the two of them learn to work together, trust each other, and become life-long friends; Kuzco is transformed by his experience as a llama, and by the time he regains human form, he has become a true man, not an overly-indulged boy.

Kuzco is spoiled. *Very* spoiled. He is so selfish and out of touch, he is not at all bothered by the fact that his plans to build himself a new summer palace (which he dubs "Kuzcotopia", further demonstrating his self-centredness) will displace an entire village. It turns out that Kuzco has summoned Pacha to the palace merely to ask him which side of the hill the village sits on is the sunniest so that he'll know where to tell the workers to build the pool. Further demonstrating his heartlessness, Kuzco glibly informs Pacha that he might want to pick up some change of address forms on his way home. When Pacha, the village's leader, asks where the people of the village are supposed to go, Kuzco's reply, delivered in a snappy, nonchalant way, is "Don't know don't care". All that Kuzco knows, at the beginning of the film, at least, is that he wants to build himself a new summer vacation palace. His only use for Pacha is to find out which side of the hill is the sunniest so that he'll know where to have his workers build the pool "complete with waterslide", and nothing else matters. He doesn't even care enough to get offended or irritated by Pacha's (very understandable) anger and defiance; the closest Kuzco comes to exhibiting an emotional reaction to Pacha's distress is to say to him with a slight degree of menace, as the guards hold Pacha back, "When I give the word, your little town-thingy will be bye-bye". All of this goes to show that, at the beginning of the narrative, everyone else's needs are too far outside of Kuzco's perception for him to even realise that he is being insensitive; he is oblivious to all around him if they are not giving him whatever he wants, and occasionally cannot even hear what they are saying over his internal monolog.

In a thematic construction which has much in common with *Beauty and the Beast* before it and *The Princess and the Frog* which would follow it, *The Emperor's New Groove* is a literalization of the symbolic "beastliness" of the selfish, spoiled man of power who must be brought low – lower than even the lowliest humans – and turned into either a deformed creature (*Beauty and the Beast*), a slimy swamp dweller (*The Princess and the Frog*; in a recurring joke in its narrative, the charge of sliminess is always corrected with the rejoinder: "It's not slime, it's mucus!"), or, in Kuzco's case, a beast of burden (he is changed into a llama). Both Naveen and Kuzco are changed into animals by an evil magician's selfish desire to usurp the "undeserved" authority conferred upon the hero by virtue of being born royal. In all three stories, a sense of revenge is present as well. A sorceress transforms the Beast because he is repulsed by her (initial) outward appearance as an old, ugly beggar woman; that her justification for the Beast's transformation is didactic is an important point, but only partially; all learn a lesson from their experience. Yzma is determined to murder Kuzco because he has fired her from her position as his advisor (and, again, Kronk spoils the attempt by accidentally adding "essence of llama" to Kuzco's drink instead of poison). Naveen is changed into a frog because his servant, Lawrence, is tired of being ordered around and disregarded by Naveen and so makes a deal with Dr. Facilier to change Naveen into a frog and assume Naveen's appearance in order to trick a wealthy woman into marriage. In all three stories as told by Disney, a strikingly similar narrative pattern can be seen:

I.   The character angers someone with magical powers

II. As an act of revenge, the character is transformed into a non-human figure

III. The character achieves self awareness, responsibility, and maturity

IV. The character commits a selfless act to save someone he loves

V.   The character earns the right to regain human form, and is restored to humanity

VI. Now a fully-actualised adult, the character proves that he is now deserving of his status as a man and as a prince

VII. The character shows in the denouement that he will continue to improve and that he has formed ties with others which will remain strong for the rest of his life.

For the Beast and for Naveen, that seventh step includes relationships which are ties of kinship and friendship, but in their narratives the most important new relationship they form is of a romantic sort: the Beast has Belle, and Naveen has Tiana. But in this respect, *The Emperor's New Groove* differs from other Disney stories; we learn that Kuzco is eighteen years old, and so according to fairy tale conventions, Kuzco is old enough to form a romantic attachment which evolves into a marriage, either by the time the film ends or with the point made clear that the marriage will come soon after the end of the on-screen narrative (though not strictly a fairy tale, *The Emperor's New Groove*, like many Disney films, *functions* as a fairy tale, as was discussed in the introductory chapter for this book). In a brief scene near the beginning of the film, we actually see Kuzco invited to inspect a line of (nearly identical) young women to choose one for his bride; he rejects all of them on the most shallow of grounds, such as not liking a hairstyle or someone's height (though, again, this is partially to emphasise Kuzco's own deep-rooted character flaws, flaws which he will overcome over the course of the film). But nowhere else in the film is any mention made of a romantic attachment. Instead, the narrative focuses on his growing friendship with Pacha, a family man some years older than Kuzco who comes to function simultaneously as a father, brother, and best friend for Kuzco.

This is a relationship which has all of the hallmarks, discussed in chapter two, of the "frienemies" relationship: the pair begin in opposition to one another, find themselves forced to work together to achieve a common goal and/or combat a common enemy, and over time, as they get to know one another, a genuine friendship develops between the two. As was said earlier, Kuzco is about to destroy Pacha's village in order to build himself a summer home. From Pacha's point of view, this is unexpected and – understandably – devastating news: not only for himself and his growing family (when we meet his wife, Chicha, we see that she is ready to give birth very soon, and also learn that they already have two young children). Though it is never stated explicitly, we are given the sense that Pacha is his village's leader. He certainly carries a weight of authority about him, lives at the highest point on the hillside where the village is built, and is the one who goes to represent the village when called upon by Kuzco. We also see that he is a good, honest, honourable, loving husband and father, and that his and Chicha's marriage is a supportive and happy one.

When Pacha realises that Kuzco – in llama form – has ended up on his cart and is now in his village, he is not pleased: he is already angry with Kuzco, and has no reason either to like or to trust him. He sees someone lost and in need, however, and no matter how he feels about Kuzco, he eventually agrees to help him. Pacha is not stupid, however: he also sees the opportunity inherent in the situation, and so makes a deal with Kuzco that, if he helps Kuzco to return to the palace, Kuzco will build his summer home somewhere else. Of course, the journey does not go as planned: it ends up taking several days longer than expected, and the evil Yzma (and the hapless Kronk) pursue Kuzco throughout their journey, which means that Pacha finds himself having to protect Kuzco on several occasions (in one particularly funny scene, Yzma and Kronk come to Pacha's home, and Chicha and the kids end up having to detain the pair so that Pacha and Kuzco can get away without being seen). Their trials force Pacha and Kuzco to trust one another in order to survive; being forced to trust each other helps them learn to tolerate each other, then like each other, until, by the end of the film, they seem not only to be best friends, but also that Kuzco has become – unofficially, of course – a member of their family.

Our last shots of Kuzco in the film, in fact, are of him vacationing in Pacha's village; he springs from the doorway of a hut similar to – but smaller than – Pacha's house, and we see Kuzco socialising with Pacha's wife, Chicha, his older children, Tipo and Chaca, and the couple's newborn (but for the audience unnamed) baby, as well as others who live in the village. It is implied earlier in the narrative (in something of a throw-away line) that this interaction may be Kuzco's first experience of true family life. In an earlier scene, Kronk mentions that Yzma practically raised Kuzco; left hanging in the air in the scene is the notion that *this* is part of why he may have turned out to be a less than upstanding young man. In a montage toward the beginning of the film, we are also given to understand that Kuzco was spoiled from infancy, but in a rather impersonal way. Baby Kuzco is seen playing with a toy which breaks; he has barely begun to cry when, immediately and from all sides of the frame, a number of hands appear holding identical copies of the toy which broke, straightaway turning baby Kuzco's sorrow at the loss of his toy to instant gratification at its replacement. We see none of the faces of those caring for the baby, though, nor is there any mention of Kuzco's parents or siblings. He is, in essence, the poor little rich boy, spoiled, the centre of the universe, but unloved and without true friends. Indeed, a large part of the growth he undergoes during the film is to learn to work in conjunction with another person, to listen to and trust that person, and to share his thoughts and emotions. That he has learned to do this is demonstrated visually by his being seen surrounded by Pacha's family in the final shot featuring him.

In the depiction of Kuzco's personality – he is clever, but selfish, objectifying, boorish, unreconstructed, and uncaring, traits which are presented with great humour and irony rather than being condemned outright – there are aspects which could be said to tie it into the "lad" culture which began to emerge in Britain in the 1990s and which, in the form of so-called "men's" magazines *FHM* in 1999 and *Maxim* in 2000,[162] rode the wave of "Cool Britannia" to America. In a discussion of this aspect of "Lad Culture" of the 1990s and early 2000s in her book *Gender and the Media*, Rosalind Gill quotes a *Sunday Times* article written about the export of the British magazine *FHM* to US consumers in their own, American-based version:

> The troops are being assembled, the invasion plans are well advanced and the general is in place ... to launch if not a full-frontal assault at least a semi-naked one, to liberate the sensibilities of the all-American male ... For Uncle Sam, the countdown to the acceptable face of party-time has begun ... A guy is a guy, wherever he lives ... A testosterone-charged British sperm is swimming across the Atlantic ... If the American 'new man' was ever house-trained by feminism to be considerate, sensitive and interested in women's minds rather than their bodies, he is about to be led wildly astray.[163]

Ariel Levy also comments on this form of masculinity as it existed around 2000 (the year that *The Emperor's New Groove* was released) in a discussion of *The Man Show* (US, Comedy Central, 1999-2004). Attending a taping of the show, she describes the audience warm up, in which men in the audience were encouraged to enact the "lad" form of masculinity:

> The night I went to a taping, there wasn't enough space to fit all the guys who had lined up outside the studio, and a team of heavy-limbed boys in matching green T-shirts from Chico State were pumped to make it into the audience.
>
> Don, the bald audience fluffer, seemed to be looking directly at them when he yelled from the stage, "A few weeks ago we had trouble with guys touching the women here. You can't just grab their asses – you don't do that in real life, do you? [Beat.] Welllll ... so do I!" The frat guys cheered, but not with the alarming gusto of the man in front of them, a scrawny computer technician who resembled one of the P's in Peter, Paul and Mary. "To the women", shouted Don, "today only, you're an honorary man! Grab your dick!"[164]

It is a kind of boisterous, self-centred and self-obsessed behaviour, oblivious to those around it, which is at the heart of this phenomenon, and one in which it seems likely that the Kuzco we meet at the start of the film would feel right at home. Yet even while the narrative's use of irony (supposedly a large part of lad culture) and humour are very much present in the depiction of Kuzco at this stage, the narrative makes clear throughout that in no way is such behaviour acceptable, let alone characteristic of how a "man" behaves. In fact, the very point of the film seems to

162 –There seem to be contradictory dates as to the start of *Maxim* in the US market. Gill says 2000, and back issues available for order on the US website for the magazine go back to 2000. However, the Wikipedia article on *Maxim* says that it began publishing in the US in 1998, and Susan J. Douglas says in *Enlightened Sexism* that its first American issue was in April 1997.

163 Quoted in Rosalind Gill, *Gender and the Media* (Cambridge: Polity Press, 2007), pp. 209-210.

164 Ariel Levy, *Female Chauvinist Pigs: Women and the Rise of Raunch Culture* (London: Pocket Books, 2005) p. 113.

be to reject this version of masculinity, holding up instead the intelligent, warm, empathetic, brave, and loyal Pacha as the true model of masculinity to be celebrated and emulated. Eventually – and without really meaning to – it is this quieter, gentler form of masculinity that Kuzco adopts; not completely – after all, he is only eighteen, and it would be surprising for him to become *exactly* like Pacha, who is older, married, and the father of three children. But in its depiction of Kuzco and Pacha, it is clear that this film is rejecting the lad culture so popular in 2000, offering up a more substantive alternative and depicting it as the happier, more fulfilled enactment of masculine behaviour and identity.

Betting on the Prince

At the start of this chapter, I quoted Sheldon Cashdan's argument that, "In contrast [to witches, godmothers, and other female characters], male figures are relatively minor figures in most fairy tales. The prince tends to be a cardboard character, almost an afterthought, who materializes at the end of the story to ensure a happy ending."[165] I began by talking about how, when looking at the Disney prince character as he exists in Disney merchandising, this would seem to be true. There is also the argument to be made that, for the first two Disney princes, The Prince from *Snow White and the Seven Dwarfs* and Prince Charming from *Cinderella*, this idea of the prince's marginality to the narrative was present in the character's function: princes were important, but nonetheless were minor characters, ultimately, in films which focused primarily on the life and trials of female heroines.

Yet as time went on, even while many of the stories featuring princes continued to spend a good portion of their narrative focused on the central female characters (Aurora, Ariel, Belle, and Tiana), increasingly – and especially during the "Disney Renaissance" era of the studio's history – the prince was brought forward and made at least as compelling as the female characters who were, ultimately, the narrative focus of the films. Prince Phillip is more than just some cipher who comes forward to kiss Aurora and break the spell that holds her, he falls for her while she is conscious, and we get to know him as an intelligent, spirited, strong, brave young man who will do anything to be with his true love. Prince Eric, too, is kindly, brave, and down to earth; captivated initially by the beauty of Ariel's voice (and all that someone's "voice" symbolically implies), he is slow to recognise his love in the (at that stage literally) voiceless young beauty he meets. He grows to know and like her, but it is still that voice – that essence which is the most important part of Ariel – which

165 Cashdan, p. 28.

183

holds his imagination and which, when she regains it, allows him to recognise Ariel immediately and know that she is the one with whom he is not only completely in love, but for whom he is willing to fight and sacrifice. As for the Beast, to paraphrase the classic Jack Nicholson line from *As Good As It Gets* (1997), Belle makes him want to be a better man (and in this film, made six years after the Disney film, Nicholson's character, Melvin, is very much depicted as the Beast opposite Helen Hunt's Carol as Beauty). In the Beast's case, his love for Belle – and her love for him – transforms him both figuratively and literally into a real man, someone who is strong, tender, loving, and caring, the true embodiment of a prince. Kuzco begins as a lad-Emperor, spoiled and almost pathologically self centred, but being brought low and forced (for the sake of his own survival) to consider someone else's needs helps him to develop empathy and true wisdom and leadership. Naveen begins as a carefree, hapless playboy with too much charm and only the "ambition" to marry a rich woman to support him in a luxury, work-free life, but being forced to fight for his survival and forming first real, true friendships, then learning through love to think of others first, helps him to value hard work and responsibility while still retaining a love of life and an appreciation of its lightness as a balance to hard work. Particularly in the cases of these last three characters – and it is interesting that they are the three most recent princes chronologically – it is striking that all three are young men whose lack of humanity is rendered literal in their narratives: they are a beast, a llama, and a frog for substantial portions of their stories, and must earn their right to be men – they learn that "Manhood" is not an entitlement.

Far from remaining the "cardboard character" of traditional fairy tales, over time Disney's princes have become hugely important figures. But why has this been recognised only by a few critics, and why have they tended to write about this is alarmist terms? One possible reason – and it is an important, valid reason – is the worry that the films in which most of these princes feature (Kuzco's story is the exception) are adaptations of traditional fairy tales which focused on the heroine; moving her to one side, essentially, could be viewed as a chauvinistic re-evaluation of the story: for such critics, making the prince a co-star in these narratives foregrounds the courtships which are important to these stories. Cummins argues in relation to this change (as she sees it) to *Beauty and the Beast* that, "if we want children to develop balanced views of relationships between men and women and of their own identities as active individuals with full access to society, we should question the messages sent by such films".[166]   166 Cummins, p. 22.

I find such a concern problematic, however. For a start, it fails to take into account studies which have looked at the interpretive nuance which fans of particular genres (such as the romance genre, in which many fairy tales fit comfortably; it is also a genre which Cummins invokes – repeatedly and with negative connotations – throughout her article) bring to their interpretations of these stories (filmic or otherwise). Perhaps even more importantly, these films which have sought to incorporate better developed, more interesting heroes as counterbalances to better developed, more interesting heroines show male and female characters who operate as equals even when they have different strengths and weaknesses. While I agree that it would be very wrong – and deeply troubling – to align specific strengths and/or weaknesses with any one sex or gender and claim that they are somehow characteristic of that sex, overall this does not seem to be the case with these films. The men and women – royalty and commoners alike – lean toward (even if they have to spend their film learning this) a valuing of intelligence, hard work and responsibility, embracing love and happiness, living with hopefulness that the hard times will come to an end and that things can and will get better, and that being true to the very best in oneself is what will help you to achieve your best and brightest goals. Admittedly, the princes as a group tend to be more prone to selfishness and laziness than the heroines, but those who suffer from these traits overcome them and do better. The prevalence of narratives in which princes are transformed into creatures would suggest that princes as a group are prone to laziness because, until a crisis befalls them (such as those which they experience in the narratives of the films under examination here), they have never had to struggle for anything. They have lived their lives in comfort, free from want, and therefore have yet to build up their inner resources or look beyond themselves. Those princes we have discussed who are the exceptions to this tendency – The Prince, Prince Phillip, and Prince Eric – begin their narratives as men of action. They are not at home in their palaces, but are adventuring, travelling far from home, and relying upon themselves to some degree. But for Prince Charming, the Beast, Emperor Kuzco, and Prince Naveen, life begins as one of privilege and indulgence, and for whatever reason(s), these young men choose to remain sheltered from the world around them, unaware of its realities and dangers. Prince Charming is the only one of these characters to not suffer and to never escape the confines of privilege: Cinderella is brought to him, not once but twice, and all he has to do to win her back is declare that he loves her: servants are dispatched immediately to find her and return her to him (presumably regardless of whether she wishes this or not; happily for her, it seems she's happy to go along with the plan). But the other six characters discussed in this chapter have to fight and struggle and search to achieve their goals. Where we do get to know them, we see that this makes them worthy of those around them, and they become princes in the archetypal sense of the word: champions who deserve the love and respect of those they lead.

4

Evil Villains

D isney does villains well. Perhaps it has to do with the fact that so many Disney villains either come directly from fairy tales, or else are inspired by fairy tales. The wicked witch in *Snow White and the Seven Dwarfs* (1937), the evil stepmother in *Cinderella* (1950), the Queen of Hearts in *Alice in Wonderland* (1951), Captain Hook in *Peter Pan* (1953), Maleficent in *Sleeping Beauty* (1959), Cruella deVil in *One-Hundred-and-One Dalmatians* (1961) ... the list goes on. We love the villains, and not just because we love to hate them: without the villain, the hero(in)es have no real incentive to move forward in their lives, to undertake their adventures, and to grow as individuals. Sheldon Cashdan, in writing about the witch (though I would argue that "the witch" in Cashdan's argument stands in for all villains), say that, "Of the many figures who make their presence felt in a fairy tale, the witch is the most compelling. She is the diva of the piece, the dominant character who frames the battle between good and evil."[167] In other words, without the villain, very often there is no story. Certainly, the villain character is seen as crucial by the animators at the Disney studio. As Frank Thomas and Ollie Johnston say in their book *The Disney Villain*, "The villains we created together at the Disney studio were memorable because they were entertaining".[168] They point out that, "On the screen we preferred to depict our examples of vileness through a strong design which eliminated realism and kept the audience from getting too close to the character".[169] A character who is bad, wicked, mean, duplicitous, and cunning is enjoyed by the audience because that character is colourful, interesting – active. Villains often are the catalyst for the action, and – conversely – create the hero(ine) we root for. After all, as Thomas and Johnston point out, "Such attacks compel the heroes to become more heroic than most people have a chance to become in a whole lifetime".[170]

167 Sheldon Cashdan, *The Witch Must Die: The Hidden Meaning of Fairy Tales* (New York: Basic Books, 1999), p. 30.

168 Ollie Johnston and Frank Thomas, *The Disney Villain* (New York: Hyperion Press, 1993), pp. 18-19.

169 Johnston and Thomas, *Villain*, p. 18.

170 Johnston and Thomas, *Villain*, p. 27.

Possibly even more importantly, the presence of the villain – and the chance for the main character(s) to be heroic – means that the narrative has the opportunity to present a victory which has been snatched from the jaws of defeat, a form of storytelling which is a necessity. As Cashdan points out, such stories "… are tales of transcendence. Once the witch dies, everyone lives happily ever after."[171] This must happen, he argues, because "For a fairy tale to succeed – for it to accomplish its psychological purpose – the witch must die because it is the witch who embodies the sinful parts of the self".[172]

This chapter, therefore, seeks to examine those male human characters in Disney's animated feature films whose job it is to goad the other characters to bravery, as well as being the characters who, in most cases, must make the ultimate sacrifice in order for the story to be satisfying for the audience. In my analysis, I have identified six basic types of male villains: Pirate Kings, Enemies of the Earth, Magically-Dangerous Villains, Criminally-Dangerous Villains, Comic Villains, and Idiot Villains. Each of these types is examined for the traits that groups of villains have in common, and, particularly in the case of "Enemies of the Earth", the rise of this particular type of villain will be considered in relation to the historical period in which he was prominent. Naturally, some of these villains have traits of more than one category: Governor Ratcliffe from *Pocahontas* (1995), is very definitely an Enemy of the Earth, given his role in deforesting and strip-mining Virginia, as well as the threat he poses to the Powhatan Indians, Pocahontas' people. Yet there are obvious comic aspects to him. However, because his villainy is such that it is not directed personally at those he opposes, but instead is about his own greed and selfishness, he is looked at for his environmental crimes primarily. Gaston from *Beauty and the Beast* (1991) is examined as comic because he targets Belle and Beast individually; yes, his motivations are selfish, but his actions are not those of an invader taking over a foreign land. Just because a villain has been classified as comic or an idiot does not mean that they are not still dangerous: the two comic villains (Gaston and Hades) and idiot villains (Goob and King Candy) commit acts which endanger lives and create havoc. However, they themselves are either greatly amusing because of how exaggerated they are (comic villains) or because there is something about how they operate which betrays a basic stupidity and ineptness which, ultimately, sows the seeds for their plans' undoing.

The characters discussed, it should be noted, are main characters in their narratives rather than secondary. This means that char-

171 Cashdan, p. 31.
172 Cashdan, p. 30.

acters such as Stromboli and the Coachman (from *Pinocchio*, 1940), Mr. Winkie (*The Adventures of Ichabod and Mr. Toad*, 1949), Horace and Jaspar Badun (*One-Hundred-And-One Dalmatians*, 1961), Edgar the Butler (*The Aristocats*, 1970), Mr. Snoops (*The Rescuers*, 1977), and Amos Slade (*The Fox and the Hound*, 1981) are not really examined. Each may play an interesting role within his narrative, but it is limited in its scope and importance to that of sidekick and/or secondary character. Some, such as Amos Slade, are only arguably villains. After all, Amos' attempts to shoot Tod, the fox, and to teach Copper, the dog, to hunt, are not villainous acts; he is a hunter, and so shooting a fox is not surprising. When Tod ends up saving Amos from an attacking bear, Amos lets him go: a life for a life. Instead, the characters I am examining in this chapter are major characters in their films: they take up a significant amount of screen time, their actions are what compel the hero(ine) to act, and without them, we would not have a story. In the words of the Magic Mirror in his narration in the classic Disney television special *A Disney Halloween*, "He's the fellow who does his best to give you his worst: the chap who gives the hero a chance to be brave!"[173]

Pirate Kings

Our first villain, both in our discussion and chronologically, is Captain Hook, who is the first human male Disney villain in a leading role. He is the pirate king who spars with Peter Pan, and of course is always bested by him. As was the tradition from the theatrical productions, the voice of Captain Hook in the Disney film was provided by the same actor, Hans Conried, who also did the voice for Mr. Darling, the father of Wendy, Michael and John. This links Hook to a controlling form of patriarchy, one usually associated with more conservative, older elements, that finds youth to be threatening and in need of control. This link is stressed by a small number of the press book articles from *Peter Pan*'s original release: in one article in particular, the link between Captain Hook and a domineering form of patriarchy is discussed at length.

> The father who forbids going to a movie, refuses to increase an allowance, or demands the lawn be mowed or leaves raked is a tyrant in childish eyes. The father, who is the foil of all the well-laid plans of younger years seems the blackest of villains to an adolescent.
>
> What more natural thing, then, to associate the *Papa Darling* with the notorious *Captain Hook*, pirate deluxe and villain extraordinary.
>
> By selecting [Hans] Conried for both parts, Walt Disney has a man who can generate with only his voice hate and fear as a pirate or warmth and

173 *A Disney Halloween*, US TV Special, ABC, Original Air Date 1 October 1983. Found at: http://www.youtube.com/watch?v=Txn1JRBObIY.

understanding as the harassed head of the *Darling's* [*sic*] Victorian household.[174]

This may be part of why it is possible to feel a degree of sympathy for Hook: his being tied so closely with the father in the story makes him seem more familiar as an individual, and therefore more relatable. Furthermore, it can be argued that Hook is outmatched in many ways: after all, the young man with whom he has this on-going battle once cut off his hand (which is why he now wears a hook), and even went so far as to feed it to a crocodile; the animal loved the taste of it so much that he has pursued Captain Hook ever since, hoping to get to eat the rest of him. Naturally, this is a feature of his life which Hook finds terribly stressful (indeed, this is shown in several instances in the Disney film; all Hook has to hear is a ticking clock (since, fortunately, the crocodile also swallowed an alarm clock at some point in the past, and so can always be heard approaching because of the constant "tick-tock" noise coming from his stomach), and he becomes terrified. His sidekick, Mr. Smee, tries hard to help Hook relax, even offering to give him a nice, soothing shave as a way to de-stress. But Hook is too tormented by Peter, and eventually resolves to destroy Peter once and for all so that he can be free of the constant worry. When we first see Hook's ship, the Jolly Roger, we see the pirate crew on the ship's deck, working and happily singing "A Pirate's Life is a Wonderful Life". However, we very quickly begin to get hints that the crew is less than happy with the captain: the camera, as it moves over the deck, comes to rest on the galley door, on which a drawing labelled "The Cap'n" has been made, and which has several knives sticking out of the drawing's belly: the pirates are using it as a target for knife throwing. Mr. Smee opens the door and comes out, cheerily wishing everyone good morning, when the pirates retort, "What's good about it, Mr. Smee? Here we are, collecting barnacles on this miserable island", (second pirate) "while his nibs plays ring-around-the-rosy with Peter Pan!" They become threatening to Smee, complaining that their skills as pirates are going to waste and that they want to get back to sailing the seas and plundering ships. When we meet Captain Hook, he is studying a map of Neverland and talking to himself, trying to figure out where Pan is hiding. That he cares nothing about his crew, only about his quest to find and destroy Peter Pan, is demonstrated when one of the pirates is suddenly heard singing a refrain from "A Pirate's Life is a Wonderful Life" in a somewhat operatic, melodramatic style, and an irritated Hook shoots him. We do not see him shot, but we see Hook look up at him with irritation, roll his eyes, then turn back to his map as he points his gun and fires.

174 Anonymous, "One 'Peter Pan' Tradition Defied in Disney Film, But Another Is Maintained", from *Peter Pan* Press Book, 1953, p. 2.

The man's singing stops abruptly, and a few seconds later, we hear a splash as his body lands in the water. Hook turns back to his map with a calmer, "Now let me see, where was I?" Smee chastises him slightly, saying, "Oh, dear, dear, dear, Captain Hook. Shooting a man in the middle of his cadenza? It ain't good form, you know." Hook loses his temper, throwing over the table in front of him and ranting, "Did Pan show good form when he did this to me?" He brandishes his hook hand angrily. Peter Pan and the crocodile are the only things which seem to make Hook emotional, but each makes him *very* emotional, even hysterical. The first time we see the crocodile in the film, its appearance turns Hook into a trembling wreck. The only thing that restores Hook to himself is the sighting of Peter Pan flying overhead. He rounds up the crew to attack him, but Peter (along with the Darling children) fly out of range in the nick of time. Later, when we find Hook again, he once more shows his contempt for human life, threatening to drown Tiger Lily, the Indian princess, if she refuses to reveal where Peter Pan's hiding place is. Hook realises that Peter is nearby and trying to trick him and Smee, and so goes after him. He sneaks up on Pan and nearly stabs him in the head with his hook: only Wendy's warning cry saves Pan's life. He nearly stabs Peter in the back with his sword, only this time Mr. Smee, who had feared Hook had been killed, cries out joyfully, and Pan turns to see Hook sneaking up on him again. Of course, Peter shows a similar disrespect for Hook's life in his willingness to feed Hook to the crocodile, kicking Hook off the cliff and into the water, where he struggles for several minutes as the crocodile tries to eat him. There seems to be very little comment made about how violent Hook is, but he is very violent indeed. Later, he will attempt to send Peter a mail bomb, disguised as a present from Wendy, in yet another attempt to murder the boy. Likewise, he is willing to kill Tiger Lily (as discussed above), Tinker Bell, Wendy and the Lost Boys, all in the cause of finishing off Peter Pan.

Hook is shown to be a vain, silly man (his long hair, fancy coat, and large hat with its huge plume, which seem inspired by the court of Charles II, his long, pencil-thin moustache and his set of "Sunday hooks" (gold and elaborate in design), as well as his melodramatic way of speaking and exaggerated actions). When attempting to bamboozle Tinker Bell into telling him the location of Pan's hideout, he plays on Tinker Bell's emotions as a "jilted woman", lamenting, "Oh, Smee, the way of a man with a maid – taking the best years of her life, and then casting her aside like an old glove!" According to Frank Thomas and Ollie

Johnston, the description given of Hook by the story department in their analysis of the character was that:

> He is a fop ... Yet very mean, to the point of being murderous. This combination of traits should cause plenty of amusement whenever he talks or acts. [There is a] danger of carrying the whimsy too far. ... If we make him a Gilbert and Sullivan type of villain, the audience may feel a lack of genuine badness.[175]

In other words, they wanted Hook to have a comic quality, but they wanted him menacing, too; otherwise, he would be unable to carry out the acts he commits against Pan and the other children. As Johnston and Thomas go on to comment,

> He needed to be an actor relishing his role as a gentleman of charm and good taste, yet he knew that underneath it all, he had as black a heart as anyone. ... [Yet] He could not be truly evil, because Peter Pan is a story of children and their games and their views of life and growing up. In this context, Captain Hook was a "bad guy" and a "scurvy villain" but only as a worthy competitor for Peter Pan.[176]

While this is no doubt an accurate reflection of the thinking behind the character's creation – after all, Thomas and Johnston, two of the famous "Nine Old Men" of the Disney studio's golden era, were part of the team who created *Peter Pan*, and therefore were eye-witnesses to the shaping of Captain Hook – it seems strange to describe a character who repeatedly attempts to murder children (and in cruel, painful ways, at that) as "not truly evil". Perhaps they hesitated to acknowledge what, arguably, are horror elements to the character (who is at least as persistent – and as vicious – as Michael Meyers in the 1978 film *Halloween*!) because he is a major character in a film which has the family and child audience so firmly in mind, and for many years there was a strong taboo (one which lingers, to a degree) against the idea of children watching, let alone enjoying horror as a genre, even in films which were aimed at the child and family audience.[177] Yet it is undeniable that Captain Hook, for all of the theatricality of his characterisation, is nonetheless a genuine threat and persistent danger to those around him. In some ways, he is one of the most violent of the Disney villains, even if he is rarely successful in his attempts to cause harm. Ultimately, Hook must be shaped with a degree of outrageousness about him so that he works as a good counterbalance to Peter Pan, who can be amusing but is never ridiculous. Hook does carry a degree of sympathy, whatever the level of violence he enacts, and so the decision was made that he not be killed off at the end of the film, but instead be chased away comically. This decision seems to have come from Walt Disney personally; his love of the story was such that he was more involved in the production of *Peter Pan* than was usually the case

175 Johnston and Thomas, *Villain*, p. 109.

176 Johnston and Thomas, *Villain*, p. 110.

177 I discuss the topic of children's horror at length in my forthcoming paper "Scaring the Children: Horror Films for the Younger Audience", to be published in Jessica McCort (Editor), *Unpleasant Tales: The Wonderland of Horror in Children's Literature and Culture* (Jackson: University of Mississippi Press, expected 2013).

for the animated features made from the early 1950s until his death in December 1966.[178] According to Johnston and Thomas,

> Walt had told us, "Instead of killing anybody we ought to get rid of them. ... Maybe with the crocodile and Hook – the crocodile is waiting for him – they have a funny chase – the last you see is Hook going like hell. That's better than having him get caught ... the audience will get to liking Hook and they won't want to see him killed."[179]

No doubt a similar thought process applied to the shaping of our next pirate villain, Mr. John Silver.

Silver is a particularly interesting addition to the ranks of the Disney villains, being the first and (so far) only cyborg. Just as the depiction of Captain Hook bore a resemblance to the character's creation in the traditions associated with the theatre, so too did an earlier, non-animated rendering of Long John Silver (as he was known in other versions) play a part in the shaping of his animated cyborg version. Silver is the first animated Disney villain to have had a Disney live-action equivalent: Long John Silver as played by Robert Newton in the 1950 Disney film *Treasure Island*, the studio's first completely live-action film. It is important to note that Robert Newton's portrayal of Long John Silver in the Disney adaptation is very possibly the single-most iconic pirate portrayal in Anglophone cinematic history. Therefore, in what in some ways was a Disney animated remake of a Disney live-action film, John Silver[180] – and Brian Murray, who provided his voice in *Treasure Planet* – could not escape Robert Newton's legacy entirely. Having said that, Murray refrains from doing a straight-forward impersonation of Newton, just as those who designed the cyborg seem to have taken their inspiration from Newton's appearance in *Treasure Island*, but avoid copying it exactly. This John Silver is missing a leg, and an arm, and an eye, and an ear, all of which have been replaced by mechanical parts (hence Silver's status as a cyborg). But there are aspects of his eyes and mouth, his girth, and his mannerism which reflect Newton's Silver. His speaking voice, too, is influenced by Newton, but in no way is an imitation; in this version, Silver's accent is not Newton's more West Country twang (the now-classic "arrgh"-inflected "pirate" accent), but instead has more occasional traces of an Irish brogue about it. Rather than being a Newtown impersonation, therefore, this cyborg-Silver is a new rendition for his new, outer space setting.

Jim is immediately suspicious of Silver, having been told by Billy Bones (from whom he acquired the map to Treasure Planet) that a cyborg is chasing him and to beware the cyborg. But when he

178 In an article written by Walt Disney that was published in the April 1953 edition of *Brief* magazine, Walt claimed that he played Peter Pan in a school production of the play when he was a young child. He writes in the article that "No actor ever identified himself with a part he was playing more than I, and I was more realistic than Maud Adams in at least one particular – I actually flew through the air! Roy was using a block and tackle to hoist me. Well, it gave way, and I flew right into the faces of the surprised audience." From Disc 2, *Walt Disney's Peter Pan, 2-Disc Platinum Edition*, Backstage Disney/"In Walt's Words: 'Why I Made *Peter Pan*,'"

179 Johnston and Thomas, *Villain*, p. 112.

180 He is never referred to in *Treasure Planet* as "Long" John Silver, only as John Silver, Mr. Silver, or "the cyborg".

asks Silver if he has ever heard of Bones, Silver of course denies it. Silver is diffident to Captain Amelia, the first mate (Mr. Arrow), and Dr. Doppler, and by turns indulgent, protective, and strict with Jim. He does everything he can to appear to be a humble ship's cook but, not long after the Legacy has set sail, we learn that Silver is in fact the true leader of the crew, and is planning to take over the ship so that he may be the one to claim the treasure on Treasure Planet, supposedly the "treasure of a thousand worlds" built up through mysterious means by the notorious Captain Flint, a figure we learn early in the film is believed by most to be more legend than real. Silver, however, knows better, and knows that the treasure they seek is also very real. Though he does not tell Jim directly, he implies – and the audience, with our superior knowledge of Silver's true intentions, are able to understand his meaning completely – that it was in pursuit of Flint's treasure that Silver was injured time and again until he became almost as much machine as he was man. Silver is shown in his dealings with the crew to be ruthless, authoritarian, cunning, and even cruel. Yet we cannot fear or hate Silver because his growing affection for Jim, begun their first night on board when Silver learns that Jim's father walked out on the Hawkins family, is genuine. In the montage which follows, we see Jim working on board ship, Silver always at his side, teaching and instructing him, his admiration for Jim growing as he sees how bright Jim is, and how hard the boy is willing to work. He remarks that he sees in Jim something of himself at the same age, and we see – again, in part of the montage – that Silver has become a father to Jim, in both his and in Jim's hearts. This duality to Silver – leader of the pirates, on the one hand, and father figure to Jim Hawkins, on the other – is what gives the character his complexity and makes him such a likeable character. The division in him is best illustrated when he comforts Jim, who has been framed for the death of the ship's first mate, Mr. Arrow. Silver says to the boy, "You've got the makings of greatness in you, but you gotta take the helm and chart your own course! Stick to it, no matter the squalls, and when the time comes and you get the chance to really test the cut of your sails and show what you're made of ... well ... I hope I'm there – catching some of the light coming off ya that day." He hugs Jim, and gives him a moment to mourn, before sending Jim off to bed, claiming that he must begin his watch. Alone with his sidekick, Morph (this version's substitute for the character's parrot), he confesses that his feelings for Jim run very deep, and worries that the other pirates will soon "be sayin' I've gone soft", thereby putting his position as their leader in jeopardy. The next morning, however, he confronts the restless crew, reasserting his strength amongst them; the pirate who cut Mr. Arrow's lifeline, Scroop, does indeed try to use Silver's affection for Jim against him, but Silver insists, "I care about one thing, and one thing only – Flint's trove". However, in our privileged position as the audience, we know that, as much as he cares about the treasure, Silver has come to care about Jim more. But to admit this would mean his and Jim's deaths, and so Silver puts on a strong show, claiming, "I cozied up to that kid to keep him off our scent. But I ain't gone soft."

Just then, a shout of "Land-ho" is heard, and the pirates rush up on deck. Silver realises he has left his spyglass in the galley, and goes back to retrieve it. He reaches the top of the galley steps just as Jim is beginning to come up them, and realises that Jim has witnessed the entire scene with the pirates and knows what is happening. Knowing that Silver's fatherly feelings towards Jim are genuine, it is doubly shocking when Silver hides his cyborg hand behind his back so that Jim won't see it transformed into a pistol; he may love the boy, but Silver's ruthlessness, however, is clearly still his dominate trait. Jim manages to get around Silver, stabbing Silver's cyborg leg so that it malfunctions, but Silver makes his way back up to the deck, transforms his cyborg hand into a machete, and announces that the mutiny is beginning. He takes the lead in blasting open the stateroom door, and leads the pirates in a chase to try and stop the captain, Doppler, and Jim from escaping in one of the long boats. Morph steals the map, thinking he's playing a game, and Silver and Jim find themselves trying to get hold of Morph and/or the map sphere before the other. Because Jim is younger, fitter, and whole bodied, he manages to get the sphere first; Silver's instinct is to transform his cyborg hand yet again, this time into a blaster, and takes aim at Jim as the boy runs to the long boat. But in the end, Silver cannot bring himself to fire the blaster, even if it means losing the map. It is meant to restore our sympathy, if not Jim's (since he has no way of knowing what has just happened), and it does, to a degree. But it is hard to forget the savagery with which Silver has threatened Jim, made all the more horrific by the fatherly role he has assumed. In this moment, he becomes like an ogre who would consume his own child; it is a moment which links Silver heavily with fairy tales and folk lore. In fact, there are numerous parallels between *Treasure Island/Treasure Planet*, on the one hand, and (in particular) "Jack and the Beanstalk", on the other. As Maria Tatar points out in her discussion of the tale, "A strong moral overlay covers nearly every aspect of this [Benjamin Tabart's 1806] version of 'Jack and the Beanstalk,' turning what probably started out as a tale of high adventure into a didactic story that molds its hero into a model for children. ... 'Jack and the Beanstalk' gives us a situation in which the fear of paternal retaliation does not take the form of an oedipal castration complex, but of the pre-oedipal dread of being devoured. Here, however, the boy never transfers the heterosexual attachment to his mother to another woman, but manages to negotiate an arrangement that allows him to stay at home as the dutiful and devoted son."[181] It is a story, once more, in which we see a brutal pirate king linked in a paternal fashion with the boy at the centre of the tale.

In the end, however, Silver's love for the boy – which is genuine and deeply felt – turns out to be his saving grace. The tide turns later when, after Flint's booby trap is triggered and the planet is destroying itself, Silver is forced to choose between saving a boatload of treasure or saving Jim, and saves Jim. This action, along with their collaboration to get the survivors of the planet's destruction safely away from it before it explodes and back to their home port, using the portal created by the map sphere to escape just in the nick of time, completely rehabilitates their relationship, and Silver's character along with it. He still manages to evade justice by escaping in one of the Legacy's longboats, but not before he and Jim have said their good-byes and parted as equals; Silver even hands Jim part of the bit of treasure he has managed to salvage in his pockets, bidding Jim to use it to rebuild the Benbow, Jim's mother's inn, which Silver and his pirates destroyed when they came after Billy Bones at the start of the film.

Silver is an interesting villain, and easily one of the more complex villains in all of the Disney cannon. While he is easily as ruthless and self-centred as any other villains we examine in this chapter, he is also the most loving and the most likeable – not just enjoyable to watch, but a character which both the audience and the film's characters are encouraged to love and even admire, even if only begrudgingly. He may be a villain, but he is a villain with a heart of gold. It is this which enables him not to only survive the narrative, which is rare enough, but for us to know that he will likely thrive. It is thanks to both the challenges and the support he has given Jim that Jim has learned to be a good, responsible, honest, worthy man, and has been saved from a life of trouble and waste, finding instead a way to make something of himself and be his best self. But equally, Jim has allowed Silver to find a way to be *his* best self. The result is a villain we can love and admire. It makes him unique amongst Disney's animated villains.

181 Maria Tatar, *Off With Their Heads: Fairy Tales and the Culture of Childhood* (Princeton: Princeton University Press, 1992), pp. 198-199

As we have seen, rendering pirate villains as sympathetic characters – and ones with some sort of paternal link to the children
they threaten – seems to be typical of pirate characters, at least as
they are portrayed in Disney. In addition to the animated characters of Captain Hook and John Silver the cyborg, we see similar
links to fatherhood being made by the 1950 *Treasure Island* as well
as by the hugely successful *Pirates of the Caribbean* franchise (to
date 2003, 2006, 2007, 2011): the pirate (Captain Hook/John
Silver/Bootstrap Bill Turner) is a threat to the hero of the tale
(Peter Pan/Jim Hawkins/Will Turner), yet he also stands in very
strongly and directly for patriarchy: Hook is always linked to the
Darling children, and therefore to fatherhood, because he is
always played by the same actor appearing in both roles; Silver
becomes a substitute father for Jim Hawkins, and helps him to
grow up and reach his full potential; Will Turner learns that he
is the son of a famous and revered pirate named Bootstrap Bill,
who will later to be found to be "alive", a member of the
enchanted crew of Davy Jones' ship, the Flying Dutchman, and
will threaten directly to kill his son, unaware of their relationship.
The idea of the murderous father is an ancient one, going back
at least to the Greek story of Kronos, the Titan who feared his
children would rise up and overthrow him, and so immediately
after each was born he would devour the child whole. Arguing
that Kronos serves as one of the probable sources for the idea of
the ogre, Marina Warner describes the ogre as a figure who "…
embodies a monstrous and anomalous paternal response to the
anxiety that his offspring would supplant him; his wicked folly
makes plain the social and human imperative that the young must
be allowed to thrive and grow".[182] These paternal pirates may fear
the youths who threatens them – this is most clearly the case with
Captain Hook's hatred of Peter Pan – but with John Silver, it is
more complicated. He recognises that Jim may discover the plot
to overthrow the ship and go after the treasure, but at the same
time, Silver comes to feel real affection for the boy, seeming to
do so in spite of himself. He continues to put himself first, by
and large, but only to a point: when Jim is in genuine danger of
dying, Silver intervenes: in the first instance, he stops the crew
from firing directly at the longboat in which Jim, Amelia and
Doppler escape the ship; later, Silver relinquishes the treasure he
has sought for years because it is the only way he can save Jim
from falling to his death. We may, as Walt Disney predicted, grow
to like Hook, but we come to care about Silver because, whatever
the nature of his many flaws, he nonetheless possesses the ability
to love, and does the right thing by the boy to whom he becomes
a father and a true friend.

182 Marina Warner, *No Go the Bogeyman: Scaring, Lulling and Making Mock* (London: Vintage, 2000), p. 77.

Enemies of the Earth

The next group of villains are characterised by the fact that their destructive ways are a direct threat first and foremost to the environment (the land, its native peoples, its native species). The stories' heroes become the villains' targets not because of any personal grudges, but instead because the heroes oppose the villains' greed and waste. Interestingly, all of the films discussed in this section come (by and large) from the 1990s: *The Rescuers Down Under* (1990), *Pocahontas* (1995), *Tarzan* (1999) and – close enough chronologically to be part of the long decade of the 1990s – *Atlantis: The Lost Empire* (2001). They fit nicely within a decade which began to see a much greater focus on environmentalism, as well as a growing fascination with the idea of multicultural-ism.[183] As Robert Gottlieb points out in his essay "The Next Environmentalism: How Movements Respond to The Changes that Elections Bring – from Nixon to Obama", "The early 1990s represented an important moment of transition for environmen-talism. This included the rise of what we today call the environ-mental justice movement; the rapid expansion in the resources of large, professional and policy-based or mainstream environ-mental groups, an expansion that had culminated in Earth Day's twenty-year anniversary extravaganza that took place in 1990 as well as a new round of policy initiatives such as the Clean Air Act Amendments of 1990 and gatherings such as the 1992 Rio Earth Summit Conference."[184] In other words, environmentalism, an important issue for several decades, was a particularly hot topic in the 1990s as it achieved a more mainstream status. To care about the health of the planet, to protect wild animals, to stand up for indigenous peoples – these were all good things and worth celebrating. To do the opposite, and engage in activities and practices which hurt the Earth and the animals and people living on it, showed at best a degree of ignorance, and at worst meant that you were just plain evil. Indeed, films such as the Oscar-nominated *Gorillas in the Mist* (1988) had highlighted a number of issues about animal conservation and the destruction of colo-nising forces and the destructiveness of the trade in wild animals, while films such as the Oscar-winning *Dances With Wolves* (1990) championed the cause of those groups of indigenous people who found themselves marginalized, persecuted and demeaned by militarily-stronger outside forces who sought to obtain their resources (usually their land).[185] The four villains in this section touch upon all of these issues, and reflect the adoption of these beliefs by the wider society; children's and family films are not known as a group for putting forward controversial messages (lest they alienate the parents in the audience), so the vilification of

183 For an in-depth discussion on this in relation to *Pocahontas*, see Amy M. Davis, "Borrowing the Earth: Saving the Planet and Disney's *Pocahontas*", in Reynold Humphries, Gilles Ménégaldo, and Melvyn Stokes, Eds., *Cinéma et Mythes*, (Poitiers: University of Poitiers, 2002), pp. 77-89.

184 Robert Gottlieb, "The Next Environmentalism: How Movements Respond to The Changes that Elections Bring – from Nixon to Obama", in *Environmental History*, Vol. 14, No. 2 (April 2009), p. 299.

185 For a discussion of revisionist westerns, see Donald Hoffman, "Whose Home on the Range?: Finding Room for Native Americans, African Americans, and Latino Americans in the Revisionist Western", in *MELUS*, vol. 22, No. 2 (Summer 1997), pp. 45-59.

the practices of hunting animals and overpowering native peoples – and treating them sympathetically when those natives rise up to fight off the interlopers – speaks volumes.

McLeach, of *The Rescuers Down Under*, is the poacher who threatens the animals of the Outback and the boy who seeks to protect them, Cody. He is possibly the most comic of the four villains in this section, yet despite the ridiculous aspects of his character, he is nonetheless a genuine danger to all around him. We first meet McLeach when Cody accidentally falls into one of his pit traps (one for which he uses a live mouse as bate, as well as an electronic system to alert him that the trap has been sprung). Everything about McLeach's arrival on the scene is shown to be destructive: we first know he is on his way because of the shaking and rumbling of the forest, then we see an overhead shot of him racing through the outback in his specially modified jeep, tearing a path through the brush in a vehicle which seems to be part army tank, part bulldozer, part monster truck. Presumably, he built it himself. McLeach tries to pretend that the hole in which Cody is trapped was dug by Joanna, a goanna lizard who serves as his sidekick, but Cody knows better and stands up to McLeach. Soon, McLeach realises that Cody has a feather belonging to the female golden eagle, Marahute, whom Cody has freed from one of McLeach's traps. Laughing hatefully, McLeach brags that he was the one who "got the father" (showing one of the male eagle's feathers, then pretending to use it as a knife to slash his own throat, a malevolent grin on his face as he makes the action). He demands that Cody tell him where the female eagle and her nest are; when Cody refuses, McLeach orders Joanna to attack him. Cody says his mother will call the rangers, but McLeach grabs Cody's backpack, throws it into a river full of crocodiles, and says, mockingly, "My poor baby boy got eaten by the crocodiles. Boo-hoo." It is at this point that the Rescue Aid Society – the mouse-run organisation, headquartered in the basement of the United Nations building in New York City, which serves to protect children all over the world – is called into action, and events ensue that will lead to Cody's rescue from McLeach's clutches.

Indeed, McLeach is shown to be a particularly despicable figure. When we see him next, he has Cody in a cage in the back of his vehicle and is heading home across a landscape which he proclaims to be abandoned opal mines. He then begins to sing a perversion of an American folk song:

> Home, home on the range!
> Where critters are tied up in chains –
> I cut through their sides,

And I rip off their hides,
And the next day I do it again!

McLeach is shown, both through this song and through his actions, to be someone who exploits the environment for his own gain. He even takes pleasure from the harm he does, and is self-centred in a way which hints strongly at his being mentally and emotionally unstable. Later, when we are inside McLeach's home/lair, we see that it is a barren, uncomfortable place the colour of dried-up earth. Furthermore, he has Cody tied up to a chair sitting in front of a large map of the local area, and he throws knives at it – on either side of and just above Cody's head – as a way to frighten and intimidate the boy. When he sees that this will not work, he then offers Cody half of the money that would come from the sale of the golden eagle, if only Cody will tell him where the nest is. Cody refuses, however, much to McLeach's fury. His reaction is one of violent anger. In his subsequent scene, he is shown to be not nearly as smart as he likes to think, when Joanna tricks him out of the eggs he has set aside for his supper, but he is able nonetheless to figure out that Cody's "weakness" is his desire to help protect the eagle's eggs, as well as the eagle herself. He follows the boy to the eagle's nest and captures the eagle, Cody, and the three mice, then exults in his success: "Look at her, Joanna – the rarest bird in the world. That bird's gonna make me rich – filthy rich!" He tells Joanna she can eat the eagle's eggs (or, as McLeach puts it, speaking to Joanna in the third person, "Does she want to make sure that bird stays rare?"), a prospect which Joanna finds exciting until she sees how hard it is to get to the nest. McLeach lowers her using a rope and harness, but when she reaches the nest and tries to eat the eggs, she realises that the nest instead has three egg-shaped stones. She throws them out of the nest (but first finds herself compelled to pretend to McLeach that she has eaten the eggs; he is shown to be intent on their destruction), and McLeach raises her back up. They set off with their prize – the captured Marahute. McLeach, describing Cody as a "loose end to tie up", drives away from Marahute's nest and back onto the plains. We next see him – again, singing a folk song ("Froggie Went a-Courtin'"; McLeach, who has Cody trussed up at the end of a rope to lower him into a river full of crocodiles, is singing "You get a line and I'll get a pole, matey ... You get a line and I'll get a pole, and we'll go fishin' in a crocodile hole …") and proclaiming his dunking of Cody into the crocodile net as "my idea of fun". Just then, with Cody dangling just out of reach of the crocodiles, the power goes out on the vehicle. McLeach sees a razorback hog run out of his truck, then sees that the keys are gone from the ignition. Refusing to be stopped, he begins shooting at the rope in order to sever it, but before he can break it completely, Joanna knocks him into the water. He fights the crocodiles, but Joanna (whose loyalty to McLeach is limited at best) abandons him and gets to shore, while the crocodiles back off just as McLeach is caught in the rapids and goes over the waterfall. Cruel and stupid to the end, his death is shown to be deserved. After his death, he is never mentioned again. His dying as a result of the wild animals and natural resources of the area (the crocodiles and the river) is a fitting punishment for someone who would destroy both without a second thought.

Ratcliffe, who is the corrupt governor of the Virginia colony in *Pocahontas* (1995), likewise stands out as a stranger in a strange land, and one who is there not because he wishes to learn and explore, but because he sees it as a chance to become filthy rich and advance to an exalted rank in the court of King James I of England. His arrival at the ship – and so his introduction in the film – shows him to be a pretentious, aloof man: dressed in an elaborate purple costume with lace cuffs, he is carried to the dock in a grand, black-painted closed coach with blue plumes on the roof and purple curtains in the windows. He steps out onto a purple carpet, an honour guard lining each side who salute him, and he waves (almost as if bored) at the crowd. He is shortly followed by his servant, who carries his equally-snobby dog, Percy, on a purple pillow. Interestingly, the music – the song "The Virginia Company", which outlines their hopes for the voyage – has as its lyrics when Ratcliffe is introduced,

> On the beaches of Virginney
> There's diamonds like debris
> There's silver rivers flowin'
> Gold you pick right off a tree
> With a nugget for my Winnie
> And another one for me
> And all the rest'll go
> To the Virginia Company!
> It's glory, God and gold,
> And the Virginia Company

It introduces Ratcliffe's ambitions perfectly. As we watch in a long shot as Ratcliffe strides up the gangplank onto the ship, closer to the camera we see a rat run across a rope onto the ship in a line that is parallel to Ratcliffe. While it is of course historically accurate to see rats creeping onto the ship, equally it is symbolic of the parasitic nature of Ratcliffe – whose name begins with Rat (a historically-accurate spelling, admittedly) – who is very much the villain at the centre of this film. This contrasts him with the film's hero, John Smith: his arrival is much livelier and more jovial: the crew know who he is, and his reputation as an adventurer makes him popular with the crew as a whole. Throughout the voyage, Ratcliffe remains aloof from the men; when a ferocious storm strikes the ship and one of the men is washed overboard and has to be saved by Smith in a daring rescue, Ratcliffe comes out, looking dry, pristine, and bored, asking, "Trouble on deck?" as if he has been completely unaware that the ship was in any difficulty, let alone that crewmembers had nearly died. He then gives a "pep talk" to the crew, reminding them that waiting for them in the "new world" is "Freedom, prosperity, the adventure of our lives. You're the finest crew England has to offer and nothing – not wind nor rain nor a thousand bloodthirsty savages shall stand in our way." The men cheer him, and he returns to his cabin. When Wiggins, his servant, complements him on his "stirring oration", his reply shows his real attitude: "Let us hope so. I'll need those witless peasants to dig up my gold, won't I?" For Ratcliffe, the crew are nothing more than expendable labour who will make him rich. Becoming rich is his most important goal, and he intends to let nothing stand in his way.

Their arrival in Virginia likewise sees Ratcliffe as incapable of viewing the landscape around them as anything other than his personal treasure trove. Rather than comment on the land's natural beauty, or even its abundant plant life and fresh water, he says only, "Look at it, Wiggins – an entire New World chock full of gold, just waiting for me." When Wiggins asks about the likelihood that they will encounter any Indians (or Savages, as he calls them), Ratcliffe's reply is equally cold-hearted: "If we do, we shall be sure to give them a proper English greeting". When Wiggins mistakes Ratcliffe's implied threat and exclaims, "Oh – gift baskets!" holding up two brimming baskets, ready to go, Ratcliffe turns back to looking out the window, muttering, "Humph! And he came so highly recommended …" He views the Native Americans not as fellow human beings, but as vermin who could become a threat that must be "dealt with", and refers to them as "Savages" and "Heathens". Not that he thinks of the British crew as being very much better: they are his servants, essentially, and he believes he can use and manipulate them as and how he thinks necessary, and that they will follow him unquestioningly. Yet he seems to be jealous of Smith, admitting to Wiggins that he has never been a popular man, complaining, "And don't think I don't know what those back-stabbers at court say about me". Wiggins' reply is played for laughs, but of course presents an accurate picture of Ratcliffe: "Oh yes, that – all that talk about being a pathetic social climber who's failed at everything …". Ratcliffe vows that he will succeed in this venture, and spends the next section of the film doggedly in pursuit of the gold and wealth he believes to be in Virginia (after all, if the Spanish found huge amounts of gold in the parts of the "New World" they "explored", then surely he will find similar riches in Virginia, despite the fact that it is a couple of thousand miles from Central and South America …).

Unfortunately for Ratcliffe, Virginia does not have gold or gems: its wealth was primarily in the plants and animals there, which offered abundant land for farming and hunting, huge resources of timber and furs and fish that could be traded, and rich, fertile soil that, later, would be used to farm crops like tobacco for export to Britain and the rest of Europe and which would make some colonists extremely rich. But the Ratcliffe we meet in this film has no knowledge of, let alone interest in, endeavours such as hunting and farming. He wants gold, and he wants it fast. When the settlers finally come ashore, he has them set to digging up the earth for gold before they even begin to build houses (he delegates one small team to unload the ship, another small team to build the fort, and the majority of the men to dig). In a montage accompanied by Ratcliffe's song "Mine, Mine, Mine" (referring both to the possessive form of "me" and to the activity of mining for minerals), he encourages the men to dig the ground and fell the trees:

> The gold of Cortez,
> The Jewels of Pizarro,
> Will seem like mere trinkets
> By this time tomorrow!
> The gold we find here will dwarf them by far,
> So with all you've got in you, boys,
> Dig up Virginia, boys!

He himself, however, does not participate in the hard work, saying in the song, "I'd help you to dig boys/But I've got this crick in my spine". The only work as such that we see Ratcliffe do is to light a cannon so that the cannonball will slice through a line of tall trees, thereby chopping them down even faster. By the end of the montage, Ratcliffe stands atop a bare earth mound at least fifteen or twenty feet tall (given that there are three lines of men circled around it, digging); the land almost appears to have been strip-mined. It is very much in contrast with the verse of the song sung by John Smith, against a backdrop of the natural wonders of the environment, about what *he* sees as the reason for coming to Virginia:

> All of my life I have searched for a land like this one!
> A wild or more challenging country I couldn't design –

Hundreds of dangers await, and I don't plan to miss one!
In a land I can claim – a land I can tame – the greatest adventure is mine!

While Smith, too, will be shown to be somewhat misguided in his attitude that the British have the right to lay claim to a land that already belongs to others, nonetheless he still stands out as the one who is there for the "right" reasons – to learn and explore and grow as a human being – whereas Ratcliffe is there only to rob the land and its people of anything of value. He also shows himself to be an unworthy, despicable person by his misunderstanding of strength and masculinity, particularly when he demeans young Thomas with the claim that "A man's not a man unless he knows how to shoot". Ratcliffe, eventually, will be shown up as the blood-thirsty savage of the film; Thomas, on the other hand, will be seen to be someone who distrusts Ratcliffe and his motives, and ultimately will rise to a leadership role within Jamestown, taking charge and ordering that Ratcliffe be restrained and deported after he tries to shoot Powhatan. Afterward, in the final scene, Thomas is standing out in front of the other British to greet Pocahontas and her delegation of Powhatan when she comes to bid farewell to John Smith. It will show the falsehood of Ratcliffe's bellicose attitude, and contrast his hatefulness against Thomas' inclination to be just and fair.

Of course, there was never gold in Virginia, so Ratcliffe's search for it is unsuccessful. He becomes increasingly frustrated, finally latching onto the idea that the Indians are hiding it for themselves; this means that the only way that he can obtain the gold is to eradicate the local tribes. For Ratcliffe, the only problem he has with this is one of strategy. Eventually, on the pretext of rescuing Smith (who has been taken prisoner by the Powhatan because they believe that he murdered Kocoum), he fires up the settlers to attack the Indians during the song "Savages", which contrasts the racial hatred, prejudice, and ignorance of the British against the racial hatred, prejudice and ignorance of the Powhatan, as each prepares to go to war in the hopes of eradicating the other side. Of course, ultimately, Pocahontas will stop the fight before it starts, preventing her father from executing Smith and making a plea for peace which he hears (partly thanks to the intervention of the spirit of Pocahontas' mother), and sees the sense of. The settlers, too, wish to avoid war, and when they see Smith released, they see no reason to fight and put down their weapons. Ratcliffe, however, is not moved. He cries out, "Now's our chance – fire!" and points his sword toward the Powhatan warriors. This time, however, the men (who have grown to distrust him as a leader) refuse to follow him, pointing out that the Powhatan have no wish to fight. But Ratcliffe will not be thwarted of his chance to remove the Indians so that he can obtain the riches he believes they are hording. Grabbing one of the men's rifles, he aims at Chief Powhatan and fires the weapon, but Smith jumps in front of Powhatan and takes the bullet. The men wrestle the gun from Ratcliffe and arrest him. At the end of the film, we see him bundled onto the ship to be returned to England; as far as the settlers are concerned, he has no place in the Jamestown settlement.

As I discuss at some length in my paper "Borrowing the Earth: Saving the Planet and Disney's *Pocahontas*", the traditional story of Pocahontas and John Smith, which began as a historical episode, over the centuries was altered and embroidered upon until it became a myth which had almost nothing to do with the real-life individuals upon whom the story was based. As myth/folklore, the story has been used to promote numerous positive messages, especially the idea that the settlers and the Native Americans, at least in the initial period of European colonization, were able to befriend one another and work together. This is shown in this myth by the supposed romance that took place between Pocahontas and John Smith, as well as by the story of Squanto's role in the founding of the Plymouth colony in the early 1620s in Massachusetts. Disney, however, in addition to this, saw the possibility of including within the film an eco-logical/environmental message, this time focusing on the evils of the idea of stripping a place of its natural resources and destroying the environment out of a misguided desire for personal wealth.[186]

In such a story, a character who is a conniving, greedy, racist, snobbish, self-obsessed petty tyrant is perfect for stressing the themes of environmentalism and racial/cultural tolerance that were so important to popular culture in the 1990s in particular. In this sense, as the ignorant representative of a greedy foreign power intent on conquest at any cost, Ratcliffe is a predictable, though enjoyable, character. It is interesting that, despite his transgressions, he does not die. It is not necessarily out of a desire to preserve historical factuality, given how historically imprecise the film is as a whole, with the ending in particular becoming ridiculously inaccurate in its claim that the only way to save John Smith's life after he is shot is to put him on a tiny ship to spend three or four months sailing from Jamestown to London. To have done away with Ratcliffe would not have been any more or less ahistorical than anything else in the film. Yet Ratcliffe survives the narrative and is returned to England – an ignominious failure, of course, but alive all the same. Nor is it squeamishness on Disney's part: after all, the villains of numerous other Disney's animated films have died, often violent, horrible deaths. Perhaps

[186] For a full discussion of this interpretation of the myth of Pocahontas and John Smith, see Davis, "Borrowing the Earth: Saving the Planet and Disney's *Pocahontas*", in Reynold Humphries, Gilles Ménégaldo, and Melvyn Stokes, Eds., *Cinéma et Mythes*, (Poitiers: University of Poitiers, 2002), pp. 77-89.

the clue lies in his dog, Percy: Percy lands in Virginia with a bump, ends up lost in the woods and in an antagonistic relationship with Meeko, Pocahontas' racoon friend, before finally becoming friends with Meeko and with Flit, Pocahontas' and Meeko's hummingbird friend. By the end of the film, Percy has not only decided to stay in Virginia without his former master, but has also lost his snotty attitude and foreign ways: we see him side-by-side with Meeko (who is now wearing Percy's fancy collar), wrapped in an Indian cloak and wearing three feathers on top of his head. He has come to know his peers in this place, and has learned to understand them and appreciate them, finally integrating himself within their society. Perhaps this is the film showing that, at some point, it can be hoped that even someone as flawed as Ratcliffe can learn the error of his ways. To kill him off because of his own intolerance might, perhaps, come across as equally intolerant. Showing that it is possible for him to reform is a more positive, hopeful message. Percy was just as hateful and predictable as Ratcliffe at the start of the film; Ratcliffe, by remaining predictably hateful, provides a reason to keep Pocahontas and John Smith apart (since in no version of the myth do they marry), and simultaneously serve as the extreme opposing force against whose example the others can become better.

Clayton, the villain of *Tarzan* is equally predictable as a type, and plays into notions of colonial entitlement and destruction of the landscape which tie him very much to the characters McLeach, the villain of *The Rescuers Down Under*, and Ratcliffe. Physically, he also bears a strong facial resemblance to Captain Hook of *Peter Pan*. He arrives on the scene with a bang – literally – when his rifle is heard echoing through the jungle by Tarzan's gorilla troop. When we first see him, it is from Tarzan's point of view: Tarzan is watching Clayton's approach from the underbrush as Clayton swings a machete back and forth to clear away the bamboo. He is every inch the great white hunter, proclaiming that it was long ago, while he was hunting wildebeests, that "I knew I was born for Africa, and Africa was created for ..." His speech fades out as he senses that he is being watched, and instead of finishing the sentence with the word "me", we hear his rifle as he fires into the jungle, very nearly hitting Tarzan. He is the epitome of the old expression "Shoot first, and ask questions later", and seems to assume that it is his right to fire indiscriminately into the jungle; anything or anyone he might hit is inconsequential. That the word "me" at the end of his sentence is replaced by the sound of gunfire – a sound which, later, Tarzan mistakenly will think is called "Clayton" – is a further symbolic linkage between Clayton as a character and the violence and destructiveness of those who hunt big game. Clayton knows nothing about the environment around him, nor does he care about understanding it. This aspect of his character is shown early on when, in reaction to Professor Porter and Jane's delight at seeing evidence that gorillas (which they have come to the jungle to study) live in family groups, Clayton sneers at them: "Family groups?! Excuse me, but these are wild beasts that would sooner tear your head off than look at you!" Clayton is equally-dismissive of Tarzan; listening to Jane describe him to her father, Clayton declares Tarzan to be a "girlish fantasy"; when, seconds later, Tarzan drops into the camp from a tree, Clayton sees that he is real, but grabs his rifle and nearly shoots him; he is prevented from doing so only by Jane's pushing the rife upward at the last second. Tarzan, upon hearing the shot, says, "Clayton!" He thinks the word means the sound of the rifle. Clayton thinks he can get Tarzan to tell him where the gorillas are, but of course Tarzan cannot understand human speech, and accidentally makes a fool of Clayton. He also does not recognise the drawing of a "gorilla" Clayton shows to him: it is a comically-bad rendition, a snarling monster rather than an accurate depiction of the animals with whom Tarzan has grown up.

For the next portion of the film, Clayton takes something of a backseat, presumably hoping that Jane and Porter, who seem to be better than he at getting through to Tarzan, will get him to show them where the gorillas live. Eventually, he is able to persuade Tarzan – who is still very much an innocent when it comes to understanding human motivations – that Jane will stay in the jungle with him if Tarzan will show her the gorillas. He agrees, and this is when Clayton comes into his own. He marks on a map the location of the gorilla encampment, and then, when Tarzan agrees to accompany Jane and her father back to England, he captures them and the good sailors, and with the help of the bad sailors, goes back to the gorilla encampment, this time to capture as many as he can to sell in England. Having been almost attacked earlier by Kerchak (who is defending his troop), Clayton decides to shoot him. Tarzan, with the help of his friends Terk and Tantor, has escaped from the ship (along with Jane, her father, and the imprisoned sailors), and shows up in the nick of time. A battle ensues, and Clayton finds himself in hand-to-hand combat with Tarzan. There is a key moment in the battle when, high up in a tree, Tarzan manages to get hold of Clayton's rifle and points it at him threateningly. Clayton taunts Tarzan: "Go ahead – shoot. Be a man." Tarzan holds up the gun, then imitates perfectly the sound the rifle makes when it is fired, momentarily frightening Clayton. Tarzan then says to him, furiously, "I'm not a man like you!" Tarzan and Clayton are polar opposites: whereas Tarzan is keenly intelligent and observant, honest and noble, generous, kind, but innocent and naïve, Clayton is of average intelligence at best (and not nearly as bright as he thinks), notices only what is right in front of him (and only when it suits him to do so), and has no problem lying and deceiving to get whatever he wants. Tarzan protects the jungle and the animals who live there, whereas Clayton thinks nothing of destroying it. He believes that an enjoyment of killing animals shows that he belongs in Africa and makes him a guide to the jungle. But he is ignorant of the jungle's secrets and its true beauty. As with McLeach, his death – caused ultimately by his own hand (Clayton becomes caught up in the vines high up in the trees, and though Tarzan tries to save him, Clayton is so intent on killing Tarzan that he falls and is hanged) – is the direct result of his lack of respect for the environment around him and for life in general. His death is not mourned, and he is never mentioned again.

As was alluded to in chapter one's discussion of Tarzan, Clayton's name clearly links him to the Burroughs character of William Cecil Clayton, who is Tarzan's cousin; Tarzan's birth name, it seems, is John Clayton. No reference is made to this at all in the film, nor is it mentioned in the "Backstage" extras on the 2013 dvd release of the film. The supervising animator on Clayton, Randy Haycock, notes that, when researching the role, "I was watching a lot of old adventure films that had big game hunters as their main characters. Forty years ago, these guys – who played the same role that Clayton plays in this film – were the heroes! But in today's climate, doing the same thing – collecting animals for the zoo – is an evil thing."[187] Haycock also claims in this short documentary that, in trying to sum up the character in one word, his choice was "suave": Clayton is polished, poised, and able to charm those around him, and does this in order to conceal his true nature and intentions, which will cause harm to those around him. This makes Haycock's claims about the character rather strange: it would be unusual for the hero of a film of any era to kidnap the film's leading lady and imprison her, her father, and her friend in the hold of a ship. While it is true that characters who, like Clayton, were big game hunters were sometimes the heroes of films and novels, it is equally true that the heroes of classic Hollywood films were rarely as dishonest, cruel, and selfish as Clayton and not considered to be at least compromised, if not the outright villain of the piece. Coming closer to an accurate description of the character is Brian Blessed, who provides Clayton's voice: "His is a life-long romance: Clayton loves himself. [He is an] Absolutely total egomaniac."[188] He is, there-

187 Backstage Disney/The Characters of Tarzan/Clayton and Sabor/"Creating Clayton". Disc 2, from *Tarzan: 2-Disc Special Edition* (Region 2/PAL, © Edgar Rice Burroughs, Inc., and Disney Enterprises, Inc., DVD release date 8 February 2013).

188 Backstage Disney/The Characters of Tarzan/Clayton and Sabor/"Creating Clayton".

fore, the perfect foil for Tarzan, an idea supplemented by this knowledge from the source material that the two men are cousins. When Tarzan refuses to be a man like Clayton, he denies in Clayton a kind of past association with colonialism; that Tarzan's accent is American – again, it is an incongruous choice, given that he is learning English from three Brits, all of whom have fairly posh English accents – in some ways associates him with the colonized, given that the British colonized America, too. Tarzan may have come from that world (after all, we do not know why his parents were travelling to Africa in the first place), but he rejects it. Clayton, however, embraces the worst of it; the natural environment is his to destroy and exploit as he chooses. He makes his living from it and – ultimately – he becomes so entangled in it that it kills him. As with McLeach, he is missed by no one.

Clayton is a character who, in seeking to destroy the troop of gorillas who raised Tarzan, could be said simultaneously to be on the verge of destroying not only endangered wild animals, but also an indigenous people; after all, for Tarzan, the gorillas are family, and we get to know them as if they were people. Our final villain in this section, Rourke, likewise is the would-be destroyer of a group of people, but in a way which is not as direct as Clayton: he attempts to rob the people of Atlantis of the force – the power – which has allowed them to function for thousands of years, and which has kept them alive and protected. Threatening anyone directly is done only to secure the power source, the Heart of Atlantis. We first meet Rourke when the film's hero, Milo Thatch, first arrives to board the vessel – captained by Rourke – which will take the group of explorers to Atlantis. Only this time, we have almost no indication that we are meeting a villain. Rourke has a folksy way about him: he chats genially with Milo and Mr. Whitmore, who is financing the exhibition, and when he sees the copy of *The Shepherd's Journal* – the book which will help them find their way to Atlantis, he comments unaffectedly, "Personally, I prefer a good Western myself". There is a slight moment of foreshadowing, when, after commenting on how much has been spent on the expedition, Milo promises that "This will be peanuts compared to what we'll gain on this expedition". Rourke's reply seems innocuous at first, but in hindsight shows that his warm exterior hides a calculating, rapacious schemer: "I'm sure we'll find this all very enriching". He seems, at least initially, to care about his crew, and is a calm, competent, strong leader who has earned the respect of those serving with him. Though he never exactly takes Milo, the newest member of the team and the least practically-oriented of the group (he is there for his linguistic abilities and academic knowledge, not because of any mechanical or weapons skills), under his wing, he does demonstrate that he values Milo's scholarly credentials and intellect; never does Rourke imply that he could be a threat. When the team first encounters the people of Atlantis, he is as surprised as everyone else to see that they have found a living civilization rather than ruins, and speaks to them warmly, as if pleased to discover that the society exists. Yet the first hint that Rourke is a cold, hardened mercenary comes shortly after they have met the Atlanteans: as they drive their vehicles into Atlantis, Helga Sinclair, his first officer on the expedition, says quietly to him, "Commander, there were not supposed to be people down here. This changes everything." Rourke's reply is spoken with a sinister hardness: "This changes nothing". On this score, Rourke is as good as his word. Not at all put off by the fact that Atlantis is alive and (mostly) well, Rourke is determined to find and bring back – for his own gain – the "Heart of Atlantis", which the expedition believes to be a great power source that allowed Atlantis to become technologically advanced by thousands of years compared to the rest of the ancient world. The idea that bringing the Heart of Atlantis back to the surface world would destroy the people of Atlantis is inconsequential: they are mere "obstacles to be overcome", by any means necessary.

Later, Milo discovers that the Heart of Atlantis is more than just an inanimate object when he swims with Kida – the princess of Atlantis and heir to its throne – to see a lost mural that tells the history of the city. When they return to the surface, he discovers that the other members of the expedition, led by Rourke, are planning to go after the Heart by force. It is then that Milo discovers Rourke's true nature:

> Milo: You think it's some kind of a diamond – I thought it was some kind of a battery – but we're both wrong. It's their life force. That crystal is the only thing keeping these people alive – you take that away and they'll die!
>
> Rourke: Well, that changes things. Helga, what do you think?
>
> Helga: Knowing that, I'd double the price.
>
> Rourke: I was thinking triple.
>
> Milo: Rourke, don't do this!
>
> Rourke: Academics. You never want to get your hands dirty. Think about it: if you gave back every stolen artefact from a museum, you'd be left with an empty building. We're just providing a necessary service to the archaeological community.

In other words, Rourke not only has no moral compunction against robbing Atlantis of its very life force – its heart – he sees no difference between the artefacts of dead civilizations and the sacred objects of living ones. Becoming increasingly forceful, and backed up not only with guns, but with soldiers (dressed menacingly in the kinds of trench coats and gas masks that have become associated with the Western front in World War I), Rourke and Helga take Kida and Milo hostage.[189]

Milo is forced to translate and interpret the book and the inscriptions around him to help Rourke find the Heart of Atlantis: he does so only because Rourke has threatened Kida directly. Soon, Rourke, Helga, Kida and Milo stumble upon an underground chamber where they see a light source (similar to the crystals the Atlanteans wear around their necks) high above them. Suddenly, and much to everyone's surprise, a blank look comes over Kida: she is drawn to stand underneath – and then is lifted up into – the glow overhead, and is transformed into a crystalline version of herself and descends to the ground. The Heart of Atlantis has chosen her, we will soon learn, and bonded with her completely. It is a sight which terrifies Milo, who has developed feelings for Kida, and astounds Helga, who watches in open-mouthed amazement. Rourke, however, seems barely moved: he watches with a look almost of irritation, chewing on a toothpick. It is as if he has no heart at all. The next thing we see, Kida has been crated into a metal box (similar to a coffin) to be taken back to the surface world. Milo berates the members of the expedition for their actions, and in most cases, his words can be seen to hit home, though not, of course with Rourke. Telling Milo to "Get off your soapbox", he implies that Milo is the one who is misguided: "You've read Darwin: it's called natural selection. We're just helping it along." Milo is livid, but is out-gunned and out-manned. But it is when Rourke punches Milo (in an unprovoked assault) that, one by one, the members of the expedition get out of the trucks and come to stand beside Milo and the Atlanteans. In response to Rourke's angry retort "You pick now to grow a conscience?" one of the secondary characters, an explosives expert named Santorini says, "We've done a lot of things we're not proud of: robbing graves, plundering tombs, double parking ... but nobody got hurt. Well, maybe somebody got hurt, but nobody we knew." Rourke is irritated, but does not argue with them. Muttering to himself as he gets into his truck, "P.T. Barnum was right",[190] he gets into the truck, ready to leave behind a group of people he has worked with for years rather than miss out on what he describes as their "biggest payday ever".

Ultimately, Rourke is destroyed: it is a key component of family cinema that good triumph, and so it does here. In fact, he is punished and destroyed in quite spectacular fashion, at the cul-

189 Indeed, the depiction of the soldiers, rendered nearly faceless – with only two large, blank, shiny glass discs instead of eyes – by their gas masks, brings to mind the soldiers depicted in the 1939 Oscar-nominated MGM short "Peace on Earth", directed by Hugh Harman, in which successions of masked human soldiers fight each other until all of humanity has been killed in senseless warfare. *Atlantis: The Lost Empire* is set in 1914, so this depiction of the soldiers' uniforms is appropriate. However, only the soldiers are covered up in this way; all of the other characters are dressed in normal clothes, some only in trousers and undershirts. This covering up of the soldiers' faces and bodies has the effect of dehumanizing them, and contributes further to the aura of menace connected to Rourke.

190 Rourke is referring to saying attributed to circus owner P.T. Barnum, who supposedly once said that "There's a sucker born every minute".

mination of a brief battle scene, when Milo uses a piece of glass from the window on Kida's "coffin" (the glass has taken on the properties of the Heart, presumably because it is a crystalline structure in close proximity to Kida/the Heart) to cut Rourke's arm, and he is transformed into a crystalline structure by it (it possesses a consciousness, so presumably it transforms Rourke in revenge for his actions) and destroyed. His death is brought about in part because Milo helps the Atlanteans figure out how to use the ancient war planes used by their ancestors, and they are able to defeat Rourke and rescue Kida before she is consumed forever by the Heart of Atlantis. One of the interesting things about Rourke is the way in which he is slowly revealed to be a villain and a mercenary who is capable of committing any atrocity so long as he can profit by it. Of course, he does not evolve into such a character: we – and the other characters – simply learn more about him, and see him pushed into revealing his true self – as the story unfolds. But while his characterisation may differ from McLeach and Clayton in that we know they are bad from the start, we are fooled by Rourke, not least because he is voiced by James Garner, an icon of American film and television who is probably best remembered for *Maverick* (1957-1962) and *The Rockford Files* (1974-80) as well as a succession of romantic/bedroom comedies in which his co-stars included Doris Day (*The Thrill of it All*, *Move Over Darling*, both 1963), Lee Remick (*Separate Beds*, 1963), Julie Andrews (*The Americanization of Emily*, 1964), Elke Sommer and Angie Dickinson (*The Art of Love*, 1965), and Debbie Reynolds (*How Sweet it Is*, 1968). So to watch as Rourke, who starts out as a tiny bit gruff but very likeable and familiar, transforms into someone so utterly heartless and despicable has a level of shock value about it. It plays upon ideas of the star persona (as discussed by Dyer in his now classic monograph *Stars*[191]), but violates those expectations in a way that is seldom found in family films.

But even more interesting than this violation of Garner's star persona and Rourke's slow reveal as the bad guy is the way in which his crime situates itself as one which is both a misuse of his authority and his violation of modern ethics about the preservation of endangered cultures and the theft of cultural artefacts. In truth, the sentiments Rourke expresses fit well within the history of "collecting" artefacts for the world's museums. In a paper on the British Museum, for example, Kelly Elizabeth Yasaitis points out that "The problem of unmitigated looting haunts museums in deciding which objects to accept or acquire and in dealing with varying levels or a lack of documented provenance".[192] But there is, in *Atlantis*, the added wrinkle that

191 Richard Dyer, *Stars (New Edition)* (London: BFI, 2007), pp.125-131.

192 Kelly Elizabeth Yasaitis, "Collecting Culture at the British Museum", in *Curator: The Museum Journal*, Vol. 49, No. 4 (October 2006), p. 456.

the Heart of Atlantis is more than just a prized possession of the Atlanteans' cultural heritage, the way the Elgin Marbles are to Greece: the heart of Atlantis is also their greatest natural resource: we are told that without it, their society will cease to function and that they will die: we get a taste of this when Rourke begins to drive away from Atlantis with the transformed Kida and we see the light begin to fade from the crystals that the people wear around their necks. Shortly after Kida/the Heart has been removed from Atlantis, the elderly king dies, further emphasising the Heart's importance. The crime Rourke is committing, therefore, is more than just a bit of tomb plundering: it is an environmental disaster with aspects of genocide about it. Furthermore, Rourke's actions are an abuse of trust and of his role as leader: he persuades – albeit temporarily – a group of basically good people to commit an atrocity against a group of people who have done them no harm. When they finally refuse to follow him further down this path, he is not even shamed or much angered: he is so twisted and selfish that he seems them as "suckers" who deserve to be left behind and forgotten. In this, Rourke is like a combination of the worst of McLeach, Clayton, and Ratcliffe: he cares for no one but himself, he is determined to achieve his ends no matter what the cost to others, and he is willing to destroy an entire civilization and way of life to do it. He is an even greater threat than this group, however, because he is no comic fool (the other three all have strong elements of the ridiculous about them), and because, initially, he fools not only the other characters, but the audience, too. He is, arguably, the most dangerous villain in the Disney canon.

Magically Dangerous

So far, the villains we have examined have been human, however inhumane their behaviour. Yet this next group of villains goes (at least) a step beyond being human because each of them has the ability to use magic to achieve his ends. Because the hero(in)es they counter are not magical, it creates a very uneven and dangerous situation for the characters who must defeat these villains. Instead, the main characters must use their intelligence, pluck, cunning, and in particular their moral and emotional strength. If anything, these villains have come to rely so much on magic that, ultimately, they fail because they think they are unbeatable. Convinced that they have the upper hands with those who would stop them from carrying out their evil plans, they allow their powers to go to their head and fail to notice the weak spot in their defences. But the heroes of *The Black Cauldron* (1985) and *Aladdin*

(1992), as well as the heroine of *The Princess and the Frog* (2009), are ready to grab the first opportunity to gain the upper hand, and each turns the villain's magical powers against himself. They demonstrate that no evil is invincible, however terrible it may be, and that good can triumph in the end, even against the least human of evil-doers.

As Disney villains go, one of the most inhuman of all time, arguably, would be the Horned King of *The Black Cauldron* (1985). While it is true that some villains change into monstrous forms, such as Maleficent in *Sleeping Beauty* (1959), their primary bodies are still humanoid. Even Ursula in *The Little Mermaid* (1989), for all that she is – technically – an octopus, and therefore not really human, nonetheless has a human upper body; she is no more monstrous, in her way, than any of the merfolk (Ariel included), as they are all half human, half sea creature. But the Horned King is different; he appears to be a living skeleton, with horns growing from his head, and is possessed of an evil which is completely devoid of the touches of humour (let alone high camp) that typically serves to mitigate the menace of most other Disney villains. It is hard to think of the Horned King as a human, given his appearance, though it is possible that, in some distant past, he may have been human. His face, devoid of flesh, is a death-head skull with "eyes" gleaming from deep within the sockets, and two horns, like thick, short antlers, stick out on either side of his head, just above where a person's ears would be. Even the animation used to create him sets him apart, as it is clear that he has been rotoscoped, a choice of technique which makes him simultaneously more realistic and more threatening, given how few animated characters, especially within Disney's house style, are created through rotoscoping.[193] The technique makes the Horned King stand out even from the background in the image, imparting to him an otherworldliness that is designed to instil menace. When we first see him, he walks toward a pile of corpses – which we learn he plans to reanimate, using the Black Cauldron, to create an unstoppable army of soldiers known as the "Cauldron Born" – and strokes the skull of one of the corpses almost lovingly, the emphasis of the shot being his bony hands with their pointy, claw-like nails. Throughout most of the short scene which serves as the film's introduction of him, the Horned King's thin, unnatural voice – created for the film by John Hurt – carries a touch of elderly frailty mixed with steely determination; he can be heard talking softly to the pile of corpses as he describes his plans for them. The scene is in sharp contrast with those on either side: the world of Dalben's and Taran's dwelling, just before it, and a leafy forest scene immediately afterward. The

193 Rotoscoping is a technique patented in 1917 by Max Fleischer whereby live-action film is shot of an actor performing a sequence, then is fed into a rotoscope, a device that allows an artist to project the image, one frame at a time, onto a drawing board so that they can "trace", essentially, the actor in the live-action film onto cels so that the cels can, in turn, be photographed in the creation of the animated film. It replaces the free-hand drawing of a character, ostensibly to make the character more realistic. In practice, however, rotoscoped characters stand out from the traditionally/hand-animated characters around them (and from the hand-drawn environment of the backgrounds) to the point that rotoscoping, rather than making the character's appearance and movement more realistic, typically renders the character Uncanny.

colours surrounding the Horned King are very limited. Greys, blacks, sickly greens, and muted purples, punctuated with blood-like reds, dominate the world of the Horned King. In fact, we never see the Horned King outside of his castle; even when he creates his army of cauldron born, he does not walk in front of them to lead them, but instead watches them from an upper window of his castle as the army sets forth on their mission to conquer the world on his behalf.

In their book on the Disney villains, Frank Thomas and Ollie Johnston have very little to say about the Horned King. Mostly, the story of the film and the character are subsumed into the story of what was a difficult transitional period in Disney studio history. Their assessment of the Horned King was that he could have been done better. They write that,

> … the Horned King, who should have been mysterious, was as ordinary as the leader of a street gang. As Roy Disney said later, their approach was "too literal-minded. He was just a guy". The use of close-ups and too much activity gave the impression that here was a man one could argue with. He should have been as unreachable and intimidating as Chernobog [the Black God from the "Night on Bald Mountain" segment of *Fantasia*, 1940]. No one should speak in his presence. The words should wither in one's throat. We should not even know if this evil creature was man, animal or demon. Here was unlimited power on the verge of taking over the world that somehow had to be stopped, and that was the special challenge to the tiny band of characters who carried the hopes of the future on their uncertain shoulders. It seemed an impossible burden for the heroic cast as well as the inexperienced staff at the studio.[194]

In many ways, they have a point: this is a character with huge potential for menace: his inhuman appearance, his eerie voice, his far-reaching authoritarian control and incredible magical powers, his unyielding determination. He should have been unstoppable. In many ways, you can see this in the animation of the character; even Thomas and Johnston concede this. But as they say, as good as the animation itself was – and many of the animators who worked on *The Black Cauldron* went on to become amongst the most respected animators of the Disney renaissance and today – the fact is that, no matter how good or interesting the art that appears on screen, "… the greatest animation in the world cannot save weak story construction or overcome the failure to develop characters who are believable and enjoyable".[195] As a character, there is something flat about the Horned King. He is the greatest threat in all of Prydain, yet the confrontation between the Horned King and Taran lasts no more than a couple of minutes. His defeat goes fairly smoothly and easily, all things considered. But this does not change the fact that he is a genuine

194 Johnston and Thomas, *Villains*, p. 170.

195 Johnston and Thomas, *Villains*, p. 170-171.

threat within his world, as well as a direct danger to the young hero of the film. He comes across as cold, calculating, and heartless. He is never silly, never bumbling. Of all the Disney villains, the Horned King is probably amongst the most humourless treatments of villainy yet created.

Jafar, our next villain, does have about him comic touches, but he is menacing and dangerous nonetheless. Overweeningly ambitious, Jafar is the sultan's vizier, but is scheming to take power for himself, one way or another. He is the first of the film's major characters we meet, and is described by the market trader (whose opening monologue leads us into the story of Aladdin) as being "a dark man with a dark purpose". Jafar is looking for a magical source of power to help him become the ruler of Agrabah, and in doing a deal with a thief he has hired to retrieve yet another magical object for him, he accidentally stumbles upon the Cave of Wonders, a place he has been seeking for years. He is warned by the cave that only someone whose inner worth is hidden by a rough exterior can enter successfully and retrieve the magic lamp hidden within; he sees that he must find someone, and so works a spell which reveals Aladdin to him. He kidnaps Aladdin and sends him into the cave; all goes well until Aladdin's monkey, Abu, touches part of the treasure and causes the cave to collapse around them. Jafar escapes, but thinks Aladdin is dead; he is not bothered about the death of a young man, however, only that he has been stopped from obtaining the lamp.

But Jafar, like all villains, is a very tenacious sort of person. Undeterred, Jafar hits upon a new plan (suggested to him by Iago, his parrot sidekick): Jafar will marry Jasmine (he finds – or at least claims to find – a clause which will allow him to marry Jasmine despite his not being a prince), kill her and the sultan, and become sultan himself. Like the Horned King before him, Jafar himself has magical ability, and also seeks out magical implements which will help him wield power over others. In Jafar's case, he has a magical golden staff (with a handle shaped like a cobra's head), and he can channel his magic through it, using the cobra's eyes to control the sultan hypnotically. Jafar is unaware that, in the meantime, Aladdin has discovered the lamp's power, released the Genie within, been transformed into Prince Ali Ababwa, and wooed Jasmine successfully, and is horrified to realise that, at last, Jasmine has agreed to marry according to the law (since now, following the law will also mean following her heart). He has Aladdin kidnapped, tied up, and thrown into a deep body of water, unaware that the magic lamp is hidden under Aladdin's turban and that Genie can and will save Aladdin's life. Putting the sultan under his control once more, he brings the sultan to Jasmine and has him order her to marry Jafar. Aladdin shows up just in time, however, and reveals what Jafar has done, both to him and to the sultan: he destroys Jafar's staff in the process. Jafar is arrested briefly, but escapes into his secret lair in the palace. But Jafar has realised an important secret: he has caught a glimpse of the lamp in Aladdin's cloak, and realised that this "prince" is the same urchin he had tried to use to retrieve the lamp for himself. Iago manages to steal the lamp and bring it to Jafar: Jafar becomes Genie's new master. He demonstrates this by knocking Genie to the floor and placing one foot on Genie's head in a gesture of pure dominance and control.

Unsurprisingly, Jafar's first wish is, "I wish to rule on high as sultan". The film cuts to an exterior of the palace as dark, menacing clouds begin to circle overhead. The sultan magically is stripped of his clothes, which refit themselves to Jafar, and Iago announces him to be the new sultan. Aladdin realises that that Jafar now has control of Genie; he pleads with Genie to stop, but Genie says sadly, "Sorry, kid; I got a new master now", as he lifts the palace up and places it atop a high, rocky mountain. Aladdin has managed to escape by jumping out of the palace and onto the magic carpet, but the sultan and Jasmine remain behind and are defiant, refusing to bow to Jafar. Furious, Jafar proclaims, "If you won't bow before a sultan, then you will cower before a sorcerer! Genie – my second wish! I wish to be the most powerful sorcerer in the world!" Genie covers his eyes and turns his head away, pointing his finger at Jafar. Aladdin begs him not to, but Genie has no choice: with a zap, Jafar is transformed into a powerful sorcerer. His cobra-headed staff reappears, and he uses it to force Jasmine and the sultan to kowtow in front of him. Jafar then reveals "Prince Ali" to be none other than Aladdin, the street urchin. He throws Aladdin into a tower of the palace, then has it take off like a rocket. Now in total command, Jafar is shown enjoying his domination of the sultan and Jasmine: Iago force-feeds the sultan crackers (Iago hated having to eat the crackers the sultan would give him), while Jafar has Jasmine dressed as a slave/concubine, her wrists in chains, forced to wait upon him. He offers to marry Jasmine, but she refuses and throws a drink in his face. Saying, "I'll teach you some respect", he is about to hit Jasmine, when an idea strikes him: summoning Genie, he announces that he wants as his third wish for Jasmine to fall desperately in love with him. Unbeknownst to Jafar, however, Aladdin, Abu, and the carpet have made it back to the palace. They return to the palace just in time to see Jafar ordering Genie, as his third wish, to make Jasmine fall madly in love with him.

Genie tries to explain that he cannot make people fall in love (it is one of the few wishes he is unable to grant, along with raising the dead and assassinating someone), but Jasmine, who has spotted Aladdin, Apu, and the carpet high overhead, decides to distract Jafar by playing along, and pretends to be mad for him, telling Jafar in her most sultry voice how wonderful he is and describing all of his "good qualities" (there is a degree of comedy to this, as she is heard describing things like the "cute little gaps between your teeth" and that his beard is "so ... twisted"). Of course, the deception is revealed: as Jasmine, still pretending to be under Genie's spell, kisses Jafar, he sees Aladdin reflected in her crown. He begins using his magical powers to stop them as Aladdin, Jasmine, Abu and the carpet try to get hold of Genie's lamp so that Jafar will no longer have control of him, imprisoning Jasmine in a giant hour glass, unravelling the carpet, and turning Abu into a wind-up toy monkey. Fed up and angry, Aladdin challenges Jafar: "Are you afraid to fight me yourself, you cowardly snake?" But with the retort "You should see how snake-like I can be", Jafar transforms himself into a giant cobra and begins trying to attack Aladdin. He wraps Aladdin in his coils, and taunts him that without the genie, Aladdin is nothing. But just as things look lost, Aladdin is inspired: he returns Jafar's taunt, reminding him that Genie is the one who made Jafar a sorcerer, and therefore can also take that power away. Jafar, drunk with rage and power, realises that Aladdin is right, and so makes his third wish: to be an all-powerful genie. Genie reluctantly grants Jafar the wish, and he is transformed into a genie: Jafar revels in the intoxicating scope of his powers, proclaiming, "The universe is mind to command – to control!" However, far below, a tiny lamp has begun forming on the end of Jafar's genie body. Aladdin picks it up, proclaiming, "Not so fast, Jafar: aren't you forgetting something? You wanted to be a genie, you got it! And everything that goes with it! Phenomenal cosmic powers ... itty bitty living space." Jafar is sucked into his own lamp, this one a dark indigo colour, indicating the evil inside. We hear the angry, muffled voices of Jafar and Iago (who was sucked into the lamp with Jafar) from inside the lamp; it is the perfect punishment for the pair. Genie throws the lamp into the Cave of Wonders, hiding them away forever.

There is no doubting the magical powers of the final villain in this section, Dr. Facilier from *The Princess and the Frog* (2009). Known around New Orleans as "The Shadow Man", Facilier is angry. It is made clear in the film's opening song, "Down in New Orleans", that Facilier feels marginalised: he sits on the side lines, enticing people with Tarot readings, and watches with undisguised envy when he sees Big Daddy La Bouff driving past in his chauffeur-driven car. Later, during the song "Friends on the Other Side", Lawrence (Prince Naveen's servant) asks why Facilier does not use his magic for himself (in other words, why does Facilier need Lawrence to help him). He replies, "Fun fact about Voodoo, Larry – can't conjure a *thing* for myself. Besides – you and I both know the real power in this world ain't magic, it's *money* – buckets of it". Facilier cannot act alone, and needs an accomplice – preferably someone weak-willed and a little stupid, so that he can control them – if he wants to bring about his plans. He has gone to great lengths, begging favours from the spirit world (his "friends on the other side") and putting himself dangerously in their debt. Facilier must find a way to seize power over New Orleans so that he can repay the spirits with the souls of the people of New Orleans, for which the Voodoo spirits are shown to be very eager indeed.

Naturally, Voodoo plays an important part in the narrative of *The Princess and the Frog*: it is what Dr. Facilier uses to transform Naveen (and by extension Tiana) into frogs, and what he also uses to transform Lawrence into Naveen. What Dr. Facilier practices is more precisely hoodoo, rather than Voodoo; hoodoo, according to Carolyn Morrow Long, is different from Voodoo because,

> While Voodoo was concerned with maintaining the spiritual well-being of worshipers who served the African deities and the ancestors, hoodoo is directed toward controlling or influencing events and people, offering health, luck, love, money, employment, protection, justice, and revenge. Hoodoo 'workers' or 'doctors' operate strictly one on one, performing rituals and formulating charms, known in Louisiana as *gris-gris*. New Orleans hoodoo resembles African-based magical practices found elsewhere in the American South, but it exhibits a decidedly Roman Catholic influence, incorporating the use of altars, candles, incense, oils, holy water, and images of saints.[196]

However, his referring to it as Voodoo seems to be historically accurate, and what a hoodoo practitioner would have done in the early twentieth century.[197] Also accurate is Tiana's knowledge of it (as a black woman from New Orleans) and her rejection of it. As Long says of the black residents of New Orleans in the late nineteenth/early twentieth century, "The newly arrived Protestant 'American Negroes' and black native New Orleanians who had converted to Protestantism equated Voodoo with devil worship and renounced it altogether".[198] Tiana is equated very easily to the groups Long describes; certainly her incredibly strong work ethic (a trait long associated with Protestantism in the United States) and her intention of using hard work to raise herself on the social ladder, as well as her distrust of a figure like

196 Carolyn Morrow Long, "Perceptions of New Orleans Voodoo: Sin, Fraud, Entertainment, and Religion", in *Nova Religio: The Journal of Alternative and Emergent Religions*, Vol. 6, No. 1 (October 2002), p. 92.

197 Long, p. 94.

198 Long, p. 92.

the Shadow Man, denotes her as being a black Protestant New Orleanian. Equally, this notion that such people "equated Voodoo with devil worship" accounts for the satanic quality of her and Facilier's interaction towards the end of the film. (This will be discussed later.)

In many ways, Facilier embodies the "Trickster" archetype. In an extensive article on the figure of the Trickster, Barbara Babcock-Abrahams argues that, "Trickster is 'at one and the same time, creator and destroyer, giver and negator, he who dupes and who is always duped himself".[199] In a list of sixteen different potential traits for trickster characters which Babcock-Abrahams lists, there are four, which apply very strongly to Facilier, which I would like to discuss:

> 2. tend to inhabit crossroads, open public places (especially the market-place, doorways, and thresholds). In one way or another they are usually situated between the social cosmos and the other world or chaos;

> 8. often have a two-fold physical nature and/or a 'double' and are associated with mirrors. Most noticeably, the trickster tends to be of uncertain sexual status;

> 12. are generally amoral and asocial – aggressive, vindictive, vain, defiant of authority, etc.;

> 14. in keeping with their creative/destructive dualism, tricksters tend to be ambiguously situated between life and death, and good and evil, as is summed up in the combined black and white symbolism fre-quently associated with them.[200]

When we first see Facilier, as mentioned previously, he sits on the sidewalk, near a crossroads (a place in and of itself which frequently is associated with the Devil), reading Tarot cards for a white man who, it turns out, is bald; Facilier blows some pink dust at him, and instantly a headful of thick, gorgeous hair springs out of the man's head. He is delighted, and instantly approaches an attractive woman. Suddenly, however, he sprouts hair – equally thick – all over his body so that he resembles a werewolf; the woman screams, hits him hard with her handbag, and runs away. So Facilier has given the man what he wants, but in such a way that he suffers for it. He is also seen lurking in doorways, watching the movements of those around him, and when he lures Naveen and Lawrence into his lair, he draws them down an alleyway; we see that the doorway to his rooms is a strange, sinister-thing, and rightfully so as it turns out to be a doorway between the world of the everyday and the world of spirit.

Visually, Facilier is a strange figure. He is noticeably thinner than the other characters: when he stands next to Naveen (whose body is well-proportioned and relatively realistic in design, at least for an animated character), he seems to be only half as wide, an effect

199 Barbara Babcock-Abrahams, "'A Tolerated Margin of Mess': The Trickster and His Tales Reconsidered", from *Journal of the Folklore Institute*, Vol. 11, No. 3 (March 1975), p. 161.

200 Babcock-Abrahams, pp. 159-160.

which exaggerates his height and gives him an other-worldly, sinister appearance. Facilier has earned his nickname amongst the film's characters, "Shadow man", presumably because he lurks in the shadows as well as having a "shadowy" nature. However, we, in the privileged position of the audience, soon learn that he has a shadow which can move completely independently from himself, and that it is not only alive, but aware and powerful, able to manipulate physical objects as well as interact with the dark, shadow-like spirit forms who help Dr. Facilier recapture Naveen when, in frog form, he escapes Facilier's clutches and runs off to the bayou. His shadow self assists Facilier on several occasions, such as when Tiana is about to break the talisman that holds Naveen's blood and allows Facilier to turn Lawrence's body into a duplicate of Naveen's human form; just as the talisman nearly hits the ground, the shadow grabs it, preventing it from being smashed and returning it to Facilier's control. Not only does Facilier have a dual form (his body and his shadow), he has also created a double: using a talisman which contains a drop of Naveen's blood, Facilier is able to transform Lawrence, Naveen's servant, into Naveen's human double (his voice remains the same, however, as does his personality). He then sets Lawrence to romancing and proposing to the (very eager to be a princess) Charlotte La Bouff, promising him wealth and power for his helping Facilier to overthrow Big Daddy La Bouff.

Facilier convinces Lawrence that this will be his chance to escape his lifetime of being put-upon by others and achieve power for himself; of course, Lawrence is too stupid to realise that Facilier, too, is using him as a piece in a much larger game. What he has done – transform Naveen into a frog and transform Lawrence into Naveen – has nothing to do with punishing Naveen's feck-lessness or fulfilling Lawrence's desires. Instead, Facilier changes these two outsiders' forms as part of a larger strategy to gain control of New Orleans by destroying Big Daddy La Bouff. In the first shots of him, before he has any lines, Facilier is shown to be watching jealously those around him, especially the white people. Big Daddy La Bouff seems to be a particular focus of Facilier, presumably because Big Daddy is very rich, very pow-erful, and very influential in New Orleans; we learn early on that this will be the fifth year in a row that Big Daddy has been declared the Mardi Gras king, denoting his particularly high status in New Orleans.[201] No further reason for Dr. Facilier's hatred of La Bouff is ever given by the narrative. Big Daddy, however, is shown to be the exact opposite of Facilier. Big Daddy is corpulent, rich, popular, prominent, beloved, kind, generous, respected, and at the pinnacle of white society; Dr. Facilier is

201 According to Sarita McCoy Gregory, this honour would have never have been bestowed five times in real life. Nonetheless, she notes that the honour of Mardi Gras King, or Rex, went only to the very top of the cream of New Orleans society, traditionally only to those who also had the "right" heritage in the city, to include being descended from "old money", anti-bellum families. See Sarita McCoy Gregory, "Disney's Second Line: New Orleans, Racial Masquerade, and the Reproduction of Whiteness in *The Princess and the Frog*", in *The Journal of African American Studies*, Vol. 14 (2010), pp. 435-36.

unusually thin, poor, reviled, marginalised, feared, hateful, vindictive, and distrusted: in many ways, he is at the bottom of black society, not least because they know him to be dangerous and duplicitous. These traits are emphasised by something else Facilier says to Lawrence, as a way to convince him to follow Facilier's plan: "Aren't you *tired* of living on the margins, while all those fat cats in their fancy cars don't give you so much as a sideways glance?" It is obvious that this is what most bothers Dr. Facilier himself; that it irritates Lawrence, too, is just fortunate for Facilier, since it allows him to manipulate Lawrence. Several times, Facilier is seen holding a Voodoo doll of Big Daddy, ready to stab it with a pin and waiting for just the right moment; happily for Big Daddy, the moment never comes.

Toward the end of the film, in a key scene both for Tiana and for Facilier, Facilier transforms Tiana back into human form, and then proceeds to tempt her (in a way which is reminiscent of the Devil's temptation of Jesus) by showing her a vision (using mise-en-scène which is vaguely reminiscent of the scene in *The Shining*, 1980, in which Jack Nicholson finds himself in the Overlook's ballroom, surrounded by elegant 1920s party-goers) of her dream restaurant: glittering and golden, hugely successful, and presided over by an elegant, richly-dressed Tiana. He will give it to her, Facilier says, if she will just hand over his talisman. We can see Tiana wavering as Facilier weaves his magic, whispering seductively in her ear about fulfilling her and her father's cherished wishes:

> "Come on now, darling, think of everything you've sacrificed ... think of all those naysayers who doubted you ... and don't forget your poor daddy – now that was one hard-working man. Double, sometimes triple shifts. Never letting on how bone tired and beat down he really was. Shame all that hard work didn't amount to much more than a busted-up old gumbo pot and a dream that never got off the back porch. But you – you can give your poor daddy everything he ever wanted. Come on, Tiana – you're almost there."

What stops Tiana from acquiescing is her realisation that, ultimately, her father "... never did get what he wanted, but he had what he needed. He had *love*! He never lost sight of what was important, and neither will I!" Though his shadow catches the talisman before it breaks and gives it to Facilier, Tiana (having been returned to frog form in punishment for not helping Facilier) manages to get it back from him using her long, sticky frog tongue. Closer to the ground this time, she smashes the talisman. The breaking of Facilier's talisman means the breaking of his deal of protection and communion with the Voodoo spirits: in revenge, and despite his pleadings and promises, they drag both his body and his shadow into their realm, through the mouth of a horned, mask-like head, leaving behind only a tombstone, a carving of his face staring from it in wide-eyed terror.

Facilier's undoing, ultimately, seems to be his arrogance in making deals with the evil forces of this world, and thinking that he is somehow their equal – that they are his "friends on the other side", and that he has some form of influence with them. In fact, just as he intended to use Lawrence to gain access to Big Daddy La Bouff's money and power, the spirits were using Facilier to gain access to the souls of humans. When Facilier abandons Lawrence after his failure, Lawrence is dragged away by the police to face earthly justice. When Facilier's deal with the spirits falls through, he is dragged away by them to face other-worldly justice. After Dr. Facilier's somewhat elongated and elaborate death, no characters mention him again. His purpose served, this trickster is forgotten as order restores itself and love triumphs over hate.

This idea of love defeating hate seems to be at least as important, if not more important, than good triumphing over evil in the narratives whose villains are magically, manically powerful. They are incapable of feeling love, and so feel only those emotions caused by love's absence: hatred (the Horned King), greed (Jafar the Vizier), and megalomania (Dr. Facilier). It is interesting that these characters all have titles which connote a sense of authority: king, vizier, and doctor. Yet each in his own way violates the leadership and wisdom implied by these roles, choosing instead to focus on the most negative and horrible aspects of the world in the deluded belief that he – perhaps because he mistakenly believes himself to be superior to others – is somehow able to control the forces around him. He becomes so caught up in his own illusion that he forgets that he is playing with a fire that he will not be able to contain for long. When he finally is burned, he is incinerated. But while he lives, he is a genuine threat to those he opposes; they underestimate him at their peril. Fortunately, each of the young hero(in)es who must fight against these villains is able to understand both the dangers these villains present, and also where these villains' greatest weaknesses lie. They can then use this knowledge to destroy the villain.

Criminally Dangerous

The criminally-dangerous villains are very similar to the magically-dangerous villains, as all are possessed of a kind of entitlement which seems to put them (at least) on the brink of insanity. However, the next two villains, Judge Frollo and Shan-Yu, possess no magical abilities at all. Their strength is derived from their twisted souls and unbalanced minds, the megalomania that convinces them that they are at the centre of their worlds, that they deserve anything they desire, and that those around them are too far beneath them to be worthy of anything but benign contempt at best, loathing and destruction at worst. Their madness is their greatest strength and their undoing – it drives them to keep going even after it is obvious that they have failed, and so it leads them to their deaths.

The villain at the heart of *The Hunchback of Notre Dame* (1996) is Judge Claude Frollo, a character who believes himself to be the guardian of righteousness and morality, but is in fact so corrupt and rotten in his soul that the evil he sees in others, we are told, is nothing more than a reflection of his own evil: "Judge Claude Frollo longed to purge the world of vice and sin/And he saw corruption everywhere except within". He is the first named character we meet in *Hunchback*; when he is arresting a group of Gypsies for entering Paris, a woman in the group runs away, clutching a bundle to her chest. He is certain that it is a bundle of stolen goods but, when the woman falls and dies, he sees that it is her baby she was clutching, and that the baby is deformed. He looks on it in horror and calls it a monster, then decides to drown it in the cathedral's well. The archdeacon sees him, and calls out to him to stop; Frollo replies, "This is an unholy demon. I'm sending it back to Hell, where it belongs." Frollo's heart is so rotten, in other words, he cannot recognise an innocent baby when he sees it; he notices only its deformities, and assumes it must be an evil, unholy thing. The archdeacon, however, is a good man; he holds Frollo to account for causing the woman's death, and tells Frollo that he must raise her child as penance. It is an exchange (done in song/recitative) that is worth quoting because it informs us so clearly of Frollo's inner darkness:

> Archdeacon: See, there, the innocent blood you have spilt on the steps of Notre Dame!
>
> Frollo: I am guiltless. She ran. I pursued.
>
> Archdeacon: Now you would add this child's blood to your guilt on the steps of Notre Dame!
>
> Frollo: My conscience is clear.
>
> Archdeacon: You can lie to yourself and your minions –
> You can claim that you haven't a qualm –
> But you never can run from
> Nor hide what you've done from the eyes …
> The very eyes of Notre Dame!

Narrator: And for one time in his life of power and control
Frollo felt a twinge of fear for his immortal soul ...

Because he is disgusted by the child's appearance, he insists that the child live secretly in Notre Dame cathedral, and comes to visit and "educate" him periodically. It is Frollo who names the infant Quasimodo (which, we are told, means "half formed"); with this name, Frollo further stigmatises the innocent baby, whom he decrees must be raised out of sight from the world, hidden in the bell tower of the church. As the prologue of the film ends, the narrator then invites us to consider "Who is the monster and who is the man?" We are expected to realise that the monster, of course, is Frollo.

Frollo is truly monstrous on the inside: he is cruel, heartless, selfish, and utterly convinced that he is morally superior to those around him. In his role as a judge, and despite his claims to be a superior Christian (in and of its self an attitude which goes against the teachings of Christ), he pays no head to the Bible verses "Judge not, that ye be not judged. For with what judgement ye judge, ye shall be judged: and with what measure ye mete, it shall be measured to you again." (Matthew, Chapter 7: Verses 1-2) Frollo's soul is an abomination; this is further demonstrated by the way in which he teaches the alphabet to Quasimodo, telling him that "A" is for "Abomination", "B" is for "Blasphemy", "C" is for "Contrition", and so forth. We also learn that Frollo has lied to Quasimodo, raising him to believe that his "heartless mother" had abandoned him, and that Frollo has raised him purely out of the goodness of his own heart. He deceives Quasimodo (and himself) by telling him that:

The world is cruel –
The world is wicked –
It's I alone whom you can trust in this whole city!
I am your only friend –
I who keep you, teach you, feed you, dress you –
I who look upon you without fear!
How can I protect you, boy, unless you always stay in here –
Away in here.

...

You are deformed (Q: Yes I'm deformed),
And you are ugly (Q: And I am ugly),
And these are crimes for which the world shows little pity.
You do not comprehend (Q: You are my one defender)
Out there they'll revile you as a monster (Q: I am a monster)
Out there they will hate and scorn and jeer (Q: Only a monster)
Why invite their calumny and consternation –
Stay in here.

This, of course, is only one side of Frollo's twisted view of the world. The other is revealed to us not long after this scene when he first encounters the young Gypsy woman, Esmeralda. He first notices her at the Feast of Fools, when she performs a dance for him and the crowd, and again, later, when he refuses to stop the crowd's humiliation of Quasimodo (Frollo considers this to be a "lesson" which Quasimodo "deserves" for defying him). Esmeralda will not stand by and watch someone suffer, and she infuriates Frollo by not only helping Quasimodo, but also shaming Frollo publically, saying to him in front of the people of Paris, "You speak of justice, yet you are cruel to those most in need of your help". She calls for justice, and mocks Frollo, saying he is the real fool. Frollo orders her to be arrested, and she uses a magic trick to get away; Frollo, however, believes she has used witchcraft. His pursuit from that moment on will be relentless, and Esmeralda is forced to claim sanctuary in the cathedral. He is furious when Phoebus refuses to drag her from the cathedral and arrest her, and livid when the archdeacon appears and comments that Frollo learned years ago to respect the sanctity of the cathedral. As Phoebus and the archdeacon walk away, Frollo sneaks up behind Esmeralda, pins her arms behind her back, and threatens her; he then takes a long, deep smell of her hair. He is aroused by her beauty and sensuality, much to her disgust. He becomes obsessed with Esmeralda from that moment on, but will not recognise that his lust is his own. He blames her, insisting that she is a witch who has put an evil spell on him. In the song "Heaven's Light/Hellfire", Frollo sings that, despite his being so much more pure than most other people, "her smouldering eyes still scorch my soul". He prays for Esmeralda's destruction; when he is informed that she has escaped the cathedral, he vows to find her himself, and sings about her, "Choose me or your pyre/Be mine or you will burn!" It demonstrates the insanity which is inherent in his character, as his search for Esmeralda intensifies and he takes to more brutal, criminal methods to find her, even ordering Phoebus to burn down the miller's home (with the miller and his family locked inside it) to make an "example" of him. Phoebus refuses to murder innocent people; Frollo sets fire to the miller's home himself, and Phoebus dashes through the flames to rescue them. Frollo then sentences Phoebus to death. Esmeralda, who has watched in horror as this scene played out, grabs a rock and hurls it at Frollo's horse, giving Phoebus a chance to escape. When Phoebus is hit by an arrow and falls into the river, he is left for dead; Esmeralda rescues him, however, and brings him to Quasimodo's bell tower, hiding him under Frollo's nose.

Frollo is able to read Quasimodo's nervousness correctly, and deduces that he is helping Esmeralda. He follows when Quasimodo and Phoebus go to warn Esmeralda and the Gypsies that Frollo will invade the Court of Miracles, and he and his men arrest those they find there. At dawn, we see him accusing Esmeralda of witchcraft and, without bothering with a trial (since his judgement is enough in his eyes), sentencing her to death out in the cathedral square; she is tied to a stake and ready to die. His twisted mind has convinced him that he can use this to offer her "redemption": really, this means her becoming his mistress. She spits in his face, so he announces that he "will send this unholy demon back where she belongs" as he lights her pyre and watches, gleefully, as she begins to die. His plan is thwarted by Quasimodo, however, who breaks free of his chains and rescues Esmeralda, carrying her to safety in the cathedral, then doing battle against Frollo. Frollo finds a way into the cathedral. He sneaks up behind Quasimodo, intending to kill him, but Quasimodo realises what is happening and turns on his "master", fighting back hard. Eventually, they are out on the roof of the cathedral, as Frollo tries to kill both Quasimodo and Esmeralda with a sword. Finally, Quasimodo is hanging from the roof, Esmeralda trying to stop him from falling. Frollo is standing on one of the rainspouts nearby: he raises his sword aloft, saying triumphantly, "And He shall smite the wicked and plunge them into the fiery pit!" These are his last words, however; his moment of judgement comes when the rainspout breaks and he falls into the pyre – the one he himself lit to murder Esmeralda for her "sinfulness" – far below. One is given the impression that the fire is the beginning of his soul's descent into Hell, and – again – it brings to mind "with what measure ye mete, it shall be measured to you again". He lit the fire to burn someone he accused of evil, and he himself dies in that fire. We see nothing more of Frollo himself, only of the puppet of him that the jester uses, this time clearly labelling it a representation of a monster.

That Frollo is a wicked man is evident throughout. What we come to realises is that he is not just twisted and misguided, he is criminally insane. He believes himself to be better than anyone else, and that it is this which gives him the right – even the duty – to cast judgement on others. When he becomes attracted to Esmeralda, he cannot bear to realise that he is just as human as the next man, and so, moving into psychopathy, he insists that he is blameless and decides either to force Esmeralda to be his mistress (though he never uses that word, his implications are clear) or else to murder her. Because he sees sex as evil and love as impossible (no doubt because he himself has never experienced it), he is unable to handle his attraction for a woman, and becomes animalistic about it, smelling her hair and, later, the scarf he has stolen from her. He will stop at nothing to deny that he has normal urges and instincts, and it is this which destroys him in the end.

Shan-Yu, the leader of the Hun in *Mulan* (1998), is another villain whose actions seem motivated by a form of criminal insanity. He is an enormous man: tall, unnaturally muscular, thick-necked, and with overly-developed limbs. His eyes are monstrous: they are elongated triangles that are too small for his face. There seem to be no eyeballs, only a black emptiness from which two glowing, bright orange irises glare forth. The Hun invasion begins in the very first scene of *Mulan*, making Shan-Yu the first named character we meet in the film. His reason for invading China is that he believes that the Chinese emperor had built the Great Wall to challenge him to invade: he even refers to the Great Wall as an "invitation" from the emperor. He and the Hun are shown to be savage, ruthless, and bloodthirsty. At one point, Shan-Yu's falcon brings him a little rag doll that it has retrieved from a village. Shan-Yu sniffs it, animal-like, as do his men, to gain from the doll clues about where it originated. He deduces that the doll came from a village in the Tung Shao Pass, and that the Imperial army is there lying in wait for the Hun. When one of the men says that the Hun can easily avoid the Imperial army, Shan-Yu's reply is touched both with logic and an evil delight in bloodshed: "No. The quickest way to the emperor is through that pass. Besides ... the little girl will be missing her doll. We should return to her." The effect is sinister, knowing that it is likely that the little girl who owns the doll will die in the battle he will incite. This fear is confirmed later, when Shang's unit comes across the burned-out ruins of the village; the doll is seen lying discarded in the snow, a tiny reminder of the dead army lying scattered across the battlefield below the village. We see Shan-Yu and his men again not long after, when they ambush Shang's troops as they make their way toward the Imperial City. The Hun outnumber Shang's men, but the Hun are stopped by Mulan's cleverness when she fires a cannonball into a snow bank on a cliff high overhead, causing an avalanche which buries the Hun and Shan-Yu. But it is Shan-Yu himself who wounds Mulan, striking her with his sword; this will reveal her to be a woman when, later, a doctor is summoned to treat her wound.

Mulan is left behind (in the company of her horse, the guardian dragon Mushu, and Cri-kee, the lucky cricket), and therefore is witness to Shan-Yu and the surviving Hun climbing out from under the snow in a way which renders them even more monstrous; they have, it seems, become the classic villains whose determination to destroy seems to exert an unnatural protection over them, like Michael Myers in *Halloween* (1978) or Schwarzenegger's character in *The Terminator* (1984). Shan-Yu is clearly offended that he was defeated, and looks down upon the Imperial City, determined to fulfil his mission. They manage to infiltrate the Imperial City and take the emperor prisoner; the men bring him to a balcony where Shan-Yu awaits. He tries to taunt the emperor, and paces around him, insisting that the emperor bow to him, referring to the emperor as an arrogant old man; it is clear that he cannot see his own arrogance, and in this scene in particular demonstrates almost psychopathic behaviour in his grandiose sense of himself and his violent, selfish, restless behaviour. He is particularly contrasted against the emperor, who is still, proud, and strong, replying to Shan-Yu's repeated orders that he bow that, "No matter how the wind howls, the mountain cannot bow to it". This infuriates Shan-Yu, who attacks the emperor, but is stopped by Shang, who leaps in front of the emperor and blocks Shan-Yu's sword with his own. He knocks out Shang, and walks past Mulan to follow after Chien-Po and the other soldiers who have slid down a rope with the emperor, getting him to safety. Mulan cuts the rope, however, causing Shan-Yu to howl like an enraged animal. Even then, he cannot see Mulan; women are meaningless to him to the point that one can be thwarting his every move and he still cannot recognise her presence. Instead he turns upon Shang, who has just regained consciousness: grabbing Shang by the throat, Shan-Yu fumes, "You took away my victory!" He only notices Mulan – and therefore is forced to acknowledge that he has been defeated by a young woman – when Mulan throws her shoe at the back of his head and calls out to him, "No! I did!" She pulls her hair back so that he will recognise her as Ping, and it is the first time he sees her. He drops Shang and goes after Mulan, but she traps him in the throne room long enough to figure out a plan. With Mushu's help, she gain's access to the fireworks meant to celebrate the victory; while Mulan holds Shan-Yu pinned to the roof with his own sword, Mushu fires the rocket at him, blowing him off the roof and killing him.

Of all the villains in Disney, Shan-Yu is probably the least developed character. He is cold, cunning, vicious, and a megalomaniac throughout. It is this set of traits which compels him to invade China in the first place, and it is the arrogance which underlies these traits which leads him to overlook and underestimate Mulan, who defeats him. The characters in the film who disregard women in general, but Mulan in particular, and never see the error of their ways, are the bad guys in *Mulan*: the emperor's counsel, Chi Fu, strays into bad-guy territory because even when Mulan has saved the emperor and defeated Shan-Yu once and for all, he dismisses her by saying, "'Tis a woman" (referring to a woman as "it", and therefore as less than human), and insisting that she is a traitor who deserves death. But what keeps Chi Fu out of the same category as Shan-Yu, ultimately, is that Chi Fu does not seek to destroy China; Shan-Yu does. Shan-Yu's reason for trying to destroy China – that the Great Wall amounted to the emperor challenging him to try to invade – is demented and ridiculous. But Shan-Yu is determined and intelligent enough to pose a genuine threat to the main characters of the film and to their nation. The only thing that will stop him is death. Killing him restores Mulan's honour, and elevates her to such a supreme position that even the emperor bows to her in a moment which serves as the climax of the film. Without the Hun invasion, Mulan would never have had her chance to become more. But his important function within the narrative does not imply that Shan-Yu can be considered anything other than a static character. He begins as a deluded monster, and he dies a deluded monster.

This is true of both the villains in this section. They are monstrous. Arguably, they are the most monstrous villains in this chapter because of the fact that they are human, and mortal, but lack normal human emotions and cannot handle anything which challenges them. They think that they are the centres of their worlds: God is watching him specially, Frollo believes, just as Shan-Yu is convinced that the emperor has built the Great Wall solely to challenge him to invade. They cannot see beyond themselves and see the world clearly, and each has managed to convince a few lesser bullies to follow him on the promise that they can be as cruel as they wish. Each is destroyed in battle (they have both lived by the sword, after all), each defeated when they think their greatest moment of triumph is at hand. Their deaths are celebrated because their dying means that a source of great evil and vice has been removed. The people they threaten – both the ordinary citizens and the heroes and heroines they face – are safe and happy with them gone.

Comic Villains

Comic villains are funny for us to watch, but they nonetheless are a force to be reckoned with. They are dangerous, powerful villains whose single-minded determination to destroy the main character(s) is such that they very nearly succeed; when they fail, it is because they come so close to succeeding that they become cocky, and this overconfidence causes them to make a mistake at the worst possible moment. The heroes are then able to seize the moment and stop the villain in his tracks. Instead, what makes the comic villain funny is his personality: he is larger-than-life, a little flamboyant, and has a great sense of humour (not necessarily about himself, but certainly about others). At least at first, before they exhibit the most despicable parts of themselves, these villains are even rather likeable, for all their obnoxiousness: we never have to deal with them ourselves, but watching them in their interactions with others is pleasurable, at least until they become so hateful and vindictive that they cease to be funny and instead become just plain dangerous.

This is certainly the case with the first of the two villains in this section, Gaston from *Beauty and the Beast* (1991). Johnston and Thomas claim that, "However self-indulgent Gaston was, he was more of a bully than a real troublemaker. It was only when he was crossed in his desires that he felt forced to be more aggressive. ... He was never an admirable person, but he had not been a complete villain until the situation went beyond anything his limited talents could handle".[202] This characterisation of Gaston, however, is a little problematic: after all, this is a character who is so comfortable with all kinds of violence, to include sexual intimidation (and he is sexually aggressive toward Belle, particularly when he "proposes" marriage to her by cornering her alone inside her house and announcing to her how lucky she is that she gets to be his "little wife"), that to justify it would never occur to him. In fact, everything that Gaston does – and he becomes increasingly violent throughout the film – has as its ultimate aim the acquisition of Belle as his wife/trophy. Never are we given the impression that he feels any genuine emotions for her; certainly there is no indication that he is even remotely in love with her. Gaston wants Belle partly because he is sexually-attracted to her (and her obvious lack of interest in him only increases his lust), but mostly because, as he himself says in his first scene, "She's the most beautiful girl in town. That makes her the best! And don't I deserve the best." As far as the town is concerned, Belle's greatest (and possibly only valuable) attribute is her beauty. In the song "Belle", the villagers note about Belle,

Well it's no wonder that her name means beauty –
Her looks have got no parallel!
But behind that fair façade
I'm afraid she's rather odd
Very different from the rest of us is Belle!

In fact, they lament that she is a "funny" (in the sense of peculiar)

girl, and hardly any of them seem to know what to make of her. But for Gaston, this is beside the point. Her beauty is enough to make her valuable. During the course of our introduction to him, Gaston indicates that he is uncomfortable with aspects of Belle's personality, in particular her love of books and her ability to use intellect and imagination. She is the opposite of Gaston, of whom we learn later in the film, when the villagers sing about him, that his great skills are spitting, hunting, fighting, biting, and shooting. In a wonderful moment, the lyrics of the song say that "No one hits like Gaston/Matches wits like Gaston", and we see him losing a game of chess and, in response, knocking the board and chess pieces flying across the room. When we first see Gaston interacting with Belle, he circles Belle, dominating the shot and her with his bulky frame and his bright red shirt (Belle, in a more sedate blue dress, is also significantly smaller than Gaston: he is about a head taller, and his shoulders and chest seem almost twice as wide has hers), and demonstrating a kind of familiarity/possessiveness toward her when he feels perfectly at liberty to pluck her book from her hands and toss it over his shoulder and into the mud. He questions the value of a book without pictures (indicating his valuing image over substance), and when Belle replies that "Some people use their imaginations" when reading pictureless books, he dismisses the notion: "Belle, it's about time you got your head out of those books and paid attention to more important things ... like me. The whole town's talking about it! It's not right for a woman to read! Soon she starts getting ideas, and thinking ..." Belle laughs at this, saying, "Gaston, you are positively primeval!" His reply, "Why thank you, Belle!" is played for laughs, but it indicates both Belle's superiority to Gaston (in case we were in any doubt) and a truth about his personality: Gaston is more body than mind, more brawn than brain, and therefore he is most at home in an environment – a more primitive, kill-or-be-killed scenario – in which a muscle-bound, hard-bodied physicality is an asset, and a propensity toward violence means survival. Even his humour is violent: when he shares a laugh with LeFou (his sidekick) as this scene closes, he slaps LeFou so hard on the back that the (significantly smaller) man flips over in mid-air and lands on his head. In the next scene featuring Gaston, when he organises an entire wedding, then announces to the assembled guests, "Now I'd better get in there and ... propose to the girl!" we see very clearly that Gaston uses his enormous frame to dominate Belle. Given that he is proposing marriage – a sexual union as much as anything else – in the scene, there can be no doubt that his behaviour toward Belle is about his lust for her; were it not for her cleverness in eluding him (and were this not a family/children's film), the threat of possible rape would be more than implied. Gaston corners her twice, her back against the wall and his hands resting on the wall on either side of her, effectively trapping her. As he moves to trap her the second time, he pushes a chair out of his way so that it falls over. None of this is rushed: he moves with the steady calm of a panther stalking its prey. But Gaston's overconfidence, combined with Belle's cleverness, means that she is able to trick him. The second time he traps her, it is against the front door, and she is able to open it and duck out from under him simultaneously as he loses his balance and is propelled forward, out of the house and landing in a puddle. He is humiliated in front of the wedding party, and stalks off, vowing, "I'll have Belle for my wife, make no mistake". His pig-headedness is made literal when, as he gets up from the deep mud puddle where he landed, it appears briefly as though he has a pig's head; he sits up all the way, and we see that he has a pig (who was presumably enjoying the mud) sitting on his shoulders. Furious, he vows to prove to the village and himself that he can conquer her; her second – and much larger – rejection of him kindles his anger, and is the first sign that he is not just threatening (albeit in a way that Belle can handle), but genuinely dangerous. It is at the end of the scene in which the song "Gaston" features that we get our first hint of the lengths Gaston will go to in order to force Belle to marry him. Realising that Belle's father, Maurice, is considered crazy by the villagers, he decides to bribe the head of the local mental asylum to commit Maurice; Gaston will then tell Belle that, if she'll marry him, he'll see to it that Maurice is set free. Just such a scenario plays itself out, only Belle refuses: they are committing Maurice because he claims that a beast is holding Belle captive. Belle, having returned home from the Beast's castle by this time, is able to prove (using a magic hand mirror given to her by the Beast) that the Beast is real. Gaston's plan changes instantly: he locks Belle and Maurice in their cellar so that they cannot warn the Beast, and he riles up the villagers to go and kill the Beast.

They make their way to the castle, and the villagers do battle with the castle's enchanted servants. Gaston, however, creeps away from the battle in search of the Beast: he finds Beast in the west wing of the castle, watching as the last petals on the enchanted rose begin to fall off, and mourning Belle's absence. Gaston fires an arrow, hitting the Beast in his back, and he roars in pain. Gaston charges him, knocking them both through the window and onto a balcony, then kicks the Beast again, sending him flying onto the roof. He begins goading the Beast, taunting him by saying, "What's the matter, Beast – too kind and gentle to fight back?" The Beast does not answer, so Gaston breaks off part of the stonework on the castle's roof, intending to use it to club the Beast to death: it is clear that Gaston is relishing this, and is rendered even more of a bully by his actions. The situation changes quickly, however, when Belle (who has escaped her cellar and ridden to the castle to help Beast) shows up and calls out to him. Realising that he does have someone to live for after all, the Beast begins to fight back, more than a match for Gaston's strength, but with more cleverness, using the gargoyles to trick Gaston. Gaston taunts him further: "Were you in love with her, Beast? Did you honestly think she'd want you when she had someone like me? It's over, Beast – Belle is mine!" At this, infuriated, Beast knocks the club from Gaston's hand, grabs him by the throat, and dangles him over the roof, ready to drop him to his death. Gaston's cowardice comes out, and he begs the Beast to release him. Beast places him on the roof, and tells him, disgustedly, to get out. He then turns toward Belle, who is on the balcony above, a look of pure joy on his face. But as Beast climbs toward her, Gaston stoops to his lowest: having just been granted mercy by the Beast, he uses the opportunity to sneak up from behind and stab the Beast in the side. But this is Gaston's undoing: shocked by the pain, Beast rears back, losing his balance. Gaston loses his balance, too, and falls backward, off the roof and into the canyon far below the castle. We do not see him die, but it is obvious that he could not survive such a fall. As with the other villains, once he is gone, no one misses him or mentions him again. His stabbing the Beast does serve an important narrative function, however: it is a death blow, and seeing him dying compels Belle to admit to herself – and to tell the Beast – that she is in love with him. This breaks the spell, and the Beast and his servants are transformed back into their original forms. Belle, who has no idea that the enchantment has a time limit (the Beast must win the love of another before the last petal falls from the enchanted rose, or he and his household will stay forever transformed), admits her love just as the last petal falls; even a few more seconds later would have been too late. So without Gaston's actions, the enchantment would have become permanent. But, naturally, Gaston has no idea that this will be the outcome of his actions (indeed, knowing this may well have made him act differently). It is a narrative device that he is used in this way, and it is a common use for a villain: he or she is the catalyst to compel the main characters to be their best selves.

Much about Gaston is comic. One of the most enjoyable scenes in the film, particularly in terms of its humour, is the song "Gaston", where we get to see just exactly how ridiculous it is that he – and the form of idealised masculinity he embodies – are valued by the society around him. In other words, the film shows Gaston to be very much a product of his culture. The villagers follow him right to the end, and we are not shown what happens to the villagers' opinions of him after the battle. So by critiquing Gaston and his enactment of hard-bodied masculinity – and unlike Beast, Gaston remains loyal to this form of masculinity right to his final moment – the film, ultimately, is criticizing the hyper-masculinity which is celebrated by many of the action movies of the 1980s. As Richard Sparks points out, "If the purposes of the action film include the visualization of a certain form of order – the challenges it undergoes, the means of its restoration or repair – then the demands made upon the hero as an agent of retribution or restoration and the evocation of the world that he inhabits necessarily stand in a dialectically intimate relation to one another. And if those surrounding conditions come to be depicted as more and more chaotic, lawless, and disorderly, then the response called forth from the hero's saving presence becomes only the more intense."[203] In this scenario, Gaston's obsession with possessing and controlling Belle creates, to paraphrase the quote, more chaos, lawlessness and disorder in the village: rather than the sunny, blue-skied version we have seen through most of the film, Gaston's rousing of the village (through the song "Kill the Beast") to attack the castle and destroy those who live there has as its backdrop the frightened faces of the villagers, torches blazing, and the beginnings of a storm (later, we will see that it is raining hard upon the Beast's castle, and Gaston and the Beast's fight takes place in pounding rain). It is a nightmare version of Belle's "poor provincial town". It is also clear that nothing will persuade Gaston to alter the path he has chosen. The hero – Beast – can restore order and repair the lives of those around him (himself included) by killing Gaston – one of (if not the) most intense responses the Beast could be called upon to enact. By this stage, Gaston has ceased to be comic. He is a threat to order and reason, pure and simple, and cannot be changed or rehabilitated. Therefore, the audience is not upset to see him die. It is shown by the narrative to be a direct result of his own actions.

Someone who is just as driven – even obsessed – as Gaston, but whose humorous depiction lasts longer in his narrative, is Hades, who seeks to destroy Hercules and defeat the gods of Olympus in the 1997 film *Hercules*. This is a very comic villain from a movie that emphasises comedy as a way to counterbalance the "stuffy" and "academic" reputation of Greek Mythology, at least according to John Musker and Ron Clements in the documentary "The

203 Richard Sparks, "Masculinity and Heroism in the Hollywood Blockbuster", from *The British Journal of Criminology*, Vol. 36, No. 3: Special Issue (1996), p. 355.

Making of Hercules".[204] Equally, the character is very much a star vehicle in a period when Disney was famous/notorious for bringing in celebrity performers to provide voices for their characters. In this case, it is James Woods who gives Hades his voice and much of his personality. Hades is obsessive, sarcastic, neurotic, fast talking, and hot-tempered to the point of maniacal. Hades is a delight to watch in the film, and much more interesting than the sweet (but admittedly somewhat dull) Hercules; when his character is in a scene (and he is in at least as many scenes as Hercules himself), he very much steals the show; Meg is the only character who seems to be able to keep up with him, quite possibly because, before she falls in love with Hercules, her cynicism is equal to Hades'. It is this very comic portrayal – along with the stereotypically tightly-wound anger of James Woods' performance – which, even while it makes him great fun as a character, also hurts his effectiveness as a villain in the film. It is obvious that he must be defeated in part because he is the villain of a Disney film, and one trait which unifies most films in the family and child market is that the villain is stopped and the hero(ine) lives happily ever after. But it is also evident from his portrayal that Hades is so tense he will snap; it is inevitable. He is an excellent balance for Hercules, and one of the most delightful villains of canon, but he has little about him as a character which is surprising.

Nonetheless, the most "useful" thing about Hades, at least in terms of the balance of the characters' personalities, is that he saves the film from being bogged down by Hercules' sweet but rather boring personality. Hercules is likeable enough, but predictable. He starts out a misfit, finds out he is the son of two Olympian gods, works hard to train and become a hero, and becomes renowned as a hero while never letting the praise go to his head. Hades, therefore, is needed. Firstly, he is the character who drives the narrative. It is on his orders that Hercules is made mortal, it is Hades who uses Meg as a honey trap and inadvertently creates a romance between Meg and Hercules, and it is Hades' obsession with defeating the gods of Olympus that puts him in opposition with Hercules. Secondly, he is the character whose antics, temper, and part "wise-guy", part "fast-talking-Hollywood-agent" speech patterns infuse the film with spirit. We never root for Hades; it is arguable that we even like him. But we enjoy him because he is the one character who makes us laugh consistently throughout the film.

Perhaps because, unlike Gaston, there is no reveal with Hades – we learn immediately just how bad Hades is when he has an

204 "The Making of *Hercules*" from *Hercules* (Region 2/PAL, © Disney, DVD release date 12 August 2002).

236

infant Hercules stolen from his cradle and made mortal so that he can be murdered on Hades' orders – he is a far less complex villain than those such as John Silver, Rourke, and Gaston. He is never really developed beyond the status of fast-talking con artist and kingpin of evil. He is there to be funny – which he is – and to create scenarios whereby Hercules and Meg have a chance to shine, grow as people, and find true love with one another – which he does. In this sense, he/James Woods steal every scene in which he appears, however briefly. He is comic because he is funny; he is not an idiot villain because, whatever his mistakes, he is focused and intelligent, and his plans, by and large, are workable. What foils him, ultimately, is that he is forced to rely upon nincompoops and dullards just when he needs the most help. Otherwise – had it not been for Hercules' noble actions (enabled by the breaking of Hades' promise that Meg would not be harmed) restoring him to godhood and restoring the balance in the fight between Zeus' allies and Hades' allies – Hades would have won.

So, though most of the villains in Disney's animated features have comic aspects, Gaston and Hades are the two who can be defined as "comic villains" because, unlike these other characters, they are more than just amusing: a large part of their function is to provide comic relief to the narrative. In this sense, they do double duty: after all, while a big part of their role is to liven up the film, they also are there to be bad – to create dangerous, difficult scenarios against which the hero must do battle. Hades is very intelligent; Gaston is less so, but he is never inept or stupid. Their comic timing is paired with obsessive natures and selfish desires, and they charm us even as they make life hard for the hero(in)es. But just when we think we can discount them, we are given a glimpse into their cunning and their ferocity, and we see how truly dangerous they can be. They amuse without being ridiculous, and fail not because their plans are bad, but because their obsession blinds them. A genuine threat to the hero(ine), each, ultimately, is an even greater threat to himself.

Idiot Villains

The greatest difference between the comic villain, discussed above, and the idiot villain is the likelihood of their plans' success. Whereas the comic villain *might* have succeeded, were he not encouraged too much by earlier successes and driven almost to insanity with his overconfidence and obsession in achieving his goals, the idiot villain lacks what it takes to succeed. He tries – he tries very hard – and he does create genuine danger for his film's main characters. But he lacks the intelligence to bring his plans to fruition, and he makes an ass of himself while trying to achieve his goals.

The Man in the Bowler Hat – whom we learn later is Goob, Lewis' roommate at the orphanage – is the strange villain who steals Lewis' memory scanner – and Wilbur's second time machine – in the 2007 film *Meet the Robinsons*. Very soon after we encounter the Man, we see that, while he may have an amazing and clever hat (it shows itself to be far more intelligent than he, and is in fact the brains of the operation), he himself is very silly and stupid. He may steal Lewis' scanner, but he has no idea what it is or what it does. He knows only that, if he can pass it off as his own, it will change the future, something he wants desperately (though why he wants this isn't revealed immediately). When he accidentally breaks the machine and goes to find Lewis to have him fix it, he comes upon Lewis' roommate, Goob (himself as a child), who has just lost his team their baseball game; Lewis had kept Goob up for several nights while he worked on his invention, and it left Goob so tired that he fell asleep during his ballgame. The boy is very calm, commenting that his coach told him to let the mistake go, and that he's probably right. The Man is adamant in his reply:

> No! Everyone will tell you to let it go and move on – but don't! Instead, let it fester and boil inside of you. Take these feelings and lock them away. Let them fuel your actions. Let *hate* be your ally, and you will be capable of wonderfully horrid things. Heed my words, Goob. Don't let it go.

As he gives this speech, choral music plays in the background, implying that this is a hugely significant moment. Goob, however, has no idea what he's talking about. The Man then goes up to the look for Lewis, and the Hat finds evidence that they are in the future. So they go back to their own time to look for Lewis. They find him at the Robinson house, but he is surrounded by the Robinson family, and the Man is too bumbling and idiotic to get him alone. He even tries bringing a dinosaur back from the past, but it tries to eat Lewis (fortunately, the Robinsons are able to stop the dinosaur, but Lewis still has to make a run for it). Wilbur realises that the dinosaur is under the control of the Man and the Bowler Hat, and is able to knock the hat off. The dinosaur (who recognises that the plan was not well thought through; this becomes a running gag in the film) is tamed, and Doris – the hat – chastises the Man.

It is later, when he tricks Lewis into fixing the memory scanner (supposedly in exchange for a trip back to see Lewis' mother drop him off at the orphanage), that we learn that the Man is none other than Lewis' roommate, Goob. Ever since his exhaustion caused him to miss the ball that lost his baseball team the game, Goob has grown angrier with each passing year. Though we are shown that no one else was bothered by his mistake, he has insisted that everyone hated him; we see him interpreting their friendliness toward him as hatred, further highlighting both Goob's obsession and his blinkeredness. When the orphanage is shut down, he stays on in the abandoned building, still sleeping in his room, living in increasing squalor, still wearing his now ridiculously out-grown little-league uniform, until he has decided to take revenge. His revenge, initially, is absurd – to throw eggs and toilet paper at the Robinson house. He is found by Doris, the bowler hat, however, and she brings him onboard to help with her plan. It turns out that Doris was invented by future Lewis to be a helping hat, but she felt her talents were being forgotten, and turns evil, especially when Lewis tries to turn her off and put her in storage. It is Doris' plan to steal the time machine; Goob's contribution is that he knows about the science fair where Lewis will demonstrate his memory scanner successfully. He also serves as a human who can front the operation and claim to be the memory scanner's and Doris' inventor. When Lewis points out that Goob has no idea what the effect on the future will be if he steals the memory scanner, Goob's response is characteristically childish: "I don't care. I just want to ruin your life!" He even says that he prefers to blame Lewis for his life rather than take responsibility for himself.

Of course, the plan goes horribly wrong. It turns out that Doris was just using Goob, and he, too, is destroyed in the dystopian nightmare that Doris wreaks once they return to the past and manage to sell both the memory scanner and Doris as Goob's inventions. Thankfully, Lewis is able to explain to him what happens and therefore can stop Goob from selling the inventions, as well as stop Doris from destroying humanity (simply by vowing to her that he will never invent her, at which point she disappears). He brings the adult Goob back to the appropriate time, and offers him a place with the Robinson family, but Goob disappears when Lewis steps aside to tell Wilbur what's going on. We see Goob looking at the Robinson house longingly, but then walk away.

In the films we have discussed, the bad guys, by and large have all been done away with (some killed, some chased away, some being forced to flee), and Goob is no exception. But rather than kill him off, or even punish him (somehow, Goob is shown to be too stupid to be deserving of punishment, and instead warrants only forgiveness). Lewis, who is not only very intelligent, but also is shown to be very wise, does something much kinder and much more effective and enlightened. Knowing that Goob felt that his life had spun out of control ever since he missed the ball in his game, Lewis makes sure to be there to wake Goob up just in time to catch the ball and win the game for his team. It is interesting that, in an earlier version of the scene (one which seems to have survived in the planning stages for a long time, given how much finished and nearly-finished animation is available to use for its inclusion as a deleted scene), Lewis stops Goob and Doris just after the successful sales pitch of the memory scanner, and then brings Goob to the fateful ball game in time for Goob to wake up his child self and catch the ball. Though the segment is introduced by the film's director, Steve Anderson, no explanation is given as to why the segment was altered in such a fundamental way.[205] To have had Goob save himself would have been much more empowering. But perhaps allowing Goob to save himself would not have allowed Lewis – the hero of the film – to redress the wrong he had done to Goob by keeping him up all night for weeks. Lewis helping Goob means that Lewis has repaid a debt and restored order; since this is Lewis' story, that would make the decision to change the scene seem sensible. In either case, the long-term effect on Goob is the same: his child self can never know who woke him up, so for him, all that matters is that he wakes up and catches the ball.

It is possible to redeem Goob, but not our final villain in this chapter, King Candy, the character who would stop Wreck-It Ralph and Fix-It Felix from helping young Vanellope in *Wreck-It Ralph* (2012). Of course, when we first meet King Candy, we have no idea that he is the villain: he is introduced as the "rightful ruler" of the "Sugar Rush" game. In that role, he presides over the nightly avatar races – in which he is also a racer – that will determine the nine avatars who will participate in the following day's game play. He is popular and beloved, and when he tries to stop Vanellope, it appears that he is doing his duty to protect the game from a glitch who will destroy it. When Ralph appears on the scene, he wrecks the spectator stands around the racetrack; he is arrested and brought back to King Candy's palace.

It is here that we get our first hint that King Candy is the villain, though upon first viewing, the clue seems to be only a comic, intertextual reference to *The Wizard of Oz* (1939): we see the guards marching outside the palace doors, chanting "Or-e-o, Oree-o" to the same tune (and mimicking the original chant, "Oh-wi-oh") used by the soldiers who guard the palace of the

205 Bonus Features/Deleted Scenes/"Bowler Hat Guy's Redemption", from *Meet the Robinsons* (Region 1/NTSC, ©Disney, DVD release date 23 October 2007).

Wicked Witch of the West – another villain who tries to stop a young girl from completing a quest. In fact, this is a very subtle foreshadow of King Candy's true nature; his status as villain, however, will not be confirmed for a little while longer. We do learn from a story that Felix tells Calhoun that, many years earlier when the arcade first opened, a racer named Turbo, from a game called "Turbo Time", became jealous that a newer game, "Road-Blasters", became more popular than his own game. He therefore abandoned his game and entered the new game; this resulted in the destruction of both games. It will be revealed that King Candy is in fact Turbo in disguise: having learned from his attempted takeover of "RoadBlasters", Turbo has reprogrammed "Sugar Rush", erasing the other characters' memories, demoting the game's actual ruler, Princess Vanellope, to the status of a glitch, and setting himself up as the game's ruler. He alone knows that Vanellope completing a race will cause "Sugar Rush's" program-ming to reset itself, restoring the characters' memories, fixing Vanellope's glitch and restoring her status as princess ... and ousting King Candy, aka Turbo, from the game. King Candy will do everything in his power to prevent this, even if it means destroying Vanellope for good and all. Of course, when King Candy tells Ralph *his* version of Vanellope's backstory, he does not explain it to Ralph this way: he reminds Ralph that glitches cannot leave their game; if she races and is seen glitching by the game's human players, they will think there's something wrong with the game, it will be shut down, the characters will be left homeless when it is unplugged, and Vanellope will be unable to escape the destruction of the world of "Sugar Rush"; she will be trapped forever in darkness. King Candy, therefore, claims that he keeps Vanellope from racing to protect the game as a whole and her in particular. He convinces Ralph that this is the truth, and Ralph agrees to try and persuade Vanellope not to race. Of course, eventually Ralph – with Felix's help – learns the truth, and together the two former combatants help Vanellope to race and win.

So what makes King Candy an idiot villain? After all, he is capable of reprogramming the code of the game, thereby altering the world around him to his own design. When he is eaten by the Cy-bug, he even manages to morph with it, becoming (he thinks) even more powerful. But King Candy cannot control his rages: it makes him behave erratically. When he joins his programming with that of a Cy-bug, he cannot even resist the bright, shiny light of the beacon Ralph creates (out of Mentos and diet cola) to attract and kill the Cy-bugs. It is this beacon which kills Turbo/King Candy/Candy Cy-bug. He may be more capable of devising a workable plan than Goob, but he nonetheless cannot keep himself under control, and therefore creates plans which, ultimately, are flawed. He is also not bright enough to see these potential problems and avoid them. All he knows is that he likes nothing better than being the centre of attention, and will do anything to stay in the limelight. It is, ironically, this very attraction to the bright and shiny that kills him. His death, followed by Vanellope's crossing the finish line and restoring the game's programming, eradicates Turbo from the story completely.

Like most villains, the idiot villain is deeply self-centred to the point of being egomaniacal. But ultimately, he is a completely ineffectual villain without the help of another character. For Goob, it is his teaming up with Doris the hat which gives him temporary success. King Candy, in some ways, is more effective, since he possesses greater knowledge of how to manipulate his world than is the case with Goob. Nonetheless, King Candy earns a place as an idiot villain because, ultimately, he allows his plans to become increasingly elaborate, and therefore out of his control. He believes that his ultimate triumph is when he morphs with one of the Cy-bugs who have invaded the "Sugar Rush" game, crowing to Ralph, "I'm now the most powerful virus in the arcade!" But the Cy-bug part is even less intelligent and less capable of reason than was the erratic Turbo; even though he realises that the beacon will destroy him, he cannot help but be drawn toward it to his death. That he decides to cross his own programming with something which is even less intelligent is a sign of his idiocy, just as surely as is Goob's poor decision to trust a hat that is intent on destroying humanity.

Conclusion

The human villains of Disney's animated films certainly cover quite a wide range of types: some are monstrous because of their inhumanity, some have magical powers, and some are nothing more or less than a dangerous obstruction to the main characters doing what is right. One even manages to take on a fatherly role, complicating his villainy and casting doubt on whether he is genuinely bad, or simply overcome with an obsession. If there are any traits which unite them as a group (besides their propensity to do bad things, of course), it is their sense of agency and their sense of entitlement. Each believes that he *deserves* whatever it is he is after – wealth, power, a woman, revenge, or some combination of these – and that the only possible outcome is that he obtain his object. In all of these cases, the villains find it impossible to see that what they are doing is wrong. Some, such as Gaston, Jafar, Ratcliffe, Frollo, Hades, Shan-Yu, Rourke, and Faciliar approach their goal so convinced that they deserve it that it comes to seem, at least in their own eyes, to be *morally* right: it is what they deserve, and anyone who stands in their way of obtaining what is rightfully deserves must be destroyed as deluded.

Of course, they must be stopped: fifteen male villains fight for what they want, and fifteen are defeated. Of those, ten die. Their deaths, according to the narratives, were what they deserved, and were the only way to put a stop to them, they had become so evil and obsessed. That so many villains die in films associated with the child/family audience may seem surprising to some, but it is a concept which goes right back to folklore and fairy tales. To repeat Cashdan's argument about why the villain dies so often in these stories, "For a fairy tale to succeed – for it to accomplish its psychological purpose – the witch must die because it is the witch who embodies the sinful parts of the self".[206] In other words, there is a link between the hero and the villain – the hero and villain often both long for some aspect of the same thing, but for different reasons – and this link means that, in a symbolic sense, they function as two different parts of the same soul. John Smith and Governor Ratcliffe, for example, both want to go to Virginia and make the most of their time there. Smith wants to explore and enjoy the challenges he will face in this wild landscape, while Ratcliffe wants to exploit the land for whatever wealth it can give him. Gaston and the Beast both want Belle: the Beast has fallen in love with her, and wants to be with her so that he can do everything in his power to make her happy and to enjoy her presence; it is his desire to make her happy that will compel him to let her leave him to save her father, and it is his recognition of her freedom that will make her able to love him in return and come back to him. Gaston's desire for Belle, however, is motivated by his lust: he wants to possess her, and would deny her freedom and force her to stay with him. Hercules and Hades both wish to prove themselves before the gods of Olympus: Hercules wishes to show that he is worthy of returning to live amongst them, and Hades wants to show that he deserves to rule over them. These are just a few examples, but they are indicative of the dichotomies inherent in each of these relationships.

Ultimately, the villain's function in the story, as was discussed at the start of the chapter, is to compel the hero(ine) to be his/her very best self: had the Hun and Shan-Yu not invaded China, Mulan would have been a failure, never finding a suitable husband or (in our eyes) worse, finding a husband who did not

206 Cashdan, p. 30.

understand her, and therefore beat down her spirit. Belle might not have found the courage in time to tell the Beast that she loved him, thereby breaking the enchantment which bound him and his servants in non-human forms. Taran would still be a frustrated assistant pig-keeper, Hercules a demi-god with no girlfriend, Tarzan would not have met Jane, and Goob would still be sitting, alone, in his former orphanage, wasting his life over his anger at missing a ball in a little-league game when he was a twelve years old. The villains force the other characters to be stronger, braver and better: the villains create the heroes.

Of the characters in this chapter, it is important to realise that, unlike the characters in the other chapters, they are not spread out – unevenly or otherwise – across the history of Disney's animated features. The earliest of them is Captain Hook, from 1953. There is then a gap of thirty-two years to 1985 and the second male villain in a leading role, the Horned King. After that, the pace picks up: human male villains appear in the films of 1990, 1991, 1992, 1995, 1996, 1997, 1998, 1999, 2001, 2003, 2007, 2009, and 2012. In other words, thirteen of the fifteen villains discussed in this chapter have appeared since 1990. Why? The simplest explanation is that the Disney studio had begun to be criticized for treating active women as villains on the grounds that such representations were anti-feminist. Disney seems to have taken this on board, and so has turned to male villains presumably as a way to avoid being deemed sexist. Naturally, it goes against feminist principles to vilify men simply because they are male; to say otherwise is to misread Feminism entirely. That Disney has begun to relax somewhat in this stance may be evidenced by a character such as Mother Gothel, from *Tangled* (2010), a wonderfully entertaining villain who – particularly frighteningly – possesses as some of her most evil traits things which are very recognisable from the everyday world, such as her way of belittling Rapunzel and then pretending that it was just a joke. She is balanced by a very strong young woman, however, who finds ways to begin to oppose Mother Gothel (though, ultimately, it is Flynn who destroys her when he cuts Rapunzel's hair, literally cutting off Mother Gothel's lifeline). The villains in these films are interesting and entertaining, regardless of their gender, and they perform the classic function of the villain within the narrative. But they also exhibit characteristics which represent what had become despicable traits in men: greed, hypermasculinity, lust, aggression, sexism, revenge, and usurpation. These men are self-obsessed, and they consider it their absolute right to assert their authority, as if they are entitled to be respected and listened to. This entitlement, in particular, is the thing which represents a trait which has come to be associated strongly with flawed masculinity since the 1990s: it is evidence that the older notion that men should be listened to simply because they are male – and the converse, that what women say and do is not worthy of attention – is an idea which is increasingly reviled. Though feminism in the early twenty-first century has much work ahead of it, this as a common trait in villains during this period is a good sign that women's participation in public life has become more normalised.

Conclusion

207 Marc Davis,
interviewed for
"You Can Fly: The
Making of Peter
Pan." Disc 2,
Backstage, from
*Walt Disney's
Pinocchio, 2-Disc
Platinum Edition*
(Region 1/NTSC,
© Disney, DVD
release date March
6, 2007).

208 *Waking Sleeping
Beauty* (2009).
Written by and
interviews
conducted by
Patrick Pacheco.
Produced by Peter
Schneider and
Don Hahn.
Directed by Don
Hahn. (Region
1/NTSC, © Buena
Vista Home
Entertainment,
Inc. DVD release
date November 30,
2010).

"If America has an art form, I'd say it's the Disney feature cartoon."
– Marc Davis (no relation), Disney Animator and one of the Nine Old Men[207]

It is in no way contentious to state that the Disney approach to feature-length animation has been successful with the public. Of course, sometimes people forget that, while some of these films were enormous critical and box-office hits when they were released (*Snow White and the Seven Dwarfs*, *Cinderella*, *The Little Mermaid*, and *Beauty and the Beast*, for example), others, such as *The Black Cauldron* and *The Rescuers Down Under*, were ... less successful. Regardless of the cost of producing these films – and they are very expensive films to make – Disney has continued to produce feature-length animation partly because there has always been an audience for it, but also because it is a crucial part of the Disney company's heritage. When asked in an interview with Diane Sawyer for *60 Minutes* in the mid-1980s, "Can you really afford to do what you wanna do in animation as much as you wanna do?" Michael Eisner's answer is important: "The answer is no, but we're doing it anyway. We have to do it in this company. We have to. That is our legacy."[208]

Of course, the situation has improved for Disney animation since that period of the studio's history. The Disney Renaissance began in the late 1980s and lasted until the end of the 1990s, and there have been successful films since then (some immediately so, like *Tangled*, others building a following over time, like *The Emperor's New Groove*). Also during that time, the field of Disney Studies as a subject of scholarly enquiry – and animation studies as a whole – has grown by leaps and bounds. I often remark to my students, at the start of the semester, that when I began my MA dissertation (which looked at representations of femininity in *Snow White and the Seven Dwarfs*, *Sleeping Beauty*, and *Pocahontas*, the most recent film featuring a female character at the time I completed the project), I owned a copy of every academic book on Disney, and they only took up about a foot or so of space on my bookshelf. Now, I have multiple shelves on Disney and American animation, and while I have a lot, I don't have it all, not least because I can't afford them all! It is a far preferable situation to be in, if less convenient. Of course, while there are some excellent, balanced, non-politically biased works, nonetheless this is an aspect of "scholarship" that Disney continues to attract, and no doubt will for many years to come. Its enormous familiarity, combined with the popularity of iconoclasm generally, makes Disney the perfect focus for those with time on their hands and an axe to grind. While, traditionally, it is the female characters who are targeted, a 2007 mash-up posted on YouTube, "Sexism, Strength & Dominance: Images of Masculinity in Disney Films", focuses on criticizing Disney's male characters. It is not at all a balanced examination. The title of the short is a hint at the biased stance it takes, and section titles such as "Violence & Dominance: Maintaining Inequality at Any Cost" show that the creator of the mash-up has an agenda he intends to fulfil at any cost. In a blog which offers a response to this, Charley Meakin points out the many problems with the film's "evidence", as she puts it. Meakin notes that one of the primary characters which the short points to is Gaston, who is offered up as the primary evidence that, "often, the message to boys both implicitly and explicitly is that men should view women as objects of pleasure, or as servants to please them".[209] As Meakin points out,

> "This is 'evidenced' in a clip of Gaston from *Beauty & the Beast* (1991) being complemented by his sidekick who claims 'no beast alive stands a chance against you, and no girl for that matter!' The clip ends here – were it to carry on, we would see said girl (Belle) refuse Gaston's hand in marriage and kick him into a muddy puddle, publically humiliating him and scoring one for the women. It's difficult to see how Newton believes that Disney wants its male audiences to wish they too could end up like Gaston, and so should objectify women in this way."[210]

She goes on to talk about Newton's use of the song "A Girl Worth Fighting For", from *Mulan*, and writes of Newton's mash-up that it, "... admittedly doesn't give the best impression".[211] Yes, the song shows men who we are coming to know as "good guys" singing about women in a way which objectifies them in various ways: one of the characters wants a woman who is physically beautiful, a second wants a woman who will admire his strength and battle scars, and a third wants a woman who is an excellent cook. When Mulan asks them (as part of the song), "How 'bout a girl who's got a brain, who always speaks her mind?" the universal response is, 'No!' Yes, as Meakin points out, The

209 Sanjay Newton, "Sexism, Strength and Dominance: Images of Masculinity in Disney Films", found at http://www.you tube.com/watch?v= 8CWMCt35oFY.

210 Charley Meakin, "'Sexism, Strength & Dominance: Images of Masculinity in Disney Films' – A Response", published 27 April 2013, https://cathpostgrad .wordpress.com /2013/04/sexism- strength-dominance -images-of- masculinity-in- disney-films-a- response/.

211 Meakin, "'Sexism, Strength & Dominance: Images of Masculinity in Disney Films' – A Response".

soldiers appear more naïve and foolish, than they do sexist."[212] But it should also be remembered that, at this stage, the men are still unaware that Mulan is a woman: they think she is a young man, Ping. It is through their experience of learning that Mulan is a woman – a woman who has been their friend and ally, the first to begin to succeed in their army training and someone who has proved herself to be a clever, brave and effective soldier – that the men begin to change. When it is revealed that Mulan is a woman, and it looks as though Shang is about to execute her, these same three soldiers, Ling, Chien-Po, and Yao, have to be restrained from coming to Mulan's defence. By the end of the film, the same three soldiers who began by objectifying women are following a woman's leadership and showing her great respect. Likewise, Shang is following orders, and supports her against Chi-Fu, who calls her a traitor (for saving the emperor ... it is not her actions which count with him, but her gender) and demands that she be executed. The characters who demonstrate sexist behaviour – who objectify women – are shown to be misguided at best, evil at worst. The good ones may start out making sexist comments, but they learn to do better by the end of the film. This is true as well of Kuzco, another character used by Newton in the piece. The scene Newton shows is when Kuzco, early in the film, rejects a line of women on incredibly shallow grounds: he does not like their hair, their height, or their looks. But this is a character who is deeply flawed at the start, and will spend the majority of the film learning not to judge appearances and treat others badly and unfeelingly. The Kuzco at the end of the film would never treat a group of people as he treats those around him at the start of the film.

Though Disney films are not perfect by any means, their track record for showing balanced representations of gender roles is improving, little by little. This fact alone means that this body of films is doing rather better than Western society in general. In 2013, there has been a wave of examples of women of all ages (and some men) expressing themselves to be fed-up with the sexist treatment that women continue to face in the second decade of the twenty-first century, nearly one-hundred years since women's right to vote on equitable terms with men first began to be recognized by law in countries such as the United States (1920) and Great Britain (1928). In a blog titled "What happened when I started a feminist society at school", Jinan Younis writes that she first began to self-identify as a feminist when she was on a school trip in Cambridge in 2012: "A group of men in a car started wolf-whistling and shouting sexual remarks at my friends and me. I asked the men if they thought it

212 Meakin, "'Sexism, Strength & Dominance: Images of Masculinity in Disney Films' – A Response".

was appropriate for them to be abusing a group of 17-year-old girls. The response was furious. The men started swearing at me, called me a bitch and threw a cup of coffee over me."[213] She goes on to say that, when she tried to begin a feminist society at her school (an all-female school), it took her a year to get the society ratified, and adds that, when the group decided to take part in a nation-wide project called "Who Needs Feminism" by posting photos of themselves on line holding up signs saying "I need feminism because ..." (with each girl's personal answer following), they were the targets of shockingly vitriolic treatment, predominately from boys their own age. The school's response? "Instead of our school taking action against such intimidating behaviour, it insisted that we remove the pictures."[214] An article by Francesca Angelini in *The Sunday Times*, "We'll Have the Last Laugh", likewise points to the rise of what has become known as "casual sexism", which stretches to the highest echelons of British society. However, this article is about how women are beginning to use the internet to name and shame those who engage in such remarks and behaviours, fighting back this creeping (and creepy) sexism to show that it is not acceptable.[215] However, in the same edition of *The Sunday Times*, an article by Christopher Goodwin, looking at women in mainstream (predominately Hollywood) cinema, notes that "A recent study of 2012's 100 highest-grossing films found that only 28% of speaking roles went to women, the lowest ratio for five years".[216]

What does all of this have to do with masculinity in Disney's animation? Context. Disney is not making its films in a vacuum: they see that films featuring leading female characters tend to be discouraged by Hollywood on the belief that no one will go to them (Goodwin claims that "Paul Feig, the director of *Bridesmaids* and *The Heat*, says he is often warned against making female-focused films".).[217] In an era when an article can appear which questions whether there are "too many" plucky girl heroines in recent Disney films (in a recent *Atlantic Monthly* article, Lindsay Lowe seems to bemoan this trend, even while she acknowledges that boys outnumber girls on screen in G-rated movies), how depictions of masculinity are being constructed in Disney's animated films is being influenced by both the attitudes at work within the film industry (of which it is a part) and by the discourses on masculinity, femininity, gender roles, feminism, and equality which are taking place in society. As was discussed in the introductory chapter, Disney is keen to do whatever they can to keep their audience, even renaming films to gender-neutral titles (and, therefore, potentially increasing the presence of the leading male characters) so that they do not alienate the male

213 Jinan Younis, "What happened when I started a feminist society at school", from *The Guardian* online, News/Education/Blogging students, published 20 June 2013. http://www.guardian.co.uk/education/mortarboard/2013/jun/20/why-i-started-a-feminist-society

214 Jinan Younis, "What happened when I started a feminist society at school".

215 Francesca Angelini, "We'll Have the Last Laugh", in *The Sunday Times*, July 14, 2013, p. 20.

216 Christopher Goodwin, "Report: Whatever Happened to the megabucks female film star?" in *The Sunday Times: Culture*, July 14, 2013, pp. 6-7.

217 Goodwin, p. 7.

audience. When articles appear in which people like Lowe can comment that "The feisty heroine may have been groundbreaking 20 years ago, but today, she's nearly as predictable as the submissive girls of early Disney years", one cannot help but wonder what a Disney and/or Pixar executive, artist, or writer would make of it.[218]

This is not to dismiss Lowe's point entirely. After all, some women and girls are feisty, some are quiet and retiring; for most of us, which of these we are probably depends on how we feel about a given situation, our mood that day, and whether we got enough caffeine that morning. After all, there is more than one type of woman. There are even more than two. So watching strong, interesting, intelligent female characters, of all ages, social levels, and nationalities/races of women and men on screen, whatever their personality, is good for all of us; it also makes for better films. This does, by and large, seem to be the direction in which Disney's animated depictions are moving. They know that audiences want to see lead characters in their films who can serve as good role models for children (and adults), and as a company, Disney has no wish to alienate their fans. But despite the emphasis on girls' merchandise, the idea of showing active female characters on screen may be appealing in theory, but it has to be balanced with a need to bring in both genders to watch the films. Disney is aware that current beliefs about men and women have set up a contradictory dichotomy between what we want to see on screen and how we purchase merchandise. Likewise, Disney is aware that it cannot be too radical with its depictions and themes: while controversial topics may be fine in some genres, they tend to be problematic in the family and children's film markets. It is not necessarily, as some would have it, that Disney "promotes" conservative ideas; rather, long experience has taught them to be careful with their level of experimentation. Go too far, and they lose the audience, lose money, and have to deal with a film which becomes a drain on the studio's resources.

This may be why, in so many of their films, Disney has tended to favour the tried and true plotlines found in traditional tales, many of which are based in romance. This creates the problem of deciding how to stick to traditional aspects of storytelling (and remember, even when an animated feature from Disney is not based on a traditional fairy tale or folklore, it nonetheless tends to *function* as a fairy tale). According to Rachel Blau DuPlessis, "The romance plot separates love and quest, values sexual asymmetry, including the division of labor by gender, is based on extremes of sexual difference, and evokes an aura around the

218 Lindsay Lowe, "Enough Feisty Princesses: Disney Needs an Introverted Heroine", from *The Atlantic* online, http://www. theatlantic.com/ sexes/archive/2013/ 03/enough-feisty-princesses-disney-needs-an-introverted -heroine/273821/

couple itself. In short, the romance plot, broadly speaking, is a trope for the sex-gender system as a whole."[219] Creating and/or reshaping characters – both male and female – who are capable of fitting traditional narratives and yet who are also acceptable to modern sensibilities has been very much an experiment of trial and error. But are traditional depictions "dangerous", as DuPlessis implies? There are those who would argue otherwise. In her discussion of scholarship on twentieth-century women's romantic fiction, Rosalind Gill points to such studies as Tania Modleski's *Loving With a Vengeance* and Janice Radway's *Reading the Romance* as earlier studies (1982 and 1984, respectively) of the genre, discussing how both – to include Radway's more ambivalent attitude towards the genre and its readers – argue, ultimately, that habitual readers of the genre read these books knowing (and taking pleasure from knowing) the formulaic twists the narrative will take, and this superior knowledge means that, far from simply reading and being duped by the narratives and the depictions of femininity, masculinity, and feminism/sexism to be found in these stories, the genre's fans read them as "fictions that engage in complex and contradictory ways with real problems – offering temporary, magical, fantasy or symbolic solutions".[220] It is my contention that Disney's films offer their multiple audiences a similar escape.

Admittedly, different sections of the Disney audience will be more familiar than others with traditional narrative structures and depictions. Those who are more knowledgeable will be better at navigating these films' "complex and contradictory ways with real problems". But this does not seem to be strictly a problem of age. After all, the mash-up by Newton discussed earlier clearly demonstrates that this was an adult man who – like a great many adults who have made similar comments before him and since him – is not familiar enough with the plot points and characters in these films to be able to understand that, when a villain says something, it probably means that it is *not* a message that the film makers want the audience to take on board as a way to live their lives. When Ursula tells Ariel that "On land it's much preferred for ladies not to say a word", the rest of the film works hard at showing the audience that Ursula was wrong, and that Eric will only be able to recognize Ariel as the love of his life when she finally opens up her mouth and *speaks*. When Gaston holds himself up as the best (and the rest are all drips!), again – those of us with a knowledge of the genre know that we should not be agreeing, but instead laughing at his self-delusion and wondering how Belle was able to put up with living for any length of time in a town like that. Instead, those in the know – those who are

219 Rachel Blau DuPlessis, *Writing Beyond the Ending: Narrative Strategies of Twentieth-Century Women Writers* (Bloomington: Indiana University Press, 1985), p. 5.

220 Gill, p. 221.

more savvy film watchers – know that we root for the hero(in)es because they behave in a way which allows them to be true to themselves, to work for what is right and good, and to succeed in their efforts. They might be led astray out of innocence or naivety, but they will learn as they go along, and will find their way towards strength, courage, and wisdom.

Disney's depictions of masculinity are not perfect. But as with their depictions of femininity and race, they are improving. These films treat the children who watch them as intelligent, discerning viewers who want and expect well-developed characters, strong stories, exciting and interesting villains, a few good plot twists, and an entertaining narrative. Likewise, they treat their adult fans as fully-fledged adults who have not lost touch with their inner child out of a mistaken belief that this will make them "mature". Disney fans tend to be lifelong fans for a reason: the films they enjoyed as children continue to be meaningful to them as adults because, like the heroes and heroines of the film, the viewer has continued to learn and grow during their journey through life. The sheer variety and diversity of types of male characters in Disney's animated feature films is continuing to improve, setting up good role models of masculinity for both the boys and the girls who are watching. As Joe Kelly and Stacy L. Smith note in their study of male characters in G-rated films as a whole, "It is important to note that children are not impacted exclusively by how characters of their *own* gender are portrayed on the silver screen. Along with expectations for themselves, children's expectations for members of the other gender, now and into the future, can be influenced by repeated viewings of characters and stories that reinforce particular notions about male and female roles."[221] In a body of films in which it is becoming habitual for there to be a balance of leading male and female characters, one can feel much optimism that there will continue to be a wide variety of male and female characters learning to become better human beings.

221 Joe Kelly and Stacy L. Smith, "G Movies Give Boys a D: Portraying Males as Dominant, Disconnected and Dangerous", A Research Brief Commissioned by the See Jane Program at Dads & Daughters, SeeJane.org, May 2006, p. 6.

Appendix A

Disney Film List - Animated Features

Subject list for *Handsome Heroes & Vile Villains*

1. Snow *White and the Seven Dwarfs* – 1937
2. *Pinocchio* – February 1940
3. *Make Mine Music* – 1946
4. *Melody Time* – 1948
5. *The Adventures of Ichabod and Mr. Toad* – 1949
6. *Cinderella* – 1950
7. *Peter Pan* – 1953
8. *Sleeping Beauty* – 1959
9. *The Sword in the Stone* – 1963
10. *The Jungle Book* – 1967
11. *The Rescuers* – 1977
12. *The Black Cauldron* – 1985
13. *The Little Mermaid* – 1989
14. *The Rescuers Down Under* – 1990
15. *Beauty and the Beast* – 1991
16. *Aladdin* – 1992
17. *Pocahontas* – 1995
18. *The Hunchback of Notre Dame* – 1996
19. *Hercules* – 1997
20. *Mulan* – 1998
21. *Tarzan* – 1999
22. *The Emperor's New Groove* – 2000
23. *Atlantis: The Lost Empire* – 2001
24. *Treasure Planet* – 2003
25. *Meet the Robinsons* – 2007
26. *The Princess and the Frog* – 2009
27. *Tangled* – 2010
28. *Wreck-It Ralph* (2012)

Appendix B

Disney's Animated Features to Date

1. *Snow White and the Seven Dwarfs* – 1937
2. *Pinocchio* – February 1940
3. *Fantasia* – November 1940
4. *Dumbo* – 1941
5. *Bambi* – 1942
6. *Saludos Amigos* – 1943
7. *The Three Caballeros* – 1945
8. *Make Mine Music* – 1946
9. *Fun and Fancy Free* – 1947
10. *Melody Time* – 1948
11. *The Adventures of Ichabod and Mr. Toad* – 1949
12. *Cinderella* – 1950
13. *Alice in Wonderland* – 1951
14. *Peter Pan* – 1953
15. *Lady and the Tramp* – 1955
16. *Sleeping Beauty* – 1959
17. *One Hundred and One Dalmatians* – 1961
18. *The Sword in the Stone* – 1963
19. *The Jungle Book* – 1967
20. *The Aristocats* – 1970
21. *Robin Hood* – 1973
22. *The Many Adventures of Winnie the Pooh* – 1977
23. *The Rescuers* – 1977
24. *The Fox and the Hound* – 1981
25. *The Black Cauldron* – 1985
26. *The Great Mouse Detective* – 1986
27. *Oliver and Company* – 1988
28. *The Little Mermaid* – 1989
29. *The Rescuers Down Under* – 1990
30. *Beauty and the Beast* – 1991

31. *Aladdin* – 1992
32. *The Lion King* – 1994
33. *Pocahontas* – 1995
34. *The Hunchback of Notre Dame* – 1996
35. *Hercules* – 1997
36. *Mulan* – 1998
37. *Tarzan* – 1999
38. *Fantasia 2000* – 2000
39. *Dinosaur (2000)*
40. *The Emperor's New Groove* – 2000
41. *Atlantis: The Lost Empire* – 2001
42. *Lilo and Stitch* – 2002
43. *Treasure Planet* – 2003
44. *Brother Bear* – 2004
45. *Home on the Range* – 2004
46. *Chicken Little* – 2005
47. *Meet the Robinsons* – 2007
48. *Bolt* – 2008
49. *The Princess and the Frog* – 2009
50. *Tangled* – 2010
51. *Winnie the Pooh* – 2011
52. *Wreck-It Ralph* – 2012

Bibliography

Primary Source Materials

Archival Materials

Story-Conference Notes for *Snow White and the Seven Dwarfs*, Dated 26 July 1934 through 8 June 1937. Transcription from the Original Story-Meeting Notes held at the Disney Studio Archives in Burbank, California, copied by David R. Williams, August 1987, and held in the collection of the British Film Institute Library, 20 Stephen Street, London.

Peter Pan's Press Pack, Library of Congress (File C-3).

The Walt Disney Company: Fiscal Year 2012 Annual Financial Report and Shareholder Letter, Online Version, Published 2013. PDF found at: http://thewaltdisneycompany.com/investors/financial-information.

Books

Eisner, Michael, with Tony Schwartz. *Work in Progress* (New York: Random House, 1998).

Irving, Washington. *The Legend of Sleepy Hollow*, Illustrated Deluxe Edition for Kindle, (Northpointe Classics, 2008).

Articles

Angelini, Francesca. "We'll Have the Last Laugh", in *The Sunday Times*, July 14, 2013, p. 20.

Anonymous. 'Sleeping Beauty'. From *Harrison's Reports*, vol. XLI, No. 5 (31 January 1959), p. 18.

Boettiger, Elizabeth F. "Families and the World Outside (1941)", in Henry Jenkins (Ed.), *The Children's Culture Reader* (London: New York University Press, 1998), pp. 499-500.

Brown, Erin R. "J.CREW Pushes Transgendered Child Propaganda", posted on Friday, April 8, 2011, 12:37pm EDT; found at http://www.mrc.org/articles/jcrew-pushes-transgendered-child- propaganda. Accessed 20 April 2011.

Chmielewski, Dawn C., and Claudia Eller, "Disney restyles 'Rapunzel' to Appeal to Boys", from *The Los Angeles Times*, 9 March 2010; found at: http://articles.latimes.com/ 2010/mar/09/business/la-fi-ct-disney9-2010mar 09

Crowther, Bosley. Film Review of *Sleeping Beauty*, 18 February 1959. From

New York Times Film Reviews, 1913-1968, vol. 5 (1959-68) (New York: *New York Times* and Arno Press, 1970), pp. 3109-10.

Drexler, Peggy. "Do Painted Toes Make the Man?" posted 16 April 2011, 5:42 ET, found at http://www.huffingtonpost.com/peggy-drexler/do-painted-toes-make-the_b_850104 .html. Accessed 20 April 2011.

Dykes, Brett Michael. "Hot pink-toenailed boy in J. Crew ad sparks controversy", found at http://news.yahoo.com/blogs/lookout/hot-pink-toenailed-boy-j-crew-ad-sparks-20110413-085113-688.html.

Goodwin, Christopher. "Report: Whatever Happened to the megabucks female film star?" in *The Sunday Times: Culture*, July 14, 2013, pp. 6-7.

Hertz, John H. "The Fiasco of Denazification in Germany", from *Political Science Quarterly*, Vol. 64, No. 4 (December 1948), pp. 569-594.

Lowe, Lindsay. "Enough Feisty Princesses: Disney Needs an Introverted Heroine", from *The Atlantic* online, http://www.theatlantic.com/sexes/archive/2013/03/enough-feisty-princesses-disney-needs-an-introverted-heroine/273821/.

Macedo, Diane. "J. Crew Ad Showing Boy With Pink Nail Polish Sparks Debate on Gender Identity", published 11 April 2011, http://www.foxnews.com/us/2011/04/11/jcrew-ad-showing-boy-pink-nail-polish-sparks-debate-gender-identity/.

Meakin, Charley. "'Sexism, Strength, and Dominance: Images of Masculinity in Disney Films' – A Response", published 27 April 2013, https://cathpost-grad.wordpress.com/2013/ 04/27/sexism-strength-dominance-images-of-masculinity-in-disney-films-a-response/.

Orenstein, Peggy. "What's Wrong With Cinderella?" from *The New York Times* online, published 24 December 2006. http://popcultureandamerican-childhood.com/wp-content/uploads/2012/04/What%E2%80%99s-Wrong -With-Cinderella_-NYTimes.pdf.

Younis, Jinan, "What happened when I started a feminist society at school", from *The Guardian* online, News/Education/Blogging students, published 20 June 2013. http://www.guardian.co.uk/education/mortarboard/2013/jun/20/why-i-started-a-feminist-society .

Websites & Electronic Sources

Text

Bush, George H. W. Acceptance speech, the Republican National Convention, New Orleans, 18 August 1988. Found at http://www.presidency.ucsb.edu/ws/index.php?pid=25955.

http://disneyworld.disney.go.com/tours-and-experiences/bibbidi-bobbidi-boutique/, accessed on 28 February 2013

Walt Disney: An Intimate History of the Man and his Magic. CD-ROM. (Santa Monica, CA: Pantheon Productions Inc, 1998). ©1998 Walt Disney Family Educational Foundation, Inc. and its licensors. All rights reserved. ©1998 Disney Enterprises, Inc. All rights reserved.

Lincoln, Abraham. Second Inaugural Speech, delivered 4 March 1865. Found at http://avalon.law.yale.edu/19th_century/lincoln2.asp.

"Death of the Seven Dwarfs: A Legend from Switzerland", Translated by D.L. Ashliman, ©1998-2013;
found at http://www.pitt.edu/~dash/dwarfs.html.

Snow-White and other tales of Aarne-Thompson-Uther type 709, translated and/or edited by D.L. Ashliman, ©1998-2013; found at http://www.pitt.edu/~dash/type0709.html.

Files/Milo, page 3-8, Disc 2, *Atlantis: The Lost Empire, 2-Disc Collector's Edition* (Region 1/NTSC, © Disney Enterprises, Inc., DVD release date January 29, 2002).

Video

A Disney Halloween, US TV Special, ABC, Original Air Date 1 October 1983. Found at: http://www.youtube.com/watch?v=Txn1JRBObIY.

"The Making of *Hercules*", Bonus Features, from *Hercules* (Region 2/PAL, © Disney, DVD release date 12 August 2002).

"The Making of *The Rescuers Down Under*", Bonus Features, from *The Rescuers Down Under* (Region 2/PAL, © Disney Enterprises, DVD release date 28 January 2002).

The Characters/"Strength of Character". Documentary Short. Disc 2, "Cogsworth and Lumiere's Library", from *Walt Disney Pictures Presents Beauty and the Beast, Special Edition – Platinum Edition* (Region 1/NTSC, © Disney Enterprises, Inc., DVD release date October 8, 2002).

Animation/" Transformation: Glen Keane", Disc 2, *Walt Disney Pictures Presents Beauty and the Beast, Special Edition – Platinum Edition* (Region 1/NTSC, © Disney Enterprises, Inc., DVD release date October 8, 2002).

"You Can Fly: The Making of Peter Pan". Disc 2, Backstage, from *Walt Disney's Pinocchio, 2-Disc Platinum Edition* (Region 1/NTSC, © Disney, DVD release date March 6, 2007).

"Sexism, Strength, and Dominance: Images of Masculinity in Disney Films", Created by Sanjay Newton, uploaded 12 April 2007. Found at http://www.youtube.com/watch? v=8CWMCt35oFY.

Bonus Features/Deleted Scenes/"Bowler Hat Guy's Redemption", from *Meet the Robinsons* (Region 1/NTSC, ©Disney, DVD release date October 23, 2007).

"The Making of *Pinocchio*: No Strings Attached." Disc 2, Backstage, from *Walt Disney Pictures Presents Pinocchio, Special Edition – Platinum Edition* (Region 2/PAL, © Disney, DVD release date 9 March 2009).

Backstage Disney/"The Characters of Tarzan", Disc 2, from *Tarzan: 2-Disc Special Edition* (Region 2/PAL, © Edgar Rice Burroughs, Inc., and Disney Enterprises, Inc., DVD release date 8 February 2013).

Waking Sleeping Beauty (2009). Written by and interviews conducted by Patrick Pacheco. Produced by Peter Schneider and Don Hahn. Directed by Don Hahn. (Region 1/NTSC, © Buena Vista Home Entertainment, Inc. DVD release date November 30, 2010).

Secondary Source Materials

Books

Allan, Robin. *Walt Disney and Europe: European Influences on the Animated Feature Films of Walt Disney* (London: John Libbey & Company Ltd., 1999).

Banyard, Kat. *The Equality Illusion: The Truth about Women and Men Today* (London: Faber and Faber Limited, 2010).

Barrier, Michael. *Hollywood Cartoons: American Animation in its Golden Age* (New York: Oxford University Press, 1999).

Biddulph, Steve. *Raising Boys* (London: Thorsons, 1998)

Blau DuPlessis, Rachel. *Writing Beyond the Ending: Narrative Strategies of Twentieth-Century Women Writers* (Bloomington: Indiana University Press, 1985).

Cashdan, Sheldon. *The Witch Must Die: The Hidden Meaning of Fairy Tales* (New York: Basic Books, 1999).

Crafton, Donald. *The Talkies: American Cinema's Transition to Sound, 1926-1931* (London: University of California Press, 1999)

Davis, Amy M. *Good Girls & Wicked Witches: Women in Disney's Feature Animation* (Eastleigh: John Libbey & Co., 2006).

Douglas, Susan J. *Enlightened Sexism: The Seductive Message that Feminism's Work is Done* (New York: Henry Holt and Company, 2010).

Dyer, Richard. *Stars (New Edition)* (London: BFI, 2007)

Feenstra, Pietsie, *New Mythological Figures in Spanish Cinema: Dissident Bodies Under Franco* (Amsterdam: Amsterdam University Press, 2011).

Gill, Rosalind. *Gender and the Media* (Cambridge: Polity Press, 2007).

James, Judi. *The Body Language Bible: The Hidden Meaning Behind People's Gestures and Expressions* (London: Vermilion, 2008).

Johnston, Ollie, and Frank Thomas. *The Illusion of Life: Disney Animation* (New York: Hyperion, 1981).

Johnston, Ollie, and Frank Thomas. *The Disney Villain* (New York: Hyperion Press, 1993).

Kurtti, Jeff. *Disney Dossiers: Files of Character from The Walt Disney Studios* (New York: Disney Editions, 2006).

Kurtti, Jeff. *The Art of Tangled* (San Francisco: Chronicle Books LLC, 2010).

Levy, Ariel. *Female Chauvinist Pigs: Women and the Rise of Raunch Culture* (London: Pocket Books, 2005).

Maltby, Richard. *Hollywood Cinema: Second Edition* (Oxford: Blackwell Publishing, 2003).

Maltin, Leonard. *The Disney Films (Fourth Edition)* (New York: Disney Editions, 2000).

McRobbie, Angela. *The Aftermath of Feminism: Gender, Culture and Social Change* (London: Sage, 2009).

Opie, Iona and Peter. *The Classic Fairy Tales* (New York: Oxford University Press, 1980).

Pallant, Chris. *Demystifying Disney: A History of Disney Feature Animation* (London: Bloomsbury, 2013).

Rebello, Stephen and Jane Healey. *The Art of* Hercules: *The Chaos of Creation* (New York: Hyperion, 1997).

Redfern, Catherine, and Kristin Aune. *Reclaiming the F Word: The New Feminist Movement* (London: Zed Books, Ltd., 2010).

Sammond, Nicholas. *Babes in Tomorrowland: Walt Disney and the Making of the American Child, 1930-1960* (Durham, NC: Duke University Press, 2005).

Solomon, Charles *The History of Animation: Enchanted Drawings* (New York: Wings Books, 1994).

Stacey, Jackie. *Star Gazing: Hollywood Cinema and Female Spectatorship* (London: Routledge, 1998).

Tatar, Maria. *Off With Their Heads: Fairy Tales and the Culture of Childhood* (Princeton: Princeton University Press, 1992)

Tieman, Robert. *The Disney Treasures* (London: Carlton Books Limited, 2003).

Walter, Natasha. *Living Dolls: The Return of Sexism* (London: Virago Press, 2010).

Ward, Annalee R. *Mouse Morality: The Rhetoric of Disney Animated Films* (Austin: University of Texas Press, 2002).

Warner, Marina. *From the Beast to the Blonde: On Fairy Tales and Their Tellers* (London: Vintage, 1995).

Warner, Marina. *No Go the Bogeyman: Scaring, Lulling and Making Mock* (London: Vintage, 2000).

Articles

Babcock-Abrahams, Barbara. "'A Tolerated Margin of Mess': The Trickster and His Tales Reconsidered", from *Journal of the Folklore Institute*, Vol. 11, No. 3 (March 1975), pp. 147-186.

Allen, Robert C. "Home Alone Together: Hollywood and the 'Family Film'", in Melvyn Stokes and Richard Maltby (Eds.), *Identifying Hollywood's Audiences: Cultural Identity and the Movies* (London: BFI, 1999), pp. 109-131.

Armstrong, Judith. "Ghosts as Rhetorical Devices in Children's Fiction", in *Children's Literature in Education* Vol. 9, No. 2 (June 1978), pp. 59-66.

Beamish, Thomas D., Harvey Molotch, and Richard Flacks, "Who Supports the Troops? Vietnam, the Gulf War, and the Making of Collective Memory", from *Social Problems*, Vol. 42, No. 3 (August 1995), pp. 344-360.

Beatie, Bruce A. "Arthurian Films and Arthurian Texts: Problems of Reception and Comprehension", in *Arthurian Interpretations*, Vol. 2, No. 2 (Spring 1988), pp. 65-78.

Cummins, June. "Romancing the Plot: The Real Beast of Disney's *Beauty and the Beast*", in *Children's Literature Association Quarterly*, Vol. 20, No. 1 (Spring 1995), pp. 22-28.

Davis, Amy M. "Borrowing the Earth: Saving the Planet and Disney's *Pocahontas*", in Reynold Humphries, Gilles Ménégaldo, and Melvyn Stokes, Eds., *Cinéma et Mythes*, (Poitiers: University of Poitiers, 2002), pp. 77-89.

deCordova, Richard "The Mickey in Macy's Window: Childhood, Consumerism, and Disney Animation", in Eric Smoodin (Ed.), *Disney Discourse: Producing the Magic Kingdom* (London: Routledge, 1994), pp. 203-213.

Fries, Maureen "How to Handle a Woman, or Morgan at the Movies", in Kevin J. Harty (Ed.), *King Arthur on Film: New Essays on Arthurian Cinema* (Jefferson, NC: McFarland & Company, Inc., 1999), pp. 67-80.

Gehlawat, Ajay. "The Strange Case of *The Princess and the Frog*: Passing and the Elision of Race", in *The Journal of African American Studies*, Vol. 14 (2010), pp. 417-431.

Glancy, Mark. "*Blackmail* (1929), Hitchcock, and Film Nationalism", in James Chapman, Mark Glancy, and Sue Harper (Eds.), *The New Film History: Sources, Methods, Approaches* (Basingstoke: Palgrave MacMillan, 2007), pp. 185-200.

Gledhill, Christine. "Women Reading Men", in Pat Kirkham and Janet Thumim (Eds.), *Me Jane: Masculinity, Movies and Women* (London: Lawrence and Wishart, 1995), pp. 73-93.

Gottlieb, Robert. "The Next Environmentalism: How Movements Respond to The Changes that Elections Bring – from Nixon to Obama", from *Environmental History*, Vol. 14, No. 2 (April 2009), pp. 298-308.

Gregory, Sarita McCoy, "Disney's Second Line: New Orleans, Racial Masquerade, and the Reproduction of Whiteness in *The Princess and the Frog*", from *The Journal of African American Studies*, Vol. 14 (2010), pp. 432-449.

Hoffman, Donald. "Whose Home on the Range?: Finding Room for Native

Americans, African Americans, and Latino Americans in the Revisionist Western", in *MELUS*, Vol. 22, No. 2 (Summer 1997), pp. 45-59.

Jeffords, Susan. "The Curse of Masculinity: Disney's *Beauty and the Beast*", in Bell, Elizabeth, Lynda Haas, and Laura Sells (eds.). *From Mouse to Mermaid: The Politics of Film, Gender, and Culture* (Indianapolis: Indiana University Press, 1995), pp. 161-172.

Keller, James R. "'Among School Children': Lacan and the *South Park* Felt Board Lesson Set", from Leslie Stratyner and James R. Keller (eds.), *The Deep End of South Park: Critical Essays on TV's Shocking Cartoon Series* (Jefferson, N.C.: McFarland & Company, Inc., 2009), pp. 167-192.

Kelly, Joe, and Stacy L. Smith, "G Movies Give Boys a D: Portraying Males as Dominant, Disconnected and Dangerous", A Research Brief Commissioned by the See Jane Program at Dads & Daughters, SeeJane.org, May 2006.

Kochert Michael N. and Karen Steenhof. "Golden Eagles in the U.S. and Canada: Status, Trends, and Conservation Challenges", in *Journal of Raptor Research*, Vol. 36, No. 1, Supplemental (March 2002), pp. 32-40.

Lester, Neal A. "Disney's *The Princess and the Frog*: The Pride, the Pressure, and the Politics of Being a First", in *The Journal of American Culture*, Vol. 33, No. 4 (December 2010), pp. 294-308.

Long, Carolyn Morrow. "Perceptions of New Orleans Voodoo: Sin, Fraud, Entertainment, and Religion", in *Nova Religio: The Journal of Alternative and Emergent Religions*, Vol. 6, No. 1 (October 2002), pp. 86-101.

Maertens, James W. "Between Jules Verne and Walt Disney: Brains, Brawn, and Masculine Desire in *20,000 Leagues Under the Sea*", in *Science Fiction Studies*, Vol. 22, No. 2 (July 1995), pp. 209-225.

Sparks, Richard. "Masculinity and Heroism in the Hollywood Blockbuster", from *The British Journal of Criminology*, Vol. 36, No. 3: Special Issue (1996), pp. 348-360.

Stabile, Carol. "Review Essay: 'First He'll Kill Her then I'll Save Her': Vampires, Feminism, and the *Twilight* Franchise", from *The Journal of Communication*, Vol. 61 (2011), pp. E4-E8.

Stone, Kay. "Things Walt Disney Never Told Us", in *The Journal of American Folklore*, Vol. 88, No. 347 (Jan.-March 1975), pp. 42-50.

Van Fuqua, Joy. "'What Are Those Little Girls Made Of?': *The Powerpuff Girls* and Consumer Culture", in Carol A. Stabile and Mark Harrison (eds), *Prime Time Animation: Television Animation and American Culture* (London: Routledge, 2003), pp. 205-219.

Yasaitis, Kelly Elizabeth, "Collecting Culture at the British Museum", in *Curator: The Museum Journal*, Vol. 49, No. 4 (October 2006), pp. 449-462.

Filmography (Chronological)

Please note that the cast and crew lists given are partial. For earlier films, the entire cast and crew were not named in the original credits. In the more recent films, the cast and crew lists are so extensive that for reasons of space, it was impossible to list them in full.

Disney Films Analysed

Snow White and the Seven Dwarfs

Rel. 1937, colour, 82 mins. Released by RKO Radio Pictures. Director: Ben Sharpsteen. Supervising Director: David Hand; Musical Directors: Frank Churchill, Leigh Harline, Paul Smith. Songs: Larry Morey, Frank Churchill. Writers: Ted Sears, Otto Englander, Earl Hurd, Dorothy Ann Blank, Richard Creedon, Dick Richard, Merrill de Maris, Webb Smith, from the fairy tale by the Brothers Grimm. Voices: Adriana Caselotti, Harry Stockwell, Lucille La Verne, Scotty Mattraw, Roy Atwell, Pinto Colvig, Otis Harlan, Billy Gilbert, Moroni Olsen.

Pinocchio

Rel. Feb. 1940, colour, 88 mins. Released by RKO Radio Pictures. Based on the story by Collodi. Supervising Directors: Ben Sharpsteen, Hamilton Luske. Sequence Directors: Norman Ferguson, Bill Roberts, Wilfrid Jackson, T. Hee, Jack Kinney. Animation Directors: Fred Moore, Franklin Thomas, Milton Kahl, Vladimir Tytla, Ward Kimball, Arthur Babbitt, Eric Larson, Wolfgang Reitherman. Story adaptation: Ted Sears, Otto Englander, Webb Smith, William Cottrell, Joseph Sabo, Erdman Penner, Aurelius Battaglia. Music and Lyrics: Ned Washington, Leigh Harline, Paul J. Smith. Voices: Dickie Jones, Christian Rub, Cliff Edwards, Evelyn Venable, Walter Catlett, Frankie Darro, Charles Jodels, Don Brodie.

Make Mine Music

Rel. 1946, colour, 74 mins. Released by RKO Radio Pictures. Production Supervisor: Ben Sharpsteen. Cartoon Directors: Bob Cormack, Clyde Geronimi, Jack Kinney Hamilton Luske, Josh Meador. Story: Homer Brightman, Dick Huemer, Dick Kinney, John Walbridge, Tom Oreb, Dick Shaw, Eric Gurney, Sylvia Holland, T. Hee, Erdman Penner, Dick Kelsey, James

Bodrero, Roy Williams, Cap Palmer, Jesse Marsh, Erwin Graham. Production Supervisor: Joe Grant. Art Department: Mary Blair, John Hench, Mique Nelson, Elmer Plummer. Cast: Nelson Eddy, Dinah Shore, Benny Goodman, The Andrews Sisters, Jerry Colonna, Andy Russell, Sterling Holloway, Tatiana Riabouchinska, David Lichine, The Pied Pipers, The King's Men, Ken Darby.

Melody Time

Rel. 1948, colour, 74 mins. Released by RKO Radio Pictures. Production Supervisor: Ben Sharpsteen. Cartoon Directors: Clyde Geronimi, Wilfrid Jackson, Hamilton Luske, Jack Kinney. Story: Winston Hibler, Harry Reeves, Ken Anderson, Erdman Penner, Homer Brightman, Ted Sears, Joe Rinaldi, Art Scott, Bob Moore, Bill Cottrell, Jesse Marsh, John Walbridge. Directing Animators: Eric Larson, Ward Kimball, Milt Kahl, Oliver Johnston, Jr., John Lounsberry, Les Clark. Cast: Roy Rogers, Luana Patten, Bobby Driscoll, Ethel Smith and the Dinning Sisters, Bob Nolan, Sons of the Pioneers. Voices: Buddy Clark, The Andrews Sisters, Fred Waring and his Pennsylvanians, Frances Langford, Dennis Day, with Freddy Martin and his Orchestra, featuring Jack Fina.

The Adventures of Ichabod and Mr. Toad

Rel. 1949. Colour, 68 mins. Production Supervisor: Ben Sharpsteen. Directors: Jack Kinney, Clyde Geronimi, James Algar. Directing Animators: Franklin Thomas, Oliver Johnston, Jr., Wolfgang Reitherman, Milt Kahl, John Lounsberry, Ward Kimball. Story: Erdman Penner, Winston Hibler, Joe Rinaldi, Ted Sears, Homer Brightman, Harry Reeves. Character Animators: Fred Moore, John Sibley, Marc Davis, Hal Ambro, Harvey Toombs, Hal King, Hugh Fraser, Don Lusk. Music Director: Oliver Wallace. Based on "The Legend of Sleepy Hollow" by Washington Irving and *The Wind in the Willows* by Kenneth Grahame. Songs for "Ichabod" segment by Don Raye, Gene DePaul. "Ichabod" segment narrated (and songs performed) by Bing Crosby. Songs for "Willows" segment written by Frank Churchill and Charles Wolcott, with lyrics by Larry Morey and Ray Gilbert. Voices in "Willows" segment: Basil Rathbone, Pat O'Malley, Claud Allister, John Ployardt, Collin Campbell, Campbell Grant, Ollie Wallace.

Cinderella

Rel. 1950, colour, 74 mins. Released by Walt Disney Pictures. Production Supervisor: Ben Sharpsteen. Special Process: Ub Iwerks. Editor: Don Halliday. Directors: Clyde Geronimi, Wilfred Jackson, Hamliton S. Luske. Original Story: Charles Perrault. Animation Directors: Milt Kahl, Ward Kimball, Frank Thomas, Eric Larson, John Lounsbery, Ollie Johnston, Wolfgang Reitherman, Marc Davis, Les Clark, Norman Ferguson. Music Directors: Oliver Wallace, Paul Smith. Songs: Jerry Livingston, Al Hoffman, Mack David. Voices: Ilene Woods, William Phipps, Eleanor Audley, Rhoda Williams, Lucille Bliss, Verna Felton.

Peter Pan

Rel. 1953, colour, 74 mins. Released by RKO Pictures. Based on the Story by J.M. Barrie. Production Supervisor: Ben Sharpsteen. Directors: Clyde Geronimi, Wilfred Jackson, Hamliton S. Luske. Story: Winston Hibler, Bill Peet, Joe Rinaldi, Ted Sears, Erdman Penner, Milt Banta, Ralph Wright. Animation Directors: Milt Kahl, Ward Kimball, Frank Thomas, Eric Larson, John Lounsberry, Ollie Johnston, Wolfgang Reitherman, Marc Davis, Les Clark, Norman Ferguson. Music Supervision: Oliver Wallace. Songs: Sammy Fain, Sammy Cahn.

Sleeping Beauty

Rel. 1959, colour, 75 mins. Walt Disney Studios. Director: Clyde Geronimi. Story Adaptation: Erdman Penner. Additional Story: Joe Rinaldi, Bill Peet, Ralph Wright, Winston Hibler, Ted Sears, Milt Banta, based on the story by Charles Perrault. Animation Directors: Milt Kahl, Frank Thomas, Ollie Johnston, Mark Davis, John Lounsbery. Editors: Roy M. Brewer, Jr., Donald Halliday Musical Adapter: George Bruns. Songs: George Bruns, Tom Adair, Winston Hibler, Erdman Penner, Sammy Fain, Jack Lawrence, Ted Sears. Sound: Robert Cook. Production Designers: Don da Gradi, Ken Anderson. Voices: Mary Costa, Bill Shirley, Eleanor Audley, Verna Felton, Barbara Jo Allen, Barbara Luddy.

The Sword in the Stone

Rel. 1963, colour, 75 mins. Released by Buena Vista. Production Supervisor: Ken Peterson. Director: Wolfgang Reitherman. Art director: Ken Anderson. Directing animators: Franklin Thomas, Milt Kahl, Oliver Johnston, Jr., John Lounsbery. Story: Bill Peet, based on the book by T. H. White. Character animators: Hal King, Eric Larson, Cliff Nordberg, Hal Ambro, Dick Lucas. Character design: Milt Kahl, Bill Peet. Music Editor: Evelyn Kennedy. Voices: Ricky Sorenson, Sebastian Cabot, Karl Swenson, Junius Matthews, Alan Napier, Norman Alden, Martha Wentworth, Ginny Tyler, Barbara Jo Allen, RIcherd and Robert Reitherman, and the Mello Men.

The Jungle Book

Rel. 1967, colour, 78 mins. Released by Buena Vista. Director: Wolfgang Reitherman. Directing animators: Milt Kahl, Granklin Thomas, Oliver Johnston, Jr., John Lounsbery. Story: Larry Clemmons, Ralph Wright, Ken Anderson, Vance Gerry, inspired by the Rudyard Kipling *Mowgli* stories. Character animators: Hal King, Eric Larson, Walt Stanchfield, Eric Cleworth, Fred Hellmich, John Ewing, Dick Lucas. Music: George Bruns. Music Editor: Evelyn Kennedy. Voices: Phil Harris, Sebastian Cabot, Louis Prima, George Sanders, Sterling Holloway, J. Pat O'Malley, Bruce Reitherman, Chad Stuart, Lord Tim Hudson, John Abbott, Ben Wright, Darleen Carr.

The Rescuers

Rel. 1977, colour, 74 mins. Released by Buena Vista Distribution Co., Inc. Directors: Wolfgang Reitherman, John Lounsbery, Art Stevens. Assistant Directors: Jeff Patch, Richard Rich. Executive Producers: Ron Miller. Producer: Wolfgang Reitherman. Production Manager: Don Duckwall. Story: Larry Clemmons, Ken Anderson, Vance Gerry, Frank Thomas, Dave Michener, Ted Berman, Fred Lucky, Burny Mattinson, Dick Sebast, based on the original stories by Margery Sharpe. Animation Directors: Milt Kahl, Frank Thomas, Ollie Johnston, Don Bluth. Music: Artie Butler. Sound: Herb Taylor. Voices: Bob Newhart, Eva Gabor, Geraldine Page, Joe Flynn, Jeanette Nolan, Pat Buttram, Jim Jordan, John McIntire, Michelle Stacy, Berbard Fox, Larry Clemmons, James Macdonald, George Lindsey, Bill McMillan, Dub Taylor, John Fiedler.

The Black Cauldron

Rel. 1985, colour, 77 mins. Released by Walt Disney Pictures. Executive Producer: Ron Miller. Producer: Joe Hale. Production Executive: Edward Hansen. Production Co-ordinators: Joseph Morris, Dennis Edwards, Ronald Rocha. Production Manager: Don Hahn. Directors: Ted Berman, Richard Rich. Story: David Jonas, Vance Gerry, Ted Berman, Richard Rich, Al Wilson, Roy Morita, Peter Young, Art Stevens, Joe Hale, based on the books by Lloyd Alexander. Voices: Grant Bardsley, Susan Sheridan, Freddie Jones, John Byner, John Hurt.

The Little Mermaid

Rel. 1989. Colour, 83 mins. Released by Walt Disney Pictures. Directors: John Musker, Ron Clements. Assistant Director: Michael Serrian. Producers: Howard Ashman, John Musker. Script: John Musker, Ron Clements, based on the original story by Hans Christian Anderson. Music: Alan Menken. Voices: Jodi Benson, Pat Carroll, Samuel E. Wright, Kenneth Mars, Buddy Hackett, Christopher Daniel Barnes, Rene Auberjonois, Ben Wright.

The Rescuers Down Under

Rel. 1990, colour, 77 mins. Released by Buena Vista Pictures. Producers: Kathleen Gavin, Thomas Schumacher. Directors: Hendel Butoy, Mike Gabriel. Supervising animators: Ruben A. Aquino, Bill Berg, Brian Clift, David Cutler, Anthony de Rosa, Russ Edmonds, Ed Gombert, Mark Henn, Renee Holt, Emily Jiuliano, Glen Keane, Marty Korth, Duncan Marjoribanks, Vera Lanpher, Nik Ranieri, Kathy Zielinski. Story: Jim Cox, Karey Kirkpatrick, Byron Simpson, Joe Ranft, based on characters by Margery Sharp. Original Music by Bruce Broughton. Voices: Bob Newhart, Eva Gabor, John Candy, Tristan Rogers, Adam Ryen, George C. Scott, Douglas Seale, Frank Welker, Bernard Fox, Peter Firth, Billy Barty, Ed Gilbert, Carla Meyer, Russi Taylor.

Beauty and the Beast

Rel. 1991, colour, 81 mins. Released by Walt Disney Pictures and Silver Screen Partners IV. Executive Producer: Howard Ashman. Producer: Don Hahn. Associate Producer: Sarah McArthur. Directors: Kirk Wise, Gary Trousdale. Screenplay: Linda Woolverton. Camera Manager: Joe Jiuliano. Editor: John Carnochan. Songs: Howard Ashman. Alan Menken. Original Score: Alan Menken. Voices: Paige O'Hara, Robby Benson, Richard White, Jerry Orbach, David Ogden Stiers, Angela Lansbury, Bradley Michael Pierce, Rex Everhart, Jesse Corti, Hal Smith, Jo Anne Worley.

Aladdin

Rel. 1992, colour, 90 mins. Released by Walt Disney Pictures. Directors: John Musker, Ron Clements. Producer: Donald W. Ernest. Script: John Musker, Ron Clements, Ted Elliott, Terry Rossio. Art Director: Bill Perkins. Music: Alan Menken, Howard Ashman, Tim Rice. Voices: Scott Weinger, Robin Williams, Linda Larkin, Jonathan Freeman, Gilbert Gottfried, Frank Welker, Douglas Seale; Singing Voices: Brad Kane, Lea Salonga.

Pocahontas

Rel. 1995, colour, 78 mins. Released by Walt Disney Pictures. Directors: Mike Gabriel, Eric Goldberg. Producer: James Pentecost. Writers: Carl Bindor, Susannah Grant, Philip LaZebnik. Musical Director: Alan Menken. Editor: H. Lee Peterson. Art Director: Michael Giaimo. Songs: Alan Menken, Stephen Schwartz. Voices: Irene Bedard, Mel Gibson, David Ogden Stiers, John Kassir, Russell Means, Christian Bale, Linda Hunt, Danny Mann, Billy Connolly, Joe Baker, Frank Welker, Michelle St. John, James Apaumut Fall, Gordon Tootoosis.

The Hunchback of Notre Dame

Rel. 1996, colour, 87 mins. Released by Walt Disney Pictures. Executive Producer: Howard Ashman. Producer: Don Hahn. Co-Producer: Roy Comli. Associate Producer: Phil Lofaro. Directors: Kirk Wise, Gary Trousdale. Art Director: David Goetz. Editor: Ellen Keneshea. Animation Story: Tab Murphy, based on Victor Hugo's novel Notre Dame de Paris. Animation Screenplay: Tab Murphy, Bob Tzudiker, Irene Mecchi, Noni White, Jonathan Roberts. Editor: John Carnochan. Songs: Music by Alan Menken, Lyrics by Stephen Schwartz. Original Score: Alan Menken. Voices: Tom

Hulce, Demi Moore, Tony Jay, Kevin Kline, Paul Kandel, Jason Alexander, Charles Kimbrough, Mary Wickes, David Ogden Stiers.

Hercules

Rel. 1997, colour, 93 mins. Released By Walt Disney Pictures. Executive Producer: Alice Dewy. Producers: John Musker, Ron Clements. Directors: John Musker, Ron Clements. Art Director: Andy Gaskill. Editor: Tom Finan. Story: Barry Johnson. Screenplay: John Musker, Ron Clements, Donald McEnery, Bob Shawn, Irene Mecchi. Music: Alan Menken. Lyrics: David Zippel. Score: Alan Menken. Voices: Tate Donovan, Joshua Keaton, Danny DeVito, James Woods, Susan Egan, Rip Torn, Samantha Eggar, Lillias White, Cheryl Freeman, LaChanze, Roz Ryan, Vaneese Thomas, Bobcat Goldthwait, Matt Frewer.

Mulan

Rel. 1998. Colour, 88 mins. Released by Walt Disney Pictures. Directors: Barry Cook, Tony Bancroft. Producer: Pam Coats. Associate Producers: Kendra Haaland, Robert S. Garber. Screenplay: Rita Hsiao, Christopher Sanders, Philip Lazebnik, Raymond Singer, Eugenia Bostwick Singer. Based on a story by Robert D. San Souci. Story: John Sanford, Chris Williams, Tim Hodge, Julius L. Aguimatang, Burny Mattinson, Lorna Cook, Barry Johnson, Thom Enriquez, Ed Gombert, Joe Grant, Floyd Norman. Music/Score Producer: Jerry Goldsmith. Songs: Matthew Wilder, David Zippel. Editor: Michael Kelly. Associate Editors: William J. Caparella, James Melton. Art Director: Ric Sluiter. Voices: Ming-Na Wen, Lea Salonga, Soon-Teck Oh, B.D. Wong, Donny Osmond, Freda Foh Shen, Eddie Murphy, Harvey Fierstein, George Takei, Jerry S. Tondo, Gedde Watanabe, Matthew Wilder, Miguel Ferrer, Frank Welker, James Shigeta, James Hong, June Foray, Pat Morita, Miriam Margolyes, Marni Nixon.

Tarzan

Rel. 1999, colour, 88 mins. Walt Disney Pictures. Producers: Bonnie Arnold, Christopher Chase, Christopher Ward. Directors: Kevin Lima, Chris Buck. Writers: Tab Murphy, Bob Tzudiker, Noni White, based on the book *Tarzan of the Apes* by Edgar Rice Burroughs. Supervising animators: Dave Burgess, Ken Duncan, Russ Edmonds, Randy Haycock, T. Daniel Hofstedt, Jay Jackson, Glen Keane, Dominique Monfery, Sergio Pablos, John Ripa, Bruce W. Smith, Michael Surrey, Chris Wahl. Musical Score: Mark Mancina. Songs: Phil Collins. Voices: Tony Goldwyn, Minnie Driver, Glenn Close, Rosie O'Donnell, Brian Blessed, Nigel Hawthorne, Lance Henriksen, Wayne Knight.

The Emperor's New Groove

Rel. 2000, colour, 79 mins. Released by Walt Disney Pictures. Producers: Prudence Fenton, Randy Fullmer, Dohn Hahn, Patricia Hicks. Director: Mark Dindal. Story: Chris Williams, Mark Dindal, David Reynolds, Stephen Anderson, Don Hall, John Norton, Roger Allers, Matthew Jacobs. Supervising animators: Debra Armstrong, Dale Baer, Tony Bancroft, Dominique Monfery, Nik Ranieri, Bruce W. Smith. Original Music: John Debney. Voices: David Spade, John Goodman, Eartha Kitt, Patrick Warburton, Wendie Malick, Tom Jones, Kellyann Kelso.

Atlantis: The Lost Empire

Rel. 2001, colour, 96 mins. Released by Walt Disney Pictures. Producers: Don Hahn, Kendra Haaland. Directors: Kirk Wise, Gary Trousdale. Story: Tab Murphy, Kirk Wise, Gary Trousdale, Joss Whedon, Bryce Zabel, Jackie Zabel. Supervising animators: Anne Marie Bardwell, Michael Cedeno, Anothony de Rosa, Russ Edmonds, Randy Haycock, Ron Husband, Shawn Keller,

Mike "Moe" Merell, John Pomeroy, David Pruiksma, Yoshimichi Tamura. Original Music by James Newton Howard. Voices: Michael J. Fox, Cree Summer, James Garner, Claudia Christian, Florence Stanley, Leonard Nemoy, John Mahony, Jacqueline Obradors, Corey Burton, Don Novello, Phil Morris, Jim Varney, David Ogden Stiers.

Treasure Planet

Rel. 2002, colour, 91 minutes. Walt Disney Pictures. Produced and Directed by John Musker and Ron Clements. Screenplay: Ron Clements, John Musker, and Rob Edwards. Producer: Roy Conli. Animation Story: Ron Clements, John Musker, Ted Elliott, and Terry Rossio. Original Score: James Newton Howard. Original Songs: John Rzeznik. Voices: Joseph Gordon-Levitt, Brian Murray, Emma Thompson, David Hyde Pierce, Martin Short, Dane A. Davis, Michael Wincott, Laurie Metcalf, Roscoe Lee Browne, Patrick McGoohan.

Meet the Robinsons

Rel. 2007, colour, 95 minutes. Walt Disney Pictures. Directed by Stephen Anderson. Screenplay: Jon Bernstein, Michelle Spitz, Don Hall, Nathan Greno, Aurian Redson, Joe Mateo, Stephen Anderson. Based upon *A Day With Wilbur Robinson* by William Joyce. Producers: William Joyce, John Lasseter, Clark Spencer, Dorothy McKim, Bill Borden, David J. Steinberg, Makul Wigert, Monica Lago-Kaytis. Editing: Ellen Keneshea. Original Music: Danny Elfman. Voices: Angela Bassett, Daniel Hansen, Jordan Fry, Matthew Josten, John H. H. Ford, Dara McGarry, Tom Kenny, Laurie Metcalf, Don Hall, Paul Butcher, Tracey Miller-Zarneke, Wesley Singerman, Jessie Flower, Stephen John Anderson, Ethan Sandler, Harland Williams, Nathan Greno, Kelly Hoover, Adam West, Nicole Sullivan, Aurian Redson, Joe Mateo, Tom Selleck, Joe Whyte.

The Princess and the Frog

Rel. 2009, colour, 95 minutes. Walt Disney Pictures. Directed by John Musker and Ron Clements. Screenplay: Ron Clements, John Musker, and Rob Edwards. Producers: John Lasseter, Aghi Koh, Peter Del Vecho, Craig Sost. Original Music: Randy Newman. Editor: Jeff Draheim. Voices: Anika Noni Rose, Bruno Campos, Keith David, Michael-Leon Wooley, Jennifer Cody, Jim Cummings, Peter Bartlett, Jenifer Lewis, Oprah Winfrey, Terrence Howard, John Goodman, Elizabeth Dampier, Breanna Brooks, Ritchie Montgomery, Don Hall, Paul Briggs, Jerry Jernion, Corey Burton, Michael Colyar, Emeril Lagasse, Kevin Michael Richardson, Randy Newman, Danielle Moné Truitt.

Tangled

Rel. 2010, colour, 100 minutes. Walt Disney Pictures, Walt Disney Animation Studios. Directed by Nathan Greno and Byron Howard. Screenplay: Dan Fogelman. Additional Story: Dean Wellins. Producers: Glen Keane, John Lasseter, Roy Conli, Aimee Scribner. Original Music: Alan Menken. Editing: Tim Mertens. Voices: Mandy Moore, Zachary Levi, Donna Murphy, Ron Perlman, M.C. Gainey, Jeffrey Tambor, Brad Garrett, Paul F. Tompkins, Richard Kiel, Delaney Rose Stein, Nathan Greno, Byron Howard, Tim Mertens.

Non-Disney Films (analysed only)

"Real Housewives of Disney" – *Saturday Night Live*, Season 37, Episode 16, Original Air Date 3 March 2012.

Index